I CHRONICLES

VOLUME 12

THE ANCHOR BIBLE is a fresh approach to the world's greatest classic. Its object is to make the Bible accessible to the modern reader; its method is to arrive at the meaning of biblical literature through exact translation and extended exposition, and to reconstruct the ancient setting of the biblical story, as well as the circumstances of its transcription and the characteristics of its transcribers.

THE ANCHOR BIBLE is a project of international and interfaith scope: Protestant, Catholic, and Jewish scholars from many countries contribute individual volumes. The project is not sponsored by any ecclesiastical organization and is not intended to reflect any particular theological doctrine. Prepared under our joint supervision, THE ANCHOR BIBLE is an effort to make available all the significant historical and linguistic knowledge which bears on the interpretation of the biblical record.

THE ANCHOR BIBLE is aimed at the general reader with no special formal training in biblical studies; yet, it is written with the most exacting standards of scholarship, reflecting the highest technical accomplishment.

This project marks the beginning of a new era of co-operation among scholars in biblical research, thus forming a common body of knowledge to be shared by all.

William Foxwell Albright
David Noel Freedman
GENERAL EDITORS

THE ANCHOR BIBLE

I CHRONICLES

INTRODUCTION, TRANSLATION, AND NOTES
BY
JACOB M. MYERS

THE ANCHOR BIBLE
DOUBLEDAY
NEW YORK LONDON TORONTO SYDNEY AUCKLAND

ISBN 0-385-01259-4
Library of Congress Catalog Card Number 65-17226
Copyright © 1965 by Doubleday, a division of
Bantam Doubleday Dell Publishing Group, Inc.
ALL RIGHTS RESERVED
PRINTED IN THE UNITED STATES OF AMERICA

12   14   16   18   19   17   15   13

BG

PREFACE

This work has been in preparation for a number of years—which may account for some repetition here and there. Certainly there can be no claim to finality or definitiveness for it. It represents only one more slight effort in furthering our understanding of the magnitude and significance of Chronicles in the light of recent study and discoveries, archaeological and linguistic.

The materials utilized are scattered in books and journals frequently difficult to obtain. Indebtedness to many authors is evident on every page and recognition thereof has, it is hoped, been duly acknowledged. Special thanks are due to G. von Rad for the loan of his valuable monograph on *Das Geschichtsbild des chronistischen Werkes;* to Professor David Noel Freedman for his guidance, interest, and many helpful stylistic and other suggestions; and to Professor W. F. Albright for awakening in the writer a continuing interest in the work of the Chronicler. However, none of these scholars are responsible for the views expressed other than those suggested in their published works—which it is hoped have been correctly understood and interpreted.

Gratitude is due also the publisher, typesetter, and others who have worked on this book, and especially to Mr. Eugene Eoyang for his unfailing kindness and innumerable helpful suggestions, and to Mrs. Patti Klein, his capable and efficient assistant, for her unsparing pains in correcting and rearranging the manuscript in the form in which it now appears.

J.M.M.

Gettysburg, Pennsylvania

To all my students, past and present,
who have inspired me and taught me so much,
this volume is dedicated in deepest gratitude.

TRANSLATOR'S NOTE

The biblical book of Chronicles is actually one book which, because of its length when translated from Hebrew into Greek, was divided into what we now know as I and II Chronicles. The division into two volumes has been retained here, but the interrelatedness of the two precluded two separate complete introductions that would, by avoiding repetition, tend to mislead the reader into thinking that I and II Chronicles were two distinct works.

Therefore, the complete Introduction for the books of Chronicles appears at the beginning of I Chronicles. The appendixes for all of Chronicles are to be found at the end of II Chronicles. Appendix I gives a complete list of the parallel and comparative passages that the Chronicler drew upon for both I and II Chronicles; Appendix II contains genealogical charts based upon the first nine chapters of I Chronicles. Each volume also includes an index of place and personal names that appear *in the biblical text of that volume,* but if a name occurs in any other of the Chronicler's works (I and II Chronicles and Ezra-Nehemiah), all of these occurrences are cited in order to illustrate the basic unity of the narrative contained in these volumes.

J.M.M.

CONTENTS

PRINCIPAL ABBREVIATIONS

1. PUBLICATIONS

AASOR Annual of the American Schools of Oriental Research
AfO Archiv für Orientforschung
AJSL American Journal of Semitic Languages and Literature
AMJV *Alexander Marx Jubilee Volume,* English section, ed. S. Lieberman. New York: The Jewish Theological Seminary of America, 1950
ANEP *The Ancient Near East in Pictures,* ed. J. B. Pritchard*
ANET *Ancient Near Eastern Texts,* ed. J. B. Pritchard*
AOB *Altorientalische Bilder zum Alten Testament,* ed. H. Gressmann*
AP *Aramaic Papyri of the Fifth Century B.C.,* ed. and tr. A. Cowley*
ARAB *Ancient Records of Assyria and Babylonia,* ed. D. D. Luckenbill*
ARI *Archaeology and the Religion of Israel,* by W. F. Albright*
BA Biblical Archaeologist
BASOR Bulletin of the American Schools of Oriental Research
BBLA Beiträge zur biblischen Landes—und Altertumskunde
BH *Biblia Hebraica,* ed. R. Kittel
BJPES Bulletin of the Jewish Palestine Exploration Society
BJRL Bulletin of the John Rylands Library
BMAP *The Brooklyn Museum Aramaic Papyri,* ed. E. G. H. Kraeling*
BP "The Biblical Period," by W. F. Albright*
BRL *Biblisches Reallexikon,* 1937
BZAW Beihefte zur Zeitschrift für die alttestamentliche Wissenschaft
CAD The Assyrian Dictionary, Oriental Institute of the University of Chicago, 1956
CBQ Catholic Biblical Quarterly
EJ *Die Entstehung des Judenthums,* by Eduard Meyer*
FAB *Festschrift für Alfred Bertholet.* Tübingen: Mohr, 1950
FSAC *From the Stone Age to Christianity,* by W. F. Albright*

* For complete reference, see Selected Bibliography.

GA   *Geschichte des Altertums,* by Eduard Meyer*
GVI   *Geschichte des Volkes Israel,* by Rudolph Kittel*
IB   The Interpreter's Bible
ICC   The International Critical Commentary
IDB   The Interpreter's Dictionary of the Bible, 1962
IEJ   Israel Exploration Journal
IPN   *Die israelitischen Personennamen im Rahmen der gemeinse-
          mitischen Namengebung,* by M. Noth*
1QH   Qumran Hymns of Thanksgiving
1QM   Qumran War Scroll
1QS   Qumran Manual of Discipline
JAOS   Journal of the American Oriental Society
JBL   Journal of Biblical Literature and Exegesis
JBR   Journal of Bible and Religion
JNES   Journal of Near Eastern Studies
JPOS   Journal of the Palestine Oriental Society
JTS   Journal of Theological Studies
KS   *Kleine Schriften zur Geschichte des Volkes Israel,* by A. Alt*
LCQ   Lutheran Church Quarterly
LGJV   *Louis Ginzberg Jubilee Volume,* English section. New York:
          The Jewish Theological Seminary of America, 1945
MGWJ   Monatsschrift für Geschichte und Wissenschaft des Judentums
          Altertumswissenschaft des heiligen Landes zu Jerusalem
OIC   Oriental Institute Communications
OTS   Oudtestamentische Studien
PEQ   Palestine Exploration Quarterly
PJB   Palästinajahrbuch des deutschen evangelischen Instituts für
QDAP   Quarterly of the Department of Antiquities for Palestine
RB   Revue biblique
TLZ   Theologische Literaturzeitung
TZ   Theologische Zeitschrift
ÜS   *Überlieferungsgeschichtliche Studien,* by M. Noth*
VT   Vetus Testamentum
VTS   Vetus Testamentum Supplements
WO   Die Welt des Orients
ZAW   Zeitschrift für die alttestamentliche Wissenschaft
ZDPV   Zeitschrift des deutschen Palästina-Vereins

* For complete reference, see Selected Bibliography.

2. Versions

Aq.	Ancient Greek translation of the Old Testament by Aquila
ATD	Das Alte Testament Deutsch
LXX	The Septuagint
LXX^A	Codex Alexandrinus
LXX^L	Codex Regius
LXX$^{\aleph}$	Codex Sinaiticus
LXX^B	Codex Vaticanus
MT	Masoretic Text
RSV	Revised Standard Version, 1946, 1952
Syr.	Syriac version, the Peshitta
Targ.	Targum, Aramaic translation or paraphrase
Vrs.	Ancient versions generally
Vulg.	The Vulgate

3. Other Abbreviations

Akk.	Akkadian
Ar.	Arabic
Aram.	Aramaic
Bab.	Babylonian
Eg.	Egyptian
Eng.	English
Fr.	French
Ger.	German
Gr.	Greek
Heb.	Hebrew
Lat.	Latin
OT	Old Testament
Phoen.	Phoenician
Sem.	Semitic
Sum.	Sumerian

INTRODUCTION

THE WORK OF THE CHRONICLER IN THE BIBLE

In many respects the work of the Chronicler—I Chronicles, II Chronicles, Ezra, and Nehemiah—has been one of the most neglected portions of the Old Testament. Where it had to be dealt with, it was done grudgingly, often with misunderstanding, misgiving, or downright hostility. However, archaeological and historical studies have now rendered it more respectable and have shown it to be at times more accurate than some of its parallel sources. Naturally the Chronicler had a particular purpose in mind and, where he found more than one source to draw from for a story he wanted to use, he followed the one most harmonious with and adequate for his purpose.

Doubtless the position of Ezra, Nehemiah, and Chronicles in both Jewish and Christian canons has had much to do with the attitude of general Bible readers toward them. Their form and content, dictated in large measure by the peculiar interests of the writer(s), makes them rather dull for the modern reader. To those without an understanding and appreciation of the historical milieu and purpose of the work, genealogies, lists, exaggerated statistics, lengthy and detailed descriptions of religious forms and institutions, etc., can be rather depressing. The contrast is striking when the Chronicler's work is compared with the immediately preceding (Christian canon) Deuteronomic history, which reads much better because it appears more in line with the methods of modern historiography.

It seems a bit strange that the Chronicler's efforts should have been dismissed so lightly in view of the fact that his work comes from just that period in Hebrew history about which so little is otherwise known. The spade of the archaeologist is beginning to fill in the gaps of that period and, with a more appreciative and controlled study of the written materials, we can now be fairly certain of a good many of the hitherto obscure references and details. Supplementing the historical materials of Samuel and Kings and carrying the history of the fortunes of the Jews down to the fourth century

B.C., these books become extremely important. Properly understood and interpreted, they throw much welcome light on this confused period.

THE TITLE OF THE HEBREW BOOKS

The title of Chronicles in Hebrew is *dibrē hayyāmīm,* that is, chronicles of events, happenings of the days, records of the days or times. It was a rather widely used expression in Kings where it occurs some thirty-two times, referring to the book or record of the chronicles of the kings of Israel and Judah; it occurs twice in Esther (x 2)—the chronicles of the kings of Media and Persia. In Esther vi 1 it is used to cite the record of the memorable events in the history of Persia. Interestingly enough, the expression is found only twice in the work of the Chronicler—I Chron xxvii 24 and Neh xii 23. The present books of Chronicles were originally reckoned as one book.

THE TITLE IN THE VERSIONS

Our present Greek and Latin versions of Chronicles are called *Paraleipomena,* that is, things left over or omitted in the histories of Samuel and Kings, especially as they involve Judah. The use of the term Chronicles goes back to Luther who took it from St. Jerome's *Prologus geleatus* which has the following notice: *Dabre Aiamim, id est Verba Dierum, quod significatius totius divinae historiae possumus appellare, qui liber apud nos primus et secundus inscribitur* (Dabre Aiamim, that is the events of the days which we might significantly call the meaning of the whole of sacred history, which book is entitled first and second by us). The Syriac follows the Hebrew.

PLACE IN THE CANON

In the Hebrew canon, the work of the Chronicler stands in the third division—the *Kethubim* (writings)—and last in that division. In our present canonical arrangement, Ezra-Nehemiah appears to be the sequel to Samuel and Kings. Though that was not originally

the case, it may have been the origin of the division at the end of
II Chronicles. Hence the history of Ezra begins just after the end
of II Kings. This also explains the order of the books, that is,
Chronicles after Ezra-Nehemiah, and accounts for the repetition of
the ending of II Chronicles at the beginning of Ezra (indicating
that the present order of the books is awkward). The separation of
Ezra from Chronicles may have resulted from the incorporation of
Ezra-Nehemiah into the Bible as a supplement to the story of
Samuel and Kings, which occurred after Samuel and Kings had been
canonized and therefore could no longer be tampered with. Chron-
icles, then, was added later. It is the last book in the Hebrew Bible
and may have been viewed as a kind of appendix to the Writings.
The Greek Bible placed Chronicles, Ezra, and Nehemiah in the
historical section in the following order: Chronicles, Esdras A,
Esdras B (our Ezra-Nehemiah). That was the order followed by
St. Jerome and Luther, and hence in our English Bibles, except
that Esdras A (apocryphal Ezra) has been relegated to the
Apocrypha while Esdras B appears as Ezra and Nehemiah.

THE INTENTION OF THE CHRONICLER

Chronicles, Ezra, and Nehemiah are so closely related in thought, language, and theology that not only must they have come from a single hand, with possibly a few exceptions, but, like the other great literature of Israel, their author must have had in view a purpose that the earlier histories of his people did not meet in the form in which they had been transmitted.

The intent of the Chronicler was neither to rewrite the history of Judah nor specifically to gather together what had not been covered by his predecessors. His work is a lesson for the people of his time and situation drawn from the history of his people.[1] It might be referred to as a series of lectures or sermons on the bearing of that history upon the needs of the hour. Benzinger has said, "The Chronicler is not at all a writer of history in our sense of the term; he does not aim to relate what took place but what serves to edify; he is not a historian but a Midrashist."[2] C. C. Torrey has written in almost the same vein.[3] But just because the Chronicler is a "Midrashist" does not necessarily mean that he is a purveyor of pure fiction; he may look at history with some bias and omit or add material when it suits his purpose.

[1] See G. von Rad, "Die levitische Predigt in den Bücher der Chronik" in *Gesammelte Studien zum Alten Testament*, pp. 248–61; *Das Geschichtsbild des Chronistischen Werkes*, pp. 133 f. (For complete references, see Selected Bibliography.)

[2] *Die Bücher der Chronik*, p. x (see Benzinger, Selected Bibliography, Commentaries).

[3] "The Composition and Historical Value of Ezra-Nehemiah," BZAW 2 (1896), 65. Cf. *Ezra Studies*, pp. 153–55, 208–13 (see Torrey, Selected Bibliography).

The Historicoreligious Situation

Without going into great detail with reference to the composition of his work (see below), it may be noted that there are several strands of material. But it is evident that the writer has in mind the postexilic period whose grave religious problems he was determined to face realistically and deal with as effectively as he knew how. The great historical writings of the Old Testament are all religious documents par excellence, composed for religious purposes. Each of the documents of the Pentateuch reflects a local situation upon which the writers brought history to bear. The latest stratum of the Penta-teuch, *P,* is closely related to the work of the Chronicler, though with certain different emphases. But the Chronicler faced a far more complex situation than that faced by the author of *P.* The Deuteron-omist was responsible for a much wider product than our book of Deuteronomy. With it went the deuteronomic history from Joshua to the end of II Kings, compiled from various sources and probably the official church history of the nation from the conquest of Canaan to the fall of Judah, including the vicissitudes of the Northern King-dom which were almost entirely ignored by the Chronicler. S. R. Driver observes that Deuteronomy "was a great manifesto against the dominant tendencies of the time. It laid down the lines of a great religious reform . . . it was a nobly conceived endeavor to provide in anticipation a spiritual rallying-point, around which, when circumstances favored, the disorganized forces of the national religion might range themselves again. It was an emphatic reaffirma-tion of the fundamental principles which Moses had long ago in-sisted on, loyalty to Jehovah and repudiation of all false gods: it was an endeavor to realize in practice the ideals of the prophets, es-pecially of Hosea and Isaiah, to transform the Judah demoralized by Manasseh into the 'holy nation' pictured in Isaiah's vision, and to awaken in it that devotion to God, and love for man, which Hosea had declared to be the first of human duties."[4] The Deuter-onomist's purpose was thus to exhibit the effectiveness of the word of the Lord in Israel's history, both as judgment and salvation, and to foster the hope of a revitalization of the promise to David

[4] *Introduction to the Literature of the Old Testament,* rev. ed., 1913, p. 89.

(II Sam vii 8–16), in the face of a weakening Assyria, if king and people heeded the lessons of the past. Cult would afford a mighty impetus in that direction.[5]

The final edition of the Deuteronomist's great history did not appear before the Exile, so that he was able to point out that the nation fell because of disobedience to the word of the Lord, though his emphasis on salvation is maintained in the final observation on the release of Jehoiachin (II Kings xxv 27–30), either deliberately omitted by the Chronicler or not present in the Samuel-Kings edition used by him (cf. Jer lii). Much of what he had thus written of the history of Judah had validity for coming generations—as may be seen from the Chronicler's use of it in his day. But the Deuteronomist's appeal and program had failed to save the nation—and a new situation confronted those who endeavored later to pick up the pieces and begin all over again. The promises of the Lord were valid but a new situation had arisen that demanded even more heroic efforts than any required earlier.

The deportation of large numbers of people from Samaria in 721 B.C. left only the poorest of the population in the land who had neither the ability nor the vitality to re-establish the old institutions. There is a possibility that some of the erstwhile inhabitants of Israel migrated to Judah. In view of the destruction of the Yahweh shrines of the north, it is quite within reason to assume that the religious leaders of Judah endeavored to evangelize certain areas of the conquered land.[6] They were doubtless influenced by the prophets drawing conclusions from the catastrophe of Israel, which led to a reformation in the south as soon as political conditions permitted (cf. II Kings xviii 4–6; II Chron xxxi 1). There are hints that the Yahweh enthusiasts did not tarry for long after the fall of Samaria to proclaim their message in deeds; Ahaz's submission to Assyria may have lent a kind of unofficial authority or prestige to their efforts to tend the religious needs of the people left in the land. The fact that the king of Assyria permitted a Yahweh priest to return to Bethel (II Kings xvii 28 ff.) is tacit recognition of some kind of religious activity conducted unofficially from the outside and which the political authorities regarded quite as dangerous as Jeroboam I had regarded the pilgrimages of his people to Jerusalem (I Kings

[5] See G. von Rad, *Studies in Deuteronomy*, 1953.
[6] See W. F. Albright, BP, p. 42.

xii 27). The sanctuary at Bethel was rehabilitated with the specific purpose of competing with that at Jerusalem. The religious
leaders of Judah were always skeptical of the religion of the
Northerners, despite the fact that their prophets never appeared to
question the legitimacy of the cultus; they did inveigh against apostasy and cultic excesses that led to the neglect of the ethical demands of Yahwism. The religion of Israel could thus be saved only
by vigorous measures taken in the south. There was no hope for the
restoration of the exiles from Samaria and the mixed population established in the north by the Assyrians, despite some Yahwist
activity (II Chron xxx 10 ff.), created a highly unfavorable cli-
mate for the pursuit of Yahwism (II Kings xvii 18 ff.). Hezekiah and
his associates attempted to remedy the situation but, in the wake of
Assyrian movements,[7] their efforts presently took a political turn
and the king was soon involved first in intrigues, then in overt action though probably not before the death of Sargon II.

The important aspect of this whole picture was the failure of
effective religious progress in the new venture in Ephraim on the
one hand and the growing strength of Yahwism in Jerusalem under
Hezekiah on the other. Indeed it is more than likely that the success of his religious reform inspired him to join with confidence in
the revolt against Assyria in 701 B.C. (II Kings xviii 13–19, 37;
II Chron xxxii 1–23; Isa xxxvi–xxxvii). The Chronicler has made a
great deal of this religious activity of Hezekiah and there is certainly much in what he says; he did not conjure up the whole idea.
It is significant that he accuses the king of pride which brought
"wrath upon himself, as well as upon Judah and Jerusalem" (II
Chron xxxii 25), though its execution was postponed until later—
an observation not found elsewhere. That pride is reflected in the
political movements of the Judean king after the death of Sargon II,[8]
especially the entangling alliances in which he became ensnared,
perhaps necessarily so, and in the ill-advised display of his wealth
before the diplomatic mission of Merodach-baladan (II Kings xx
12–19). But the fact remains that Hezekiah and his advisers developed and maintained a vital interest in the religious fortunes of

---

[7] Sargon II kept affairs pretty well under control in his empire but the
western provinces became increasingly restive under the heavy tribute imposed
upon them during his northern campaigns from his sixth to tenth years (715–
711 B.C.). Cf. D. D. Luckenbill, ARAB, II, pp. 4–13; M. Noth, *The History of
Israel*, p. 264 (see Selected Bibliography).

[8] Albright, BP, pp. 43 f.

their impoverished brethren in the north, a policy continued by his successors.[9] They regarded themselves as the true representatives of the Yahweh cult centered in Jerusalem and hence responsible for their brothers.

The reigns of Manasseh and Amon (687–640) marked a reaction against the reforms of Hezekiah, and the leaders of Yahwism doubtless went underground; that they relinquished their activity altogether is unthinkable in light of the vigorous reassertion of the Yahwists in the reign of Josiah. We need only recall the prophets whose life and schooling must have begun in that period—Zephaniah (630), Huldah (II Kings xxii 14; II Chron xxxiv 22) and even Jeremiah, though he may have been moved to prophesy by Zephaniah's gloomy message. The outburst of such intense scribal activity points to pent-up force ready to be released at the opportune time. The functioning of the *am-ha-aretz* (the people of the land, i.e., the free landholders) in the enthronement also indicates the presence of sociolegal principles still operative in the minds of the landholders of Judah. Their function in maintaining the Davidic throne was of paramount importance for both political and religious stability in Judah.[10]

In any case, Josiah (640–609) turned to the Lord early in his reign—like Joash, he may even have been tutored secretly by the priests. A priestly regency may have been established during the years of his minority. If the date of II Kings (xxii 3 ff.) for the beginnings of the reformation be accepted, we must assume a period of preparation for some years, which may have been induced by the awesome declarations of the coming day of the Lord by Zephaniah (Zeph i). However, the Chronicler asserts that "During the eighth year of his reign, while he was still a youth, he [Josiah] began to seek the God of David his father" (II Chron xxxiv 3) and four years later began to purge the land of its Canaanite religious vestiges. That would correspond in general with his assumption of the full powers of rule and the relinquishing of effective Assyrian control over the Palestinian provinces attendant upon the death of Asshurbanipal around 627/6 B.C. That his purge extended to the north, beyond the boundaries of Judah and Benjamin, is attested in both

---

[9] As appears from the fact that Amon and Eliakim (Jehoiakim) were descendants of Galilean mothers (II Kings xxi 19, xxiii 36). Cf. F. M. Abel, *Géographie de la Palestine*, II, p. 366 (see Selected Bibliography).

[10] E. Würthwein, *Der 'amm ha'arez im Alten Testament*, 1936, pp. 30–46.

Kings (II Kings xxiii 15, 19 f.) and Chronicles (II Chron xxxiv 6 f., 33). It was only through his vigorous reforming activity, probably as a nominal vassal of the Assyrians—there is no indication of a rupture with Assyria in the early portion of his reign, nor of a military conquest directed against the north—that Josiah was able to consolidate the religious parties of all Israel. The Deuteronomic reformation was at least partially successful in the re-establishment of true Yahwism at Jerusalem and in centering it in the cult at the temple. There was no effective opposition from the only quarter it could have come—Bethel—and hence the idea of one true center of pure and official Yahwism was further accentuated.

The death of Josiah dealt a severe blow to the scheme of Josiah and his officials to remake the kingdom after the Davidic pattern. As a matter of fact, the tragic end of the reforming king cast a shadow over his reformation; there is at least a suspicion though it ought not be pressed too strongly that the circumstances of Josiah's death may have led the Chronicler to shift some of the glory of Josiah to Hezekiah. Nevertheless, the Deuteronomic history of the nation, interpreted from a strictly prophetic point of view, will ever stand as a memorial to the valiant attempt of Josiah and his associates to apply the law of Moses to the changing fortunes of the people. But the failure of that reapplication of the law to save the nation from disaster could not be obscured; it did, however, drive another peg into the structure of the legitimacy of the cult of the south, where the chief exponents of Yahwism lived and whence authentic teachings emanated.

After 609 B.C., in spite of the proclamations of prophets like Jeremiah and Habakkuk, the decline was rapid. Deuteronomy may have contributed thereto unwittingly by the creation of a misdirected sense of security on the part of officials who trusted in externals to the exclusion, or nearly so, of a deep inner commitment to the will of God. At least that seems to be the main burden of Jeremiah's temple sermon (vii, xxvi) delivered at the beginning of the reign of Jehoiakim (609–597). However wrong officials and cult prophets were during the reign of Zedekiah and despite the growing weakness of the moral aspects of Jerusalem's religion, they embodied the only legitimate Mosaic tradition. That is amply demonstrated by religious developments in Babylon after the exiles had learned their lesson and under the persistent prodding of men like Ezekiel. Those left in the land after the second deportation might have recaptured the spirit of the Deuteronomic ideal if they had chosen to follow the advice of Jeremiah and the leadership of Gedaliah. But that was not to be, for Ishmael, a Davidide, wrought havoc among the chiefs of Mizpah which resulted in the withdrawal of what respectable elements remained to Egypt where they ultimately became part of the nucleus of the Elephantine community of Jews (II Kings xxv 25–26). There is some evidence for a third Babylonian deportation (Jer lii 28 f.; cf. Josephus *Antiquities* X.ix.7); if so it means that Judah was divested of its most substantial citizens no less than three times in about fifteen years (597–582). The depopulating of the land was thus devastating because the best classes of people were involved. Yet there were still some Israelites of standing in the land for, it is to be observed, no outsiders were brought in to fill in the vacuum.[11] Alt is surely right in his belief that the Judean territory was added to Samaria;[12] the southern portion was apparently given to Edom. According to Jer xli 5, certain Yahwists from Shechem, Shiloh, and Samaria had brought offerings to the Lord at the time of the murder of Gedaliah. When they learned of that event, they returned to their respective homes. It is well to note that in the fifth century Samaria was governed by a Yahwist, perhaps a descendant of earlier Yahwist governors.

There is virtually no explicit information on the religious situation in Palestine during the Exile. As noted above, Jer xli 5 informs us that worshipers from the north came to bring offerings "to present at the house of Yahweh." Hence the site must have been regarded as sacred, though the temple structure lay in ruins. That such offerings continued may be assumed.[13] Zech vii 5 speaks of regular fasts being held for seventy years; whether they were held at Jerusalem or elsewhere is not stated.[14] In the latter case the reason for the repudiation of the offerings of people of the land by the returnees was their manifest connection with other shrines nearer home, their practice of a kind of syncretism such as prevailed at Elephantine. They may have been prevented from taking measures

[11] Cf. A. Alt, "Die Rolle Samarias bei der Entstehung des Judentums," KS, II, p. 326.

[12] KS, pp. 328 f.

[13] Noth, *op. cit.*, p. 290; J. Bright, *A History of Israel*, p. 345 (see Selected Bibliography).

[14] Cf. E. Janssen, *Juda in der Exilszeit*, (Göttingen, 1956), pp. 94–104, and J. N. Scofield, "'All Israel' in the Deuteronomic Writers," *Essays and Studies Presented to Stanley Arthur Cook* (London, 1950), pp. 25–34, especially p. 27.

toward reconstructing the Jerusalem center of worship out of fear or because of the lack of dynamic leadership—all the Jerusalem officials were in exile.

Religious conditions in Babylon were quite different, as might be expected. The fires of religion were at first fanned by Ezekiel: later by such enthusiasts as the Second Isaiah whose emphasis on universalism was fused with a powerful conception of nationalism. Under the spell of hope generated by the movements of Cyrus II, the great prophet proclaimed a message of expectation and restoration (Isa xliii 1–7, xliv 26, 28, lii 7–9, lxi 4 ff.). To be sure, the exiles acquired a new slant on religion and developed somewhat away from the sacrificial (xliii 22 ff.) but they were fired with a fresh zeal for Zion. They familiarized themselves with the ancient stories of their people, studied the laws and prophecies of the fathers, and increased their faith in the God of the fathers as they observed the religious practices of the people around them. Theirs was the living God who did not have to be carried about in religious processions like the gods of Babylon (xliv 9–20, xlvi 1–13); he was the fulfiller of his promises to those who were obedient to him (xlviii 1–9, xlix 14 ff.). The prophet looked forward to the glories of the new or renewed Zion under an everlasting covenant, even "the sure mercies of David" (lv 3). It is striking indeed that the noblest conception of religion in the Old Testament came from the exilic community in Babylon.

In all probability, the prophet of the Exile was impressed by the advances of Cyrus the Great, whose phenomenal career began around 550 B.C. when he became ruler of Media. Within a few years he had extended his rule to include all the territory east of the Tigris River and was soon lord of North Mesopotamia and the former kingdom of Croesus (Lydia) in western Asia Minor. In 539 Babylon fell into his hands. There was an almost immediate release of subject peoples in line with the enlightened and benevolent policy of the Persian king.[15] The edict of Cyrus (Ezra i 2–4, vi 3–5) is fully in harmony with that policy. How wide the response to that edict was (cf. Josephus Antiquities XI.i.1 f.) we do not know but it is certain that some of the more pious Jews accepted it with alacrity (Ezra i 5 ff.). It may even be that the

[15] See the Cyrus Cylinder in ANET, pp. 315 f.; E. Meyer, Kleine Schriften, II, pp. 69–100 (see Selected Bibliography); R. de Vaux, "Les decrits de Cyrus et de Darius sur la reconstruction du Temple," RB 46 (1937), 29–57.

XXVI INTRODUCTION

descendants of the Davidic line and the priests were instrumental
in procuring the document of release. At any rate, those who did
accept the challenge were apparently directed by Sheshbazzar (*Sin-
ab-uṣur*),[16] the fourth son of Jehoiachin (I Chron iii 18 where he
is called Shenazzar), who came to Jerusalem (Ezra i 8) and laid
the foundations of "the house of God" (Ezra v 16). He was named
the first governor (*peḥah;* Ezra v 14). What happened to him is
unknown, though we may surmise that he died sometime between
538 and 522 when we find Zerubbabel, son of Shealtiel and the
nephew of Sheshbazzar in charge of affairs.[17] The latter apparently
served as regent for Zerubbabel during his minority.

With the returnees was also Joshua, the high priest. That some
sort of religious system was set up at once may be regarded as
certain, though it was not as elaborate as the Chronicler would
have us believe (Ezra iii). There is nothing inherently improbable,
however, in the establishment of an altar for their immediate religious needs. That was not because there was none present during
the Exile but because the returned exiles regarded that one as
impure and contaminated. The erection and use of an altar also
required ritual that was doubtless rather simple. Those who returned were poor, and conditions in the land were anything but
conducive to the establishment and maintenance of an elaborate
sacrificial system such as that envisioned by Ezekiel or the Chronicler. That progress was slow and tortuous is demonstrated by the
prophecies of Haggai and Zechariah: they were compelled to take
the people to task for their apparent lethargy (Hag i 4). It is
possible that the political authorities moved very cautiously to the
manifest displeasure of the religious zealots. The erection of an altar
with provision for simple services would not have aroused the suspicion of the Persian authorities, but the construction of a temple
would be something else again. The temple with its ecclesiastical
organization centering around the anointed ones—the high priest
and messiah—would have had political implications, which was precisely what Zerubbabel wanted to avoid.[18]

The confusion resulting from the death of Cambyses and the
accession of Darius I, when there was rebellion everywhere in the

[16] Albright, BP, p. 62, n. 119.
[17] On the Sheshbazzar-Zerubbabel situation see R. A. Bowman in IB, III,
1949, pp. 574 f., 612 f.
[18] Cf. Albright, BP, pp. 49 f.

empire,[19] was taken advantage of by Haggai and Zechariah to whip up the religious fervor of the people.[20] They responded to the prophetic appeal and by 515 the temple was completed, but the Davidic line had come to an end in the eclipse of Zerubbabel. Though a semblance of the Davidic line was maintained and there were family scions, they played no active part, so far as we know, in the events of the fifth century B.C. Henceforth political control was largely in the hands of the priesthood who guided the affairs of the little community until the time of Nehemiah.

The exact course of events from the completion of the temple until the coming of Nehemiah is far from clear. If the date of Joel and Malachi were certain, some further information might be available. Still, the over-all picture would not be radically changed: only its outlines would be more clearly drawn. The lack of progress made during the period indicates that the devoted servants of the Lord had a hard time, a fact substantiated by the records preserved in Ezra-Nehemiah. Joel speaks of plagues (i 2 ff.) and drought (i 19), the lack of religious fervor (ii 12 ff.) and complications with surrounding peoples (iii 4–8). Malachi reflects difficulties with Edom, which took over much of the southern portion of Judah in the wake of advancing Arabs (i 2–4); the lack of religious zeal (i 6–14); and the lethargy of many of the priests, possibly because support for them had virtually ceased (ii 1–9), resulted in opportunist marriages (ii 10–16). Such conditions are just what might be expected in view of the report on Jerusalem received by Nehemiah shortly after the middle of the fifth century (Neh i 3).

The Chronicler's view, as recorded in Ezra, seems to disregard the above explanations of the situation almost entirely. He thinks the cause for the sad state of affairs at Jerusalem was limited to opposition from the people of the land, that is, those who had assumed control during the Exile. As is well known, opposition did come, chiefly from Samaria, though later it came also from other quarters. The population of Samaria had been heterogeneous in character since the days of Sargon II; it had been augmented by other peoples settled there by Esarhaddon (Ezra iv 2). These peoples are represented as worshipers of Yahweh since that time— probably a syncretistic cult somewhat like that at Elephantine. The

[19] Cf. A. T. E. Olmstead, *The History of the Persian Empire* (University of Chicago Press, 1948), Ch. VIII.
[20] Albright, BP, p. 50.

rather strange verse in Ezra iii 3—"They set up the altar upon its bases—for they were afraid of the peoples of the land—and offered burnt offerings to Yahweh . . ."[21]—may indicate more than physical fear of surrounding peoples; it may very well reflect a religious fear of joining them in what the returnees regarded as illegitimate worship. It has been pointed out that Haggai (ii 14) already regarded the people of the land as unclean. They were held in disdain by the purists who refused to have anything to do with them. Such an attitude would naturally create tension and ultimately covert and overt opposition on the part of those who had been rejected. "The people of the land weakened the hands of the people of Judah and deterred them from building; they also hired counselors against them to frustrate their purpose . . ." (Ezra iv 4–5). To "weaken the hands" means to undermine or subvert the morals of the people of Judah, the returnees. The whole outlook of the Chronicler is religious and he makes everything subservient to his purpose. Again and again he calls attention to the consequences of religious compromise and that is why he apparently thinks of it as the impediment to progress toward rebuilding the temple at Jerusalem. Furthermore, he regarded the unfavorable conditions prevalent there in the first half of the fifth century as arising from the gradual and effective, though tragic, influx among the people of the land of the descendants of the exiles who had returned with Zerubbabel.

The mission of Nehemiah was not merely to assist the community by providing physical protection for itself but also to help it regain its religious foothold in Jerusalem. The Chronicler is concerned chiefly about the re-establishment of the pure community of the Lord, which meant complete independence from the people of the land and the religious sanctification of the community. In their effort to survive, many of the families of the returnees had intermarried with the local families of standing,[22] perhaps being lured or compelled to do so by economic circumstances. There must have been more than normal tendencies at work when so many of the upper classes intermarried—priests, Levites, and important families (Ezra x 18–44). Just what effect this had on religion is not indicated, since there is no direct proof that the people of the land participated in formal religious rites. Little is said directly of Jewish maidens marrying foreigners (Neh x 30; Ezra ix 12), though there

---

[21] See interpretation of Josephus in *Antiquities* XI.iv.1.
[22] Würthwein, *Der 'amm* . . . , pp. 57–70.

were doubtless instances of it. The reference to Solomon (Neh xiii 26) with his foreign wives makes clear the whole purpose the writer had in mind, that is, to guard the faithful from apostasy. Hence, what appears to us as a ruthless and heartless procedure was simply a stern measure on his part to save the religion of Yahweh from serious contamination, possible extinction. The reference to intermarriage with Ashdod, Ammon, and Moab (Neh xiii 23; Ezra ix 2 may be a later addition from Deut vii), especially the emphasis on the mixture of language, points to an attempt to hold the returnees to nationalistic purity, which for the Chronicler was essential for religious purity. He visualized a Jewish national state with its center of worship in Jerusalem, from which the dispersed Jews of the world could draw their inspiration and guidance and which they in turn would support in every way[23]—a situation, comparable in many ways, to modern Zionism.

The relationship between Nehemiah and Ezra is historically quite complicated and cannot be dealt with here extensively. That Ezra followed Nehemiah may be taken as fairly certain, because the politico-economic conditions with which the latter dealt so effectively were no longer present for Ezra. Ezra had authority to set up local government on the basis of the Mosaic law (vii 25–26, x 8) and to enforce that law. Actually he was commissioned by the king of Persia to establish a kind of Jewish commonwealth operating within the empire. That became necessary by virtue of the rebuilding of the temple, the city, and its enclosure and the reinstitution of a functioning religious system that included social regulations of various types. Thus for the first time the vacuum left by the Babylonian captivity was filled. Nehemiah had come mainly to improve physical conditions (Neh i 5, 8); Ezra to organize the religio-social life of Judah. However, the power to initiate and regulate the organization of people for purposes he came to achieve was also wielded by Nehemiah as shown by his work-defense plans (Neh iii–vi)— after all he was governor (v 14, viii 9, x 1). During the first period of his incumbency he appears to have operated by persuasion; he was much sterner during the second period (xiii)—perhaps he was armed with more authority then.[24]

[23] Cf. E. J. Bickerman, "The Historical Foundations of Postbiblical Judaism," *The Jews: Their History, Culture, and Religion*, ed. L. Finkelstein, 1949, I, pp. 70–110, especially p. 72.

[24] On the dates see Bowman, IB, III, p. 807; W. Rudolph, *Esra und Nehemia* (Tübingen, 1949), pp. 203 f.

For our present purposes, it is sufficient merely to call attention to conditions in Palestine in the last half of the fifth century. Certainly much was accomplished under difficult circumstances. The power vacuum at Jerusalem and the old district of Judah was filled when the walls of the city were rebuilt and a Persian governor installed. With it came a reinstitution of the cultus and necessary reforms under the authority of the Persian king. So Jerusalem became once more the religious center from which emanated all legal (Mosaic law) authority for Jews throughout the diaspora, with the exception of those at Elephantine and Samaria. It is worth noting that the Jerusalem cultus was set up along lines developed through the Babylonian golah (i.e., those who returned from Babylon) and supported by foreign funds: yet it became the center from which Jews all over the world received religious direction.

THE AIM OF THE CHRONICLER IN THE LIGHT OF HIS SITUATION

It must already be apparent that the Chronicler had more in mind than a recounting of the history of Israel (Judah) in the several aspects utilized by him. But he did not deliberately distort history to fit his purpose; he employed those phases that were apropos and, at numerous points, he manifestly relied on sources sometimes more accurate than those used by the Deuteronomist. In view of that fact one cannot accuse him of writing imaginative history, as has been charged so often. That he had his own way of filling in the gaps, with some embellishments no doubt, was due to the interests of his cause. The political aspect of the Davidic line had come to an end and there was no hope of re-establishment, at least not so far as he could see. Hope for Israel lay in the fortification of the religious institutions that survived the tragic experiences of 587 B.C. and the long years of the Exile. For the Deuteronomist the kingdom was promised to David and his descendants—"I will establish the throne of his kingdom forever" (II Sam vii 13).

Despite the fact that it had almost ceased to exist, the Davidic house was important for the Chronicler. So also was his kingdom. Hence the Davidic monarchy receives full treatment and David himself is given quite extensive coverage. Yet, after the Exile there is markedly less emphasis upon the Davidic line, though the Davidic cultic tradition seems to be maintained (Ezra iii 10, viii 20; Neh xii 24, 36, 45). Sheshbazzar and Zerubbabel are still regarded as Davidides but then the line drops out of the main stream of events. However, the Davidic line is continued in I Chronicles iii, which shows that there was still some interest in the genealogy, even though the Davidides played no discernible role in the history of the commonwealth after the time of Zerubbabel until the time of the Qumran community and the New Testament when the situation was entirely different. Thus there seems to be an anomaly between the conception of Chronicles and that reflected in Ezra-Nehemiah. The different points of view could be explained by postulating an original author whose overriding interest was the restoration of the kingdom with a Davidic scion at the head. By the time of Ezra-Nehemiah the whole situation had altered considerably, so that these men who were not primarily historians and writers but men of action simply dealt with current problems in terms of the most appropriate remedies—law, priesthood, and the temple. Their memoirs were left in terms of what they had seen and done. The amalgamation of Chronicles with Ezra-Nehemiah was the product of someone—a little later or, perhaps, contemporaneous because the story ends abruptly in this period—whose main interest was in continuity and legitimacy and who emphasized the continuity of the community of the Lord from Adam to Ezra-Nehemiah and the Jewish commonwealth centering about Jerusalem. His chief concern, then, was Jerusalem and the Jewish community, with the Davidic line on the throne of Judah only an important episode. That may be the import of the genealogy of I Chronicles iii which fits neither Chronicles nor Ezra-Nehemiah, who at least minimize the Davidic line. The final editor was influenced by *P,* many of whose ideas and expressions he incorporated in his work.[25]

On the other hand, the author of Chronicles (except I Chron i–ix) and Ezra-Nehemiah (into which the Ezra-Nehemiah memoirs were incorporated) was certainly aware that the situation of his time called for resolute action. He could not pass over lightly the facts of history, however he might embellish or interpret them. This he did by taking hold of the Davidic religious institutions—Jerusalem, the temple, the cultus—through which the people of the Lord could operate as a community once more. That he stressed the Davidic kingdom is clear from the fact that he quoted II Sam vii 13 but

[25] This is the view of D. N. Freedman, "The Chronicler's Purpose," CBQ 23 (1961), 436–42.

had come to terms with life by substituting the Persian authorities, represented by the governors, for the Davidic kingdom. Here he simply followed the Second Isaiah. Some elements of Ezra-Nehemiah and I Chron i–ix were added later, possibly when disillusionment with the Persians set in. In any case, the desire of the writer was to strengthen the things that remained and to do so he had to set forth the developments of this side of the nation's life, thus minimizing to a large extent its purely political vicissitudes because they were more or less irrelevant to his purpose. Three aspects of the Chronicler's work significantly reveal his point of view.

(a) One of the chief purposes of the Chronicler, in view of the situation to which he was addressing himself, was to demonstrate that the true Israel was the one perpetuated in Judah—the one which began in the Davidic kingdom, continued right through the history of Judah, and more to the point, was now represented in the exilic community. From that community came the founders of the restored religious institutions at Jerusalem and in that community resided the only hope for the perpetuation of those institutions. It is no accident that such emphasis is placed on David whose dynasty was continued in the Southern Kingdom. The very fact that the returnees came from the exiles of that kingdom appeared proof of the divine blessing bestowed upon it—still further confirmed, they believed, by the acts of the Persian king's support of the program and work of restoration.[26]

The rupture with the Northern tribes was due to the recalcitrance of their leaders. The Chronicler's attitude is clearly expressed in II Chron x 19: "So Israel has remained in rebellion against the house of David until today." In other words, he interpreted the ongoing situation of division as the result of disobedience and sin, thus accentuating a significant feature of the preaching of the prophets. That is not to say that the same tendencies in some representatives of the Davidic line were ignored—he refers repeatedly to the evil done by the rulers of the south (II Chron xii 1, 14, xvi 7–10, xx 33, 35, xxi 4, 6, 11, 16 ff., xxii 3 ff., xxiv 17 ff., xxv 2, 14, 27, xxvi 16 ff., xxviii 1 ff., 22 ff., xxxii 25, 31, xxxv 22, xxxvi 5, 9, 12)—but that the kingdom was saved because of the Lord's covenant with David (II Sam vii 11–16 ∥ I Chron xvii 11–14; II Chron xxi 7) or because king and people humbled themselves before the Lord

[26] See W. Rudolph, "Problems of the Books of Chronicles," VT 4 (1954), 401–9, especially pp. 404 f.

(II Chron xii 6, 12, xxxii 26, xxxiii 12, xxxiv 27). Of course in many of those references he merely followed his main source.

According to our author, the attitude that the division was the result of evil was stubbornly maintained except in a few instances (e.g., II Chron xxx 10–11). For him the Northern Kingdom was conceived in sin, born in iniquity, and nurtured in adultery. There was only one way to salvation for its rulers and people and that was to recognize their sins of defection, humble themselves, and submit to the appointed way of the Lord which was through the Davidic dynasty and the temple of the Lord at Jerusalem. Rudolph[27] is clearly right when he points out that the Chronicler was interested not only in showing how the theocracy had developed in the politico-religious institutions of the Davidic and Solomonic periods but in emphasizing, in the light of that development, that there could be no compromise with the Samaritan community of his time. Even in the lists in the introductory chapters of I Chron (i–ix), the families of David and Judah precede those of the other tribes who separated themselves from the true community by their willfulness and sin, and hence forfeited their rights ever afterward unless they humbled themselves before the Lord. The Chronicler further asserts that after the rebellion of Jeroboam I and his followers "the priests and Levites all over Israel came from their domain and placed themselves at his [Rehoboam's] disposal. The Levites left their pasture grounds and their property and went to Judah and Jerusalem because Jeroboam and his sons had excluded them from the priesthood of Yahweh" (II Chron xi 13–14). This is confirmed by I Kings xii 31 which refers to Jeroboam's ordination of a new priesthood not of Levitic descent. At the instigation of the man of God, Amaziah cancelled his contract with Ephraimite warriors whom he had hired to assist him in the campaign against Edom (II Chron xxv 5 ff.), a move bitterly resented by them. When Hezekiah invited the Northerners to participate in the passover celebration, the couriers were laughed at and ridiculed. However, "a few men from Asher, Manasseh, and Zebulun humbled themselves and came to Jerusalem" (II Chron xxx 10). None who came from the north were barred from participation, though they had not followed prescribed regulations (II Chron xxx 18 f.). The historicity of Hezekiah's passover does not concern us here; it is the Chronicler's point of view that is significant. The Davidic line was the true one and Jerusalem was

---

[27] *Chronikbücher*, p. ix (see Rudolph, Selected Bibliography, Commentaries).

the sanctuary of the Lord; and while there could be no joint religious enterprises from his vantage point, there was always the possibility of participation in the cultus on the basis of humility and the acceptance of the historic tradition with its stipulations and requirements. So much appears clear from his reference to the situation in the time of Hezekiah. Even in the passover celebration under Josiah, some people from Israel were present and participated in that event (II Chron xxxv 18). The Chronicler has both passovers take place at Jerusalem—an important departure from the original local family procedure (Exod xii 1–14).[28] Kings, though it does not mention such a rite in connection with Hezekiah, supports the cultic institution of the passover at Jerusalem in the time of Josiah (II Kings xxiii 21 ff.)—an outgrowth of the Deuteronomic reform. In this matter the Chronicler followed the Deuteronomist, as indeed he did in many others. But the double celebration recorded in Chronicles emphasizes the writer's view of the position of Jerusalem as the cult center of the nation. It is just one more plank in the religious structure of the Judean capital as the official cult place and reinforces the belief in the unauthenticity of all rites performed at other places.

(b) Having detailed the Judean religious development from David to the fall of the Southern Kingdom, our author presses home the meaning of it all for the community and period for which he is writing. He is at great pains in Ezra-Nehemiah to authenticate the continuity of that development in the postexilic age. While he does on occasion stress the inclusion of all Israel within the purview of his religious scheme, though speaking of Judah and Benjamin specifically (Ezra i 5, iv 1, x 9; cf. II Chron xxxi 1, xxxiv 9), he allows no doubt as to the right place for true worship or the proper religio-political atmosphere. For him the dwelling place of God is Jerusalem (Ezra i 3), as it was for the later prophets of Judah. In agreement with Haggai and Zechariah, he asserts that the returnees "built the altar of the God of Israel to offer burnt offerings upon it as prescribed in the law of Moses, the man of God" (Ezra iii 2). The author of Ezra refers frequently to the house of God *at Jerusalem* (i 4, 5, ii 68, iii 8, iv 24, v 2, 16, 17, vi 3, 5, 12, 18, vii 15, 16, 17, 27, viii 29, 30).[29] Such accentuation upon the specific

[28] See A. C. Welch, *The Work of the Chronicler*, pp. 108 f. (see Selected Bibliography).
[29] Cf. also references to Jerusalem as the holy city in Neh xi 1.

place of the house of God must have special significance; it seems
to point directly and emphatically to the belief that it was the only
legitimate place for worship. There can be no doubt that the Chronicler was interested chiefly in the religious institution—the house of
God or the temple of God—as may be seen from the numerous
occurrences of the term in Ezra-Nehemiah (upward of forty-five
times). That interest, together with his overt emphasis upon Judah
and Jerusalem, reveals his conception of the continuity of worship
in the old Judean cult center. As noted above, such a point of view
is of particular consequence when it is recalled that there was, in
all probability, a peristence of some kind of worship at Jerusalem
during the Exile though it may not have been regarded as adequate
for various reasons (cf. Ezra iv 2). Since Bethel was not destroyed
in the campaigns of Nebuchadnezzar,[30] the old shrine there may
have been repaired after its demolition by Josiah (II Kings xxiii
15; II Chron xxxiv 6 f.) and utilized by the people of the area until
its destruction in the late Neo-Babylonian or early Persian period.
There may be a hint of worship by the people of the land, perhaps
after the burning of Bethel, at Jerusalem in Ezra iii 3.[31] But the
Chronicler would, of course, have looked upon either with disfavor.

Along with the insistence upon true worship as confined to the
house of God at Jerusalem went emphasis upon the proper personnel
in the right social conditions. The lists indicate that both Ezra and
Nehemiah were concerned about the pedigree of the participants
(Ezra ii 59 ff.; Neh vii 61 ff.).[32] They had to be able to furnish the
proper credentials to admit them to the true community of worshipers and as functionaries of the cult. Ezra ii 1 appears to limit
them to those whom Nebuchadnezzar had exiled, though strictly
speaking that does not seem to have been quite the case (Ezra vi 21
—"all those who had separated themselves from the impurities of
the nations of the land" indicates clearly that others, perhaps of
their relatives who had remained in the land, were permitted to
join in religious celebrations). Even though, for the most part,
Judeans were involved, they thought of themselves as representatives
of all Israel, the true Israel (Ezra vi 17, viii 24, 35).

[30] W. F. Albright, ARI, pp. 172 ff.

[31] Cf. Rudolph, *Esra und Nehemia*, p. 29.

[32] On the relation of these lists see H. L. Allrik, "The Lists of Zerubbabel
(Neh 7 and Ezra 2) and the Hebrew Numerical Notation," BASOR 136
(1953), 21–27; K. Galling, "The Gola-List according to Ezra 2 / Nehemiah 7,"
JBL 70 (1951), 149 ff.; and the commentaries.

Particularly important is the list of those accompanying Ezra (viii 1–14) which consists of twelve groups of laymen with the priestly and Davidic groups.[33] This list affords welcome insight into the Chronicler's conception of the organization of the returned golah. It was composed of laymen, priests, and officials. The note that Sheshbazzar was a prince of Judah (Ezra i 9), the reference to Zerubbabel as political leader (Ezra ii 2, iii 2, 8; iv 2, 3, v 2; Neh vii 7, xii 1, 47; Hag i 1, 12, 14, ii 2, 4, 21, 23; Zech iv 6, 7, 9, 10), to Nehemiah as governor of Judah (Neh viii 9, x 1, xii 26; supported by the powers he seems to have had), the pains taken by them to show that the building enterprises were in accordance with the royal decrees, and the regard for David (Ezra iii 10, viii 20; Neh xii 24, 36, 45, 46)—all reflect the political phase of the whole movement, as the Chronicler sees it. All in all it was an attempt to refill the vacuum left in Judah and Jerusalem (Ezra i 3, ii 1, v 1, vii 14, ix 9, x 7) after the events of 587, which had been occupied to some extent by the surrounding peoples who spilled over into the area abandoned by the captives. The expression Judah and Jerusalem occurs frequently in Jeremiah, and the arrangements of his time may have been the pattern followed by the writer. The new community visualized by Haggai, Zechariah, and Ezra i–vi was intended to resume where the one exiled in 587 left off, as may be seen from the attempt to connect the leaders of the first returnees with the Davidic dynasty. The picture of the restored community emerging in Ezra vii through Nehemiah is somewhat different. Here the Davidic element, except in cultic matters, is replaced by Nehemiah.

Thus the Chronicler sees Jerusalem as the authentic place of worship, the returnees as the legitimate successors of the people of Judah and the cult personnel, and the community established by them as the true Israel. The Exile was but an interlude in the ongoing history of Judah and Jerusalem, though the organization and governing powers were a bit different.[34]

---

[33] The twelve groups of laymen symbolize the twelve original tribes (also lay), and support the view that the writer regarded the returnees as the true representatives of "all Israel." The connection with the Qumran community ought not to be overlooked. It too was composed of lay, priestly, and Davidic elements. The Qumran organization was based largely on Ezekiel and the *P* regulations of the wilderness, in addition to some influences from Ezra-Nehemiah.

[34] Albright, BP, p. 50.

(c) A third factor operative in the whole situation requires special emphasis. That was the necessity for an institutional structure such as that envisioned in Ezra-Nehemiah because of the manifest political and social pressures exerted upon the new community. The postexilic writers sometimes leave us cold and unresponsive because we fail to grasp the importance of institutions that are strong and vigorous enough to offset those pressures in difficult times. There is a certain analogy between medieval monasticism and the separatist movement of Ezra-Nehemiah. Both were a bulwark against forces that could easily have wrecked what they stood for and what they regarded as essential for themselves and the world of their time. Brief comment upon some of the forces militating against the religion of the Jews in the late sixth and early fifth centuries is necessary.

An excellent illustration of the headway made by those forces may be seen in a comparison between the high ideals set forth in Second Isaiah and the degenerate practices reflected in the book of Malachi. Almost everything detrimental to the purity and vigor of religious devotion is to be found there. So careless, probably not without cause, had the people of Judah become that only the poorest animals were offered in sacrifice (Mal i 8) and then not wholeheartedly; they manifested a certain weariness in their religious obligations (Mal i 13), and with it came a breakdown of morality and common decency (Mal ii 14). The tithe for the service of the Lord's house was neglected or only intermittently paid (Mal iii 8 ff.). The extent of such lethargy in religious matters appears in the rebuke the prophet administered to the priests who were unorthodox in their teaching (Mal ii 7). In place of knowledge and instruction in the way of the Lord, so as to turn people away from their evils and wrongdoing, there was actual misdirection (Mal ii 8). Instead of being the messengers of the Lord, they turned out to be exponents of convenience, failed to keep the Lord's way, and exhibited partiality in the application of the Torah (Mal ii 9). How deeply ingrained the tendency toward deviation was may be seen from the fact that when Nehemiah had left Jerusalem for a time, the high priest Eliashib unlawfully provided a room in the temple for Tobiah (Neh xiii 4–9). Nehemiah's and Ezra's insistence upon a pure religion, thoroughly orthodox, though seemingly restrictive, was absolutely essential in coping with the inclination toward a watered-down, half-hearted faith.

Of course the roots of the difficulty were sunk deep into the subsoil of the social and economic life of the time. As noted above in the discussion of the historical situation, the returnees were confronted with all sorts of adverse conditions. Poverty, crop failure, harassment by hostile groups, and political involvements took their toll. But the greatest danger of all, and one that ultimately required heroic measures to combat, was that of absorption in the sociopolitical structure of neighboring people. It was observed earlier that the golah was threatened by Samaritans who wanted to share in the building of the temple (Ezra iv 2) and who, when their overtures were rejected, offered all sorts of difficulties. Such a compromise would have meant syncretism like the one prevailing at Elephantine and therefore could not be accepted. Yet they persisted even to the point of deception (Neh vi 1 ff.) and subversion (Neh vi 10 f.). Marriages with the people of the land were doubtless an outgrowth of economic necessity,[35] but necessities have a way of undermining character and faith. The most distressing feature of the whole situation was that the officials and chiefs were uppermost in this unfaithfulness (Ezra ix 2, and cf. the list in x 18–44). The ordinary citizens, by virtue of their status, were not required to wrestle with the problem so much, though the Nehemiah passage (xiii 23 f.) suggests a fairly widespread practice of intermarriage and warns of the dangers of social laxity among the Jews of the period. What might seem to us an unreasonable demand—forcing the divorce of foreign wives married by the upper classes—can be understood in the light of the emphasis on purity in the Hebrew conception of the family. Had the practices continued unabated over an extended period of time, the Judaism of the returnees might have evaporated without a trace. The problem was an intensely practical one, and the simplest solution was to identify the religious community with the genealogically pure. This was doubtless a distortion and oversimplification imposed by the desperate condition of the Jewish community around Jerusalem. Identification by heredity rather than by faith had a permanent effect upon the Jewish community. The two were always present; the prevalence of now the one and now the other was probably due to the circumstances at the time. Both are reflected also in the New Testament.

Another point that appears to be emphasized by the Chronicler is the authority of those whom he invests with cultic functions.

[35] Würthwein, *Der 'amm* . . . , pp. 64 ff.

There is no doubt about the high priests in his time (cf. list in I
Chron vi 1–15, 50–53; Neh xii 10–11): they were the spiritual
and temporal heads of the new community after the debacle under
Zerubbabel. His chief interest in the clergy was the Levites,[36]
probably necessitated by local conditions. The Deuteronomic reformation located the official cultus at Jerusalem and while Josiah is
said to have brought all the local priests to Jerusalem (II Kings
xxiii 8), many of them could not or would not come to fulfill their
functions there (II Kings xxiii 9). It is likely that among those who
remained in the land were many of the local cult functionaries.
Those who were taken to Babylon enjoyed their status to such an
extent that they were reluctant to return to Jerusalem. Only 341
Levites and 392 temple servants as against 4289 priests returned
with Zerubbabel (Ezra ii 36–58); no Levites appeared in response to
Ezra's invitation until pressure was exerted and then only 38 Levites
and 220 temple servants showed up (Ezra viii 15–20). It was thus
imperative that the status of Levites be clarified since in Ezekiel's
program there was a sharp distinction between priests and Levites
(xliv 10 ff.). Proper service at the new temple demanded that cultic
rites be handled by authenticated persons or groups; their authentication depended, in part at least, upon a definite recognition of their
status. Moreover, their assent and loyalty to the cult was in some
measure contingent upon the concession of their rights and privileges.
Such recognition won support from them and at the same time
curbed the power of the Zadokites.

Strict cult orthodoxy, exclusivism and the support of a more
broadly based cult personnel were of the utmost importance if the
community was to succeed in its efforts. There could be no deviation

---

[36] Cf. R. H. Pfeiffer, *Introduction to the Old Testament* (New York, 1941),
pp. 792 ff. He observes that the position of the Levites is shown by a pointing
up of their function in history, which was not limited to temple worship. Note
the prominent position they occupy in the Davidic arrangements (I Chron xv
2–27, xxiii 3–5). They had charge of the sacred vessels and objects (I Chron
ix 26–32). They performed certain cultic duties (I Chron xxiii 28–32); they
were teachers of the law (II Chron xvii 7–9) and served as judges (II Chron
xix 8–11). They played a significant role in the coronation of Joash (II Chron
xxiii 2–20), co-operated enthusiastically in Hezekiah's reformation (II Chron
xxix 4–19) and passover (II Chron xxx 13–17), as well as in those of Josiah
(II Chron xxxiv 9–13, xxxv 3–18). Individual Levites served as scribes (I
Chron xxiv 6; II Chron xxxiv 13) and prophets (I Chron xxv 5; II Chron
xx 14). According to II Chron xvii 8 f., xxxv 3, they handled the law. They
are even described as holy (II Chron xxiii 6, xxxv 3).

in view of the circumstances and the presence of powerfully de-
structive forces operative on all sides.

The intention of the Chronicler in meeting the needs of his time
was to show that the true Israel was the one perpetuated in Judah
from the period of David to Ezra. Those who returned from the
Exile were, therefore, the true successors of the Judah governed by
the Davidic dynasty. The re-established institutions required the
strictest loyalty and devotion to the ideals of its founders and every
effort had to be exerted to keep the community pure and orthodox
if it was to survive the many-sided onslaughts then being launched
against it. Curtis and Madsen correctly observe that "in his day
his message rendered a most important service."[37]

[37] *A Critical and Exegetical Commentary on the Books of Chronicles*, p. 16;
a good assessment of the religious value of Chronicles. (See Curtis and
Madsen, Selected Bibliography, Commentaries.)

LITERARY CONSIDERATIONS

One of the most vexing problems of almost every Old Testament book or broader composition such as that of the Deuteronomist has to do with sources and literary structure. This problem is perhaps less difficult in the work of the Chronicler than elsewhere since we have some comparative materials to guide us. Yet there are sections and nuances which do offer considerable trouble for the serious student. Space limitations prevent a full discussion of all views that have been put forth on the subject; it must suffice to point out general lines along which the discussion has moved in recent years. But it is necessary first to survey the general content of Chronicles.

CONTENT OF CHRONICLES

I Chron i–ix, which introduces the work of the Chronicler, is composed of a collection of tables which is not an integral part of a book at all. *P*'s genealogies are usually introduced by connecting links, but the bald way in which these lists begin suggests that it was really a file prefixed to the Chronicler's work and then tied in rather clumsily at the end. The date of the file as it now stands can be determined by the Davidic genealogy and the chapter on the returned exiles.[38] It begins with the broadest possible reference to the genealogies from Adam to Israel (Jacob), with an Edomite interlude (i 35–42) and an account of Edomite chiefs (i 43–54). The genealogy of Israel follows and continues to the end of chapter viii. It traces the descendants of Judah (ii 3 f.), through Perez (ii 5), Hezron (ii 9–17), Caleb (ii 18–24), and Jerahmeel (ii 25–41), and localizes the children of Caleb (ii 42–50a) and Hur (ii 50b–55). Then comes the family of David (iii 1–9) through Solomon

---

[38] I owe this suggestion to Professor Freedman.

to the postexilic sons of Elioenai (iii 10–24). As David was a Judahite, the family of Judah is again taken up (iv 1–23). Simeon, closely identified with Judah, follows (iv 24–43). The Transjordan Reuben, Gad, and the half-tribe of Manasseh are dealt with in v 1–26. Next comes the compiler's favorite group—the descendants of Levi, with a list of pre-exilic high priests (vi 1–15), the Levite genealogy (vi 16–30), the Levitical musicians and functionaries (vi 31–53) and their allotment among the tribes (vi 54–81). Chapter vii deals with the descendants of Issachar (1–5), Benjamin (6–12), Naphtali and Manasseh (13–19), Ephraim (20–29), Asher (30–40); chapter viii returns to the Benjaminites at Geba (1–7), in Moab, Ono, and Lod (8–12), in Aijalon, Gath, and Jerusalem (13–28), in Gibeon and Jerusalem (29–32), as a prelude to the genealogy of Saul (33–40); ix 1ab forms the conclusion to the preceding chapters; ix 1c–34 (cf. Neh xi 3–23) has to do with the inhabitants of Jerusalem after the Exile (1c–16) and the functions of the Levites (17–34); ix 35–44 is another version of the list of Benjaminites living at Gibeon (cf. viii 33–38), probably an introduction to the story of Saul's death and burial in the following chapter.

I Chron x–xxix deals with the central character in the Chronicler's history, David. It begins with a circumscribed narrative of Saul's last battle with the Philistines which ended in his death (x). Next comes the anointing of David and the capture of Jerusalem—to become the capital of his empire (xi 1–9)—followed by the list of his heroes introduced through the Philistine struggle (xi 10–47). The building of David's army and its strength follow (xii 1–40). Then comes one of the prime events in David's career: the bringing of the ark to Jerusalem. The first attempt failed (xiii 1–14); the second, after proper precautions were taken, succeeded and was marked with great pomp and ceremony (xv 1–xvi 43). Between the narratives of the two attempts stands a description of the building of the palace, an enumeration of his wives and an account of the Philistine wars (xiv). Chapter xvii tells of David's desire to build a temple, his colloquy with Nathan, and his prayer. Then comes a reference to the Philistine campaign, wars with Aram and Edom, and a list of David's officials (xviii). Chapters xix–xx give an account of the Ammonite wars and another brush with the Philistines at Gezer. Chapters xxi–xxviii describe the plans for the temple and the organization of its staff. Chapter xxi recounts the census story merely as the occasion for the selection of the temple site;

chapters xxii–xxiii set forth the plans for the temple with provisions for its worship; chapters xxiv–xxvi portray the organization of the staff of officials for the cultus. The royal administrative orders form the subject matter of chapter xxvii; the following chapter (xxviii) presents David's last address to the congregation, his prayer, the anointing of Solomon as king, and chapter xxix, a brief evaluation of the years of his reign.

II Chron i–ix is devoted to the activities of Solomon. It begins with the new king's establishing himself in his position and his prayer for wisdom (i 1–17) and then proceeds immediately to a particularization of preparations for the construction of the temple (ii 1–18) and the formation of the corvée. The plans for the temple (iii), provision for its equipment (iv) and the dedication (v 1–vii 10) follow. Solomon's vision, administrative activity—both secular and religious—(vii 11–viii 18), the visit of the queen of Sheba (ix 1–12) and an inventory of the royal revenue and trade activity (ix 13–31) conclude the part. In the estimation of the Chronicler, Solomon is an extension of David, that is, the one who carried out the directions issued by the great king, though he did reflect wisdom and piety in his own right.

II Chron x–xxxvi rehearses the story of Judah as seen by the writer and enacted through its kings. In some respects, this story is the fulfillment of the divine promise to David by Nathan (I Chron xvii 13) and reaffirmed by Yahweh to Solomon (II Chron vii 18). In line with his method of dealing with history, this part centers about personalities, generally kings of Judah. The story begins with an account of the attitude of Rehoboam which led to a division of the kingdom (x) and a report on the progress of his plans for a separate administration—dissuasion from attacking Jeroboam, construction of fortress cities, the gravitation of the Levites to his territory (xi). Chapter xii deals with the invasion of Shishak with its consequences and the Chronicler's emphasis on the submission of the king in harmony with the demands of prophecy; it closes with the usual notice of the king's character, years of reign, death, and burial. The reign of Abijah is covered in a single chapter (xiii) which limits itself almost entirely to that king's campaign against Jeroboam which ended disastrously for the latter. The Chronicler's narrative of Asa includes a note on the ten years of peace at the beginning of his reign, his active participation in the religious purification of the land, and a more lengthy reference to Asa's defense

against Zerah the Ethiopian (xiv). Chapter xv contains the prophecy of Azariah, son of Oded, and its results. The third chapter (xvi)
devoted to Asa describes his altercation with Baasha of Israel,
which involved an alliance between the former and Benhadad of
Damascus against Baasha, and the prophecy of Hanani against Asa
and its consequences. One of the favorite characters of our author
was Jehoshaphat (xvii 1–xxi 1) whose exploits are set forth at
some length. Chapter xvii begins with a general summation of Jehoshaphat's reign and then enumerates some of the deeds of the
king—the instruction of the people (7–9), the tribute received by
him (10–13) and the garrisoning of the fortified cities of Judah
(14–19). His association with Ahab, king of Israel, in the Ramoth-
gilead campaign, the prophecy of Micaiah ben Imlah associated
with it and the outcome of the battle are related in chapter xviii.
Jehoshaphat was rebuked for participating by Jehu ben Hanani (xix
1–3) a prophet. The judicial reform (xix 4–11) was of great
significance. The campaign against the Transjordan confederation
composed of Ammonites, Moabites, and Mennites is the subject of
xx 1–30. The summary of Jehoshaphat's reign, his alliance with
Ahaziah, the maritime fiasco at Ezion-geber, and his death and
burial are recounted in xx 31–xxi 1. The remainder of chapter xxi
deals with the reign of the wicked Jehoram, who slew his brothers,
was allied by marriage with the house of Ahab, defeated the Edomites, received a letter from Elijah, suffered an invasion by Philistines and Arabs, and was the victim of a loathsome disease. Chapter xxii presents the story of Ahaziah, his death at the hands of
Jehu, and the usurpation of the throne by Athaliah, his mother.
The purge was not long in coming, as we learn from the success of
Jehoiada in putting Joash on the throne (xxiii). Things went well
while Jehoiada lived (xxiv 1–16), but after his death the king defected. When Zechariah, son of Jehoiada, reprimanded him, Joash
put Zechariah to death. An Aramaean invasion followed and Joash
was killed, the victim of a palace intrigue (xxiv 17–27). Joash
was succeeded by Amaziah who, in accordance with prophetic advice, rejected Israelite assistance in his war with Edom. But, like his
father, he turned away from Yahweh and became proud. The end
was defeat, humiliation, and capture at the hands of Joash of Israel.
Finally Amaziah was slain, by conspirators, at Lachish (xxv). The
reigns of Uzziah and Jotham are of more than ordinary importance.
The former was apparently a successful ruler (xxvi 1–15), but, like

many others, overstepped his bounds (xxvi 16–23). Jotham's policy
was a continuation of his father's (xxvii). The rule of the wicked
Ahaz is dealt with most unsympathetically (xxviii). As in the case
of Jehoshaphat, four chapters are devoted to Hezekiah (xxix–
xxxii). The first act of Hezekiah was to issue orders for the cleansing of the temple (xxix) and the reinstitution of orderly worship. The
Chronicler's ascription of a magnificent passover celebration to this
king is given in chapter xxx; the following chapter (xxxi) is devoted to the religious reformation of Hezekiah. Chapter xxxii 1–23
is concerned with the invasion of Sennacherib and Hezekiah's reaction to it—his strengthening of the capital and his and Isaiah's
prayers about the insults of the Assyrians hurled against the city
and people—and the miraculous deliverance of Jerusalem. A summary statement on the achievements of the king follows (xxxii
24–33). Manasseh, the son of Hezekiah, acted haughtily toward
Yahweh, followed the Assyrian cult, and desecrated the house of God
(xxxiii 1–9). Finally there is the account of his capture by the
Assyrians, his repentance and amends, and an evaluation of his
reign (xxxiii 10–20). Nothing good is said about Amon who re-
verted to the evils practiced by his father before his repentance.
He was slain by his own servants (xxxiii 21–25). Josiah is portrayed in almost the same glowing terms as Hezekiah. As soon as he
reached the proper age he began the general reform (xxxiv 1–7)
that led to the repair of the temple and finding the book of the law,
which became the program for further cultic reformation (xxxiv
8–33). A spectacular observance of the Passover followed (xxxv
1–19). The account of Josiah closes with the king's death at Megiddo
where he attempted to thwart Pharaoh Neco in his hasty march to
the Euphrates to assist the Assyrians against their opponents (xxxv
20–27). Succeeding reigns are passed over rapidly (xxxvi 1–21).
Chronicles ends with a reference to the rise of Cyrus and his benevolent attitude toward the captive Jews in Babylon (xxxvi 22–23).

THE SOURCES REFERRED TO IN CHRONICLES

Our present books of Chronicles refer explicitly to sources used
by the compiler. Those sources can only be listed under the categories into which they appear to fall and characterized in so far as
our present state of knowledge permits.

Official records

Into this category fall what appear to be the accounts of the deeds and acts of kings, perhaps the record kept in the royal archives or in the temple. Mentioned specifically are the following:

The book of the chronicles of King David (I Chron xxvii 24)

The chronicles of the kings of Israel and Judah (II Chron xxvii 7, xxxv 27, xxxvi 8)

The chronicles of the kings of Judah and Israel (II Chron xvi 11, xxv 26, xxviii 26, xxxii 32)

The Chronicles of the kings of Israel (I Chron ix 1; II Chron xx 34)

The records of the kings of Israel (II Chron xxxiii 18)

The treatise (midrash) of the chronicle of the kings (II Chron xxiv 27)

The decree of David the king of Israel and the decree of Solomon his son (II Chron xxxv 4)

Whether the Chronicler had direct access to these records or whether they were taken from the Deuteronomic compilation is a matter of debate. In all instances where notices of sources occur in the Kings parallels, the reference there is to the "chronicle of the acts of the kings of Judah" (I Kings xiv 29, xv 7, 23, xxii 45; II Kings xiv 18, xv 6, 36, xvi 19, xx 20, xxi 17, xxiii 28, xxiv 5). Just why the Chronicler should refer to his sources in precisely the way he does is not clear, nor is it certain what is meant by his "midrash of the chronicle of the kings." There has been much speculation on the subject but no convincing solution.

Official genealogical lists

The following are expressly noted:

They had an official genealogy (the descendants of Simeon) (I Chron iv 33)

All of them were included in the official genealogy (the descendants of Gad) (I Chron v 17)

Their official genealogy (descendants of Benjamin) (I Chron vii 9)

Their official genealogy (descendants of Asher) (I Chron vii 40)
Officially registered (of all Israel) (I Chron ix 1)
Officially registered (of doorkeepers) (I Chron ix 22)
Official genealogy (of Rehoboam) (II Chron xii 15)

The writer was doubtless in possession of these lists and others he does not specify—since this is one aspect of his work in which he was particularly interested, as was the author of the *P* document before him. It is more than likely that he took most of his early lists (I Chron i–ix) directly from the already compiled Pentateuch, with additions here and there.

Prophetic records

Here the interests of the writer are once more quite evident:

The records of Samuel the seer (I Chron xxix 29)
The records of Nathan the prophet (I Chron xxix 29; II Chron ix 29)
The records of Gad the seer (I Chron xxix 29)
The prophecy of Ahijah the Shilonite (II Chron ix 29)
The visions of Iddo the seer concerning Jeroboam the son of Nebat (II Chron ix 29)
The records of Shemaiah the prophet (II Chron xii 15)
The visions of Iddo the seer (II Chron xii 15)
The treatise (midrash) of the Prophet Iddo (II Chron xiii 22)
The records of Jehu ben Hanani (II Chron xx 34)
The history of Uzziah which Isaiah the prophet, the son of Amoz, has written down (II Chron xxvi 22)
The vision of Isaiah, the son of Amoz, the prophet in the chronicle of the kings of Judah and Israel (II Chron xxxii 32)
The records of his seers (referring to Manasseh) (II Chron xxxiii 19)

Some of these prophecies were undoubtedly written down either in separate documents or in connection with longer records; the language of the author is too definite to assume otherwise. And the structure of the prophetic books that have come down to us indicates the transmission of some of their contents either as independent bodies of oral material or as written documents.

Other official documents

In this category belong the following:

Message of Sennacherib to Hezekiah (II Chron xxxii 10–15)
Other letters of Sennacherib (II Chron xxxii 17)

Many of these documents were included in and formed a part of larger sources employed by the Chronicler, such as the memoirs of Nehemiah and Ezra, and the Deuteronomist.

Others

The words of David and Asaph (II Chron xxix 30)

These may refer to Psalms attributed to them, though none is actually quoted by the Chronicler. The Psalm portions used in I Chron xvi 8–36 (cf. Pss cv 1–15, xcvi, cvi 1, 47 f.) are not identified.

The document with plans for the temple (I Chron xxviii 19)[39]
The Lamentations (II Chron xxxv 25)

These are obviously the Lamentations of Jeremiah—indeed Jeremiah is reported to have uttered some lamentations for Josiah which are said to be quoted there (in the same verse). The Book of Lamentations was thus in existence and known as such when the Chronicler wrote, though its subject matter consists of lamentation for Jerusalem rather than for Josiah as reported here.

Whatever may be one's view as to the historical accuracy of the Chronicler, one cannot totally disregard his references to materials extant in his time or earlier. How much the stories or elements taken over from those sources were embellished by him is something else again, but wherever his work can be checked it is found to contain an element or elements of truth, as may be seen from the following analysis.

[39] See J. A. Bewer, "Textkritische Bemerkungen zum Alten Testament," FAB, pp. 75 f.

USE OF THE SOURCES[40]

One of the most difficult problems arising from the study of the literary composition of Chronicles, Ezra, and Nehemiah is the origin and use of the compiler's sources. Can his references to the sources noted in the previous section be taken seriously or were they already present in the anthology employed by him? The answer to that question will, to some extent, determine the evaluation placed on materials transmitted by the Chronicler which are not found elsewhere. R. H. Pfeiffer thinks he draws about one half of his material from earlier biblical books, while the other half consists, for the most part, of more or less historical fiction.[41] B. Maisler thinks that both Kings and Chronicles were dependent on "the words" of the prophets and famous personalities to a very large extent and to a lesser degree on the temple chronicles and official records.[42] The Chronicler's use of his sources is closely related to his purpose, his theology and general point of view,[43] which in turn depend on one's interpretation.[44] In the following resume only the barest facts can be stated, but it is absolutely essential for purposes of evaluation of the problem. For the sake of convenience, the outline follows the one above on content.

Genealogical introduction to Chronicler (I Chron i–ix)

The genealogical introduction to Chronicles parallels material appearing in the completed Pentateuch and the Deuteronomist's history (Joshua through II Kings, except Ruth).[45] The compiler was of course interested chiefly in Judah because of the historical circumstances of his time and deals with other phases of Israel's

[40] Based on M. Noth's analysis in ÜS, pp. 131–50.
[41] *Introduction to the Old Testament*, pp. 803 ff.
[42] "Ancient Israelite Historiography," IEJ 2 (1952), 82–88.
[43] See A. M. Burnet, "Le Chroniste et ses sources," RB 60 (1953), 481–508; RB 61 (1954), 349–86.
[44] Cf. Noth, ÜS, pp. 110–80. Also Rothstein and Hänel, *Kommentar zum ersten Buch der Chronik*, Teil 2, pp. ix–lxxxii; Galling, *Die Bücher der Chronik, Esra, Nehemia*, pp. 8–12; Rudolph, pp. x–xxiv; Goettsberger, *Die Bücher der Chronik oder Paralipomenon*, pp. 6–17; Curtis and Madsen, pp. 17–26; and the various introductions (for complete references, see Selected Bibliography, Commentaries).
[45] This suggestion I owe to Professor Freedman.

experience only where it impinges upon that of Judah. He begins, therefore, by showing how Judah was related to Israel (Jacob), Israel to Abraham, Abraham to Shem, and Shem to Adam.

i 1–4, from Gen v, except vs. 4, possibly from Gen x 1 (*P*)

i 5–7, from Gen x 2–4 (*P*)

i 8–10, reproduces Gen x 6–8 exactly, except for a few spellings (*P*)

i 11–16, from Gen x 13–18a (*J* or *JE,* and *P* [vs. 11])

i 17–23, from Gen x 22–29, but omits "and the sons of Aram" before Uz (17) and Meshech for Mash at end of verse; Ebal for Obal in vs. 22 (*J* and *P*)

i 24–28, based on Gen xi 10–26 (*P*)

i 29–33, mostly from Gen xxv 12–16a, 2–4 (*P* and *J* or *E*)

i 34–42, probably from Gen xxxvi 4, 5a, 11–12a, 20–28 (*P*), with considerable abbreviation and spelling variants

i 43–54, from Gen xxxvi 31–43 (*P*), with few omissions

ii 1–2, condensation of Gen xxxv 23–26 (*P*); cf. Exod i 1–6 (mostly *P*). Chronicler follows a different order

ii 3–4, from Gen xxxviii 2–7 (*J*), 29–30 (*J*); xlvi 12 (*P*); Num xxvi 19–20 (*P*). Again with much simplification

ii 5, from Gen xlvi 12b; Num xxvi 21 (*P*). Does not gloss over the sin of Er

ii 6–8, with some variations from Josh vii 1 (cf. I Kings v 11 [iv 31E][46])

ii 9–17, cf. Ruth iv 19–22; I Sam xvi 6–13; II Sam ii 18, xvii 25. The Chronicler connects the family of David with Judah through Hezron

ii 18–24, unparalleled genealogy of Caleb, son of Hezron

ii 25–41, unparalleled genealogy of Jerahmeel, the oldest son of Hezron

ii 42–55, unparalleled genealogy of Caleb (the second one) and Hur the son of Caleb by Ephrathah

iii 1–9, cf. II Sam iii 2–5, v 5, xiii 1. The Chronicler has Daniel for Chileab as the second son of David born at Hebron, and omits "over all Israel and Judah." After the list of the first four sons born at Jerusalem, he adds, "to Bathshua the daughter of

---

[46] Chapter and verse numbers which differ in the Hebrew and English versions are designated by an "E" or an "H."

Ammiel"; for the other sons of David he has a different order, two Eliphelets, and adds Nogah

iii 10–24, follows the Kings order, except for the omission of the name of Athaliah and the expansion of the family lists from Josiah to Elioenai. This is the genealogy of the house of David. It gives the names of the kings as well as those of the heirs apparent or presumptive and their relatives of the royal line

iv 1–4, vss. 1–2 follow the Judah genealogy of ii 52, vss. 3–4 may be intended to supplement ii 51b as the descendants of Hareph

iv 5–8, supplementary to ii 24, the Calebite clan

iv 9–10, supplementary to ii 55a, the Calebite clan through Jabez

iv 11–12, supplementary to ii 55b, as shown by LXX reading of Rechab for Recah (iv 12)

iv 13–15, supplementary to ii 22, amplifying the Calebite line (cf. Num xiii 6; Judg i 13; Josh xv 13 ff.)

iv 16–20, supplementary to ii 42–50a, further amplifying Caleb's descendants combining persons and place names. Probably from local sources

iv 21–23, supplementary to ii 3, with information concerning the third son of Judah, Shelah, who was the ancestor of the potters. From an ancient record

iv 24–43, the descendants of Simeon and their place of occupation. List of sons departs somewhat from those in Gen xlvi 10 and Exod vi 15. It follows Num xxvi 12–14 except for Jarib, there Jachin. The place names (28–33) are parallel, with some variations, to Josh xix 1–8, itself dependent on Josh xv 26 ff. where they are reckoned to Judah.[47] Verses 34–37 represent an expansion of the Simeon list at a time when they were half nomads

v 1–10, the Reubenite clan, based on Gen xxxv 22 and Num xxvi 5–6 (cf. Gen xlvi 9; Exod vi 14; all *P*) but expanded here

v 11–17, independent of any known source. Taken from official lists from time of Jotham and Jeroboam II. Purpose of the writer was to treat the Transjordan tribes together

v 18–22, an expansion of vs. 10, detailing an Israelite campaign against Transjordan peoples

[47] Verses 28–33 represent one of the three transmissions of this list which indicates its age. Cf. F. M. Cross, Jr., and G. E. Wright, "The Boundary and Province Lists of the Kingdom of Judah," JBL 75 (1956), 214 f.

v 23–26, begins with a reference to the half-tribe of Manasseh (the tribe of Manasseh was divided into two groups, one of which resided in Transjordan and the other in Cesjordan) and ends with an account of the captivity under Tilgath-pilneser which may have been taken in part from II Kings xv 19, 20, xvii 6, xviii 11; but the theology of the writer is quite evident (vs. 25), as above in vs. 20

vi 1–15 [v 27–41H], a list of pre-exilic high priests which takes its departure from Exod vi 16–23 (cf. Gen xlvi 11; Num xxvi 57–60; iii 2, 17). Twenty-six high priests are named from Levi to Jehozadak

vi 16–30 [vi 1–15H], the Levitical list (cf. Num iii 17–20, xxvi 57–62a; Exod vi 16–19), other than the high priestly descendants

vi 31–48 [vi 16–32H], the Levitical musicians

vi 49–53 [vi 33–38H], the Aaronite functionaries. Parallels list from Aaron to Ahimaaz in vss. 1–15. Probably supplementary to the preceding section, but observe the position

vi 54–81 [vi 39–66H], the Levitical cities paralleled in Josh xxi and dated by W. F. Albright to the time of David or Solomon[48]

vii 1–5, the family of Issachar (cf. Num xxvi 23–25; Gen xlvi 13), with genealogy of oldest son (Tola) only

vii 6–12, the family of Benjamin (cf. Gen xlvi 21; Num xxvi 38–41), may be a later official register. Verse 12b is a fragment of a Danite list

vii 13, the Naphtali descendants (cf. Gen xlvi 24; Num xxvi 48–49)

vii 14–19, the Manassites (cf. Num xxvi 29–33), with some additions, notably the reference to the Aramaean wife, perhaps to show how the Samaritans of his day were following the old ways—no scruples against mixing with the people of the land[49]

vii 20–29, descendants of Ephraim. Expansion of Num xxvi 35–36 which names only four families. Of importance is the genealogy of Joshua and a fragment of an early story of the conquest in which Ephraim suffered reverses.[50] Cf. the situation

---

[48] "The List of Levitic Cities," LGJV, pp. 49–73, and ARI, pp. 121 f.
[49] Cf. Rudolph, p. 70.
[50] See W. Albright, BASOR 35 (October 1929), 6; FSAC, p. 211; A. Alt, PJB 35 (1939), 100–4.

in Gen xxxiv (Jubilees xxxiv). The conquest of Palestine continued for a long time, beginning with the patriarchal age and was completed in the Davidic age. Verses 28–29 list the towns in possession of Ephraim (Joseph)

vii 30–40, the Asher list (cf. Num xxvi 44–46 and especially Gen xlvi 17 which may have been the basis for the Chronicler's list)

viii 1–40, expanded list of Benjamin. A combination of lists devoted to Saul, perhaps in preparation for what follows in chapter x: (a) 1–7, the Benjaminites of Geba; (b) 8–12, those in Moab, Ono, and Lod; (c) 13–28, those in Aijalon, Gath, and Jerusalem; (d) 29–32, with those in Gibeon and Jerusalem; (e) 33–40, with the family of Saul (cf. I Sam xiv 49 ff., xxxi 2 and the list in ix 35–44). The list may represent the situation in the Josiah period[51]

ix 1–44, list of returnees to which is appended the Gibeon list of Saul and his family. The former may be dependent, in part, on Neh xi. The order of laymen, priests, and Levites is followed, though the names differ in numerous instances—for meaning see COMMENT on Sec. 9

The history of David (I Chron x–xxix)[52]

x 1–14, introduction to the history of David, describing the death and burial of Saul. Dependent upon I Sam xxxi; last two verses are the Chronicler's

xi 1–9, based on II Sam v 1–10 with some modification, especially in vs. 6

xi 10–47, based on the same source as II Sam xxiii 8–39 but considerably expanded;[53] expansions may come from another list, or a supplementary list (41b–47) may have been utilized

xii 1–22, a special source whose authenticity there is no good reason to dispute

xii 23–41, a schematic composition in the Chronicler's style but based on good sources

[51] Rudolph, p. 77.
[52] For a detailed discussion of this section see J. Botterweck, "Zur Eigenart der chronistischen Davidgeschichte," Festschrift für Prof. Dr. Viktor Christian (Vorderasiatische Studien), 1956, pp. 12–31.
[53] K. Elliger, "Die dreissig Helden Davids," PJB 31 (1935), 29–75.

xiii 1–14, based on II Sam vi 2–11; Chronicler placed vss. 1–5 before it. Probably pieced together from various evidence found elsewhere, though not invented material. Note interest in ark tradition

xiv 1–17, a miscellany of materials (cf. II Sam v 11–25). For the list of David's sons the writer leans upon II Sam v 14 f., to which he adds the names Eliphelet and Nogah after Elishua, possibly a correction on the basis of I Chron iii 5–8

xv–xvi—The ceremonies connected with the removal of the ark to Jerusalem. Most scholars think these chapters are based on II Sam vi 12 ff. with numerous additions by Chronicler and later hands. Chapter xv 4–10 is an expanded list of religious officials summoned by David, as shown by vs. 11. The same is true of vss. 16–24. Cf. the religious motive for the removal of the ark[54] as over against the one stated in II Sam; also the legislative order attributed to David. Chapter xvi 1–3 is from II Sam vi 17–19; but note further orders (xvi 4–7) and the Psalms used in the celebration (xvi 8–22 ‖ Ps cv 1–15; xvi 23–33 ‖ Ps xcvi 1–13; xvi 34–36 ‖ Ps cvi 1, 47 f.). Emphasis upon the Levites and their functions is consistent with Chronicler's views and though the story was composed by him, it is in all probability based on true tradition or material.[55] The Psalm represents the practice at the time of the writer. Chapter xvi 43 ‖ II Sam vi 19b–20a. Verses 37–42 are a continuation of the Levite orders pertaining to instrumentalists as well as vocalists

xvii, based on II Sam vii 1–29, with necessary omissions and alterations. Note Messianic undertone in vs. 14[56]

xviii–xx—David's wars. Chapter xviii 1–17 ‖ II Sam viii 1–18; xix 1–xx 3 ‖ II Sam x 1–xi 1, xii 26–31; xx 4–8 ‖ II Sam xxi 18–22. The gruesome details with reference to the Moabites (II Sam viii 2) and Ammonites (II Sam xii 31) are omitted; the hocking of the chariot horses may be a reflection of Deut xvii 16. Cf. omission of Hadadezer of Zobah (II Sam viii 12b) and attribution of conquest of Edom to Abishai instead of to David himself (II Sam viii 13). He makes the sons of David assistants rather than priests (II Sam viii 18c ‖ I Chron xviii 17c). Cf. different version of the slaying of the giant (II Sam

[54] In Burnet, RB 60 (1953), 501.
[55] See Albright, ARI, pp. 119–29; BP, p. 25.
[56] Von Rad, Das Geschichtsbild . . . , pp. 128 f., and Welch, The Work of the Chronicler, pp. 47 f.

xxi 19; I Chron xx 5). There are a few other subtractions or additions; of special interest are the omission of the Bathsheba episode (II Sam xi–xii), the family situation of David (II Sam xiii–xiv) and the handling of Jonathan's son (II Sam ix)

xxi—The census and its aftermath (cf. II Sam xxiv) curtails some and embellishes other aspects of its source. Satan is introduced as the instigator of the census which is more strongly opposed by Joab. Levi and Benjamin were not counted (vs. 6). The angel of Yahweh is accentuated. The price of the threshing floor goes from fifty shekels of silver to six hundred of gold— gold is the only worthy contribution and the fifty shekels is multiplied by twelve for the twelve tribes of Israel. David's offering is stressed (cf. COMMENT on Sec. 21, vss. 24, 26, on the acceptable sacrifice offered by David) and an explanation given as to why David did not go to Gibeon during the plague

xxii–xxix, the final activity of David, has no parallels elsewhere.

(a) xxii 1–19, preparations for building the temple, is obviously the Chronicler's since he attributes to David (and not to Solomon as the Deuteronomist did) the plans which Solomon executed

(b) xxiii 1–32, census and service of Levites is cultic in character; David is made the authority for the establishment of the temple cultus and the service orders of the Levites (cf. I Chron xvi 4 ff.; Neh xii 24). It has been suggested that the chapter is composed of three parts (a) 3–6a, (b) 6b–24, (c) 25–32, a and b reflecting pre-Chronicles and c post-Chronicles conditions[57]

(c) xxiv 1–9, the temple staff, priests with their twenty-four orders of service. This is the only list in OT in which Jehoiarib stands in first place (cf. Neh xi 10); he was regarded as the ancestor of the Maccabees (I Maccabees ii 1, xiv 29)[58]

(d) xxiv 20–31, the assignment of later Levites to temple duties. May be a late list. The placing of Levites after priests may be of some significance. Was it the work of a priest?

(e) xxv, the orders of Levitical singers, the work of one of them. The twenty-four orders are schematized to make Levites equal to the priests. Hence authority for them is traced to David[59]

[57] E.g., Rudolph, in loco.

[58] For a discussion of the priestly order system see E. Meyer, EJ, pp. 171 f., and for dating, P. Ackroyd, "Criteria for the Maccabean Dating of the Old Testament," VT 3 (1953), 126 f.

[59] See Albright, ARI, pp. 125 ff. On verse 4b see Rudolph, in loco.

(f) xxvi 1–19, the gatekeepers (janitors). May not come from Chronicler, though that is by no means certain

(g) xxvi 20–32, the Levites charged with the temple treasures and external affairs. The latter duty mentioned only here and is doubtless based on authentic information

(h) xxvii, David's administrative organization. A summary of lists brought together from various sources, forming an addition to the preceding chapter on the external affairs of the Levites, and reflects the situation in the Chronicler's period

(i) xxviii, David's final assembly and charge to his officials, presentation of temple plans to Solomon, and final charge to him. Takes up the story of xxiii 2a and ends with the Chronicler's favorite theme—plans for the construction of the temple

(j) xxix, a rapid summary of acts concluding David's reign, with record of sources from which material was drawn

Solomon's reign and activity (II Chron i–ix)[60]

i—Solomon's prayer with Yahweh's response (i 7–12 || I Kings iii 5–15; i 14–17 || I Kings x 26–29; i 5 || Exod xxxviii 1 ff.). Note resort to Gibeon for sacrifice where altar of Bezalel was located at the tent of meeting. Jerusalem had not yet attained its later status. The ark was at Jerusalem, but was associated only with musical service and not with sacrifices

ii–vii—Temple affairs (ii 3 || I Kings v 3 ff.; ii 7 || v 6; ii 11 || v 7; ii 16–17 || v 13–18, not very close; iii || vi, vii, not close; iv 2–5 || vii 23–26; iv 10–22 || vii 39–50; v 1–14 || vii 51–viii 11; vi 1–40 || viii 12–53; vi 41–42 || Ps cxxxii 8–10; vii 1–10 || viii 54–66, not verbally close; vii 11–22 || ix 1–9; vii 1–3a || Exod xl 34 f. and Lev ix 24). Nearly all commentators agree that the writer's source here was the Deuteronomic book of Kings. There may be a few minor additions such as v 11b–13a, vii 6, 9, vii 12b–15. But the author has not lost sight of his aim, that is, the temple, and has omitted matters apparently irrelevant to him (cf. rest of the records and II Chron ix 29); he has transmitted the tradition in his own words

viii–ix, External matters pertaining to Solomon: his campaign to Hamath-zobah, corvée, fulfillment of religious obligations in ac-

---

[60] Noth is certainly correct in assuming that the material of this section is pretty much as it left the hand of the Chronicler—ÜS, pp. 116 f.

cordance with the commands of David, shipping and trade through Ezion-geber, the visit of the queen of Sheba which reminds the writer of the wealth of Solomon made to minister to the glory of God (ix 11). Omissions and inclusions may be seen from the following: viii 1–18 ‖ I Kings ix 10–28; ix 1–28 ‖ I Kings x 1–29 (ix 26 ‖ I Kings v 1 [iv 21E]); ix 29–31 ‖ I Kings xi 41–43[61]

Other kings of Judah (II Chron x–xxxvi)

x–xii, Rehoboam's reign (x 1–19 ‖ I Kings i–xx [Chronicles omits vs. 20]; xi 1–4 ‖ I Kings xii 21–24; xi 5–17 ‖ I Kings xii 25–33). Chronicles expands and omits in last passage. The list of Rehoboam's fortified cities is historically trustworthy.[62] The Levitical exodus from Israel to Jerusalem fortifies the Chronicler's conception that only at Jerusalem is true Yahwism to be found and thus is doubtless tendentious, though it rests on a factual basis as may be judged by Jeroboam's construction in his kingdom of religious centers with a more conservative tendency (I Kings xii 27 ff.). The family list of Rehoboam[63] is derived from a special source and is at least partially historical. Chapter xi 23 indicates that he carried out the policies of his father (I Kings iv 8–19). xii 1–12, the invasion of Shishak, depends on I Kings xiv 25–28; xii 13–14 ‖ I Kings xiv 21–22; xii 15–16 is a variant of I Kings xiv 29–31, but not because different sources are mentioned

xiii—Abijah. Greatly expanded from I Kings xv 1–8. Abijah's successful war with Israel is probably historical,[64] though it has some typical Chronicler touches. The Northerners were probably more numerous and powerful than the Judeans— as was the case between Samaritans and returnees in the time

---

[61] On II Chron viii 2–6 see C. H. Gordon, IEJ 5 (1955), 88.

[62] G. Beyer, "Das Festungssystem Rehabeams," ZDPV 54 (1931), 113–34; K. Elliger, ZDPV 57 (1934), 87 ff.; Alt, "Festungen und Levitenorte im Land Juda," KS, II, pp. 306–15; W. F. Albright, "The Judicial Reform of Jehoshaphat," AMJV, pp. 66 f. Whether the fortification took place before or after the Shishak invasion is not clear, but R. Kittel, (GVI, II, p. 223) suggests it was afterward.

[63] See Noth, ÜS, p. 143, n. 1.

[64] Cf. Kittel, GVI, II, pp. 224 f. Noth, *The History of Israel*, p. 233, attributes it to Rehoboam. Cf. Noth, ÜS, p. 142. Bright, *A History of Israel*, p. 215, and Rudolph, pp. 235–39, also think it is historical.

of the writer. Abijah's victory was due to an alliance with the Aramaeans (cf. I Kings xv 19) and brought Benjamin into the camp of Judah. Observe the theological tendency of Abijah's address to Jeroboam. In the reign of Asa, a portion of Benjamin was in Southern hands, thanks to the intervention of Ben-hadad (I Kings xv 19–22).[65] The best proof of the Chronicler's assertion is Baasha's attempt to retake some of the lost territory (I Kings xv 17)

xiv–xvi—Asa (xiv 1 ‖ I Kings xv 8; xv 16–19 ‖ I Kings xv 13–15; xvi 1–6 ‖ I Kings xv 17–22; xvi 11–14 ‖ I Kings xv 23–24). The Chronicler has greatly embellished the material found in Kings, for which he had other unutilized sources at his command. Albright thinks an Egyptian colony composed of Cushites was settled between Egypt and Judah by Shishak. This was the force that Asa subdued in part (xiv 9–15), but he did not succeed in taking their capital at Gerar. Since the booty included camels, the Cushites were doubtless assisted by the bedouin.[66] In view of this fact it is within the range of possibility that Asa built, perhaps rebuilt, fortified cities (xiv 6). That he engaged in reforming activity is attested also by Kings[67]

xvii–xx—Jehoshaphat (xviii 1–34 ‖ I Kings xx 1–36; xx 31–37 ‖ I Kings xxii 41–47). The Kings parallels may safely be regarded as representing the Chronicler's views of the received tradition. The judicial reform is factual.[68] The miraculous deliverance of Jehoshaphat from a coalition of Moabites, Ammonites, and Arabs sounds very much like the Israel-Aramaean affair described in II Kings vii. Behind it lies a historical nucleus,[69] though it is difficult to get at the precise facts. As usual the story is shot through with Levitical themes of the Chronicler—the piety of Jehoshaphat, the message of the Levitical prophet (xx 14), the Levitical praises (19 f.), singers appointed to praise Yahweh (21) and the valley of Beracah

[65] On Ben-hadad's first invasion of Israel (II Chron xv 19–xvi 6) see W. F. Albright in BASOR 87 (October 1942), 27 f.

[66] W. F. Albright, "Egypt and the Early History of the Negeb," JPOS 4 (1924), 146 f.

[67] Albright, ARI, pp. 157–59.

[68] Albright, AMJV, pp. 74–82. I Chron xvii 7–9 may be a doublet describing the reform movement.

[69] M. Noth, "Eline palästinische Lokalüberlieferung in 2 Chron. 20," ZDPV 67 (1944/45), 45 ff.

(blessing). Note the reasons given for the failure of the maritime venture (36–37; cf. I Kings xxii 47–50a)[70]

xxi—Jehoram (xxi 1 ‖ I Kings xxii 51[50E]; xxi 2–11 ‖ II Kings viii 16–22). Apparently the Chronicler had another source besides Kings since he reports Jehoram's slaying of his brothers, which is not beyond belief because other kings had done the same and because they may have objected to his policies (cf. II Chron xxi 13). The revolt of Edom and Libnah is reported also in Kings. The defection of Philistine areas (submissive under Jehoshaphat, II Chron xvii 11) and the restlessness of the bedouin in the south is quite possible under such unstable conditions—a legitimate assumption on the basis of other revolts successfully carried out against the king of Judah[71]

xxii—Ahaziah and Athaliah (xxii 1–6 ‖ II Kings viii 24b–29; xxii 7–9 ‖ II Kings ix 20, 21, 27, 28; xxii 10–12 ‖ II Kings xi 1–3). The slaying of Ahaziah's sons is utilized by the writer as retaliation for Jehoram's slaying of his brothers (xxii 1). His enthronement was probably the act of Jerusalem's officialdom who assumed the function of the *am-ha-aretz*. The latter had apparently been pushed into the background by the adoption of Northern policy in Judah because of the close relationship with the Ahab dynasty. That policy was doubtless followed by Athaliah. The rest of the material is from Kings

xxiii—Jehoiada's acts in behalf of Joash (xxiii 1–21 ‖ II Kings xi 4–20, with some additions by the Chronicler). The additions are interesting; the priests and Levites participate in the plot to thwart Athaliah whereas in Kings only the Carians and guards are mentioned[72]

xxiv—The reign of Joash (‖ II Kings xii). In addition to the three facts mentioned in Kings, the Chronicler supplies from his source the reference to his family (vs. 3), the death of Jehoiada (vss. 15–16) and the murder of Zechariah, the priest's son (vss. 20–22). In connection with the restoration of the temple, the Levites occupy the center of the stage rather than the priests. The Aramaean invasion is toned down con-

[70] Cf. N. Glueck in BASOR 79 (October 1940), 8.
[71] Cf. Kittel, GVI, p. 264, n. 6.
[72] On the whole episode see W. Rudolph, "Die Einheitlichkeit der Erzählung vom Sturz Atalja," FAB, pp. 473–78, and Würthwein, *Der 'amm* . . . , pp. 22 ff.

siderably. These additions may well be historical, at least in
essence; the Zechariah incident reflects the writer's interest in
the prophets though, if historical, was given a peculiar religious
twist.

xxv—Amaziah (xxv 1–4 ‖ II Kings xiv 1–6; xxv 11 ‖ II Kings
xiv 7; xxv 17–24 ‖ II Kings xiv 8–14; xxv 25–28 ‖ II Kings xiv
17–20). Theologizing is very evident at two points: the prophet
forbidding the use of Israelite mercenaries because Yahweh is
not with Israel, and the statement that Amaziah served the gods
of Edom which he had captured and brought to Jerusalem.
There may have been some provocation for Amaziah's challenge
of Joash (vs. 13), though the allegory of the thistle and the cedar in both accounts strongly suggests the pride of the former.
The defeat of Amaziah and the conspiracy against him are interpreted as punishment for his failure to heed the prophet

xxvi—Uzziah (Azariah) (xxvi 1–2 ‖ II Kings xiv 21–22; xxvi
3–4 ‖ II Kings xv 2–3; xxvi 20–23 ‖ II Kings xv 5–7). A whole
mass of information is preserved here that is not found in Kings.
Archaeological discoveries offer ample evidence of great building activity in this period. Towers were constructed in the wilderness and cisterns carved out.[73] Eloth was rebuilt and Jerusalem fortified. The position of the priests is shown by their
rebuke of Uzziah for overstepping his bounds in offering incense[74]

xxvii—Jotham (xxvii 1–3 ‖ II Kings xv 33–35; xxvii 7 ‖ II Kings
xv 36; xxvii 9 ‖ II Kings xv 38). The Chronicler notes that
Jotham continued the policies of his father. That appears pretty
well established by archaeological results. His success is attributed to the fact that "he did what was right in the sight of Yahweh" and did not go into the temple

xxviii—Ahaz (xxviii 1–5 ‖ II Kings xvi 2–5; xxviii 16 ‖ II Kings
xvi 6–7; xxviii 20 ‖ II Kings xvi 9; xxviii 26–27 ‖ II Kings xvi
19–20). Chapter preserves some historical material not in Kings.

---

[73] Cf. F. M. Cross, Jr., and J. T. Milik, BASOR 142 (April 1956), 5–17.
They favor the age of Jehoshaphat but admit that the activity in the Judean
Buke'ah could have taken place under Uzziah. Iron II sherds and an inscribed
ostracon were found at Qumran (RB 61 [1954], 567); also an Israelite installa-
tion and cistern attributed by Father de Vaux to Jotham or Uzziah (RB 63
[1956], 535 f.). Cf. the fortress at Hurvat 'Uzzah; see Y. Aharoni, "The Negeb
of Judah," IEJ 8 (1958), 37. For an archaeological summary, see F. Feuillet,
VT 11 (1961), 270–91.
[74] See further the discussion in the COMMENT on Sec. 26.

The Edomite-Philistine uprising is quite plausible in the light of Assyrian inscriptions.[75] The list of Ephraimite chiefs came from the source. Of interest is the notice of the prophet Oded and his declaration of Israel's guilt; so also the reference to the Israelites as brothers of the Judahites (vss. 8, 11, 15), which may be due to his theology

xxix–xxxii—Hezekiah (xxix 1–2 || II Kings xviii 1–3; xxxi 1 || II Kings xviii 4; xxxii 1–2 || II Kings xviii 13, Isa xxxvi 1; xxxii 9–15 || II Kings xviii 17, 19, 22, 35, 33, 29, Isa xxxvi 2, 4, 7, 14, 20, 18; xxxii 20–21 || II Kings xix 15, 35–37, Isa xxxvii 36–38; xxxii 24 || II Kings xx 1–2, Isa xxxviii 1–2; xxxii 31 || II Kings xx 12–13, Isa xxxix 1–2; xxxii 33 || II Kings xx 20–21). The Chronicler reflects only eighteen verses of Kings; the other material is his own (approximately 100 verses). He regards Hezekiah as more than a descendant of David; he is virtually a second David. The Levites figure prominently in his special material; he combines the musical services with sacrifices at the temple. Emphasis is placed on the king's observance of the commandments of David. There is nothing improbable in the outline of Hezekiah's reforming and missionary activity.[76] The fortification of Jerusalem and preparations for siege are doubtless historical

xxxiii 1–20—Manasseh (xxxiii 1–10 || II Kings xxi 1–10; xxxiii 18–20 || II Kings xxi 17–18). The Chronicles source included the story of Manasseh's conversion, an attempt to explain the long reign of Judah's worst king.[77] Some of the story may be true, especially that dealing with the Assyrian captivity

xxxiii 21–25—Amon (|| II Kings xxi 19–24). Source here was Kings, which was somewhat curtailed

xxxiv–xxxv—Josiah (xxxiv 1–2 || II Kings xxii 1–2; xxxiv 8–28 || II Kings xxii 3–20; xxxiv 29–33 || II Kings xxiii 1–3; xxxv 1 || II Kings xxiii 21; xxxv 18–19 || II Kings xxiii 22–23; xxxv 20 || II Kings xxiii 29; xxxv 24 || II Kings xxiii 30a). Of the fifty verses of II Kings, some thirty are paralleled in II Chronicles. The Chronicler has expanded the story by using materials un-

[75] See references in COMMENT on Sec. 28.
[76] Chapter xxx has been unduly suspected (cf. W. F. Albright, JBL 58 [1939], 185). On the whole situation see Albright, BP, p. 42; Kittel, GVI, II, p. 376.
[77] E. Meyer, GA, III, p. 60, n. 1. For other references see COMMENT on Sec. 36.

known or rejected by the Deuteronomist. Josiah's reforming activity began in his twelfth year (ca. 629 B.C.), a few years before the death of Ashurbanipal, and the relative inactivity of the Assyrians in the west. His concern for the people of the north follows that of Hezekiah. His conflict with Neco is correctly interpreted (xxxv 20) and must come from this source.[78] Josiah aspired to become another David and his religio-political activity is, in general, correctly reflected by the writer. He brings in his favorite Levites and mentions the prophetess Huldah. The Levites were the teachers of all Israel (xxxv 3) and participants in the preparations for the passover

xxxvi 1–4—Jehoahaz (|| II Kings xxiii 30b–34). Source curtailed

xxxvi 5–8—Jehoiakim (|| II Kings xxiii 34–37; xxiv 1, 5, 6). Also somewhat shortened. His being bound in chains is connected with a revolt against Nebuchadnezzar after the latter's indecisive campaign against Egypt in 601 B.C.[79]

xxxvi 9–10—Jehoiachin (|| II Kings xxiv 8–10, 16b–17). A greatly condensed version of the essentials as given in Kings and now known from the Weidner texts[80]

xxxvi 11–21—Zedekiah (11–13a || II Kings xxiv 18–20, Jer lii 1–3). The twenty-five verses of Kings have been condensed to eleven and the historical events theologized. The writer's reference to the duration of the Exile (20) marks a good transition point for the last verses, which were added after the completion of the work

xxxvi 22–23 || Ezra i 1–3a

Conclusion

The Chronicler had at his disposal the priestly redaction of the tetrateuch and the great history of the Deuteronomist, which included the books of Deuteronomy, Joshua, Judges, Samuel, and Kings. The fact that he omitted much material indicates only that it did not contribute to his purpose—not that he rejected it as

[78] Cf. Couroyer, "Le litige entre Josias et Nechao," RB 55 (1948), 388–96; M. B. Rowton, "Jeremiah and the Death of Josiah," JNES 10 (1951), 128–30; D. J. Wiseman, *Chronicles of Chaldaean Kings (626–556 B.C.) in the British Museum*, 1956, pp. 18 ff.

[79] He may have bought off Nebuchadnezzar. See Wiseman, *op. cit.*, pp. 29 f.; D. N. Freedman, *The Biblical Archaeologist Reader*, 1961, pp. 113–27.

[80] W. F. Albright, "King Jehoiachin in Exile," BA 5 (1942), 49–55.

untrue; it was clearly available to him, as his use of surrounding matter demonstrates. The inclusion of material supplementary to that of the Deuteronomist does not of itself mean that he wanted to add to the sum total of historical knowledge; it may indicate only that additions or omissions supported his main thesis in a given situation. Where he followed the Deuteronomist exactly, it may be presumed to have represented his point of view.

It is fairly certain that he was in possession of copies of official documents and memoirs (Ezra and Nehemiah), as well as of official lists of various types which he may have completed partly from oral tradition and partly from studies and collections of his own. The availability and use of some independent prophetic materials appear quite plausible. Moreover, sources of information not found elsewhere but which were drawn from the archives of the temple and were authentic, as can be shown from archaeological discoveries and topographical studies, were utilized.

The matter of recensions is difficult and no firm conclusion is possible. That there were later additions to some stories, perhaps whole stories compiled and inserted, can hardly be doubted, but it seems unwise to conclude that there was wholesale revision or major rewriting of the original work. It would appear that the work is pretty much as it was when it left the hands of the author, with the exception of the additions which may have been intended to bring it up to date or make it applicable to a slightly later period. Furthermore, within the limits of its purpose, the Chronicler's story is accurate wherever it can be checked, though the method of presentation is homiletical. The only valid objection to the foregoing statement could be his numbers which, by any interpretation, are impossibly high. This fact perhaps more than any other has made the Chronicler's work suspect.

THE THEOLOGY OF THE CHRONICLER

The lengthy section on the theology of the Chronicler contributed by Hänel[81] deals exhaustively with the subject. Taken in conjunction with von Rad's excellent study[82] we have just about all that can be said about it in the present state of knowledge. The Chronicler's theology, however, was not *basically* at variance with that of the other biblical historians, though there were variations on certain themes and perhaps different emphases. Yahweh was still the God of Israel and Israel was still his people. Worship, while more elaborate and institutional in character, was just as essential in the Chronicler's time as in that of *J* or *P*. The centrality of the law of Moses is evident on almost every page of his work but its application follows a somewhat different pattern. The fundamental demands of the Lord have not changed—they have been particularized and applied to the writer's situation in the hope of achieving that relationship between the Lord and his people envisaged by the prophets and exemplified in the exalted moments of the Davidic kingdom.

THE CHRONICLER'S CONCEPTION OF GOD

The Chronicler's conception of God follows that of the Deuteronomist fairly closely. The Lord is an active God, vitally interested in the affairs of his people. Special stress is laid upon the fact that he was the God of the fathers—an indication of the continuity of the nation as his people (I Chron xxix 20; II Chron xiii 18, xv 12, xix 4, xx 6, xxi 10, xxiv 18, 24, xxviii 6, 25, xxix 5, xxx 7, 22, xxxvi 15; Exra vii 27, viii 28, x 11, etc.). The evidence of God's hand is everywhere apparent, as may be seen in almost every chapter of

[81] Rothstein and Hänel, Teil 2, pp. ix–xliv.

[82] *Das Geschichtsbild* . . . ; cf. A. Noordtzij, "Les intentions du chroniste," RB 21 (1940), 161–68; A. M. Burnet, "La théologie du Chroniste théocratie et messianisme," *Sacra Pagina*, I (1959), 384–97.

the Chronicler's work (cf. II Chron xxi 16 f., xxii 7, xxv 8, xxxii 8).

The Lord judges both Israel and the nations (I Chron xvi 33 ‖ Ps xcvi 13; II Chron vi 23 ‖ I Kings viii 32; II Chron vi 35, 39, xix 6, 8, xx 12); he is the helper of his people (I Chron xii 18, xv 26; II Chron xiv 11, xviii 31, xxv 8, xxvi 7, xxxii 8) in times of need and they are exhorted to rely on him, for other helpers are vain and unreliable. It is he who gives victory to them over their enemies (I Chron xi 14, xviii 6, 13, xxii 18; II Chron xiii 15 ff., xiv 12, xx 22 ff.). He is always in communication with his people, speaks to them and acts on their behalf. He keeps his promises (II Chron i 8 ff., vi 4, 10, x 15) and what he says comes to pass (I Chron xvii 27; II Chron vi 15, x 15, xxxvi 21 f.; Ezra i 1)—all of which indicates his concern for the life and fortunes of his people.

Though he is a God who dwells in the midst of his people (I Chron xxiii 25), he is also transcendent. His dwelling place is heaven (II Chron vi, vii 14, xx 6, xxx 27, xxxii 20; Ezra i 2; Neh ix), yet his eye is ever on his people. The Chronicler has taken over the Deuteronomic name-theology in which the "name of Yahweh" appears hypostatically, particularly in connection with the temple (I Chron xxii, xxviii 3, xxix 16; II Chron ii 1, 4, vi, vii, xii 13, xx 8, 9; Neh i 9). There is a tendency toward indirect communication with Israel through the spirit (I Chron xii 18, xxviii 12; II Chron xv 1, xx 14, xxiv 20; Neh ix 20, 30). In earlier times the spirit of God was more frequently a power, a dynamic, enabling those upon whom it came to perform mighty deeds (e.g., Judg xiv 6, 19) or act in other than normal ways (I Sam x 6, 10). Of special interest is the place of the Satan in connection with the census of David (I Chron xxi 1); the Samuel parallel attributes to the Lord the incitement to number the people directly (II Sam xxiv 1). Hänel may be right in suggesting that here is a further development of the Satan, from that of accuser to that of a tempter.[83] If such is the case it represents another step in the development of the idea of God; incitement to evil comes from the Satan, the Lord being no longer the direct cause.

Though it is not said in so many words, for the Chronicler the Lord was a holy God as may be seen from the description of numerous things and persons associated directly with him. His people are a holy people (Ezra viii 28). Jerusalem, the place chosen for his name (his earthly dwelling place) is called the holy city. The

---

[83] Rothstein and Hänel, Teil 2, p. xvi.

offerings brought to him and the vessels employed in their presentation were holy too. So was the ark and those who ministered before
it or bore it. The Lord also had a holy day (Sabbath). The Levites
were required to keep themselves holy—the Lord was to be wor-
shiped in holy attire (I Chron xvi 29; II Chron xx 21). The whole
of the Chronicler's attitude toward God as holy reflects that of *P* and
H codes, which appear to circumscribe somewhat his wider interests.
To be sure he is the universal God and beside him there is no god
(II Chron ii 5 f.), but non-Israelites came within his purview only
as their activity ministered to the needs and desires of his people or
were used to chastise them. There was apparently little or no concern
for their salvation or provision for their participation, even as sojourners (*gērīm*), in the blessings of Israel.

Prayer was accentuated in the work of the Deuteronomist; it is
also evident in that of the Chronicler. In fact it seems to be stressed
even more by him, as may be seen from the incidents not paralleled
in sources drawn upon by him in so far as they are known (I Chron
iv 10, v 20, the prayer—blessing of David, xxix 10 ff.; II Chron
xiv 11 f., xx 6–12, xxxiii 13, 19). Ezra and Nehemiah further substantiate that observation (Ezra vi 10, viii 23, ix 6–15, x 1; Neh i
4–11, ii 4, iv 9, ix 6–37, xi 17). Thus the Lord is a God who hears
and answers prayer.

He is also a God of love (*'hb*), love exercised in his dealings with
Israel (II Chron ii 11, ix 8 ‖ I Kings x 9; Neh xiii 26) who responds
to him in kind (Neh i 5). The Chronicles passages, interestingly
enough, report the observation of God's love for his people as coming from outsiders (Hiram and the queen of Sheba). He is bound
to them in the covenant (thirty-four times) which operates under
conditions of steadfast love (*ḥesed*)—a term that occurs some
twenty-three times in the Chronicler's work, some, of course, taken
from his sources. But unless he meant to accentuate the idea he
would not have used the term.

Another striking feature of the writer's theology was that the Lord
used outsiders to announce his will and purpose. It was a well-known
article of faith that he employed them for the carrying out of his
purposes in other ways—to punish his people for their defections or
to deliver them from captivity. But nowhere else is he said to have
used foreigners to deliver his word. In II Chron xxxv 22, the words
of Neco are said to have been uttered at the instigation of the

Lord.[84] The proclamation of Cyrus permitting the Jews to return to their homeland was due to the spirit of the Lord (II Chron xxxvi 22–23; Ezra i 1–4). To say the least this is a very remarkable illustration of the writer's monotheism.

WORSHIP

The God so closely affiliated with his people, who communicated with them in sundry ways and dwelt in their midst, was yet the God of heaven, and inspired them to a sense of awe, respect, reverence, and worship. That was one of the central concerns of the Chronicler. The God who gave so lavishly to Israel evoked from them response in worship. The content of that response is clearly spelled out by the writer. In truth the cardinal elements in the reciprocal relationship between Israel and the Lord were quite simply blessing and worship—blessing from the Lord and worship from the people.

The Sanctuary

The Chronicler, like the Deuteronomist, recognizes one central sanctuary at Jerusalem. Here the time of writing must be kept in mind. Other religious centers such as Samaria and Elephantine were regarded as highly illegitimate because of the precedents of revelation and history. David made Jerusalem his capital and brought to it the ark of the convenant, the symbol of the Lord's presence. There he set up a system of worship and directed Solomon to build the house of the Lord. The Lord's anointed lived in the Lord's city, that is, he was a member of the household of the Lord whose earthly dwelling place was the sanctuary at Jerusalem. It is hardly accidental that so frequently when the house of the Lord is mentioned, in Jerusalem or at Jerusalem is added[85] (I Chron vi 10, 32; II Chron i 13, iii 1, vi 6, xxx 1, xxxiii 4, 7, 15, xxxvi 14, 23; and a score of times in Ezra). Neither Bethel nor Dan, sanctuaries of the north, are mentioned. Nor is there any reference to Josiah's destruction of

[84] See comments on this passage, *in loco*, J. M. Myers, *II Chronicles*, 1965, Sec. 40.

[85] The name Jerusalem occurs some 235 times in Chronicles, Ezra, and Nehemiah as against only 123 times in Samuel and Kings.

the altar at Bethel (II Kings xxiii 15). This is pretty good evidence
that the Chronicler never recognized it as a sanctuary of the Lord.

Since kingdom and sanctuary were so closely associated, the king
and the Lord must have been on intimate terms. That is precisely
the writer's position. The king was a scion of the Davidic dynasty
whose founder was the recipient of the divine promise that his house
(II Sam vii; I Chron xvii) and throne should endure forever. There
are many complexities in those chapters, but it must suffice here to
call attention to the fact that David was the originator of the temple
idea for Israel and contrived elaborate plans for its construction
under his successor. As Moses had once received plans for the
tabernacle, so David now received plans for the temple from the
Lord (I Chron xxii 1, xxviii 19); and the place was designated by
the angel of the Lord (I Chron xxi 18 ff.). But what the house of
the Lord stood for is the important thing. It signified the presence of
the Lord at the seat of Israel's government. Hence its precincts became the place for worship on every occasion desired by the Lord
or dictated by the experiences and needs of his people. On its altar,
smoking sacrifices were offered, from its incense altar arose sweet-
smelling savor that filled the house, and on its table of presence
bread, fresh loaves were set every day. Its courts resounded with
music and praise as the daily services were conducted. In short,
this was the eternal trysting place between the Lord and his people
as represented by king, priests, Levites, and temple servants. It was
the heart of the nation's life, beating rapidly and joyfully, or slowly
and erratically, but beating nevertheless throughout her life. That
was the basic concern of the Chronicler, whose portrait is not merely
that of a symbol or lifeless formality; the temple was the life center
of the people of God, the hub of the Lord's kingdom on earth.

Personnel

The position of the cultus sketched by the Chronicler required an
extensive organization of personnel. He was meticulous about the
proper character, appointment, and service of those who officiated
because of the serious view he took of the demands of the Yahwistic
religion of his time. He wanted, above all else, to avoid the dangerous miscalculations of the past and to maintain a holy relationship
with the Lord so that the congregation of Israel might please the

Lord and continue to enjoy his blessings in the land given to the fathers (cf. Neh ix 13–15).

Certain of these personnel arrangements, such as that of the Levites for carrying the ark (I Chron xv 15) and others dealing with the position of priests and Levites (II Chron xxx 16; Ezra vi 18), are ascribed to Moses. But most of the priestly, Levitical, and other personnel appointments in connection with the temple cultus are attributed to David, who was virtually a second Moses. The standing of the priests and Levites follows the traditional pattern, with the former preceding the latter in the genealogical lists and in the service lists. Yet there is a distinct bias in favor of the Levites throughout the work. They are charged with minor laxities on occasion (II Chron xxiv 5, xxx 15) but never with serious faults.

Certain orders of priestly and Levitical services were performed when the ark was removed from the house of Obed-edom. That there was considerable ceremony involved in the operation is reflected already in II Sam vi and the Chronicler is probably correct in stressing the preparations made for it. According to P (Num i 50 ff.), the Levites were in charge of the tabernacle, while the priestly family of Kehath were in charge of the ark and the appurtenances for worship such as the table of the presence bread, lampstand, altars, etc. (Num iii 31). Nevertheless, the Levites were under the general supervision of Eleazar. I Sam vi 15 reports the Levites took the ark from the cart that bore it from Beth-shemesh to the field of Joshua. The Chronicler maintains the sharp distinction between priests and Levites initiated by Ezekiel and the P code but he invests the latter with more than menial tasks. They were the bearers of the ark (I Chron xv 15; II Chron v 4 f.), singers (I Chron xv 16–22; II Chron v 12), and porters (I Chron xv 23). There is some evidence that they were invested with priestly functions, at least on certain occasions (II Chron xxix 5 ff.). They were thus important cult functionaries, though, for the most part, under the direction of the priests (I Chron xxiii 27–32). With the priests, the Levites were organized into regular service orders (I Chron xxiv 20–31), the two most significant being that of the musicians (I Chron xxv 1–31) and that of the porters (I Chron xxvi 1–19).[86] In addition to those offices, they performed other roles, as: judges (II Chron xix 8, 11), prophets (II Chron xx 14 f.),

[86] See COMMENTS on I Chron. xxv, xxvi, Secs. 25 and 26.

royal functionaries (I Chron xxvi 20–30), cleaners of the temple (II Chron xxix), fund raisers (II Chron xxiv 5 ff., xxxiv 9), foremen for temple construction (II Chron xxxiv 12 f.).[87] Again and again it is stated that they acted on the orders of the king (i.e., David, or his successors following his precedent; cf. II Chron viii 15, xxix 25 f., xxxv 3 ff., 15). There can scarcely be any doubt that certain basic duties were assigned to the Levites by David (cf. also Jer xxxiii 17–21), especially in view of the fact that he recognized the religion of Israel in connection with the establishment of the capital at Jerusalem and his provision for the ark. Some of the functions attributed to them were doubtless due to the exigencies of the politico-religious situation in the postexilic period.

The priests were not actually demoted by the Chronicler; they continued to be the chief religious officials. But there can be no doubt that they are treated with much less enthusiasm than their brothers, the Levites. This may be seen from the order of I Chron vi where, in the genealogy of Levi, the high priests are listed first, then the Levites, and finally the sons of Aaron (the priests), and in the recurrent expressions of displeasure with them (II Chron xxvi 19, xxix 34, xxx 3, 15; Ezra x 18; Neh ix 34, xiii 28 ff.). Nevertheless the priests still carried on their traditional duties as trumpeters (I Chron xvi 6; II Chron v 12, vii 6, xiii 14, xxix 26; Ezra iii 10; Neh xii 35, 41); they ministered in the inner sanctuary (II Chron v 14, xxix 16); they offered sacrifices on the altar (II Chron xxix 21) and sprinkled the blood of the paschal offering (II Chron xxx 16, xxxv 11); they also burned incense (II Chron xxvi 18) and served, with the Levites, as teachers of Torah (II Chron xv 3, xvii 8). The priestly functions were more closely guarded and hedged about by the Chronicler than by the Deuteronomist. The founder of the temple and its services (David) wore priestly vestments when the ark was moved to Jerusalem (I Chron xv 27). He also blessed the people (I Chron xvi 2) and offered sacrifice upon the hastily constructed altar on the threshing floor of Ornan (I Chron xxi 26). Only once is Solomon said to have blessed the people (II Chron vi 3); at the time of the dedication of the temple there was no royal (priestly) blessing as in I Kings viii 55. The Deuteronomist reports David's sons to have been priests (II Sam viii 18) but the Chronicler refers to them simply as chiefs (I Chron xviii 17). Perhaps the

[87] See footnote 33.

most telling incident is that of Uzziah's attempt to offer incense (II Chron xxvi 16 f.) which had serious consequences for the king.

The temple cult was directed by *the* priest (*hakkōhēn*), a term used some thirteen times by the Chronicler. He is referred to as the leader (*nāgīd*) of the house of God (I Chron ix 11; II Chron xxxi 13; Neh xi 11). Later he was called chief priest (*kōhēn rō'š*— I Chron xxvii 5; II Chron xix 11, xxiv 11, xxvi 20, xxxi 10; Ezra vii 5) or great priest (*kōhēn gādōl*)—II Chron xxxiv 9; Neh iii 1, 20, xiii 28). He was doubtless the spokesman for the priests (II Chron xxvi 17), the one who acted for the nation in time of crises (II Chron xxiii), and the one who generally took the lead in religious matters, especially in consultation with the political leaders.[88]

A third group of religious functionaries was the temple servants (*neṯīnīm*) whose origin is traced to David (Ezra viii 20). Outside of Ezra (where it occurs six times) and Nehemiah (nine times), the term itself occurs only once, in I Chron ix 2 in the list of returnees. They were the lowest class of temple servants (Neh vii 73) and were the assistants of the Levites (Ezra viii 20). They had their own residence in Ophel (Neh iii 26, 27) or in the cities of the Levites (Neh xi 3). They were apparently organized after the pattern of other groups (Neh xi 21).[89]

Offerings

The three elemental offerings were observed—the burnt offering, the peace offering, and the meal offering. The burnt offering (Lev i) is mentioned most frequently and was celebrated regularly morning and evening and on festival occasions such as new moon and sabbath (I Chron xvi 40; II Chron ii 4, xiii 11, xxxi 3; Ezra iii 4, 5, etc.; Neh x 33). Peace offerings (Lev iii) were presented by David at the time of the transfer of the ark to Jerusalem (I Chron xvi 1–2) and on the threshing floor of Ornan when the plague was stayed (I Chron xxi 26). They were offered also at the time of the dedication of the temple (II Chron vii 7) and in connection with the cleansing of the temple by Hezekiah (II Chron xxix 35) and his passover (II Chron xxx 22). The meal offering (Lev ii) was also offered by David at the threshing floor of Ornan (I Chron xxi 23);

[88] Cf. R. de Vaux, *Les Institutions de l'Ancien Testament*, II, 1960, pp. 266–74.
[89] *Ibid.*, I, p. 139.

it was employed regularly in the daily sacrifices along with the burnt offering (I Chron xxiii 29; Ezra ix 5; Neh x 34). There was a room in the postexilic temple for storing supplies for it (Neh xiii 5, 9).

Wine is mentioned in connection with offerings (I Chron ix 29) and associated especially with David's final blessing (I Chron xxix 21) and Hezekiah's passover (II Chron xxix 35). There was obviously some religious significance in David's libation of the water from the well at Bethlehem (I Chron xi 18). The guilt offering ('šm) is referred to only in Ezra x 19 and the atonement offering in I Chron vi 49 (v 34H); II Chron xxix 24; Neh x 33. The wood offering (qurbān hā-'ēṣīm) referred to twice in Nehemiah (x 34, xiii 31) is simply the provision of wood used in the burnt offering or the altar fires (cf. Lev vi 12).

The times for the offerings were similar to those observed in other portions of the Old Testament. Often referred to are the regular morning and evening oblations (I Chron xvi 40; II Chron ii 4, viii 12, xiii 11, etc.; Ezra iii 4–5), the festival offerings on new moons, Sabbaths and feast days (I Chron xxiii 31, etc.), occasional sacrifices in connection with particular events such as the staying of the plague noted above, the dedication of the temple, the removal of the ark to Jerusalem, the anointing of the king, the refurbishing of the temple after periods of neglect, and celebrations of victory over enemies.

The Chronicler's conception of worship affords an excellent insight into his whole idea of religion. The Deuteronomist was concerned with the book—the law book—which was for him the guide to the nation's relationship with the Lord in the promised land now occupied by Israel. The Chronicler, on the other hand, emphasized the aspect of God's presence in the practice of worship. He was aware of the acts of God in history, especially the history of his people, as evidenced by his reliance upon Samuel and Kings for so much of his information. But he was even more interested in the continuity of the cult which symbolized the abiding presence of God in the midst of his people and which had been interrupted only by relatively short periods of apostasy.[90] The morning and evening sacrifices, the seasonal and special festivals, the orderly functioning of the clergy, the smoking altar, the sweet-smelling in-

---

[90] The Deuteronomist writes more from a political point of view; the Chronicler from that of the church of Israel. Cf. Procksch, *Theologie des Alten Testaments*, 1950, p. 368.

cense, the concourse of throngs of grateful and dedicated worshipers—these were evidences of a blessed people among whom the Lord dwelt in all his glory and devotion. The history of the nation was not just a series of isolated acts of God in the past; it was centered rather in a continuous institution manned by lineal descendants of those who served in the times of Moses and David, the ongoing family or church of God. There were, of course, times when this organism malfunctioned because of the epidemics of sin. The Deuteronomist had effectively pointed out that disobedience brings disaster and obedience victory, a moral stressed also by our author. But the latter argued that sin had not yet proved utterly fatal since recovery had thus far always followed temporary disaster. However, illnesses of the past should serve as a warning and be avoided in the future. The only way they could be avoided was by the maintenance of a healthy rapport with the Lord which in turn could be accomplished only through purity of worship in a living institutional milieu.

ISRAEL AS GOD'S PEOPLE

The division of the kingdom and the Exile of both Israel and Judah presented a serious challenge to the basic conception of the nation as *the* people of God. The "children of Israel" stands, in reality, for more than nation; it implies that the descendants of Jacob-Israel are a people, a family, held together by blood ties as well as religion. As such it was the people of God, a common expression in the Bible, but far more than that. It was a theological dogma based on a very vital religious experience in patriarchal times which the religionists attempted to keep alive at all cost. They were quite conscious of the problems raised by the disruption of the kingdom; but with the fall of Samaria when all hope for reconciliation and possible re-establishment of a united people of God seemed to have evaporated, these difficulties became extremely acute. The efforts of Hezekiah (II Chron xxxi) and Josiah (cf. II Chron xxxiv 33) to reconstruct the old religion and state for "all Israel" offers ample testimony to the hopes and dreams of the nation's leaders. The same attitude is reflected in the Kings narrative of Josiah who had definite ambitions of becoming a second David.

The Chronicler caught the vision of a united Israel along the lines of the Davidic kingdom with its capital at Jerusalem. That is why he took advantage of every opportunity to speak of evangelistic missions to the seceded tribes. Israel as a united people under a king of the Davidic line was his ideal. There could, therefore, be only one Israel consisting of all the tribes (cf. II Chron xi 16). Earlier the Deuteronomist gave considerable weight to "all Israel."[91] That phrase occurs about forty-one times in Chronicles and eight times in Ezra and Nehemiah. It is found only six times in parallel passages in Samuel and Kings; in other places it is rendered by such phrases as "all the tribes of Israel," "all the select men of Israel," "all the people," "all the house of Israel," "all the children of Israel," "all the land," and once (I Kings xii 23 ‖ II Chron xi 3) "all the house of Judah."

What the writer had in mind may be seen from the fact that the phrase "all the congregation [qāhāl] of Israel" appears some twenty-two times (once with 'ēdāh) in Chronicles, Ezra, and Nehemiah, whereas it occurs only four times in Kings. His interest was centered on a complete Israel represented by the Davidic kingdom perpetuated at Jerusalem with but a short interlude during the captivity. Whenever the opportunity presented itself, he pointed out that Northerners came to Jerusalem: that is, David issued an invitation to "our brothers who remain in all the regions of Israel together with their brothers" (I Chron xiii 2) to assist in the ceremonies of removing the ark to Jerusalem and at the time of the disruption of the kingdom, the priests and Levites from "all Israel" went along with Rehoboam (II Chron xi 13 f.).[92] Abijah dwelt on that point (II Chron xiii 9 ff.) when he observed that the South had the true cult of Yahweh. II Chron xv speaks of many from Ephraim, Manasseh, and Simeon living with their brothers in the kingdom of Judah and who had defected from Jeroboam when they saw that Yahweh was with Judah. Hezekiah's invitation to the pass-

[91] The phrase occurs, in one form or another, some seventy-five times in Samuel and Kings though it frequently refers to the Northern Kingdom in Kings. That it was more than a slogan may be seen from the fact that it is used fifteen times in Deuteronomy itself. Cf. the emphasis on David as king of all Israel in the synagogue panel at Dura Europas. C. H. Kraeling, *The Synagogue*, 1956, Pl. xxxv.

[92] In connection with the prophecy of Shemaiah against Rehoboam, the expression "the captain of Israel" is used even though "the captains of Judah" are referred to in the preceding verse (II Chron. xii 6).

over was extended to Northerners; though it elicited little response, a few did accept (II Chron xxx 10–12, 18, 25). Josiah's interests too were focused on all Israel and he apparently met with some success in his efforts at reform in Manasseh and Ephraim (II Chron xxxiv 9; cf. II Kings xxiii 15, 19, 20) and priests and Levites from "all Judah and Israel" were present at his passover (II Chron xxxv 18).

Though nation and religion were one and inseparable, the Chronicler accentuated religion, since it remained the one possibility for meeting the situation prevalent in his time. By virtue of the threat to the religious unity of his people, it was imperative for him to fortify his convictions by laying great weight upon the Jerusalem cultus with its history and precedents. God's people, a united congregation, were lineal descendants of those invested by David to carry on the service of the sanctuary at Jerusalem, which was the only legitimate one, located in the chosen place from "all the tribes of Israel." The writer's long lists of names may have been included, at least in part, to establish that continuity. It is altogether possible that the legitimacy of the cult questioned by Tobiah and the Samarians had to be authenticated by the documentation of family connections provided by the genealogies. Obviously the problem of intermarriage also required such data.

THE PROPHETS AND THE TORAH

Almost every page of his work reveals the Chronicler's respect for the prophets and the Torah, but his view of them differs somewhat from that of the Deuteronomist. They were authoritative for both and yet the purpose of each determined his particular conception and use of them.

The Prophets

As indicated above the Chronicler relied heavily upon prophetic materials which might have already been incorporated in his source of Kings. Kings, in turn, never mentions any such collection of prophetic oracles. Though Samuel, Nathan, Gad, Shemaiah, and Jehu the son of Hanani were mentioned by name by both Deuteronomist and Chronicler, only the latter refers to a collection of oracles from each of them. Crediting the prophets with such material, the Chronicler offers clear testimony of his respect for them. Besides, in the course of his work, he refers not only to the prophets mentioned in Samuel and Kings[93] but to five others.[94] What is more, he has Zechariah, the son of Jehoiada the priest, prophesying (II Chron xxiv 20); he has a Levite giving an oracle in the assembly (II Chron xx 14–17); and he designates Heman (I Chron xxv 3, 5), Asaph (II Chron xxix 30) and Jeduthun (II Chron xxxv 15) as seers (hōzēh).

As purveyors of the word of the Lord, the prophets spoke with authority. The word of the Lord came to Nathan (I Chron xvii 3) who delivered it to David. Shemaiah relayed the message of the Lord to Rehoboam not to undertake a campaign against Jeroboam (II Chron xi 2); and later when the Lord exercised restraint in carrying out his judgment against Jerusalem through Shishak (II Chron xii 7), the word was given to Shemaiah. Jeremiah also was entrusted with the Lord's word when he spoke of the duration of the Exile (II Chron xxxvi 21–22; Ezra i 1). The oracles of the prophets were interpreted as commandments (II Chron xxix 25; Ezra ix 11).

Closer examination of the oracles of the prophets recorded here reveals a somewhat different outlook or, rather, a different emphasis from those in Kings. Virtually all are lacking in specifically moral content and have to do almost entirely with oracular matters related to the cult or with a declaration of the principle of *quid pro quo*. Two oracles deal specifically with the relationship between the two kingdoms of brothers. Shemaiah advises Rehoboam not to take up arms against Jeroboam because the rebels are his kinsmen (II Chron xi 4). In the time of Ahaz the situation was just the reverse: then Obed warned Ephraim not to bring further destruction upon their brothers in Judah (II Chron xxviii 9–11). Those oracles reflect the writer's feeling for "all Israel," the people of the Lord. The principle of equivalent returns is the burden of Shemaiah's prophecy against Rehoboam: "You have forsaken me, therefore I have forsaken you to Shishak" (II Chron xii 5); when he humbled

[93] Samuel, Nathan, Gad, Shemaiah, Ahijah, Micaiah, Elijah, Jehu the son of Hanani, Isaiah, and Huldah. On the Chronicler and prophecy, see Welch, *The Work of the Chronicler*, pp. 42–54.

[94] Iddo, Azariah the son of Oded, Eliezer (II Chron xx 37), Jeremiah, and Noadiah (Neh vi 14); and, of course, Haggai and Zechariah who were too late for inclusion in Kings.

himself the Lord relented accordingly. So also Azariah told Asa that the Lord was with him because he was true and drew the general lesson that the Lord forsakes those who forsake him but is found by those who seek him (II Chron xv 2–7). Hanani's rebuke of Asa for calling in the Syrians to assist him against Baasha is based on the same principle. The Lord helped him against the Ethiopians because he called and relied upon him, but now since he has appealed to the sword of the foreigner he shall have war (II Chron xvi 7–9). Zechariah told Joash that his abandoning of the Lord in cultic affairs meant that the Lord would forsake him (II Chron xxiv 20). Amaziah, accused of serving foreign deities, was lured into defeat at the hands of Joash of Israel (II Chron xxv 15 f.).

Jahaziel delivered an oracle of victory in the name of the Lord to Jehoshaphat (II Chron xx 15–17) because he was a good king. Because of the possible contamination of Judah by the wicked—those not in good standing according to the writer's views—Jehoshaphat received a comparatively mild rebuke from Jehu (II Chron xix 2–3) for his participation in Ahab's campaign against Ramoth-gilead. For the same reason Amaziah was cautioned not to permit Ephraimites to accompany him on his expedition against Edom (II Chron xxv 7–9).

The Chronicler borrowed only one prophetic story from the Deuteronomist (that of Micaiah son of Imlah), yet a prophet is somehow involved in every significant movement in Judah. The prophets were the prime movers in rebuking error or deviation and the Lord's appointed representatives in holding the kings in line. Not only so, but they were the ones who pronounced the final judgment upon the kingdom; however, they also announced the return from exile and the hope for a new beginning. The individual messages of the prophets are watered down considerably and all of them say almost the same thing, but the value of these independent men of God was as great as that of any in the history of the nation. In some instances they appear to be royal officials (seers of the king) but they are regarded without exception as men of God, delivering his message and his judgments to the house of David.

The Torah

Despite the fact that the Chronicler stresses throughout his work the cultic arrangements instituted by David and Solomon, there is a much stronger emphasis upon Moses and the Torah than in the corresponding books of the Deuteronomist. The name of Moses occurs only twelve times in Samuel and Kings but thirty-one times in the works of the Chronicler. The term Torah is found only twelve times in the former and about forty times in the latter. The Chronicler refers to the Torah of Moses seven times, the Deuteronomist only twice.

There is relatively strong emphasis on the Torah as a book (nine times as against three times in Kings), and, as such, written (eight times as against three times in Kings). Fourteen times it is spoken of as the Torah of the Lord, or of God, or of the Lord God (only once so denominated in Kings). Thus it was regarded as a fixed, authoritative body of material and refers to Pentateuchal legislation of one kind or another. Interestingly enough, only once is the command of David put on a par with that of the Torah (II Chron xxiii 18).

A number of toroth, or laws, deal with cultic matters of various sorts. There is the injunction to carry on the burnt offering continually (I Chron xvi 40; II Chron xxiii 18), the observation that Hezekiah's portion was given for burnt offerings for regular and seasonal occasions (II Chron xxxi 3) and that Ezra's altar was erected for the same purpose (Ezra iii 2). The festival of booths was celebrated in the time of Nehemiah in accordance with the regulations of the law of Moses (Neh viii 14). Provision is made for wood to keep the burnt offering fired (Neh x 34). The offering of firstlings is enjoyed in harmony with Torah provisions (Neh x 36). During festival celebrations the celebrants occupied their legally appointed places (II Chron xxx 16).

More weight is placed on the Torah as an instrument of instruction for the guidance of the community in worship and presumably in other matters as well. The delegation of political and religious officials sent by Jehoshaphat to instruct the people of Judah took with them the Torah book of the Lord (II Chron xvii 9). Ezra brought with him a book of the Torah (Neh viii 1) which he read to the people (viii 8) and to which they listened with intent (viii

9).[95] He took pains to assist them in comprehending it (viii 13). Ezra "set his mind on the law of Yahweh to observe it and to teach Israel its statutes and judgments" (Ezra vii 10). The priests and Levites were the appointed interpreters of the Torah, for they were to devote themselves to it (II Chron xxxi 4). Ezra is reported to have been especially skilled in the Torah of Moses (vii 6). Guidance and direction were given from it for the conduct of festivals (Neh viii 18) and it formed part of the regular worship program on such occasions (ix 3).

The Torah was thus the official standard according to which the life and activity of nation and individuals were judged. Solomon was urged by his father to observe the Torah of the Lord so that his rule might prosper (I Chron xxii 12)—here the Torah is thought of as a body of statutes and ordinances set for the guidance of the nation. Amaziah, upon becoming king, removed those responsible for the death of his father but did not harm their children because that is what the Torah book prescribed (II Chron xxv 4; cf. Deut xxiv 16). Much is made of the portion of the Torah in the law book of Josiah (II Chron xxxiv 14, 15, 19); it became the program for his reforms, and his life was modeled after the requisites of the law of the Lord (II Chron xxxv 26). The Jerusalem community in the time of Nehemiah bound itself by "a solemn oath to follow the law of God which had been transmitted through Moses the servant of God, and to observe and act in accordance with all the commands of Yahweh our God, with his judgments and statutes" to maintain purity in marriage and to keep strictly the sabbath regulations (Neh x 30–32). Observance of the Torah thus became a mark of distinction between the Jews and the peoples of the land (Neh x 28).

The profound sense of the meaning of dedication of the community to God's will evidenced by the writer indicates that he was steeped in every aspect of the Torah. He had much to say about the cultic worship of the Lord but it was more than a ceremonial matter; it had to do with inner community relationships as well. The doctrine of Israel's separateness was based on a recognition of a distinctly higher conception of God and his moral demands than prevailed elsewhere and would account for the wide use of such

[95] Nehemiah viii 2 speaks of those who could listen intelligently to the reading of the law, while certain designated persons instructed the people (viii 7).

terms as statutes, judgments, commandments, and the like. Such concepts reveal a keen consciousness of sin[96] against God (e.g., I Chron xxi 7, 17; Neh i 6; Ezra ix 6, 7, 13) and man (cf. II Chron xix 10). The positive side appears in the declaration of God's righteousness (II Chron xii 6; Ezra ix 15; Neh ix 8, 33) and the observation that David (I Chron xviii 14) and Solomon (II Chron ix 8), the chosen of the Lord, executed justice and righteousness.

The importance of the Torah may be judged by the fact that kings and kingdom, cult and ministrants were under its judgment. The prophets sternly rebuked any or all who violated it. Moreover, the Chronicler scrutinized every phase of politics and religion for possible violations of its demands, which he applied rigorously to all life and conduct. The Torah ideal was imbedded deeply in his whole religious outlook. The early community of Israel centered about the dual leadership of Moses and Aaron and it is hardly an accident that religious and political aspects of the kingdom of the Lord from David to the governors after the Exile were so closely connected. The handling of the Torah in the way that the writer does may have been due, in some measure, to the Mosaic claims of the Samaritans. But its effectiveness and authority were not diminished thereby, for hidden behind the exhortation to trust in the Lord, the injunction to call upon him in times of need, and the demand to seek him, which are enjoined upon all, lay the experience of Moses.

MESSIANISM

The presence of messianic features in the work of the Chronicler has been recognized by nearly all commentators, but the features are somewhat different from those appearing elsewhere because of the historical circumstances at the time of writing. Evaluation of these features depends on one's definition of the term.

[96] Cf. use of such roots as *ḥāṭā'* (27 times), *'wh* and *'āwōn* (6 times), *ma'al* (24 times), *rā'ā* (44 times), *'āšam* (12 times), and *ṭāmē'* (5 times); they are concerned, for the most part, with sins against God and are generally of a cultic nature. Forgiveness becomes, therefore, a largely formal and cultic matter and has to do with wrongs committed against God. The terms employed for forgiveness too are mostly cultic (*kāpar* and *ṭāhar*), though *sālaḥ* does occur a number of times in the Deuteronomic chapter of II Chron vi; *kāsāh* and *'āvar* occur only once each in this sense.

The Kingdom and the King

The kingdom was the Lord's, according to the Chronicler. That is clear from his peculiar rendering of I Chron xvii 14—"I will set him over my house and my kingdom forever." The Deuteronomist's version in II Sam vii 16 is: "Your house and your kingdom shall remain secure before me forever." In David's address to the assembled officials and servants of his house, Solomon is said to have been chosen "to occupy the throne of the kingdom of Yahweh over Israel" (I Chron xxviii 5) and in his blessing of Yahweh David says, "Yours is the kingdom and you have exalted yourself as head over all . . . you rule over all; in your hand are power and might" (I Chron xxix 11–12). Abijah speaking to Jeroboam says, "Now you propose to hold your own against the kingdom of Yahweh which is in the hands of the sons of David" (II Chron xiii 8)—and so Jeroboam failed in his venture against Judah.[97]

The Lord chooses whom he will to rule over his kingdom. Thus he took it from Saul and gave it to David (I Chron x 14). Even Cyrus owed his position to the Lord (II Chron xxxvi 23; Ezra i 2). Nehemiah (xiii 26) affirmed that Solomon "was loved by his God and God made him king over all Israel." Hence the throne was the Lord's (I Chron xxix 23; II Chron ix 8; cf. Ps xxix 10) who was the real king (I Chron xvi 31).[98] The king of Israel was then an official or vicegerent of the Lord, (cf. I Chron xi 2, xvii 7, xxix 22; II Chron vi 5 f.) who owed his position to the Lord and was always subject to the Torah.[99]

Because of the close relationship between the Lord and David,

---

[97] Cf. Procksch, *op. cit.*, pp. 369–71; G. von Rad, *Theologie des Alten Testaments*, I, 1957, pp. 347 ff. Also Rehm, *Die Bücher der Chronik*, p. 47, n. 14 (see Selected Bibliography, Commentaries). "The kingdom of Yahweh" is equivalent to "the kingdom of God" in the New Testament.

[98] This is a quotation from Ps xcvi 10; the idea of the Lord's reigning occurs in a number of Psalms (x 16, xxii 28, xxiv 10, lxxxiv 3, xcvi 10, xcvii 1, xcix 1, cxlvi 10) though most of them have a wider significance than merely reigning over Israel.

[99] Cf. von Rad, *Das Geschichtsbild* . . . , pp. 128 f.; A. C. Welch, *Post-Exilic Judaism*, pp. 192 ff. (see Selected Bibliography); Welch, *The Work of the Chronicler*, pp. 47 f.

the latter occupied a unique position in Israel.[100] He was the *one* sitting upon the Lord's throne, which was the focal point of his earthly dominion. So there is great significance to the Chronicler's beginning his work with David rather than with Moses, as his predecessors had done. In his time there was no king in Israel. In so doing he emphasized the old Davidic tradition, though mainly, as will appear, only one side of it. Its regal aspect was not played up, possibly because of the delicate situation at the time and because the writer did not want to stir up antagonism or even arouse the suspicion of the Persian government, whose annals doubtless contained adverse references to the troubles that had taken place more than a century earlier.[101] Nevertheless a semblance of the political line was kept alive through the governors of the district of Judah who shared in the direction of the community with the high priest. But the disappearance of Zerubbabel ended the effective reign of the royal seed of David's line after which Judah was more or less in the hands of the priests, whose power grew steadily under the Persians. Of course, one of the aims of Chronicles may have been to keep alive the Davidic tradition in the hope of revival at an opportune time,[102] a theme played down very effectively, so far as the royal angle is concerned, by Ezra and Nehemiah.

There are also a few references to the promises of the Lord to

[100] The verb to anoint (*mšḥ*) occurs only five times in Chronicles (not at all in Ezra-Nehemiah) and "messiah" only twice (none at all in Ezra-Nehemiah). Anointing of kings is referred to only in connection with David, Solomon, Joash, and Jehu of the Northern Kingdom (II Chron xxii 7). Solomon refers to himself as "your anointed one" (II Chron vi 42). The other occurrence is in I Chron xvi 22, which is a quotation from Ps cv 15; the Chronicler applies it to David. A. R. Johnson (*Sacral Kingship in Ancient Israel*, 1955, p. 12, n. 2.) thinks the emphasis on the Davidic line, the close relationship between the king and the Lord as illustrated by David's concern for the ark and the temple, and the reforming activity of later kings reflects a strong messianic tendency in the Chronicler's work. For views of other scholars see J. de Fraine, *L' aspect religieux de la royaute israelite* (Rome, 1954), *passim*. W. F. Stinespring ("Eschatology in Chronicles," JBL 80 [1961], 209–19) argues for an eschatological purpose along the line of the David of history and the David of faith.

[101] For the difficulties attending the premature messianic stirrings in the time of Haggai, Zechariah, and Zerubbabel, see Bright, *A History of Israel*, pp. 351–55. That there was some brush with the Persian authorities cannot be doubted but just what its immediate effect was is not clear, though the long range one was sterility, poverty, indecision and retrogression as may be seen from the oracles of Malachi.

[102] Cf. von Rad, *Das Geschichtsbild* . . . , pp. 128 f.

David (I Chron xvii 26; II Chron i 9, vi 4, 10, 16, 20) and one
to the effect that he would not destroy the house of David because
of his promise (II Chron xxi 7). The kingdom had been con-
ferred upon David and his sons forever by a covenant of salt (II
Chron xiii 5). That covenant was reaffirmed by the Lord in Solomon's vision (II Chron vii 18). But, on the whole, there are
surprisingly few references of this kind in Chronicles, and only one
of them outside the David-Solomon narratives.

The Cultus

The other side of the Davidic tradition has to do with specifically
religious matters and is represented in the sacred institutions. David
was regarded as the progenitor of both the royal and cultic traditions of Israel. For the Chronicler the latter was the more immediately important, largely because of external conditions already referred to. Israel (Judah) was, in a way, reverting to a theocracy
in which the ecclesiastical element was naturally in the ascendancy.
Much emphasis was therefore laid on the origin of Jerusalem as
the worship center of Israel and the cultus established there by
David. Certainly the main interest of the writer was to connect
David with the ecclesiastical structure pertinent in his time.

The monarchy was non-existent and prophecy quiescent; in their
absence there was a return to the old ideal of revelation (direction)
through the purely cultic institutions. God's will was made known
or applied in and through the religious officials. In contradistinction
to the line taken by the *P* code, the writer dwells on the ark and
the temple, with the accent upon the Levites as the chosen ministers of the Lord (cf. I Chron xxiii 27–32), the Aaronites falling
distinctly into the background. David was the founder of the temple
at Jerusalem. In preparation for the establishment of the cultus
there, the ark was moved to a tent set up for it. The Levites
officiated in accordance with the regulations of the Torah. In addition certain rites were performed at the time, centering chiefly
around music and musical instruments. The Levites were appointed
to that service by the king (I Chron xv 16–25), which became a
permanent part of the temple liturgy (I Chron xxiii–xxvi). Thus great
weight is given to the work, commandment, order, and direction
of David in respect to cultic matters—he is even said to have performed priestly functions himself (I Chron xv 27, xvi 2) which

were acceptable to the Lord. Hence his authority for worship arrangements was drawn upon to substantiate the order and practice of the cultus in the time of the writer.

The Chronicler regarded election as important and applied the term to the choice of the king, with the cult center and the tribe of Levi acting as functionaries.[103] Precedents for the cultic community of Israel as it now operated were traced to David, who had been placed in charge (selected by the Lord) of his people in a new and saving relationship. That relationship revolved around the cultus as the divinely designated way to maintain and strengthen it. One means for achieving that end was the maintenance of a healthy and vital rapport with the Lord through worship, which was essentially a confessional service acknowledging him as Savior and Lord. The cult-centered community in living fellowship with him was the saved community in which the will of the Lord was done and his blessings enjoyed. That was to be the standard in later days when the Hasmoneans ruled, and they were descendants of the tribe of Levi.

Character of the Chronicler's Messianism

The Chronicler can hardly be said to have been a proponent of ordinary messianism as conceived in other portions of the Old Testament, notably by the prophets. He did not look into the distant future for the realization of a majestic dream in which Jerusalem was seen as the center of the world governed by Israel and to which all nations were welcomed. It was rather a conception of the saved people, those who had returned from exile, joined by those who had remained in the land and who were ready to accept the returnees' direction and rule, dwelling in the chosen place of the Lord and maintaining their relationship with him in purity and in a kind of magnificent isolation from other peoples.

While those who returned probably cannot be said to have been satisfied completely with the status quo, they did conceive of themselves as the favored of the Lord. The dark days of Malachi were behind them and they were enjoying the peace of the Persian empire and, indeed, some of its material blessings.

Then, too, they had attained more or less community solidarity

[103] Von Rad (*Theologie des Alten Testaments*, I, pp. 349 f.) points out that to choose (*baḥar*) is used eleven times without parallel in the sources.

under the leadership of Nehemiah and Ezra. The impure were
expelled from their midst, worship services restored in accordance
with the command of David, and economic conditions mainly
favorable. The wide horizons of the prophets were no longer evident. The little community, the remnant of a more ambitious period,
had barely escaped and now looked in another direction for self-
realization.

One may argue that the Chronicler reflects certain inconsistencies
in regard to messianism. In Chronicles it appears in connection
with the house of David, the Temple, and the prophetic orders.
The close association of the three outlines the hope of the Chronicler and, if he is to be connected with Haggai and Zechariah,[104]
what he hoped for can be documented more exactly. In Ezra-Nehemiah, on the other hand, messianism has all but evaporated, as
indicated above. If, however, the complex of Chronicles-Ezra-Nehemiah was basically the work of one man (with the exceptions
already noted) who wrote toward the end of the fifth century, then
the messianic hope expressed in Chronicles is more apparent than
real. Later on, the Hasmoneans attempted to incorporate more of
the monarchial elements and to appropriate the Davidic hope to
further their own ambitions; at the same time, they maintained the
cultic pattern described in the preceding paragraph.

[104] See Freedman, CBQ 23 (1961), 441.

AUTHORSHIP AND DATE

Authorship and date are closely related in these books. The basic material was gathered together and forged into a unified document —with certain later additions and expansions—by a single hand writing at a specific time and with a specific purpose, as noted above. The general, long-range period is perfectly clear: it was postexilic. But, in what segment of that extended period, more precisely, did our author do his work? Before attempting to answer that question, it may be helpful to set down what we know about the man responsible for it.

The author

The Chronicler was a man with a consuming desire to justify and maintain the hard-won victory over the forces of opposition, disintegration, and despair that bedeviled the Jewish community in Judah from the moment the returnees set foot upon its sacred soil until his own time, when the issue was, in some measure, resolved. The way was rugged and hard and the removal or surmounting of its obstacles far from easy. A plan, a program devised by one of clear vision and carried through by resolute action finally brought a semblance of security and hope to that struggling community.

The identity of the man with such vision, insight and determination must, at present, remain an unproved surmise. Whether or not it was Ezra cannot be demonstrated with absolute finality. Torrey[105] and Albright[106] agree that, on the basis of language, literary man-

---

[105] *Ezra Studies*, Ch. vii, especially pp. 243 ff.
[106] "The Date and Personality of the Chronicler," JBL 40 (1921), 119–24; AMJV, pp. 72–74. Cf. also Noth, ÜS, p. 111—he insists upon an individual personality as the author, over against the claims for a circle or school. V. Pavlovsky ("Die Chronologie der Tätigkeit Esdras," *Biblica* 38 [1957], 450 f.) thinks Chronicles through Ezra vi was written by Ezra in response to his commission from the Persian king (Ezra vii 25). To carry out that commission Ezra appointed (Levitical?) helpers for whom he wrote the above noted history for guidance and direction in understanding the true Israel.

nerisms, and religious interests, the person who wrote the Ezra memoirs was responsible also for the Chronicler's work. Certainly the author was one steeped in the history of Israel, a persistent student of her religious traditions, and a capable organizer. He had the capacity to capture the imagination of those around him, to win their confidence in the basic correctness of his plans and aims, and to inspire them to put forth the tremendous efforts required to achieve the goal set before them.

He was above all else a churchman of the highest order inasmuch as he proposed to carry out his scheme for the preservation and progress of his people through a living religious institution rather than through the royal messianism proclaimed by the prophets —a messianism which had signally failed in the early stages of the postexilic community. He was aware not only of the history of that well-intentioned experiment but also cognizant of the dangers of possible political repercussions in his time if that experiment were to be repeated. Hence he sought out a new way by tracing out, with great dexterity, and emphasizing the other half of the Davidic tradition—that of ark, temple, and cultus. So effective was his work that not only did Judah take on a new lease of life but she was able to establish herself so firmly and decisively in the Torah of the Lord, operative and applicable in the cultus, that she was able to withstand the enormous pressures of disintegration unleashed against her in the Hellenistic period.

The author of Chronicles, Ezra, and Nehemiah was thus an ecclesiastical official of knowledge, insight, wisdom, courage, organizing ability, and determination to put through his plan. He was in essence a reformer whose success may be judged by the fact that the Jewish community ever afterward—with a brief interlude—remained basically a religious community.

The date

Most scholars have located the work of the Chronicler in the Greek period (after 333 B.C.).[107] However, there is now evidence

[107] For recent arguments see Noth, ÜS, pp. 150–55; he places it between 300 and 200 B.C., in the Ptolemaic age. Cf. also diagram in Torrey, *Ezra Studies*, p. 35, for details. The presence of Chronicles, Ezra, and Nehemiah fragments among the Qumran cave 4 materials makes a third-century date difficult to maintain.

that makes it almost imperative to place his activity in the Persian period (ca. 538–333 B.C.). It is impossible to deduce here all the arguments in favor of the latter date or to go into detail with reference to any one of them. A simple listing of the most significant data must suffice.[108]

Since the publication of the Elephantine materials[109] there can no longer be any doubt as to the date of the Aramaic section of Ezra. Syntax, vocabulary, idioms and expressions are virtually identical. Spelling variants do occur but that is not a unique phenomenon in the transmission of such materials. The Hebrew of the Chronicler sounds altogether like a living language having all the marks of current usage, though it is strongly influenced by Aramaic as might be expected in the Persian empire of the period.[110]

One of the striking features about the Chronicler's work is the presence of a comparatively large number of Persian words (especially in Ezra) whose usage in the West declined rather rapidly in the Greek period[111] and the absence of Greek words, as Albright has demonstrated.[112] The sole apparent exception is the word *darkᵉmōnīm* (drachma, always in plural),[113] but the Attic drachma or imitations of it appear in Palestinian excavations in the Persian period, some of which bear the inscription *yᵉhūd*. Thus the Jews had the right of coinage and the Chronicler's references need be neither late nor anachronistic in this instance.

Then, too, the latest Persian king mentioned is Darius II (423–405 B.C.), who was a contemporary of the high priest Johanan (Neh xii 22–23).[114] The latest high priest named is Jaddua (Neh xii 22), but he is not listed as such—the Chronicler's list included the names of the high priests only as far as Johanan (Neh xii 23),

---

[108] Presented by Albright; see footnote 106.
[109] A. Cowley, AP; E. G. H. Kraeling, BMAP; G. R. Driver, *Aramaic Documents of the Fifth Century B.C.* (Oxford, 1954); J. Kutscher, "An Aramaic Leather Scroll of the Fifth Century B.C.," *Kedem* (Jerusalem, 1945), II, 66–74; Torrey, *Ezra Studies*, pp. 161–66.
[110] See A. Kropat, *Die Syntax des Autors der Chronik* (BZAW) (see Selected Bibliography); Curtis and Madsen, pp. 27–36; M. Rehm, *Textkritische Untersuchungen zu den Parallelstellen der Samuel-Königsbücher und der Chronik*, pp. 102–8 (see Selected Bibliography).
[111] Albright, JBL 40 (1921), 117.
[112] *Ibid.*, pp. 113–15, and AMJV, pp. 64 f.
[113] Occurs in Ezra ii 69; Neh vii 70–72—four times. Cf. Albright, AMJV, pp. 64 f.
[114] See letters 30, 31 in AP.

who occupied that position around 410 B.C.[115] When Jaddua took office is not known, but Josephus (*Antiquities* XI.vii.8) speaks of a Jaddua who was a contemporary of Alexander the Great (356–323) and was apparently an old man at the time; he died soon after Alexander.[116]

A final piece of evidence is the Davidic genealogy in I Chron iii 10–24 which is traced down through seven generations from Jehoiachin (598 B.C.) which, on the basis of an average of twenty-five years for a generation, would bring the birth of Elioenai's eldest son to about 420 B.C. and the youngest somewhere around 405. Hence our list could hardly be much later than 400 B.C.[117]

All indications point, therefore, to a date around 400 B.C. for the composition of the Chronicler's work, though there were doubtless some later additions or expansions at certain points, as noted above and in the COMMENTS, and, perhaps, a revision but hardly an extended one.

A Note on Chronicles in the Light of Qumran

So far only one copy of Chronicles has turned up at Qumran; it contains a quite small portion of the book with only four legible words.[118] Of the Samuel material so far published only the following parallels occur in Chronicles:

1Q Sam	cf. II Sam xxi 16–18; vs. 18	I Chron xx 4
1Q Sam	cf. II Sam xxiii 9–12	I Chron xi 12–14
4Q Sam[a]	cf. II Sam xxiv 16b–17a	I Chron xxi 15b–17a[119]

The Kings manuscripts reported to date provide only one parallel with Chronicles—I Kings xxii 29–31 ‖ II Chron xviii 28–30. They are said to be "notably different from MT."[120] Qumran Samuel reflects a close relationship to the Greek tradition, and where the passages in Chronicles parallel those in Samuel, 4Q Sam[a] represents

---

[115] A letter from Elephantine addressed to the governor of Judah in the seventeenth year of Darius II (ca. 407) refers to messages directed to Johanan and his colleagues three years earlier. See Cowley, AP, letter 30, line 18; and H. H. Rowley in *Ignace Goldziher Memorial Volume,* I (Budapest, 1948), pp. 135 ff.

[116] See Albright's discussion in JBL 40 (1921), 122.

[117] Cf. also Albright's calculations, *ibid.,* pp. 110 f. and comments below on I Chron iii in the light of the Weidner texts.

[118] F. M. Cross, Jr., *The Ancient Library of Qumran,* rev. ed., 1961, p. 41.

[119] *Ibid.,* pp. 188 f., n. 40a.

[120] BA 19 (1956), 82.

a text nearer to that employed by the Chronicler than that transmitted through the Massoretes.[121] The Chronicler appears to be supported invariably by the Greek in those passages paralleled in 4Q Sam where he deviates from the present Samuel recension.

[121] Cf. Cross, *op. cit.*, p. 41; BA 19 (1956), 84; BASOR 141 (February 1956), 11.

SELECTED BIBLIOGRAPHY

COMMENTARIES

Barnes, W. E., *The Books of the Chronicles* (Cambridge Bible for Schools and Colleges). Cambridge, 1899.

Benzinger, I., *Die Bücher der Chronik* (Kürzer Hand-Commentar zum Alten Testament). Tübingen und Leipzig: Mohr, 1901.

Cazelles, H., *Les Livres des Chroniques* (La Sainte Bible). Paris: Cerf, 1954.

Curtis, E. L., and Madsen, A. A., *A Critical and Exegetical Commentary on the Books of Chronicles* (The International Critical Commentary). New York: Scribners, 1910.

Elmslie, W. A. L., "The First and Second Books of Chronicles" in *The Interpreter's Bible*, III, pp. 339–548. New York and Nashville: Abingdon Press, 1954.

Galling, K., *Die Bücher der Chronik, Esra, Nehemia* (Das Alte Testament Deutsch, XII). Göttingen: Vandenhoeck & Ruprecht, 1954.

Goettsberger, J., *Die Bücher der Chronik oder Paralipomenon* (Die heilige Schrift des Alten Testaments, XII). Bonn: Peter Hanstein, 1939.

Haller, M., *Chronik* (Die Schriften des Alten Testaments: II, 3, pp. 330–54). Göttingen: Vandenhoeck & Ruprecht, 2d ed., 1925.

Kittel, R., *Die Bücher der Chronik und Esra, Nehemia und Esther* (Handkommentar zum Alten Testament). Göttingen: Vandenhoeck & Ruprecht, 1902.

Noordtzij, A., *De Boeken der Kronieken* (Korte Verklaring der Heilige Schrift). Kampen: J. H. Kok, 2d ed. (2 vols.), 1957.

Rehm, M., *Die Bücher der Chronik* (Echter-Bibel). Würzburg: Echter-Verlag, 1934.

Rothstein, J. W., and Hänel, J., *Kommentar zum ersten Buch der Chronik* (Kommentar zum Alten Testament). Leipzig: A. Deichert, 1927.

Rudolph, W., *Chronikbücher* (Handbuch zum Alten Testament). Tübingen: Mohr, 1955.

Slotki, I. W., *Chronicles* (Soncino Books of the Bible). London: the Soncino Press, 1952.

Van Den Born, A., *Kronieken* (De Boeken van Het Oude Testament). Roermond en Maaseik: J. J. Romen & Zonen, 1960.

Van Selms, A., *I-II Kronieken* (Tekst en Uitleg). Groningen-Batavia: J. B. Wolter, 1939, 1947.

Other Works

Abel, F. M., *Géographie de la Palestine*. Paris: Gabalda, 1933, 1938.

Albright, W. F., *Archaeology and the Religion of Israel* (abbr. ARI). Johns Hopkins Press, 1942.

——, *From the Stone Age to Christianity* (abbr. FSAC). New York: Doubleday Anchor Books, 1957.

Alt, A., *Kleine Schriften zur Geschichte des Volkes Israel* (abbr. KS). Munich: Beck, 3 vols., 1953, 1959, 1964.

Bright, John, *A History of Israel*. Philadelphia: Westminster Press, 1959.

Cowley, A., ed. and tr., *Aramaic Papyri of the Fifth Century B.C.* (abbr. AP). Oxford: Clarendon Press, 1923.

Ehrlich, A. B., *Randglossen zur hebräischen Bibel*, VII. Leipzig: Hinrichs, 1914.

Gressmann, H., ed., *Altorientalische Bilder zum Alten Testament* (abbr. AOB). Berlin and Leipzig: Walter de Gruyter, 2d ed., 1927.

Junge, E., *Die Wiederaufbau des Heerwesens des Reiches Juda unter Josia*. Stuttgart: Kohlhammer, 1937.

Kittel, R., *Geschichte des Volkes Israel* (abbr. GVI). 3 vols., 1923–29: Vols. I, II (Gotha: Leopold Klotz Verlag, 1923, 1925); Vol. III. (Stuttgart: Kohlhammer, 1927, 1929).

Kraeling, E. G. H., ed., *The Brooklyn Museum Aramaic Papyri* (abbr. BMAP). Yale University Press, 1953.

Kropat, A., *Die Syntax des Autors der Chronik (Beihefte zur Zeitschrift für die alttestamentliche Wissenschaft)*. Giessen: A. Töpelmann, 1909.

Kugler, F. X., *Von Moses bis Paulus* (pp. 234–300). Munster: 1922.

Luckenbill, D. D., ed., *Ancient Records of Assyria and Babylonia* (abbr. ARAB). University of Chicago Press, 1926, 1927.

Meyer, E., *Die Entstehung des Judenthums* (abbr. EJ). Niemeyer: Halle a. S., 1896.

——, *Geschichte des Altertums* (abbr. GA). Darmstadt: Wissenschaftliche Buchgemeinschaft, 1953–58 (reprint), 3d ed., 1954.

——, *Kleine Schriften*. Halle: Niemeyer, 2d ed., 1924.

Noth, M., *Die israelitischen Personennamen im Rahmen der gemeinsemitischen Namengebung* (abbr. IPN) *(Beiträge zur Wissenschaft vom Alten und Neuen Testament)*. Stuttgart: Kohlhammer, 1928.

————, *The History of Israel.* New York: Harper, 1958.

————, *Überlieferungsgeschichtliche Studien* (abbr. ÜS). Tübingen: Niemeyer Verlag, 2d ed., 1957.

Pritchard, J. B., ed., *The Ancient Near East in Pictures Relating to the Old Testament* (abbr. ANEP). Princeton University Press, 1954.

————, *Ancient Near Eastern Texts Relating to the Old Testament* (abbr. ANET). Princeton University Press, 2d ed., 1955.

Rehm, M., *Textkritische Untersuchungen zu den Parallelstellen der Samuel-Königsbücher und der Chronik* (Alttestamentliche Abhandlungen). Münster i. W.: Aschendorff, 1937.

Torrey, C. C., *Ezra Studies.* University of Chicago Press, 1910.

————, *The Chronicler's History of Israel.* Yale University Press, 1954.

Vannutelli, P., *Libri Synoptici Veteris Testamenti seu Librorum Regum et Chronicorum loci paralleli.* Rome: Pontificio Instituto Biblico, 1931.

von Rad, G. *Das Geschichtsbild des Chronistischen Werkes* (Beiträge zur Wissenschaft vom Alten und Neuen Testament). Stuttgart: Kohlhammer, 1930.

Welch, A. C., *The Work of the Chronicler.* London: The British Academy, 1939.

————, *Post-Exilic Judaism.* Edinburgh and London: William Blackwood, 1935.

ARTICLES

Albright, W. F., "The Biblical Period" (abbr. BP), *The Jews: Their History, Culture, and Religion,* ed. L. Finkelstein (New York: Harper, 1949), I, pp. 3–69.

————, "The Date and Personality of the Chronicler," JBL 40 (1921), 104–24.

————, "The Judicial Reform of Jehoshaphat," *Alexander Marx Jubilee Volume,* English section (abbr. AMJV). New York: The Jewish Theological Seminary of America, 1950.

————, "The List of Levitic Cities," *Louis Ginzberg Jubilee Volume,* I, English section (abbr. LGJV). New York: The Jewish Theological Seminary of America, 1945.

Bea, A., "Neuere Arbeiten zum Problem der biblischen Chronikbücher," *Biblica* 22 (1941), 46–58.

Beyer, G., "Das Festungssystem Rehabeams," ZDPV 54 (1931), 113–34.

Burnet, A. M., "Le Chroniste et ses sources," RB 60 (1953), 481–508; RB 61 (1954), 349–86.

————, "La théologie du Chroniste. Théocratie et messianisme," *Sacra Pagina*, I (1959), 384–97.

Freedman, D. N., "The Chronicler's Purpose," CBQ 23 (1961), 436–42.

Klein, S., "Kleine Beiträge zur Erklärung der Chronik," MGWJ 70 (1926), 410–16; MGWJ 80 (1936), 195–206.

Noordtzij, A., "Les intentions du Chroniste," RB 21 (1940), 161–68.

North, R., "The Cain Music," JBL 83 (1964), 373–89.

————, "Theology of the Chronicler," JBL 82 (1963), 369–81.

Richardson, H. N., "The Historical Reliability of Chronicles," JBR 26 (1958), 9–12.

Rudolph, W., "Problems of the Books of Chronicles," VT 4 (1954), 401–9.

von Rad, G., "Die levitische Predigt in den Bücher der Chronik," *Gesammelte Studien zum Alten Testament* (Munchen: Kaiser Verlag, 1958), pp. 248–61.

Zimmerman, F., "Chronicles as a Partially Translated Book," JQR 42 (1951–52), 265–82, 387–412.

I. THE GENEALOGICAL LISTS

1. GENEALOGICAL LISTS FROM ADAM TO ISRAEL (JACOB)
(i 1–54)†

Antediluvian patriarchs

I ¹ Adam, Seth, Enosh. ² Kenan, Mahalalel, Jared. ³ Enoch, Methuselah, Lamech. ⁴ Noah,ᵃ Shem, Ham, and Japheth.

The line of Japheth

⁵ The sons of Japheth were Gomer, Magog, Madai, Javan, Tubal, Meshech, and Tiras. ⁶ The sons of Gomer were Ashkenaz, Diphath,ᵇ and Togarmah. ⁷ And the sons of Javan were Elishah, Tarshish, Kittim, and Rodanim.

The line of Ham

⁸ The sons of Ham were Cush, Mizraim, Put, and Canaan. ⁹ The sons of Cush were Seba, Havilah, Sabta, Raama, Sabteca; the sons of Raamah were Sheba and Dedan. ¹⁰ And Cush bore Nimrod who became ᶜthe first tyrantᶜ on the earth. ¹¹ Mizraim bore the Ludim, the Anamim, the Lehabim, the Naphtuhim, ¹² the Pathrusim, the Casluhim, and the Caphtorim whence came the Philistines. ¹³ Canaan bore Sidon, his first-born [son] and Heth, ¹⁴ the Jebusites, the Amorites, the Girgashites, ¹⁵ the Hivites, the Arkites, the Sinites, ¹⁶ the Arvadites, the Zemarites, and the Hamathites.

† I Chron i 1–4 ‖ Gen v; 5–7 ‖ Gen x 2–4; 8–16 ‖ Gen x 6–8, 13–18; 17–28 ‖ Gen x 22–29, xi 14–26; 29–31 ‖ Gen xxv 13–16; 32–33 ‖ Gen xxv 2–4; 34–37 ‖ Gen xxv 19, 24–26, xxxvi 10–19; 38–42 ‖ Gen xxxvi 20–28; 43–54 ‖ Gen xxxvi 31–43.

ᵃ LXX adds "the sons of Noah," which may have fallen out of MT by haplography.
ᵇ LXX and many Hebrew manuscripts have "Riphat." Cf. Gen x 3.
ᶜ⁻ᶜ LXX "a mighty hunter."

The line of Shem

17 The sons of Shem were Elam, Asshur, Arpachshad, Lud, Aram, Uz, Hul, Gether, and Meshech. 18 Arpachshad bore Shelah and Shelah bore Eber. 19 Two sons were born to Eber: the name of the one was Peleg for in his days the earth was divided into districts; his brother's name was Joktan. 20 Joktan bore Almodad, Sheleph, Hazarmaveth, Jerah, 21 Hadoram, Uzal, Diklah, 22 Ebal, Abimael, Sheba, 23 Ophir, Havilah, and Jobab; all these were the sons of Joktan. 24 *d*Shem, Arpachshad, Shelah,*d* 25 Eber, Peleg, Reu, 26 Serug, Nahor, Terah, 27 Abram, that is Abraham. 28 The sons of Abraham were Isaac and Ishmael.

Abraham's descendants through Ishmael

29 These are their descendants: Ishmael's first-born [son] was Nebaioth, then Kedar, Adbeel, Mibsam. 30 Mishma, Dumah, Massa, Hadad, Tema, 31 Jetur, Naphish, and Kedemah; these were the sons of Ishmael.

Abraham's descendants by Keturah

32 The sons of Keturah, Abraham's concubine, whom she bore were Zimran, Jokshan, Medan, Midian, Ishbak, and Shuah. The sons of Jokshan were Sheba and Dedan. 33 The sons of Midian were Ephah, Epher, Enoch, Abida, and Eldaah: all these were the sons of Keturah.

Abraham's descendants by Sarah

34 Abraham fathered Isaac. Isaac's sons were *e*Esau and Israel.*e* 35 The sons of Esau were Eliphaz, Reuel, Jeush, Jalam, and Korah. 36 The sons of Eliphaz were Teman, Omar, Zephi, Gatam, Kenaz, Timna, and Amalek. 37 The sons of Reuel were Nahath, Zerah, Shammah, and Mizzah.

---

d–d LXX begins the summary of the preceding genealogy in preparation for its continuation with Abraham with "the sons of Shem [were]."
e–e LXX[B] "Jacob and Esau" but MT is preferred because the Chronicler always has "Israel" for "Jacob" except in the poem of I Chron xvi 3.

The families of Seir

38 The sons of Seir were Lotan, Shobal, Zibeon, Anah, Dishon, Ezer, and Dishan. 39 Lotan's sons were Hori and Homam, and Timna was Lotan's sister. 40 The sons of Shobal were Alian, Manahath, Ebal, Shephi, and Onam, and the sons of Zibeon were Aiah and Anah. 41 Anah's son *was Dishon; the sons of Dishon were Hamran, Eshban, Ithran, and Cheran. 42 The sons of Ezer were Bilhan, Zaavan, and Jaakan; the sons of Dishon were Uz and Aran.

Edomite kings and chiefs

43 These are the kings who reigned in the land of Edom before a king reigned over the Israelites: Bela, son of Beor, the name of whose city was Dinhabah. 44 When Bela died, Jobab, son of Zerah from Bozrah became king in his place. 45 When Jobab died, Husham from the country of the Temanites became king in his place. 46 When Husham died, Hadad son of Bedad who defeated Midian in the land of Moab became king in his place; the name of his city was Avith. 47 When Hadad died, Samlah from Masrekah became king in his place. 48 When Samlah died, Saul from Rehoboth by the river became king in his place. 49 When Saul died, Baal-hanan son of Achbor became king in his place. 50 When Baal-hanan died, Hadad became king in his place; the name of his city was Pai and the name of his wife was Mehetabel the daughter of Matred the daughter of Mezahab. 51 Finally Hadad died. The chiefs of Edom then were chief Timna, chief Aliah, chief Jetheth, 52 chief Oholibamah, chief Elah, chief Pinon, 53 chief Kenaz, chief Teman, chief Mibzar, 54 chief Magdiel, and chief Iram—these were the chiefs of Edom.

---

*MT and Vrs. read "the sons of Anah were Dishon." Either some name or names dropped out or the Sebir (a variant reading, from the so-called corpus of *Sebirim* [variant readings or explanations]) is correct: "son of Anah."

NOTES

i 5. *Tubal, Meshech*. Tabal and Meshech occur as the names of countries in Assyrian inscriptions and letters from the ninth and eighth centuries B.C.

7. *Rodanim*. Gen x 4 has "Tarshish and Dodanim."

12. *Philistines*. Tradition preserved also in Amos ix 7.

19. *districts*. Cf. Akk. *puluggu, pulungu*, meaning "district"; hence a
geographic designation.

46. *Avith*. See Gen xxxvi 35.

50. *Hadad*. Gen xxxvi 39 has "Hadar." Chronicles has the more accurate rendering of the name.

COMMENT

The first nine chapters of I Chronicles deal with genealogies of
great significance for the history and religion of Israel. While many
of them cannot be dated, others can; these shed some light on the
period from which they come. But perhaps of paramount importance
is their revelation in these chapters of the aim and method of the
writer. For him they served to validate the figure and position of
David, who occupies the central position in this work. For the
Deuteronomist Moses occupied that position. But the new situation
faced by the Chronicler called for a new method of approach in
which he follows that of the priestly writer who introduces his work
by referring to the generations of the heavens and the earth. His
story of Noah is prefaced by an extensive genealogy, as is that of
Abraham (Gen xi). Authority, for him, rested upon family relationships and continuity, both of which were important to maintain
the pure Israelite religious community in his day. To him these lists
were not just dry family registers; they represented living persons in
the great chain of Israel's religious history. One should compare
these lists to the genealogical chapters of Matthew and Luke in the
New Testament, whose authors had in mind the same general purpose in identifying the Messiah. The Chronicler's lists read like sermon notes to be filled in by the speaker as he pointed out their
relevance to his subject. Little attention is paid to side lines or other
details because he wants to get to the main point of his argument as

quickly as possible—the new messianic implications centering in David and his line on the one hand and on the other the direct and connected line of the descent behind the Israel of his day.

[From Adam to Noah, i 1–4a]: These verses list only the bare names of the line from Adam to Noah in precisely the order of Gen v 1–31. The Cainite and Sethite lines (Gen iv 17–25) were ignored, though that does not imply that the writer did not know them.

[The sons of Noah, 4b]: LXX begins the more detailed account of Noah's descendants by inserting the words "the sons of Noah [were]" (cf. Gen v 32) and follows with the genealogy of each of the three.

[The line of Japheth, 5–7]: Of the seven sons of Japheth the genealogies of only two, Gomer and Javan, are carried further.

[The line of Ham, 8–16]: The descendants of Ham are treated more fully (only Put is without detail) probably because the Hebrews had more dealings with this group than with the Japhethites, at least in their early history. Nimrod is characterized simply as a hero or tyrant; the reference to the mighty hunter is omitted. For the Genesis list see Gen x 6–8, 13–18.

[The line of Shem, 17–28]: The Shemites are traced from Shem through Arpachshad, Shelah, Eber, and Joktan; the source was Gen x 22–29, xi 14–26; it ends with the Nahor, Terah, Abraham succession where it narrows down to Abraham, who was the center of interest for the writer and who marks the end of the main line— Adam, Noah, Abraham. Verses 17a–24a are omitted by LXX[B] through homoioteleuton (see Noth, ÜS, p. 117, n. 2, and Goettsberger, *in loco*).

[Abraham's descendants through Ishmael, 29–31]: Curiously enough the side line is followed first as if to get it out of the way so that the main one may be continued, just as is the case above with Japheth and Ham before Shem. It corresponds exactly to the source in Gen xxv 13–16. The Ishmaelites were North Arabians. (See J. A. Montgomery, *Arabia and the Bible,* 1934, index, for names and possible identification of the Ishmaelites.)

[Through Keturah, 32–33]: The Genesis genealogy refers to Keturah as Abraham's second wife, taken after the death of Sarah. To the Chronicler she is his concubine, though his children by her are the same as in the Genesis list (Gen xxv 2). Only the descendants of Jokshan and Midian are listed, those of Dedan being ignored (cf. Gen xxv 3–4), possibly because the situation had changed by his time. They were South Arabians.

[Through Sarah, 34a]: The shortest possible designation of Abraham as the progenitor of Isaac (Gen xxv 19b).

[The line of Esau and Seir, 35–42]: The reason for the association of the two reflects the tradition of the relationship between the groups in the territory of Edom. The sons of Esau are the same as those listed in Gen xxxvi 10, 14; so are those of Eliphaz except for the spelling of Zephi and the fact that Timna here is a son of Eliphaz, whereas Gen xxxvi 12 says Timna was a concubine of Eliphaz and the mother of Amalek. On sons of Reuel, cf. Gen xxxvi 13. Without indicating that the Seirites were coinhabitants of the land (Gen xxxvi 20), they are simply listed by name, with some variant spellings or order from the Genesis list (xxxvi 20–28) and the omission of the name of Oholibamah, the daughter of Anah.

[Edomite kings and chiefs, 43–54]: This list follows almost verbatim that of Gen xxxvi 31–43a. It is obviously an old one, somewhat magnifying the position of Edom while Israel was struggling to maintain itself. On the date of these kings, especially Hadad, see ARI, p. 206, n. 58. Note that the listing reflects no dynastic line since each king's residence was at a different location. Also where the father's name is given it does not correspond to the former king. The same circumstances as prevailed in Israel in the period of the judges when the leaders were residents of local centers appear to have obtained in Edom. These Edomite kings were no more than "judges." The transition in Edom seems to have been gradual, as in Israel, and the line not a sharp one between "judge" and "king" until after the establishment of a strong dynasty. (On the kings of Edom see B. Moritz, "Die Könige von Edom," *Le Muséon* 50 [1937], 101–22; G. L. Robinson, *The Sarcophagus of an Ancient Civilization*, 1930, Chs. 23, 24; F. Buhl, *Geschichte der Edomiter*, 1893; A. Alt, article on "Edomiter," in *Reallexikon der Vorgeschichte*, ed. M. Ebert, III, pp. 10 f.; *Encyclopaedia Biblica*, I, 1950, pp. 99–103 [in Hebrew]; E. Meyer, *Die Israeliten und ihre Nachbarstämme*, pp. 370–86.)

2. THE LINE OF JUDAH
(ii 1–55)†

The sons of Israel (Jacob)

II ¹ These are the sons of Israel: Reuben, Simeon, Levi, Judah, Issachar, Zebulun, ² Dan, Joseph, Benjamin, Naphtali, Gad, and Asher.

The line of Judah

³ The sons of Judah were Er, Onan, and Shelah, the three being born to him by Bathshua the Canaanitess. Er, Judah's first-born son, was so evil in the sight of Yahweh that he slew him. ⁴ Also Tamar, his daughter-in-law, bore him Perez and Zerah, so that he had five sons in all. ⁵ The sons of Perez were Hezron and Hamul. ⁶ The sons of Zerah were Zimri, Ethan, Heman, Calcol, and Dara*ᵃ*—all together five. ⁷ The sons of Carmi were Achar who brought misfortune upon Israel when he violated the ban. ⁸ The son*ᵇ* of Ethan was Azariah. ⁹ The sons of Hezron who were born to him were Jerahmeel, Ram, and Chelubai.

The ancestors of David

¹⁰ Ram fathered Amminadab and Amminadab fathered Nahshon, prince of the sons of Judah. ¹¹ Nahshon fathered Salma and Salma fathered Boaz. ¹² Boaz fathered Obed and Obed fathered Jesse. ¹³ Jesse fathered Eliab his first-born son, Abinadab

† **I Chron ii 1–2** ‖ Gen xxxv 23–26; **3–9** ‖ Gen xxxviii 2–5, 7, 29–30, xlvi 12, I Kings v 11 (iv 31E), Josh vii; **10–17** ‖ Num i 7, Ruth iv 19–22; **18–24** ‖ I Chron ii 42–49, 50–55; **25–41**: cf. I Sam xxvii 10, xxx 29.

ᵃ I Kings v 11 (iv 31E) has "Darda" for "Dara" but Vrs. support MT, which is correct.
ᵇ MT and Vrs. "the sons of Ethan." Either a name has dropped out or the Sebir is correct: "the son of Ethan."

the second, Shimea the third, 14 Nethanel the fourth, Raddai the fifth, 15 Ozem the sixth, and David the seventh. 16 Their sisters were Zeruiah and Abigail; the sons of Zeruiah were Abishai, Joab, and Asahel, three in number. 17 Abigail bore Amasa—the father of Amasa was Jether the Ishmaelite.

Descendants of Caleb

18 Caleb son of Hezron fathered children by Azubah his wife and Jerioth; these were her sons: Jesher, Shobab, and Ardon. 19 After Azubah died, Caleb married Ephrath; she bore him Hur. 20 Hur fathered Uri and Uri fathered Bezalel. 21 Afterward Hezron married the daughter of Machir the father of Gilead; he married her when he was sixty years old and she bore him Segub. 22 Segub fathered Jair, who had twenty-three cities in the land of Gilead. 23 But Geshur and Aram took from them the tent villages of Jair and Kenath and its dependencies, sixty towns. ᶜAll of these belonged toᶜ the sons of Machir the father of Gilead. 24 After the death of Hezron, ᵈCaleb married Ephrathahᵈ the wife of Hezron his father who bore him Ashhur the father of Tekoa.

The Jerahmeelites

25 The sons of Jerahmeel, Hezron's first-born son, were Ram, his first-born son, Bunah, Oren, Ozem, and Ahijah. 26 Jerahmeel had another wife by the name of Atarah; she was the mother of Onam. 27 The sons of Ram, Jerahmeel's first-born son, were Maaz, Jamin, and Eker. 28 The sons of Onam were Shammai and Jada, and the sons of Shammai were Nadab and Abishur. 29 The name of Abishur's wife was Abihail who bore him Ahban and Molid. 30 The sons of Nadab were Seled and Appaimᵉ. Seled died leaving no sons. 31 The sonᶠ of Appaimᵉ was Ishi, the son of Ishi was Sheshan, and the sonᶠ of Sheshan was Ahlai. 32 The sons of Jada, the brother of Shammai, were Jether and

ᶜ⁻ᶜ So with LXX; Heb. "All these were the sons of . . ."
ᵈ⁻ᵈ With LXX; Heb. "in Caleb Ephrathah."
ᵉ LXXᴮ "Ephraim."
ᶠ So with Vulg. and the Sebir; MT "sons of."

Jonathan; Jether died leaving no sons. 33 The sons of Jonathan were Peleth and Zaza. These were the sons of Jerahmeel. 34 *Sheshan had no sons* but daughters. Sheshan had an Egyptian servant by the name of Jarha. 35 Sheshan gave his daughter to Jarha his servant as wife who bore him Attai. 36 Attai fathered Nathan, Nathan fathered Zabad, 37 Zabad fathered Ephlal, Ephlal fathered Obed, 38 Obed fathered Jehu, Jehu fathered Azariah, 39 Azariah fathered Helez, Helez fathered Eleasah, 40 Eleasah fathered Sismai, Sismai fathered Shallum, 41 Shallum fathered Jekamiah and Jekamiah fathered Elishama.

Another list of Calebites

42 The son*h* of Caleb, brother of Jerahmeel, was Mesha*i* his first-born son who was the father of Ziph *jwhose son* was Mareshah the father of Hebron. 43 The sons of Hebron were Korah, Tappuah, Rekem, and Shema. 44 Shema fathered Raham the father of Jorkeam*k* and Rekem fathered Shammai. 45 The son of Shammai was Maon and Maon was the father of Bethzur. 46 Ephah the concubine of Caleb bore Haran, Moza, and Gazez; Haran fathered Gazez. 47 The sons of Jahdai were Regem, Jotham, Geshan, Pelet, Ephah, and Shaaph. 48 Maacah the concubine of Caleb bore Sheber and Tirhanah. 49 She bore also Shaaph the father of Madmannah and Sheva the father of Machbenah and the father of Gibea. Caleb's daughter was Achsah. 50 These were the sons of Caleb. The sons*l* of Hur, the first-born son of Ephrathah, were Shobal the father of Kirjath-jearim, 51 Salma the father of Bethlehem and Hareph the father of Beth-gader. 52 The sons of Shobal the father of Kirjath-jearim were Haroeh*m*, the half of Menuhoth, 53 and the families of Kirjath-jearim, the Ithrites, the Puthites, the Shumathites,

g–g See vs. 31, which attributes one son, Ahlai, to Sheshan.
h So for MT "sons" because of context.
i LXX "Maresha."
j–j Uncertain; Heb. "the sons of Mareshah the father of Hebron."
k LXXA "Jerkaan"; LXXB "Jaklan"; LXXL "Jerekam." Josh xv 56 has "Jokdeam."
l So with LXX and Vulg.; Heb. "son."
m Perhaps "Reaiah," as in iv 2.

and the Mishraites. The Zorathites and Eshtaolites descended from these. ⁵⁴ The sons of Salma were Bethlehem, the Netophathites, Atroth-beth-joab, the half of the Manahathites, the Zorites, ⁵⁵ the families of Sopherim who lived at Jabez, the Tirathites, the Shimeathites, and the Sucathites. They were the Kenites who descended from Hammath the father of Bethrechab.

NOTES

ii 7. *Achar.* The reference is to Achan in Josh vii, with a play on words. The verse is defective as may be seen from Josh vii 1, 18.

10. Cf. Num i 7, and on verses 10 ff., see Ruth iv 19–22; see I Sam xvi 6–13.

40. *Sismai.* See COMMENT.

49. *Sheva.* Name occurs also in BMAP 13:1, 9; cf. 40:1 in AP.

55. *Sopherim.* Possibly not a proper name. Cf. *Eretz Israel: Archaeological, Historical and Geographical Studies,* V (Jerusalem: Israel Exploration Society, 1958), p. 90.

Hammath. S. Talmon suggests "family-in-law," IEJ 10 (1960), 178.

COMMENT

The lists in chapters ii to iv are far more complicated than those in chapter i because they have been expanded at several points with secondary materials. For a discussion of the literary-historical problem see M. Noth, "Eine siedlungs-geographische Liste in I Chr. 2 und 4," ZDPV 55 (1932), 97–124; "Die Ansiedlung des Stammes Juda auf dem Boden Palästinas," PJB 30 (1934), especially 42 ff.; ÜS, pp. 118 ff.; and the commentaries. While the technical details need not detain us, the following discussion is based on the results of Noth's work, with modifications.

[The sons of Israel (Jacob), ii 1–2]: The list is based on Gen xxxv 23–26 with a different order following Zebulun. Here Dan follows Zebulun, and Joseph and Benjamin come between him and Naphtali (may be simply a copyist's error). The Genesis list places the sons of the handmaids last, those of Bilhah preceding those of Zilpah. But the Chronicler significantly shifts the order in his later and fuller treatment of them, in chapters iv–viii, where Judah stands first. Here the two verses are probably meant to be taken with the genealogies of the preceding chapter since then the same order of treatment would obtain—Japheth, Ham, Shem; Ishmael and Abraham's sons by Keturah, Isaac; Esau, Jacob—in a descending order. Thus an ascending order is followed, beginning with Judah, because of the interest in the Davidic line.

[The descendants of Judah, 3–9]: This piece is doubtless taken from Num xxvi 19–21 || Gen xlvi 12, with some material drawn from Gen xxxviii. That the writer did not slavishly follow one document is evident from the complexion of the list. His theological view appears in vss. 3, 7; Judah is said to have married a Canaanitess which does not affect his standing as the ancestor of David. On the other hand Er was so persistent in his evil that Yahweh slew him. Achar by his act brought guilt upon all Israel in his violation of the ban. Membership in the covenant community does not automatically confer salvation. (See Rudolph, *in loco*.) God is the God of both judgment and mercy.

Of special interest here is vs. 6—the line of Zerah, which is not given fully elsewhere (cf. Josh vii 1; I Kings v 11 [iv 31E]). The Chronicler's interest in Zerah's line lies in its connection with the musical guilds (ARI, pp. 126 f.). The relation of these musical guild heads to Zerah (Ezrah) makes them descendants of pre-Israelite families. Cf. I Kings iv 31. "Darda" in the Kings verse is correct. "Achar" for "Achan" in vs. 7 represents a play on words; it has the same consonants as the participle *'okēr*, "who brought misfortune."

[The ancestors of David, 10–17]: They were naturally of paramount concern for the Chronicler. In vs. 5 Hezron was listed as one of the sons of Perez who in turn was one of the twins of Judah born by Tamar, his daughter-in-law. Verse 9 follows through by noting the three sons of Hezron, two of whom are the progenitors of the indeterminate clans of Jerahmeel and Caleb and whose line is taken up later. Since the procedure is reversed here it may be that we have to do with a later expansion (cf. Rudolph, *in loco*); from now on, however, the main line of descent is presented first (cf. Simeon, iv 24 ff., Reuben, v 1 ff., etc.). Though there is an almost exact correspondence between vss. 10, 11 and Ruth iv 19–22, this list, as the additional material indicates, was not copied from Ruth; nor is Ruth dependent on our passage directly since it extends back to

Perez (Goettsberger, p. 38). Both lists may go back to an original
temple source. According to Num i 7, Nahshon the son of Amminadab (cf. Exod vi 23) was the Judahite representative who assisted in the census and was a *nāśī'*, that is, representative or leader
of the tribe, one of the staff officials serving with Moses and Aaron
(Num ii 3). (See M. Noth, *Zwölf Stämme Israels,* 1930, pp. 155 ff.)
The Samuel tradition speaks of eight sons of Jesse (I Sam xvi 10 f.,
xvii 12) while our list contains only seven names. Only here do
we learn that Zeruiah and Abigail were sisters of David (cf. I Sam
xxvi 6; II Sam xvii 25), brought in because they figure in the
history of the latter later on. A brother of David (Elihu) is mentioned in xxvii 18.

[The Calebites, 18–20]: The purpose of this notice is probably
the connection with Bezalel who played a major role in the construction of the tabernacle furniture and equipment (Exod xxxi 2–
11, xxxv 30–35, xxxvi, xxxvii, xxxviii; II Chron i 5) which was
transferred to the Solomonic temple. In the Exodus account (xxxi 2,
xxxv 30) Hur is associated with the tribe of Judah. The Caleb referred to here is not Caleb the spy, though the latter too was a Judahite (Num xiii 6). There is a great deal of uncertainty in this section
since we know nothing further about either places or people except
Bezalel, and possibly Ephrathah (cf. ii 50, iv 4).

[Hezron, 21–24]: After the Caleb expansion, Hezron is taken
up (vss. 5, 9, 10; Gen xlvi 12; Num xxvi 6, 21; Ruth iv 18, 19).
While the place names, except Segub, are mostly known, what they
have to do with the Hezron of Judah is not certain. The list may
reflect an obscure relationship with the Transjordan places in the
time of the writer or there may be some confusion with the Hezron
of Reuben (Gen xlvi 9; Exod vi 14; I Chron v 3). (See EJ, p. 160.)
Concealed in the list may be the relation of David to Geshur through
Maacah (II Sam iii 3; I Chron iii 2). The tent-villages of Jair are
elsewhere associated with Manasseh (Num xxxii 41); so also
Kenath. (Cf. M. Noth, "Beiträge zur Geschichte des Ostjordanlandes," BBLA [1949], 11–12, n. 4. Something of the seminomadic
character of the Southern clans may be reflected here. Cf. A. Alt,
"Erwägungen über die Landnahme der Israeliten in Palästina," PJB
35 [1939], 26 f.; Albright, BASOR 125 [February 1952], 30.) According to Judg x 3 f., Jair was a Gileadite and because of what is
said there about the oppression of Gilead, the Chronicler's theology
may have crept into his genealogy.

Verse 24 is an explanation of vs. 19. This is the only reference to a double marriage of Ephrathah; Noth thinks vs. 24 should come between iv 4 and iv 5 (ZDPV 55 [1932], 107 f.).

[The Jerahmeel line, 25–33]: The names are apparently personal, as far as we know, and about all that can be said here is that traditionally Jerahmeel early became associated with Judah and was one of the Southern groups that cast in its lot with the people among whom they lived (I Sam xxvii 10, xxx 29). Noth thinks they formed an amphictyony with Judah, Caleb, Simeon, Othniel, and Kain, with their center at the Calebite city of Hebron. The religious factor was noticeable in the names Ahijah and Jonathan. Meyer is of the opinion that they may have been associated, at least in border areas, with the Edomites (*Die Israeliten und ihre Nachbarstämme*, p. 340).

[The progenitors of Elishama, 34–41]: Not much can be made of the list of names here except to say it is probably an addition to the preceding list since vs. 31 says Sheshan had a son (or sons) while vs. 34 says he had no sons but daughters, one of whom he married to his Egyptian servant. Of Elishama we know nothing definite. The name Sismai now appears as the name of a Phoenician deity in an Aramaic incantation text from Arslan Tash. See *Mélanges Syriens offerts à Monsieur René Dussaud* (Paris, 1939), pp. 421–34; and W. F. Albright, BASOR 76 (December 1939), 7, n. 9.

[The line of Caleb, 42–50a]: This is the first section of one of the most significant lists transmitted by the Chronicler. The Calebites, like Jerahmeel, were a Southern group (I Sam xxx 14) and Kenizzites (Num xxxii 12; Josh xiv 6, 13; Judg i 13). (P found no difficulty in reconciling Caleb and Judah, for the former was claimed as a Judean [Num xiii 6]. Whereas he remains the son of Jephunneh in P, he is here regarded as an integral part of the Hezron line and so brought into a closer relationship with the Davidic ancestors.) Early the Calebites became closely identified with Judah and occupied Hebron (Josh xiv 13, xv 13; Judg i 20), perhaps as their chief city, and by right of conquest, though Judg i 10 attributes that to Judah, perhaps a reflection of early identification between the two groups. The form of the genealogy is interesting. Caleb's line is followed through a wife and two concubines which means that from the writer's point of view it consisted of a main stem with two branches. But the most important aspect of it is the name of persons associated with places of settlement. There continue to be reminiscences of Edomite (Korah—i 35; Shammah—i 37) and even

Midianite relationships (Ephah—i 33; Gen xxv 4). There are elements of very important pre-exilic materials in the list. See Noth, ZDPV 55 (1932), who dates it in the period of David or Solomon and thinks it was drawn up as a military reserve list for Judah. Albright points to the archaeological results as demanding a later date, in the seventh century (AMJV, p. 65). Cf. the lam-melek stamps, an abundance of which have appeared in archaeological sites all over Judah; two of the centers mentioned are Ziph and Hebron, which were important store cities in the eighth–seven centuries (see tables in Olga Tufnell, *Lachish III: The Iron Age,* 1953, p. 342, and C. C. McCown, *Excavations at Tell En-Nasbeh,* I, 1947, p. 161; W. F. Albright, AASOR, 21–22 [1943], 74–75). That the list cannot refer to the postexilic period is shown by the fact that the southern boundary of Judah extended only as far as Beth-zur (see G. E. Wright and F. V. Filson, *The Westminster Historical Atlas,* 1956, Pl. VII, D.). Cf. Meyer, *Die Israeliten . . . ,* p. 404.

[The line of Caleb through Hur, 50b–55]: That the line was connected with Ephrathah and the district to the north and southwest is clear from the place names known. The three regions connected with the sons of Hur were Kiriath-jearim, Bethlehem and Beth-gader and their surrounding areas, some of which cannot be identified. "The families of Sopherim" may have been scribal guilds, though the whole verse is unintelligible as it stands. (See the proposals of G. Richter, "Zu den Geschlechtsregistern I Chr. 2–9," ZAW 49 [1931], 263; Rehm, p. 13; S. Klein, MGWJ 70 [1926], 414; A. Ehrlich, *Randglossen zur hebräischer Bibel,* VII, *in loco* [see Selected Bibliography].)

3. THE LINE OF DAVID
(iii 1–24)†

The descendants of David to the Exile

III 1 These are the sons of David who were born to him at Hebron: his first-born son was Amnon by Ahinoam the Jezreelitess, the second Daniel[a] by Abigail the Carmelitess, 2 the third Absalom the son of Maacah, daughter of Talmai king of Geshur, the fourth Adonijah son of Haggith, 3 the fifth Shephatiah by Abital, and the sixth Ithream by Eglah his wife. 4 Six were born to him at Hebron where he was king for seven years and six months; then he was king at Jerusalem for thirty-three years. 5 The following were born to him at Jerusalem: Shimea, Shobab, Nathan and Solomon—the four of them by Bathshua[b] daughter of Ammiel. 6 Then there were Ibhar, Elishama, Eliphelet, 7 Nogah, Nepheg, Japhia, 8 Elishama, Eliada, Eliphelet—nine. 9 All these were sons of David, not counting the sons of the concubines and their sister Tamar.

List of kings of Judah

10 Solomon's son was Rehoboam, his son Abijah, his son Asa, his son Jehoshaphat, 11 his son Joram, his son Ahaziah, his son Joash, 12 his son Amaziah, his son Azariah, his son Jotham, 13 his son Ahaz, his son Hezekiah, his son Manasseh, 14 his son Amon, and his son Josiah. 15 The sons of Josiah were his first-

† **I Chron iii 1–9** ‖ II Sam iii 2–5, I Chron xiv 3–7.

[a] LXX^AB in II Sam iii 3 has "Dalouia"; here LXX^A has the same, while LXX^B has "Damniel." MT at II Sam iii 3, however, has *Kil'ab* ("Chileab"). How the two names, Kil'ab and Daniel, for the same person arose is obscure. The original form of the name in II Sam iii was *ykl-'b* ("the father prevails"). Cf. *ykl-yh* in II Kings xv 2 ‖ II Chron xxvi 3. The initial *yod* frequently drops off in personal names. I owe this suggestion to Professor Freedman.
[b] LXX and Vulg. have "Bath-sheba."

born son Johanan, the second Jehoiakim, the third Zedekiah, and the fourth Shallum. 16 The sons of Jehoiakim were Jeconiah his son and Zedekiah his son.

Postexilic line of descent

17 The sons of Jeconiah the captive were Shealtiel his son, 18 then Malchiram, Pedaiah, Shenazzar, Jekamiah, Hoshama, and Nedabiah. 19 The sons of Pedaiah were Zerubbabel and Shimei; the sons of Zerubbabel were Meshullam and Hananiah; Shelomith was their sister. 20 Then there were Hashubah, Ohel, Berechiah, Hasadiah, and Jushab-hesed—five. 21 The sons of Hananiah were Pelatiah and Jeshaiah; also there were the sons of Rephaiah, the sons of Arnan, the sons of Obadiah, and the sons of Shecaniah. 22 The sons of Shecaniah were Shemaiah and the sons of Shemaiah were Hattush, Igal, Bariah, Neariah, and Shaphat—six. 23 The sons of Neariah were Elioenai, Hizkiah, and Azrikam—three. 24 The sons of Elioenai were Hodaivah, Eliashib, Pelaiah, Akkub, Johanan, Delaiah, and Anani—seven.

NOTES

iii 17. *Jeconiah the captive.* Albright reads "[while he was] a captive" (BA 5 [1942], 50), i.e., his sons were born during his captivity.

18. *Shenazzar.* The leader of the first returnees or the regent who acted because Zerubbabel was too young to take charge of affairs personally in 538 B.C. The name is defective writing for *šn'b'ṣr* (Bab. *Šin-ab-uṣur*), the *'b* having fallen out by haplography. See Albright, JBL 40 (1921), 108 ff. Perhaps both "Shenazzar" (vs. 18) and "Sheshbazzar" (Ezra i 8, 11, v 14, 16) are corruptions, each in a different way approximating the correct Babylonian form, which falls somewhere between them.

20. *Then there were.* Apparently two periods or places of children are involved.

COMMENT

Apparently this is a later addition in the spirit of the Chronicler whose chief concern centered about David. One would expect it to follow ii 17 where the ancestors of David are given. The sons born to him at Jerusalem are listed in I Chron xiv 3–7 also, while those born at Hebron are not referred to elsewhere in Chronicles. The other name of Azariah (vs. 12), Uzziah, is used in II Chron xxvi, xxvii; and Jeconiah (vss. 16, 17) is called Jehoiachin in II Chron xxxvi. Zerubbabel's father here is Pedaiah (vs. 19); in Ezra iii 2, 8, Shealtiel. Note, however, the numbering of the sons of David (1–3) and the sons of Josiah (15) and the same pattern followed with reference to the sons of Jesse (ii 13–15), though this may not indicate a literary relationship. (As Rothstein and Hänel, p. 44, think it does; but cf. Rudolph, p. 26.) On this chapter (iii) see J. Liver, *The House of David* (Hebrew) (Jerusalem, 1959), Chs. I and II. If chapters i–ix are a collection of archival material the position of this chapter is understandable.

[The descendants of David, iii 1–9]: Verses 1–3 are nearly identical with II Sam iii 2–5, with the exception of the name of the son of Abigail which is Daniel here but *Kil'ab* (Chileab) there.

Verses 4–9 list the sons born at Jerusalem, which follows in general the one in I Chron xiv 3–7. In each case thirteen names are given; eleven are in II Sam v 14–16. Eliada is Beeliada in I Chron xiv 7 and may have been influenced by the Samuel list. On the other hand Elishama (1) is Elishua both in Sam and I Chron xiv 5. The names omitted in Samuel are Eliphelet (1) and Nogah. The first four sons are said to be by Bathshua (Bathsheba), the daughter of Ammiel (the daughter of Eliam in II Sam xi 3, a reversal of the position of the two elements composing the name). Some commentators read seven for nine, omitting Eliphelet and Nogah, with Samuel, but the author's expansion of the list demands that the latter number remain. He includes Tamar (II Sam xiii) because wives, concubines and daughters are mentioned in his source (II Sam v 13).

[Davidic dynasty to the Exile, 10–16]: The source for the dynastic order is the Deuteronomic book of Kings, for the most part. The reason for the omission of Athaliah is obvious. The throne name of Uzziah-Azariah, and probably Shallum-Jehoahaz (see J. A. Montgomery and H. S. Gehman, *The Books of Kings* [in ICC], 1951, p. 446), is used, as is the more formal Abijah for Abijam in Kings (cf. *ibid.*, p. 273, note on I Kings xiv 31; for form and meaning of name see Noth, IPN, p. 234). Note the use of double names elsewhere—Jedidiah-Solomon, Eliakim-Jehoiakim, Mattaniah-Zedekiah —and the fact that Assyrian kings frequently changed their names upon taking the throne. Verses 15–16 are difficult. Josiah's son Johanan is not mentioned elsewhere, nor is there any explanation for Shallum-Jehoahaz as the successor of Josiah except that offered in II Kings xxiii 30 ‖ II Chron xxxvi 1 (see Würthwein, *Der 'amm . . . ,* pp. 33 ff.). Rudolph thinks Johanan may have died before his father. Then Jehoiakim, who was friendly to Egypt, would have been the natural successor to Josiah but "the people of the land" intervened, probably because of that fact, in behalf of Shallum-Jehoahaz. But why Zedekiah was bypassed is also uncertain unless it was because of the officials' knowledge of his vacillating character, which appears later during his reign. In the name Jeconiah there is another transposition of the theophoric element of the name Jehoiachin. There are three interpretations of "Zedekiah his son"—(a) that he was the son of Jeconiah, (b) that he was the son of Jehoiakim (cf. II Chron xxxvi 10, MT), (c) that "his son" means his successor. The second is doubtless right and Zedekiah is thus the nephew of Zedekiah the king and named after him.

[The postexilic line, 17–24]: On Jehoiachin see II Chron xxxvi 9 ff. The seven sons were born while he was in captivity. The Weidner texts speak of five sons for whom rations were provided by the Babylonian authorities (*Mélanges Syriens offerts à M. René Dussaud,* II, pp. 923–28). These texts date from 595 to 570, the crucial one from the thirteenth year of Nebuchadnezzar (ca. 592) which means that the oldest son of Jehoiachin was born not later than 597 B.C. Since Pedaiah falls third in the list, and allowing twenty-five years for a generation, it means that he was born around 595 B.C. (see Albright, JBL 40 [1921], 110 f.). The following table indicates the approximate dates for the birth of the persons named:

Pedaiah	ca. 595 B.C.
Zerubbabel	ca. 570 B.C.
Hananiah	ca. 545 B.C.
Shecaniah	ca. 520 B.C.
Shemaiah	ca. 495 B.C.
Neariah	ca. 470 B.C.
Elioenai	ca. 445 B.C.
Hodaviah	ca. 420 B.C.
Anani (last son)	ca. 405 B.C.

The fact that the line of descent ends with them, and that it is so reasonable in itself, has a very important bearing on the date of the Chronicler. One of the difficulties is that Pedaiah is said to be the father of Zerubbabel, whereas in other places his father is Shealtiel (Hag i 12, 14, ii 2, 23; Ezra iii 2, 8, v 2; Neh xii 1). LXX, probably for that reason, alters Pedaiah to Shealtiel (Salathiel). But either Shealtiel died early, after which Pedaiah became the head of the family (Goettsberger), or the latter may have married the childless widow of the former (Rudolph, following Neteler), in which case Zerubbabel would have been regarded as Shealtiel's son in accordance with Levirate marriage rules. The names were apparently common in the period as may be seen from their appearance on seals, letters, and other lists: Pedaiah (Ophel seal of sixth century and Elephantine Papyri, AP, 43); Jekamiah (fifth century, seal, D. Diringer, *Le Iscrizioni antico-ebraiche Palestinesi,* 1934, p. 210; eighth century, I. Ben-Dor, QDAP 13 [1948], 90); Igal (O. R. Sellers, *The Citadel of Beth-Zur* [1933], pp. 60 f.; O. R. Sellers and W. F. Albright, BASOR 43 [1931], 8 f.); Meshullam (Lachish III, Pl. 47A, 4–6; Elephantine, AP, 8, 9, 19, 22, 25; BMAP, 2, 5, 7–12; Shemaiah (Lachish Letters 4:6; 19:4); Hananiah (often; see *Hebrew Inscriptions and Stamps from Gibeon,* ed. J. B. Pritchard, 1959); Nedabiah (as Nedabel, Diringer, *op. cit.,* p. 189; A. Reifenberg, PEQ [1942], 110–11); Pelatiah (Elephantine, AP, 5, 10; BMAP 6); Anani (BMAP, 1, 2, 4, 6, 7, 9–13); Hodaviah (Lachish Letters 3:17; Elephantine Papyri 2, 10, 19, 22, 44, 46, 65). Cf. Albright, AMJV, p. 66. On Anani, see ANET, p. 492. The data listed above indicate strongly that this material does not come from a time later than the end of the fifth century B.C.

The following is a genealogy of the Davidic line:

THE DAVIDIC FAMILY AND LINE
ACCORDING TO I CHRON iii

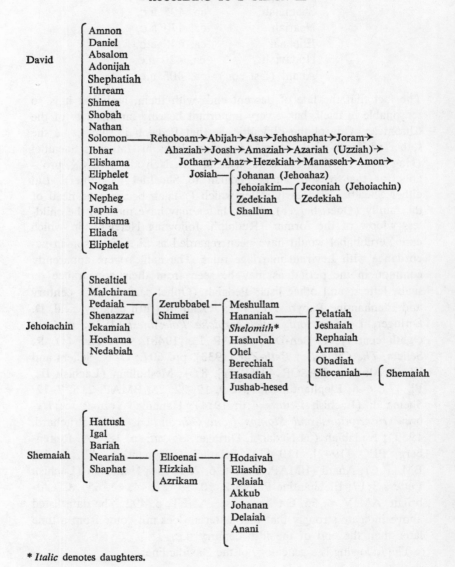

* *Italic* denotes daughters.

4. SOUTHERN TRIBAL LISTS
(iv 1–43)†

The sons of Judah and Shobal

IV ¹ The sons of Judah were Perez, Hezron, Carmi, Hur, and Shobal. ² Reaiah the son of Shobal fathered Jahath and Jahath fathered Ahumai and Lahad. These were the families of the Zorathites.

The sons of Hur

³ᵃThese [were the sons of Hareph: . . .] the father of Etam,ᵃ Jezreel, Ishma, and Idbash, and their sister's name was Hazzelelponi. ⁴ Penuel was the father of Gedor and Ezer was the father of Hushah. These were the sons of Hur the first-born son of Ephrathah the father of Bethlehem.

The sons of Ashhur

⁵ Ashhur the father of Tekoa had two wives, Helah and Naarah. ⁶ Naarah bore to him Ahuzzam, Hepher, Temeni, and the Ahashtarites—these were the sons of Naarah. ⁷ The sons of Helah were Zereth, Zohar, and Ethnan. ⁸ Koz fathered Anub, Hazzobebah, and the families of Aharhel the son of Harum. ⁹ Now Jabez was more worthy of honor than his brothers; his mother had named him Jabez saying, "I have borne him in pain." ¹⁰ But Jabez called upon the God of Israel saying, "May you indeed bless me, enlarge my territory, let your hand be with me and prevent evil from hurting me." And God granted what he asked.

† **I Chron iv 11–20** ‖ Num xiii 6, Judg i 13; **24–43** ‖ Gen xlvi 10, Num xxvi 12, Josh xix 1–8.

ᵃ⁻ᵃ LXX has "and these were the sons of Etam." The reconstruction is that of Noth, ZDPV 55 (1932), 103. Syriac has "these were the sons of Abinadab" and Vulg. "this too is the line of Etam."

Descendants of Caleb

11 Chelub[b] the brother of Shuhah fathered Mehir who was the father of Eshton. 12 [c]Eshton fathered Beth-rapha, Paseah, and Tehinnah, the father of Ir-nahash. These were the men of Recah[c]. 13 The sons of Kenaz were Othniel and Seraiah. The sons of Othniel were Hathath [d][and Meonothai][d]. 14 Meonothai fathered Ophrah and Seraiah fathered Joab the father of Ge-harashim, for they were artisans. 15 The sons of Caleb the son of Jephunneh were Iru, Elah, and Naam. [e]The son of Elah was[e] Kenaz. 16 The sons of Jehallelel were Ziph, Ziphah, Tiria, and Asarel. 17 The sons of Ezrah were Jether, Mered, Epher, and Jalon. She conceived Miriam, Shammai, and Ishbah the father of Eshtemoa. 18 His Judean wife bore Jered the father of Gedor, Heber the father of Soco, and Jekuthiel the father of Zanoah. These were the sons of Bithiah the daughter of Pharaoh whom Mered had married. 19 The sons of the wife of Hodiah the sister of Naham the father of Keilah the Garmite and Eshtemoa the Maacathite . . . 20 The sons of Shimon were Amnon, Rinnah, Ben-hanan, and Tilon. The sons of Ishi were Zoheth and Ben-zoheth.

Descendants of Shelah

21 The sons of Shelah the son of Judah were Er the father of Lecah, Laadah the father of Mareshah, the families of linen makers of Beth-ashbea, 22 Jokim, the men of Cozeba, Joash, and Saraph who married Moabites and then returned to Bethlehem (these traditions are old). 23 They were the potters who dwelt at Netaim and Gederah; they resided there in the service of the king.

[b] Vrs. read "Caleb." LXX reads "Caleb the father of Aska."
[c-c] LXX "He fathered Bethraiah, Bessee, and Thaimah, the father of the city of Nahash, the brother of Eselon of the Qenizites. These are the men of Rekab."
[d-d] So with LXX[L] and Vulg.
[e-e] MT reads "the sons of Elah and Kenaz"; LXX reads "the sons of Ada (Ala) [were] Kenaz."

Descendants of Simeon

24 The sons of Simeon were Nemuel, Jamin, Jarib, Zerah, Saul, 25 his son Shallum, his son Mibsam and his son Mishma. 26 The sons of Mishma were Hammuel his son, Zaccur his son and Shimei his son. 27 Shimei had sixteen sons and six daughters but his brothers did not have many sons so that all their families did not have as many sons as Judah. 28 They lived in Beer-sheba, Moladah, Hazar-shual, 29 in Bilhah, in Ezem, in Tolad, 30 in Bethuel, in Hormah, in Ziklag, 31 in Beth-marcaboth, in Hazar-susim, in Beth-biri, and in Shaaraim; these were their cities until David became king. 32 Their settlements were Etam, Ain, Rimmon, Tochen, and Ashan—five cities, 33 together with all their dependencies which were round about these cities *as far as Baalath*. These were their dwelling places and they had an official genealogy. 34 Meshobab, Jamlech, Joshah the son of Amaziah, 35 Joel, Jehu the son of Joshibiah, the son of Seraiah, the son of Asiel, 36 Elioenai, Jaakobah, Jeshohaiah, Asaiah, Adiel, Jesimiel, Benaiah, 37 Ziza the son of Shiphi, the son of Allon, the son of Jedaiah, the son of Shimri, the son of Shemaiah— 38 These above named were princes in their families and the house of their fathers. They multiplied greatly 39 and went as far as the entrance of Gedor*, to the east side of the valley in search of pasture for their flocks. 40 There they found luxuriant and excellent pasture and the land extensive on both sides, as well as quiet and peaceful, for the earlier inhabitants there were Hamites. 41 These, who were recorded by name, arrived in the days of Hezekiah* king of Judah and razed their tents and lodgings which were found there. They banished them to this day and occupied their place because there was pasture there for their flocks. 42 Five hundred men of them, of the sons of Simeon went to Mount Seir, their leaders being Pelatiah, Neariah,

- So with LXXᴮ; cf. Josh xix 8.

ᵍ LXX has "Gerara" ("Gerar"), which is undoubtedly right. See II Chron xiv 9 ff., and cf. Y. Aharoni, "The Land of Gerar," IEJ 6 (1956), 26–32.

ʰ Hebrew reads "Jehizkiah," but context indicates that "Hezekiah" is intended.

Rephaiah, and Uzziel, the sons of Ishi. 43 They exterminated the remnant of the Amalekites which had escaped and they have lived there until this day.

NOTES

iv 7. *and Zohar.* Reading "[and] Zohar" with Qere for "Izohar."

10. For an example from Canaanite literature see W. F. Albright, BASOR 94 (April 1944), 30 f.

11. *Mehir.* On possible name of Mehir on seal see A. Dupont-Sommer's note in Tufnell, *Lachish III: The Iron Age*, p. 358.

12. *Ir-nahash.* Could also be rendered "city of Nahash," more likely "city of smiths or craftsmen" (see COMMENT, vss. 14, 21–23). Has been identified with Khirbet Nahaš in Wadi Arabah.

15. *The son of Elah was Kenaz.* A name or names may have fallen out; or with Rothstein and Hänel, and Curtis and Madsen, a transposition of "the sons of Kenaz" with "Elah" as a demonstrative pronoun ('lh-'elleh-these), it could be read "these were the sons of Kenaz" and thus refer to the foregoing names.

16. *Tiria, and Asarel.* For identification of Tiria and Asarel see Albright, BASOR 125 (February 1952), 30 f.; but cf. S. Yeivin in *Mélanges Bibliques rédigés en l'honneur de André Robert*, n. d., p. 100. Observe the curious position of Simeon in II Chron xxxiv 6; Ezek xlviii 24, 25, 33, and the reference to his being scattered throughout Jacob and Israel in Gen xlix 7; cf. Num ii 12.

17. *Epher.* Albright, *loc cit.*, identifies "Eber" with 'Apiru or with Epher in I Chron v 24, and "Asarel" in the preceding verse with Asriel of Manasseh.

She. I.e., Bithiah, daughter of Pharaoh (cf. vs. 18).

Miriam. On Miriam see JTS 38 (1897), 403.

19. A difficult and uncertain verse. In Neh viii 7, ix 5, x 11, 14, 19, Hodiah is said to be one of the Levites assisting Ezra; Naham is mentioned nowhere else.

21. *families.* I.e., guilds of weavers.

22. *Bethlehem.* With a slight change in pointing and the addition of "beth" (cf. Ruth i).

22–23. Translation follows, in part, Cazelles, *Les Livres des Chroniques*, p. 44 (see Selected Bibliography, Commentaries). Verses are difficult. LXX is noncommittal and apparently transliterates the last part of vs. 23. Unless we think of Joash and Saraph as governors in the time of the United Kingdom, it seems better to regard the situation as similar to that pertaining in Ruth i. Tur-Sinai goes too far (*Eretz Israel*, V, pp.

87 f., English résumé) in his forced treatment of the words "these traditions are old," which are better left as they stand, thus calling attention to the antiquity of the traditions.

23. On this verse see, in addition to the references below, Albright in AASOR 21–22 (1943), 74 f.; McCown, *Excavations at Tell En-Nasbeh*, I, pp. 156–61; Sellin in ZDPV 66 (1943), 216–32; D. Diringer in PEQ (July 1941), 89 f.

31. *Shaaraim.* Sharuhen. How this change came about is explained by Albright, JPOS 4 (1924), 134 f.

32. *Ain, Rimmon.* Ain-Rimmon should be (properly) a single place name, as in Josh xix 7.

41. *their tents.* Rudolph, *in loco,* suggests "the people of Ham," but cf. II Chron xiv 15.

lodgings. Another translation is "Meunites" (cf. II Chron xx 1).

COMMENT

As has been noted above, chapter iv is part of the Judahite list which dates from pre-exilic times, but contains additions drawn from other sources or even sometimes repetitions of what has gone before. It contains much pre-exilic material and hence is another valuable criterion for the authenticity of the Chronicler's work. It fills in the details or, perhaps better, provides elements not given in chapter ii. Noth (ZDPV 55 [1932], 97–124; PJB 30 [1934], 31–47) thinks of four sections in the whole list of the family of Judah: (a) the line of Judah through Shelah, iv 21–23, and localized in the western highland; (b) the line of Hur (through the marriage of Hezron with Ephrathah), ii 50a, 53, iv 2, ii 54–55, iv 3, 16–19, 4b, located in the north; (c) the line of Caleb, son of Jephunneh (through marriage with Ephrathah after death of Hezron), ii 24, iv 5–7, 11–12, the Calebite-Judahite interrelated families; (d) the other sons of Caleb, ii 42–50a, comprising Calebite families of the south.

[More on Judah and Shobal, iv 1–2]: This is an expansion of Judah's progeny through Shobal mentioned in ii 50, 52. Verse 1 is introductory and traces both Hur and Shobal to Judah, though the latter is the son of the former by Ephrathah. The purpose of the supplement is to explain the background of the Zorathites (ii 53), which was not through Kirjath-jearim but through Reaiah. Of the persons named as sons of Reaiah nothing further is known. Perhaps there was need for explaining the origin of Zorah in view of its importance (cf. II Chron xi 10; Neh xi 29) later.

[Descendants of Hur, 3–4]: Something has fallen out at the beginning of vs. 3, between "these" and "the father of Etam." The reason for the extension is to complete the genealogy of Hur (vs. 4b). Etam (present-day Khirbet el Khokh, one of the towns fortified by Rehoboam (II Chron xi 6), was southwest of Bethlehem; Gedor (Kh. Judūr), a few miles north of Beth-zur and west of Tekoa; Hushah (Husan), some five or six miles west of Bethlehem. Jezreel may reflect the northward penetration of the Jezreelites from a place south of Hebron (cf. Josh xv 58). The others are probably personal names. "Father of Bethlehem" may be a reflection of ii 51, where Salma is said to be the father of Bethlehem, and meant to refer to Bethlehem's progenitor Hur.

[Descendants of Ashhur, 5–8]: Ashhur is the son of Caleb and Ephrathah (so also ii 24). Chapter ii 19 is apparently another tradition. The combination of Caleb with Tekoa points to an amalgamation of southern elements with Judah. Most of the list is obscure, though some of the names suggest southern connections, for example, Temeni, Tekoa, Zohar (cf. Gen xlvi 10; Exod vi 15 where it is the name of a son of Simeon); Anub and Koz are uncertain, though the former has been associated with Anab (Josh xi 21, xv 50). The Persian derivation of Ahashtarites is very doubtful (cf. C. C. Torrey, "Medes and Persians," JAOS 66 [1946], 7 f.). The list may be given because of the prominence of the Tekoites, who participated in the rebuilding of the walls of Jerusalem (Neh iii 5, 27), and the appearance of significant references to Tekoa elsewhere in Chronicles.

[Note on Jabez, 9–10]: This little pericope is theological in meaning though it may have been intended as a comment on ii 55 where Jabez is a place name. Here it is a personal or family name. The play on words which is not apparent in translation—between Jabez and pain ('ōṣeb)—is due to popular etymology and is preparatory to the main element here, vs. 10. The name was fraught with consequences (cf. Gen xxxv 18) that could be altered only by the giving of another name. The Chronicler therefore breaks with tradition and resorts to prayer to change the fortunes of life—"hurting" is the same root as "pain" in the preceding verse (see Introduction, The Theology of the Chronicler). He thus emphasizes that God listens to genuine prayer. This is a case of prayer without vow, which may have fallen out. But it appears that the Chronicler has rejected the idea of the vow since the term does not occur in his writings. (Cf., however, H. L. Ginsberg, "Psalms and Inscriptions," LGJV, p. 164, n. 14.)

[Further on Calebites, 11–15]: Noth thinks vss. 11–12 were introductory to ii 42 ff. (see above, ZDPV 55 [1932], 97–124). His reconstruction, based on the formula, X (person) the father of Y (place), is probably the best interpretation available at present, but the persons and places are not otherwise identified. On the relation between Kenaz and Othniel see Josh xv 17; Judg i 13, iii 9, 11, which may be reflected by the writer. The Ge-harashim cannot be separated from Neh xi 35. The occurrence of Ophrah and perhaps Maon (in Meonothai) may be due to pastoral seasonal migrations (see Alt, PJB 35 [1939], 26 ff.). Ir-nahash, "city of smiths," is connected with the Arabah by N. Glueck, *Rivers in the Desert* (New York, 1959), pp. 134, 156. The Kenites were wanderers (*ibid.*, p. 134).

[Judahite-Calebite clans, 16–20]: That the list is pre-exilic is shown by the fact that numerous places not included in the province of Judah in Nehemiah's time, which extended only as far south as Beth-zur, are included here, for example, Ziph and Eshtemoa. Whether Keilah, Zanoah, Soco were in the south or in the west hill country is not certain. For opposing views see Noth, ZDPV 55 (1932), 109 ff. Jether may be connected with Jattir, modern Kh. Attir, southeast of Hebron. If the northern places of Zanoah and Soco are meant, Gedor would be near them; if not then it may be the modern Kh. Judūr, southwest of Bethlehem (Josh xv 58). Otherwise we know nothing of the names or places except that they obviously indicate the tenacity of old traditions and their pastoral character.

[The descendants of Shelah, 21–23]: This little note on Judah's third son Shelah either became separated from ii 3 or is an afterthought expansion. Of the places named, Mareshah was one of Rehoboam's fortified cities (II Chron xi 8) on the southwest border of Judah (Tell Sandaḥannah); Cozeba may be Achzib of Josh xv 44 (cf. Mic i 14), some five miles north of Mareshah, but Elliger, ZDPV 57 (1934), 124, identifies it with en el-Kezbe near beit Neṭṭif. Gederah has been identified with Tell ej-Judeideh, a few miles north of Mareshah, and Naṭaim with the modern Arab village of Kh. en-Nuweiṭi slightly north of Gederah (cf. W. F. Albright, "The Administrative Divisions of Israel and Judah," JPOS 5 [1925], 50, and AASOR 21–22 [1943], 74 f., 112 f.; McCown, *Excavations at Tell En-Nasbeh,* I, pp. 156–61; Sellin, ZDPV 66 [1943], 216–32). Several very important considerations grow out of an examination of this list. The name Jokim, though not of the same person, is now known from a seal (BASOR 31 [1928], 11). The references to families of linen workers and potters (cf. scribal guilds, ii 55) are illuminated now through a study of pottery and pottery marks. These are distinctive in character because they were royal potters (I. Mendelsohn, "Guilds in Ancient Palestine," BASOR 80 [1940], 17–21, and especially references cited there; Albright, JPOS 5 [1925], 50 f.). The connection of Judah and Moab is of some interest because of the marriage of Elimelech's sons to Moabite girls, a practice forbidden after the Exile (Ezra ix 1; Neh xiii 23). Here is more than genealogy in the strict sense of the word; it is rather more of a reference to the founders of various guilds whose names were associated with localities where their trade was carried on possibly for centuries.

[The family of Simeon, 24–43]: The first portion of this family genealogy is based on Num xxvi 12–13 and amplified by the Simeonite list of Josh xix 1–8 (cf. also Gen xlvi 10 which differs somewhat from both). Comparison with Judah is doubtless a commentary on Josh xix 9. The orderliness of the presentation is noteworthy: (a) the family list, 24–27; (b) their towns and cities, 28–33; (c) the movements of their leaders and clans, 34–43.

The genealogy of Simeon has been transmitted through four lists (Gen xlvi 10; Exod vi 15; Num xxvi 12–13; and here). The Pentateuchal materials belong to *P.* The Genesis and Exodus lists correspond exactly; both Numbers and Chronicles omit Ohad; Chronicles has Jarib for Jachin; and both Chronicles and Numbers have Zerah for Zohar. According to Genesis and Exodus, Saul was the son of a Canaanite woman, and Gen xxv 13 (cf. I Chron i 29, 30) attributes Mibsam and Mishma to Ishmael. See R. Dussaud, *La pénétration des Arabes en Syrie avant l'Islam* (Paris: Geuthner, 1955), p. 175, and A. Musil, *Arabia Deserta* (New York: American Geographical Society, 1927), p. 479. The list is carried further than in the Chronicler's source, and his observation that Simeon was not so prolific as Judah reflects the absorption of Simeon by Judah. Simeon lost its identity quite early (Josh xix 1, 9; cf. Gen xlix 5–7; note its absence in blessing of Moses in Deut xxxiii and from the list of places to which David sent booty in I Sam xxx 27–31).

The interest in Simeon may be due to the writer's conception of the ideal Israel illustrated by his emphasis on the twelve (Ezra viii 24) and all Israel (Ezra vi 17, viii 35 and often elsewhere) and certainly stresses his strong sense of history for his purposes.

The list of towns and cities has been dealt with by Albright (JPOS 5 [1925], 149–61. See also Cross and Wright, JBL 75 [1956], 214 f., and Aharoni, IEJ 8 [1958], 26–38) who points out that there are a number of Simeon lists in the Bible. The earliest one (Josh xix 2–7) dates from before the time of Judah's absorption of Simeon, the next oldest (Josh xv 26–32, 42) from the period of Judah's greatest extent, and the third, our list, which comes from the Chronicler and possibly because his edition was copied less frequently transmits the names in the most accurate form. The references in I Sam xxx 27 f. need not be considered here though they doubtless point to a contemporary tradition. In Neh xi 26 ff. there is a list of reoccupied cities in so far as they pertained to the situation in the time of the Chronicler. Many of the sites have been identified, at least tentatively. That the list is old is indicated by the remark in vs. 31—"these were their cities until David became king" (Aharoni [IEJ 8 (1958), 31] sees no reason to question this comment)—and is supported by the further statement of the existence of an official genealogical register.

The final portion of the chapter deals with the Simeonite chiefs who for natural reasons sought sustenance elsewhere (vss. 38–39, 41). There is no religious motive expressed here; it is simply a matter of overpopulation and the need for pasture for flocks. They expanded in two directions; the first one was westward toward Gerar (see textual note *f*) whose lands were in the hands of Egyptian puppets. Gerar was probably established as the center of a kind of buffer state by Shishak (Albright, JPOS 4 [1924], 146 f.) and remained so even after the time of Asa (II Chron xiv). Gerar was outside the tribal system and the invaders came only so far as the city itself—"to the east side of the valley." These outlying areas could be taken only because the people of Gerar were reveling in contentment as the people around Laish had been when Dan struck (Judg xviii 7). The period from which the movement stems is given as that of Hezekiah. The second movement was in the opposite direction and displaced the Amalekite elements residing in the Akaba region among the Edomites since their dispersal in the time of Saul (I Sam xv 7 f.) and David (I Sam xxx 18).

5. LISTS OF TRANSJORDANIAN TRIBES
(v 1–26)†

Descendants of Reuben

V 1 The sons of Reuben the first-born son of Israel—though he was the first-born son, when he defiled his father's bed his birthright was given to the sons of Joseph, the son of Israel, and he was not included in the official genealogy according to birthright. 2 Although Judah grew superior to his brothers and a leader came from him, the birthright was Joseph's. 3 The sons of Reuben the first-born of Israel were Enoch, Pallu, Hezron, and Carmi.

Descendants of Joel

4 The sons of Joel were Shemaiah his son, Gog his son, Shimei his son, 5 Micah his son, Reaiah his son, and Baal his son. 6 Beerah his son, whom Tilgath-pilneser[a] king of Assyria exiled, was the prince of the Reubenites. 7 His brothers, [b]by families[b], were included in the official genealogy according to their descendants. Jeiel was first, then Zechariah and 8 Bela the son of Azaz, the son of Shema, the son of Joel who lived in Aroer and as far as Nebo and Baal-meon. 9 His occupation extended eastward to the edge of the desert and the Euphrates River, for they had many cattle in the land of Gilead. 10 In the time of Saul they made war on the Hagrites who fell into their hand and who then resided in their tents on the eastern frontier of Gilead.

† I Chron v 1–3 ‖ Gen xxxv 22, xlvi 9, Exod vi 14, Num xxvi 5–6; 23–26: cf. Num xxxii 39, II Kings xv 19 f., xvii 6, xviii 11.

[a] So for MT "Tillegath-pilneeser."
[b–b] Heb. "his families."

Descendants of Gad

11 Opposite them, in the land of Bashan as far as Salecah, lived the sons of Gad. 12 Joel was the first, Shapham the second, then Janai and ᶜShaphatᶜ in Bashan. 13 Their brothers, according to their families, were Michael, Meshullam, Sheba, Jorai, Jacan, Zia, and Eber, seven. 14 These are the sons of Abihail the son of Huri, the son of Jaroah, the son of Gilead, the son of Michael, the son of Jeshishai, the son of Jahdo, the son of Buz. 15 Ahi the son of Abdiel, the son of Guni was the head of their families. 16 They inhabited Gilead, Bashan and its dependencies and also all the pasture lands of Sharon on their extremities. 17 In the time of Jotham king of Judah and in the time of Jeroboam king of Israel all of them were included in the official genealogy. 18 The sons of Reuben, Gad and the half-tribe of Manasseh had warriors, men armed with shield and sword, who could draw the bow and who were trained for war, to the number of forty-four thousand seven hundred and sixty fit for service. 19 They made war on the Hagrites, Jetur, Naphish, and Nodab. 20 When they received support against them, the Hagrites and all their allies fell into their hand for they cried unto God during the battle and he answered them because they trusted in him. 21 They captured of their possessions fifty thousand camels, two hundred fifty thousand sheep, two thousand asses and one hundred thousand men. 22 Because the war was of God, many were slain. They continued to live in their territory until the Exile.

Descendants of the half-tribe of Manasseh

23 The sons of the half-tribe of Manasseh lived in the land from Bashan to Baal-hermon, Senir, and Mount Hermon; they were quite numerous. 24 These were the heads of their families: Epher, Ishi, Eliel, Azriel, Jeremiah, Hodaviah, and Jahdiel —warriors, men of renown, and heads of their families. 25 But since they were unfaithful to the God of their fathers and played

ᶜ–ᶜ LXXᴮ "scribe." It has been suggested that "Janai, the judge in Bashan" be read.

the harlot by going after the gods of the peoples of the land whom God had exterminated before them, 26 the God of Israel incited the spirit of Pul, king of Assyria, even the spirit of Til-gath-pilneser, king of Assyria who deported them—the Reuben-ites, the Gadites, and the half-tribe of Manasseh—and brought them to Halah, Habor, Hara and the river of Gozan, *d*where they remain to this day*d*.

d-d Hebrew reads simply "to this day."

NOTES

v 6. *Tilgath-pilneser*. Tilgath-pilneser III (745–727). The Reubenite clan of Joel was exiled during the first of his conquests to the west in 734 B.C.

16. *Sharon*. Here not the plain by that name located south of Carmel, but an unknown place in Transjordan. See line 13 of the Mesha In-scription.

20. *When they received support*. The help came from God, not from allies, as indicated later in the verse.

22. *their territory*. I.e., the territory of their enemies.

23. *half-tribe*. A tribe divided into two parts, each one of which re-sides in a different locality.

Baal-hermon. Cf. Judg iii 3. The Hermon of Baal, which as a place name became Baal-hermon—like Baal-lebanon, Baal-hammon, Baal-zaphon—and was a surrogate for the mountain itself. Cf. Abel, *Géog-raphie de la Palestine*, I, p. 348; H. Th. Bossert, AfO 19 (1960), 147 f.

24. *Epher . . . Azriel*. On identification of the sites see Albright, BASOR 125 (February 1952), 30 f.

26. *Tilgath-pilneser*. Pul and Tilgath-pilneser refer to the same person. Assyrian kings who also ruled over Babylonia frequently bore two names, one as king of Assyria and one as king of Babylonia. For ex-ample, Tilgath-pilneser III's Babylonian name was Pul; Shalmaneser V's Babylonian name was Ululaia. Cf. also the dual names of the kings of Judah: Uzziah-Azariah; Jehoahaz-Shallum; Eliakim-Jehoiakim; Mat-taniah-Zedekiah. See NOTES on II Chron xxvi with references.

COMMENT

In his zeal for maintaining the position of Judah, the tribe of David, as the center of national religious institutions, the Chronicler does not lose sight of other tribes, even remote and long extinct ones. Here he takes up the Transjordan tribes of Reuben, Gad, and the half-tribe of Manasseh. This is one more point in his conception of postexilic Hebrew universalism in which Jerusalem and Judah figure as the true center and perpetuator of Israel. Judah is, therefore, treated first and Simeon, because of the close relationship to and absorption by Judah, comes next.

[The descendants and locale of Reuben, v 1–10]: The writer is factually correct in reckoning Reuben as Jacob's oldest son, by Leah (Gen xxix 32, xxxv 23, xlix 3; Exod vi 14; Num i 20, xxvi 5). But he calls attention to the sin of Reuben (Gen xxxv 22, xlix 4b; cf. Josh xxii 11 ff.) and posits it as the reason for the ascendancy of the sons of Joseph. Hence it was that Reuben was no longer reckoned according to birthright in the official genealogical register of Israel.

On the problem of the status of the first-born and the possible shift of rights to others see I. Mendelsohn, "On the Preferential Status of the Eldest Son," BASOR 156 (1959), 38–40. Joseph was the first-born son of the favorite wife. The father could presumably designate the "oldest" son, especially if the normal heir did something to impair his claim. This conception of the birthright with its concomitant privileges is reflected in the common view in the Bible that Joseph constituted two tribes (Ephraim and Manasseh), and thus held two portions of the inheritance of Jacob. This is in line with the rule that the eldest son received the first (the best) portion and then shared equally with the other brothers in the distribution of the remainder. For example, if there were two brothers the older would get two shares (the birthright and another) while the other brother would get one share. With twelve sons, the "oldest" would get the birthright, and then share with the other eleven, thus producing thirteen shares in all, of which he would hold two. The commingling of traditions could account for the variations in the tribal listings, that is, there were twelve sons but thirteen tribes, counting both Ephraim and Manasseh, and Levi. In the distribution of the territory, the number of shares was reduced to twelve (Joseph re-

ceiving two) with Levi deprived of a regular portion for special reasons and compensated in other ways. In this way the conflicting
traditions were reconciled. The application of birthright principles to
territorial allotment may not have historical foundations but it does
represent the mode by which the tribal-territorial history was ac-
commodated to the family traditions of the patriarchs. The list here
must have been handed down from earlier times, since the Chronicler would hardly have glorified the Joseph tribes at the expense of
Judah.

Doubtless underlying the pronouncement of Reuben's sin was
the position occupied by Joseph in the period of the divided kingdom
and the blessing given him by Jacob (cf. Gen xlix 26, xlviii 18 f.).
Nevertheless, the Chronicler thought that Joseph's birthright had
been nullified by the apostasy of North Israel and the failure of the
remnants to maintain their legal status (the Samaritans) and that
the choice of David (the leader, or messiah) had indicated the shift
of blessing and power (cf. II Sam vii 8 ff., where the same word for
leader is used and Ps lxxviii 67–68). The Chronicler may have had
in mind the Psalm of the great historical cult (lxxviii) which is
certainly pre-exilic and in all probability reflects the tragic downfall
of the Northern Kingdom in 722 B.C., possibly also the Judean
deliverance from the siege of Sennacherib in 701 B.C. If that is
correct, it is one more example of his cultic concern. Rudolph suggests a slight emendation of the text (vs. 2) so as to make it read:
"for Judah became the mightiest among his brethren so that *to him,
not* Joseph belonged the birthright." But in view of the writer's feeling for religious history, it is hard to see why he might have altered
the plain situation portrayed in the records. The actual list of the
four sons of Reuben follows the written tradition (Gen xlvi 9; Exod
vi 14; Num xxvi 5). The descendants of Reuben given here differ
from those in Num xxvi 8 ff. where Dathan and Abiram, the opponents of Moses, are listed with others as descendants through
Pallu. How Joel was related to Reuben is not stated and it appears
that the writer's chief concern centers upon Beerah who was deported by Tilgath-pilneser III (cf. II Kings xv 29). This is further
confirmation of the shift of blessing from Joseph to Judah. All that
can be said about the line is that it was regarded as Reubenite, for it
must be remembered that "son" does not always mean literally
child; it can mean simply descendant. The inclusion of the name
Baal points to an old tradition. Baal names are generally confined

to the period of the United Kingdom or thereafter to the Northern
Kingdom (cf. G. B. Gray, *Hebrew Proper Names,* 1896, pp. 120 ff.;
Noth, IPN, pp. 116 ff.) except where Baal is obscured as in Baanah,
Baasha, Baara. Some of the place names occur in the Mesha Inscription—Baal-meon, Aroer, Nebo—and were in the hands of
Moab in the third quarter of the ninth century B.C. According to
Jer xlviii they were still Moabite in the prophet's time though he
predicted their destruction. Consequently the list contains elements
not later than ca. 850 B.C. and is based on Num xxxii 37 f. That
some of the clans of Reuben remained in Gilead, migrating north
in the wake of the Moabite and Ammonite pressure, until the Assyrian conquest is altogether possible. Even in other lists the situation
in Transjordan appears quite fluid (see M. Noth, "Beiträge zur
Geschichte des Ostjordanlandes," PJB 37 [1941], 98–101). The
Reubenites were absorbed quite early by Gad since the Mesha Inscription mentions the latter but not the former. Because of the
character of these tribes, they may have remained as seminomadic
herdsmen and roamed the entire range of territory on the desert
frontier as indicated in vss. 9, 10. The Hagrites were Arabs who
appear at several points in the history of Israel (see Meyer, *Die
Israeliten* . . . , pp. 326–28). The conflict mentioned may refer to
the Ammonite wars of Saul (I Sam xi). Psalm lxxxiii 6 places the
Hagrites in the vicinity of Moab.

[The Gadites, 11–17]: There is no connection between this list
and those of Gad elsewhere (Gen xlvi 16; Num xxvi 15–18; cf. list
of those in David's army, I Chron xii 9–13) which indicates use of
an unknown source. The territory occupied by Gad as delimited in
Deut iii 10 is the source upon which the writer here draws. Bashan is
the area northeast of the Jabbok to beyond the Yarmuk River; it is
substantially the same as Gilead, which later took in more or less all
Transjordan. Salecah may have been east of Edrei (cf. Josh xiii 11)
on the Yarmuk River. Sharon is unidentified but is here located on
the extremities of Gilead and Bashan, doubtless toward the east.
The important point to be noted here and in the Reubenite list is
the references to their many cattle and pasture lands which fit the
geographical locale quite well. The mention of Jotham with Jeroboam II is simply the writer's way of saying that his list was the
official one at that time (i.e., between 750 and 745 B.C.) and he
includes the name of the former to accord with his scheme of mak-

ing the Davidic dynasty the chronologico-religious backbone of his work.

[The Transjordan wars with Arab peoples, 18–22]: The numbers are generally fantastically large, reflecting the writer's tendency to exaggerate on this point, though the number of those "fit for service" is not nearly so large as that given in the census lists of Numbers (i, xxvi). The date of this tradition is indicated by the recognition of the separate tribal existence of Reuben, Gad, and the half-tribe of Manasseh. The recognition had long ceased when the Mesha Stone was inscribed (late ninth century B.C.), since the tribe of Gad is there said to have occupied what was earlier the territory of Reuben "from of old" (mē'ōlām). The fortunes of Jetur reflected in the Bible show clearly the fluid situation, especially in the lands to the north and east of Palestine proper. Genesis xxv 15 locates Jetur in North Arabia; I Chron i 31 and the present passage place it in Transjordan. In Luke iii 1, Jetur (Iturea) is situated in the Antilibanus region (cf. Dussaud, *La pénétration des Arabes en Syrie avant l'Islam,* pp. 176 f. and references cited there). The Hagrites, Naphish, and Nodab (Nadab) are found in Assyrian documents (see W. F. Albright, "The Biblical Tribe of Massa . . . ," *Studi orientalistici in onore di Giorgio Levi della Vida,* I, 1956, pp. 1–14, especially pp. 12–14) and the activity of the Transjordan tribes against the Arabs is just what might be expected in the eleventh century (cf. vs. 10). The exile mentioned in vs. 22 in all probability refers to Tilgath-pilneser's conquest in 734 B.C. (cf. II Kings xv 29) when Gilead became the center of the Transjordan district (cf. Alt, "Das System der assyrischen Provinzen," KS, II, pp. 188–205; Albright, JPOS 5 [1925], 44). The theology of Chronicles is applied in the affirmation that Yahweh was with the Israelites because they trusted in him.

[The half-tribe of Manasseh and the captivity of the Transjordan Israelites, 23–26]: As if to emphasize the common lot of the tribes on the other side of the Jordan, this list is introduced here despite the fact that the tribe of Manasseh is treated in vii 14–19. According to Num xxxii 39 ff. and Josh xiii 8–13, the tribal allotment for the two and a half eastern tribes covered the territory from the Arnon to Mount Hermon, and Manasseh was the one farthest north. The list must refer to a time of Israelite supremacy and then to the loss of the region in the campaign of Tilgath-pilneser III in 734. After the division of the kingdom and the early struggles of each section to perpetuate itself, the more distant portions of the Northern Kingdom must have come under attack from Damascus, and the Transjordan portions were in constant danger. Some cities were taken from Omri (I Kings xx 34). The only time peace reigned between Israel and Damascus was when both were threatened by Assyria (cf. the western movement of Shalmaneser III). Ahab's sally against Ramoth-gilead indicated that that region was then under control of Damascus (I Kings xxii). Joram asserted his claims against Ramoth-gilead (II Kings viii 28) and Jehu was the Israelite general in command of the forces to hold it against the enemy (II Kings ix). Hazael wrought havoc against Bashan and Gilead (Amos i 3; II Kings x 32–33). Under Jehoahaz Aram's success continued (II Kings xiii 3) but the situation may have changed for the better (xiii 5). The last stroke of victory over Damascus came under Jeroboam II (II Kings xiv 25, 28). The region delimited here runs westward from Bashan to Mount Hermon; Baal-hermon (cf. Judg iii 3) is otherwise unknown. Senir is the old name for Hermon (cf. Deut iii 9). Verses 25–26 set forth again the theology of the writer. On exile see the paragraph above on vs. 22. It is to be recalled that two kings of Israel, Shallum and Menahem, were Transjordanians (II Kings xv 13, 17). The substance of these verses was taken from II Kings xv 19, 29, xvii 6, xviii 11.

6. THE DESCENDANTS OF LEVI
(vi 1–81)†

The chief priests

VI ¹ The sons of Levi were Gershon, Kehath, and Merari. ² The sons of Kehath were Amram, Izhar, Hebron, and Uzziel. ³ The children of Amram were Aaron, Moses, and Miriam; the sons of Aaron were Nadab, Abihu, Eleazar, and Ithamar. ⁴ Eleazar fathered Phinehas, Phinehas fathered Abishua, ⁵ Abishua fathered Bukki, Bukki fathered Uzzi, ⁶ Uzzi fathered Zerahiah, Zerahiah fathered Meraioth, ⁷ Meraioth fathered Amariah, Amariah fathered Ahitub, ⁸ Ahitub fathered Zadok, Zadok fathered Ahimaaz, ⁹ Ahimaaz fathered Azariah, Azariah fathered Johanan, ¹⁰ Johanan fathered Azariah—he is the one who served as priest in the house that Solomon built at Jerusalem—¹¹ Azariah fathered Amariah, Amariah fathered Ahitub, ¹² Ahitub fathered Zadok, Zadok fathered Shallum, ¹³ Shallum fathered Hilkiah, Hilkiah fathered Azariah, ¹⁴ Azariah fathered Seraiah, Seraiah fathered Jehozadak, ¹⁵ and Jehozadak went away into exile when Yahweh exiled Judah and Jerusalem by the hand of Nebuchadnezzar.

The sons of Levi

¹⁶ The sons of Levi were Gershom, Kehath, and Merari. ¹⁷ These are the names of the sons of Gershom: Libni and Shimei. ¹⁸ The sons of Kehath were Amram, Izhar, Hebron, and Uzziel. ¹⁹ The sons of Merari were Mahli and Mushi. These are the Levitical clans according to families: ²⁰ of Gershom were Libni his son, Jahath his son, Zimmah his son, ²¹ Joah

† I **Chron vi 1–15** ‖ Gen xlvi 11, Exod vi 18, Num xxvi 59–60; **16–30** ‖ Num iii 17–20, I Sam i 1; **54–81** ‖ Josh xxi.

his son, Iddo his son, Zerah his son, and Jeatherai his son.
22 The sons of Kehath were Amminadab his son, Korah his
son, Assir his son, 23 Elkanah his son, Ebiasaph his son, Assir
his son, 24 Tahath his son, Uriel his son, Uzziah his son, and
Saul his son. 25 The sons of Elkanah were Amasai and Ahimoth*a*; 26 Elkanah his son*b*, Zophai his son, Nahath his son,
27 Eliab his son, Jeroham his son, and Elkanah his son. 28 The
sons of Samuel were Joel*c* his first-born son and Abijah his second. 29 The sons of Merari were Mahli, Libni his son, Shimei
his son, Uzzah his son, 30 Shimea his son, Haggiah his son, and
Asaiah his son.

The Levitical singers

31 These are the persons whom David appointed as song-lead-
ers in the house of Yahweh after the ark had come to rest there.
32 They were ministers in song before the tabernacle of the
tent of meeting until the time when Solomon built the house of
Yahweh at Jerusalem and they carried on their duties in accordance with their custom. 33 These were the persons who
served together with their sons: among the sons of the Kehathites were Heman the cantor, the son of Joel, the son of Samuel,
34 the son of Elkanah, the son of Jeroham, the son of Eliel, the
son of Toah, 35 the son of Zuph, the son of Elkanah, the son of
Mahath, the son of Amasai, 36 the son of Elkanah, the son of
Joel, the son of Azariah, the son of Zephaniah, 37 the son of
Tahath, the son of Assir, the son of Ebiasaph, the son of Korah,
38 the son of Izhar, the son of Kehath, the son of Levi, the son
of Israel. 39 His brother was Asaph who stood at his right side.
Asaph was the son of Berechiah, the son of Shimea, 40 the son
of Michael, the son of Baaseiah, the son of Malchijah, 41 the
son of Ethni, the son of Zerah, the son of Adaiah, 42 the son of
Ethan, the son of Zimmah, the son of Shimei, 43 the son of
Jahath, the son of Gershom, the son of Levi. 44 The sons of
Merari their brother who stood on the left side were Ethan

---

a Perhaps "Mahath," as in vs. 35. But cf. LXX, Vulg., and Syr.
b So with LXX, for Heb. "Elkanah the sons of Elkanah."
c Inserted with I Sam viii 2 and LXX*L*. Omission due to haplography.

the son of Kishi, the son of Abdi, the son of Malluch, 45 the son of Hashabiah, the son of Amaziah, the son of Hilkiah, 46 the son of Amzi, the son of Bani, the son of Shemer, 47 the son of Mahli, the son of Mushi, the son of Merari, the son of Levi.

Other Levites

48 Their Levitical brothers were appointed for all the other duties of the tabernacle of the house of God, 49 while Aaron and his sons offered sacrifices on the altar of burnt offering and on the incense altar; they were responsible for all the tasks affecting the holy of holies and for making atonement for Israel in accordance with everything that Moses the servant of God had commanded. 50 These were the sons of Aaron: Eleazar his son, Phinehas his son, Abishua his son, 51 Bukki his son, Uzzi his son, Zerahiah his son, 52 Meraioth his son, Amariah his son, Ahitub his son, 53 Zadok his son, and Ahimaaz his son.

Locations of Aaronites and other Levites

54 These were their locations for their encampments within their prescribed territory: to the sons of Aaron of the Kehathite family—for the first lot came out for them—55 they gave Hebron in the land of Judah with its surrounding pasture grounds. 56 But the arable land of the city and its dependencies they gave to Caleb the son of Jephunneh. 57 To the sons of Aaron they also gave the cities of refuge: Hebron, Libnah with the pasture grounds, Jattir, Eshtemoa with its pasture grounds, 58 Hilen with its pasture grounds, Debir with its pasture grounds, 59 Ashan with its pasture grounds and Beth-shemesh with its pasture grounds; 60 and of the tribe of Benjamin Geba with its pasture grounds, Alemeth with its pasture grounds and Anathoth with its pasture grounds. All their cities distributed among their families numbered thirteen. 61 To the rest of the sons of Kehath they gave ten cities by lot from the family of the tribe, that is, from the half-tribe[d] of Manasseh. 62 To the sons of Gershom according to their families they gave thirteen

d Omit "half" of MT, with Vulg.

cities from the tribe of Issachar, from the tribe of Asher, from the tribe of Naphtali and from the tribe of Manasseh, in Bashan. 63 To the sons of Merari according to their families they gave by lot twelve cities from the tribe of Reuben, from the tribe of Gad and from the tribe of Zebulun. 64 The sons of Israel gave to the Levites both the cities and their pasture grounds. 65 They also gave to them by lot, from the tribe of the sons of Judah, from the tribe of the sons of Simeon, and from the tribe of the sons of Benjamin, *these cities which have been named*. 66 Some of the families of the sons of Kehath also received cities of their region from the tribe of Ephraim. 67 They gave to them the cities of refuge: Shechem in Mount Ephraim with its pasture grounds, Gezer with its pasture grounds, 68 Jokmeam with its pasture grounds, Beth-horon with its pasture grounds, 69 Aijalon with its pasture grounds, and Gath-rimmon with its pasture grounds; 70 and from the half-tribe of Manasseh they gave to ʹthe rest of the familiesʹ of the sons of Kehath Aner with its pasture grounds and Bileam*g* with its pasture grounds. 71 To the sons of Gershom according to their families they gave from the half-tribe of Manasseh Golan in Bashan with its pasture grounds and Ashtaroth with its pasture grounds; 72 from the tribe of Issachar, Kedesh with its pasture grounds, Daberath with its pasture grounds, 73 Ramoth with its pasture grounds, and Anem with its pasture grounds; 74 from the tribe of Asher, Mashal with its pasture grounds, Abdon with its pasture grounds, 75 Hukok with its pasture grounds, and Rehob with its pasture grounds; 76 from the tribe of Naphtali, Kedesh in Galilee with its pasture grounds, Hammon with its pasture grounds, and Kiriathaim with its pasture grounds. 77 To the rest of the sons of Merari they gave from the tribe of Zebulun, Rimmono with its pasture grounds and Tabor with its pasture grounds; 78 from Transjordan at Jericho, to the east of the Jordan from the tribe of Reuben, Bezer in the desert with its pas-

e-e So with LXX[B].

f-f So with LXX[L].

g So for "Ibleam" in LXX[AL] and Targ. This is another case of the *yod* being dropped from a personal name. See textual note *a*, Sec. 3.

ture grounds, Jahzah with its pasture grounds, 79 Kedemoth with its pasture grounds and Mephaath with its pasture grounds; 80 from the tribe of Gad, Ramoth in Gilead with its pasture grounds, Mahanaim with its pasture grounds, 81 Heshbon with its pasture grounds and Jazer with its pasture grounds.

NOTES

vi 15. *into exile.* Adding *bag-golah,* as in Amos i 15; Jer xlviii 11, etc.

22. *Amminadab.* Possibly a mistake for "Izhar." Cf. vss. 18, 37 f., though the passage may conceal a confusion of the Amran and Izhar lines.

32. The Chronicler was profoundly concerned about worship (cf. chs. xvi, xxvi) and the temple service which he traces to David, the central personality in his scheme.

39. *Asaph.* Name appears on a seal found at Megiddo, belonging to the period of Jeroboam II, ca. 786–746.

54. *the first lot.* Add with Josh xxi 10.

57. *the cities of refuge.* Cf. Josh xxi 13. While the cities named, with the exception of Hebron, were not, strictly speaking, cities of refuge, the Chronicler so regards them because they were Levitical cities. All of the cities of refuge are included later. For a list of these cities see Josh xx 7–8; Deut iv 43. Num xxxv 13–15 specifies the number, three on each side of the Jordan, but does not give their names.

66. *of their region.* Josh xxi 20 has "of their allotment."

67. *cities of refuge.* Cf. Josh xxi 21. See NOTE on vs. 57.

68. Josh xxi 23 adds: "from the tribe of Dan, Elteke with its pasture grounds and Gibbethon with its pasture grounds."

70. *Aner.* Josh xxi 25 has "Taanach," which is correct.

71. *To the sons . . . families.* Cf. Josh xxi 27.

81. *Jazer.* See G. M. Landes, "Fountain at Jazer," BASOR 144 (December 1956), 30 ff., for possible identification of the site.

COMMENT

This chapter contains a number of lists all dealing in a general way with the priests and Levites. For the writer the chief interest must have centered around the nucleus of vss. 17 to 20 which called forth the various aspects of the position and function of the Levites given in the successive parts of the chapter. But the whole of that

material is prefaced by an account of the high-priestly line from
Levi to the Exile, matching the postexilic list in Neh xii 10–11.

[Pre-exilic high-priestly line, vi 1–15 (v 27–41H)]: The list may
be divided into two parts, vss. 1–3 dealing with the descendants of
Levi and vss. 4–15 with those of Eleazar (see K. Möhlenbrink, "Die
levitischen Überlieferungen des Alten Testaments," ZAW 52
[1934], 184–231, but especially pp. 197 f.). All of the genealogies
agree on the sons of Levi (Gen xlvi 11; Exod vi 16; Num iii 17,
xxvi 57), and are in the same order, but there the parallels of the
section end, except for the Kehathites. Both Exod vi 16 f. and
Num iii 17–21 take up the descendants in the order of the direct
sons of Levi. Here, however, Gershon and Merari are ignored,
probably because the writer's main interest is in the Aaronite line.
The use of the name "Gershon" is found only twice in Chronicles
(here and I Chron xxiii 6, though Gershunnites appears about five
times elsewhere); in other places the form "Gershom" is employed.
The Kehath genealogy follows the sources without deviation.

The other portion of the list, vss. 4–15, purports to give the names
of the chief priests directly through the Eleazar line without taking
into account the Ithamar priests or even family connections in the
chosen line. The sentences are uniformly verbal in form as over
against the nominal form in the preceding verses, which argues
against the unity of the passage. The Kehath genealogy is set forth
again below in vs. 18. Miriam appears to be an addition unless we
render the Heb. $b^e n \bar e$ as children, though LXX follows MT. But
the list from Eleazar to Jehozadak occurs only in the Chronicler's
work. According to Num xx 25 ff., Eleazar succeeded his father
Aaron and Phinehas was the son of Eleazar (Num xxv 11 ff.)
whose line was invested with the priesthood forever. But the list is
generally not carried further. The Chronicler, or an editor, repeats
the list three times, with variations—(in I Chron vi 1–15; I Chron
vi 50–53; and Ezra vii 1–5). The last one is usually thought to be an
independent list intended to support the position of Ezra and was
then utilized here and in vss. 50–53. The addition of the names from
Amariah to Johanan may be part of another, possibly later, tradition; otherwise it corresponds exactly with Ezra vii 1–5 with the
exception of Jehozadak who is replaced in Ezra by Ezra. The list in
I Chron vi 50–53 follows the one here as far as Ahimaaz which
may offer a clue as to its purpose: to connect Zadok with the
Aaronite line. Möhlenbrink (ibid., pp. 204 f.; cf. Rudolph, pp.

52 f.) points out that I Chron ix 10–13 does not attempt to do this and hence is older than II Sam viii 17. The comment on Azariah (vs. 10) is based on I Kings iv 2. Hilkiah (II Kings xxii 4 ff.), Seraiah (II Kings xxv 18), Jehozadak (Hag i 1, 12, 14, ii 2, 4; Zech vi 11; Ezra iii 2, 8, v 2, x 18; Neh xii 26) are noted elsewhere as important priests. On the other hand Jehoiada (II Kings xi, xii) and Urijah (II Kings xvi 10 ff.) are not found in the list, for what reason we can only speculate. Whether on chronological grounds Amariah (II Chron xix 11) and Azariah (II Chron xxvi 17, 20, xxxi 10) can be equated with those of like name here is beyond us at present. The only certain conclusion with reference to the whole list is that the introductory element (1–3) is based on common tradition and that the body of it represents a mixture of names some of which agree with those in other lists. That we do not have a full list here is beyond doubt.

[Levitical line, 16–30 (vi 1–15H)]: Verses 16–19a follow almost verbatim the list in Num iii 17–20 (cf. Exod vi 16–19; Num xxvi 57–61). The Gershom tradition is followed through Libni for a total of seven generations; that of Kehath through Amminadab (see NOTE on vs. 22) with ten; that of Merari through Mahli for seven. Asaiah is mentioned again in I Chron xv 6, 11 as one of the Levites, which may suggest that the writer intended his list to carry only so far as David, inasmuch as the Levitical cities enumerated later are probably to be referred to that period. The most significant element in these verses is the inclusion of Samuel among the Levites. The genealogy is based on I Sam i 1, viii 2. Here is clearly expressed the old tradition that Levites need not be specifically blood descendants of Levi nor priests blood descendants of Aaron. Samuel was actually an Ephraimite but was reckoned with the Levites because of his special services (I Sam iii 15) in connection with the tabernacle and performance of priestly duties (I Sam ii 11, 26, vii 9 f.); cf. Albright, ARI, pp. 109 f. The genealogy may be artificial, at least in part derived from I Sam i 1, viii 2 and from other members of the Kehathite group (II Chron xxix 12; cf., here, vss. 34–36).

[The Levitical singers, 31–47 (vi 16–32H)]: The list is undoubtedly schematic, built around the three sons of Levi (see Möhlenbrink, ZAW 52 [1934], 202 f.). The introductory verses refer to David as the one who organized the Levitical musical guilds for service in the tabernacle, a practice transferred to the temple. The traditional acceptance of David as the organizer of the guilds must not be cast aside lightly; in fact it is, in all probability, substantially true and the Chronicler insists upon it in more than one place (cf. I Chron xv 16, 27, xxv 1 ff.; II Chron xxix 26 ff.; Neh xii 46 f.). David was a musician of note (I Sam xvi 14–23; II Sam i 17 ff., vi 5, 14) and tradition attributes many psalms to him. Solomon is reported to have continued the practice of composing songs (I Kings iv 32). For further dicussion see ARI, p. 126; note especially the strong evidence for the early presence of musical guilds, likely of Canaanite origin.

[Other Levitical and priestly officials, 48–53 (vi 33–38H)]: The purpose of this insertion is manifestly twofold: (a) to point out that other Levites had equally responsible duties in connection with the worship service (cf. Num iii 6–8, xviii 2 ff.), and (b) to confirm further the position and duties of the Zadokites. With vss. 4–8, with which it agrees, though with a different formula, this list endeavors to connect Zadok with the line of Aaron. Since David's name occurs above (31) it brings down the line only to his time. On the vexing problem of the Zadokites see Möhlenbrink, ZAW 52 (1934), 202 f., and Albright, ARI, p. 110 and n. 46, p. 205. Möhlenbrink thinks the oldest list is that of I Chron ix 10 ff., the next I Chron vi 1–15, the latest, this one. All that we know of Zadok from other sources is that he was the son of Ahitub (II Sam viii 17) and that Ahimaaz was his son (II Sam xv 36, xviii 19, 27), as was Azariah, Solomon's priest (I Kings iv 2). For further discussion of Zadok see H. H. Rowley, "Zadok and Nehushtan," JBL 58 (1939), 113–41, and "Melchizedek and Zadok," FAB, pp. 461–72.

[The Levitical cities, 54–81 (vi 39–66H)]: The list here, as in Josh xxi, combines the cities of refuge with the Levitical cities. Both lists follow the familiar pattern of allotment to the Kehathites, Gershunnites, and Merarites, in that order because the Aaronite line is represented by Kehath, followed by Gershom as the oldest of the sons of Levi and Merari as the youngest. The numbers are not reliable, as Albright has indicated (LGJV, pp. 53 ff.), but a secondary intrusion into the list. Chronicles represents one recension of an original list which can be readily determined by a comparison of the two surviving lists—Josh xxi and this one (*ibid.*, pp. 54 f.). The arguments for the date of the original list are for the most part Albright's. See further B. Mazar, "The Cities of the Priests and the

Levites," in Oxford Congress Volume, VTS, VII (Leiden, 1960), pp. 193–205, and "The Cities of Dan," IEJ 10 (1960), 70 f.

There are certain criteria which point to the origin of the Levitical city arrangement in the period of David or Solomon, more likely the former. For one thing the Canaanite cities named could hardly have been included before David's time because they were not yet incorporated into the Israelite system, for example, Bileam (Ibleam), Rehob, Gezer, Jokmeam, and others. According to Judg i 27 ff., Taanach, Ibleam, Gezer, Rehob, and Nahalol were not subdued at the time of the invasion. Jokmeam was outside the tribal allotment of Zebulun (Josh xix 11). On Gezer, see Josh xvi 10. On the other hand, it cannot be later than around 900 B.C. because Gezer was destroyed by Shishak in the last quarter of the tenth century and not reoccupied by Hebrews until the Persian period (see W. F. Albright, BASOR 92 [December 1943], 17 f.). Golan and Ashtaroth were doubtless among the cities in Bashan taken from Israel by Benhadad (I Kings xv 20) early in the ninth century and remained under Aramaean control until the destruction of the cities of Bashan by the Assyrians in 733 B.C. (Albright, LGJV, p. 57, nn. 19, 20). Bezer was in ruins when Mesha took it; he also captured Jahaz during his campaign against Israel, as he says in his inscription. Moreover, Judah and Simeon were reckoned together and Heshbon, which was allotted to Reuben, is here attributed to Gad (see COMMENT on Sec. 5, v 1–10. On Alemeth see W. F. Albright, AASOR 4 [1924], Appendix vii).

A strong argument in favor of the Davidic period is the general observance of the tribal system, which was replaced by the administrative districts of Solomon, and the fact that David also catered to the priestly elements, partly as a matter of principle but perhaps more for political reasons: he was aware of their prestige and therefore utilized them in making the transition from the disorganized period of the Judges and Saul, possibly because he could better keep them under surveillance and content by giving them definite assignments. The list reveals that the Levites were scattered throughout the whole territory of Israel at the time.

7. THE NORTHERN TRIBES
(vii 1–40)†

The descendants of Issachar

VII ¹ The sons*a* of Issachar were Tola, Puah, Jashub, and Shimron—four. ² The sons of Tola were Uzzi, Rephaiah, Jeriel, Jahmai, Jibsam, and Samuel, chiefs of their families, of Tola; in the time of David the warriors of their descendants numbered twenty-two thousand six hundred. ³ The sons of Uzzi were Izrahiah; the sons of Izrahiah were Michael, Obadiah, Joel, and Isshiah—five—all of them chiefs. ⁴ The descendants of their families had *b*thirty-six thousand troops for warfare, because they had more wives and sons, ⁵ *c*than their brothers*c*. All the families of Issachar had eighty-seven thousand warriors, all included in the official genealogy.

The descendants of Benjamin

⁶ The sons*a* of Benjamin were Bela, Becher, and Jediael—three. ⁷ The sons of Bela were Ezbon, Uzzi, Uzziel, Jerimoth, and Iri—five, chiefs of families and warriors. Their official genealogy included twenty-two thousand thirty-four members. ⁸ The sons of Becher were Zemirah, Joash, Eliezer, Elioenai, Omri, Jeremoth, Abijah, Anathoth, and Alemeth—all of these were the sons of Becher. ⁹ Their official genealogy according to the descendants of the chiefs of their families included twenty thou-

---

† I Chron vii 1–5 ‖ Gen xlvi 13, Num xxvi 23–24; **6–12** ‖ Gen xlvi 21, Num xxvi 38–40; **13** ‖ Gen xlvi 24, Num xxvi 48–49; **14–19:** cf. Num xlvi 29–33; **20–29** ‖ Num xxvi 35–36; **30–40** ‖ Gen xlvi 17, Num xxvi 44–46.

a So with LXX^A; Heb. "to the sons of."
b Heb. "beside them."
c–c Heb. "and their brothers," taking the Heb. word *'hyhm*, "their brothers," with the next verse. The preposition "from" was lost by haplography.
d "Sons" dropped by haplography, but preserved in many manuscripts.

sand two hundred warriors. 10 The son*e* of Jediael was Bilhan, and the sons of Bilhan were Jeush, Benjamin, Ehud, Chenaanah, Zethan, Tarshish, and Ahishahar. 11 All these were the sons of Jediael, the chiefs of families; the warriors ready for combat numbered seventeen thousand two hundred, 12 and Shuppim and Huppim were the sons of Ir; Hushim was of the sons of Aher.

The descendants of Naphtali

13 The sons of Naphtali were Jahaziel, Guni, Jezer, and Shallum; they were the sons of Bilhah.

The descendants of Manasseh

14 The son*f* of Manasseh was Asriel whom his Aramaean concubine bore; she [also] bore Machir the father of Gilead. 15 Machir took a wife for Huppim and Shuppim and his sister's name was Maacah*g*. The name of the second son was Zelophehad but Zelophehad had only daughters. 16 Maacah the wife of Machir bore a son whom she named Peresh; the name of his brother was Sheresh whose sons were Ulam and Rekem. 17 The son*h* of Ulam was Bedan. These were the sons of Gilead, the son of Machir, the son of Manasseh. 18 His sister Hammolecheth bore Ishhod, Abiezer, and Mahlah. 19 The sons of Shemida were Ahian, Shechem, Likhi, and Aniam.

The descendants of Ephraim

20 The sons of Ephraim were Shutelah, Bered his son, Tahath his son, Eleadah his son, Tahath his son, 21 Zabad his son, Shutelah his son, and Ezer and Elead whom the men of Gath, natives of the land, killed when they came down to carry off their cattle. 22 Ephraim their father gave himself to mourning for a long time and his brothers came to console him. 23 Then he cohabited with his wife who conceived and bore a son whose

e So for MT "sons."
f So for MT "sons."
g LXX reads "Moocha" here and in the next verse.
h So with Vulg.; MT "sons of."

name he called Beriah because misfortune had come to his house. 24 His daughter was Sheerah who built lower and upper Beth-horon and Uzzen-sheerah. 25 Rephah was his son, as well as Resheph, Telah his son, Tahan his son, 26 Ladan his son, Ammihud his son, Elishama his son, 27 Non his son, and Joshua his son. 28 Their possession and their location was Bethel and its dependencies from Naaran on the east to Gezer and its dependencies on the west, together with Shechem and its dependencies as far as Aijah and its dependencies. 29 Under control of the sons of Manasseh were Beth-shean and its dependencies, Taanach and its dependencies, Megiddo and its dependencies, and Dor and its dependencies. In these places lived the sons of Joseph the son of Israel.

The descendants of Asher

30 The sons of Asher were Imnah, Ishvah, Ishvi, and Beriah, and Serah was their sister. 31 The sons of Beriah were Heber and Malchiel who was the father of Birzvaith. 32 Heber fathered Japhlet, Shomer, Hotham, and Shua their sister. 33 The sons of Japhlet were Pasach, Bimhal, and Ashvath. These were the sons of Japhlet. 34 The sons of Shemer his brother*i* were Rohgah, Jehubbah, and Aram. 35 The sons*j* of Helem his brother were Zophah, Imna, Shelesh, and Amal. 36 The sons of Zophah were Suah, Harnepher, Shual, Beri, Imrah, 37 Bezer, Hod, Shamma, Shilshah, Ithran, and Beera. 38 The sons of Jether were Jephunneh, Pispa, and Era. 39 The sons of Ulla were Arah, Hanniel, and Rizia. 40 All these were the sons of Asher; they were heads of families, select men, warriors, and chiefs of princes. Their official genealogy included twenty-six thousand men mobilized for combat.

i So for "Ahi" of MT; cf. vs. 35.
j So with many manuscripts.

NOTES

vii 1. *Tola . . . Shimron.* The families of Issachar were apparently early connected with the hill country of Ephraim (Judg x 1). Cf. KS, I, p. 126, n. 4, p. 168. The hill of Shemer (later Samaria) was occupied in the Early Bronze Age and there were a few remains from the Early Iron Age that may point to the existence of a small place (cf. *The Buildings at Samaria*, J. W. Crowfoot et al., 1942, p. 94; Abel, *Géographie de la Palestine*, II, p. 444; IEJ 8 [1958], 179, n. 35) but identification of Shamir with the supposed village of Shemer is quite uncertain.

12. *Shuppim and Huppim.* Cf. Num xxvi 39.

Hushim . . . Aher. See COMMENT on 12b.

14. Cf. Albright's translation: "The sons of Manasseh; Asriel . . . ; his Aramaean concubine bore Machir the father of Gilead and his [Machir's?] sister Hammoleket bore Išhod and Abiezer and Maḥlah. And the sons of Shemidaʿ were Aḥyan and Sekem and Leqḥi and Aniʿam [error for Abino ʿam?]—" JPOS 5 (1925), 28, n. 28; see also sketch on p. 41. Rudolph, p. 70, also proposes a translation on the basis of a reconstructed text of vss. 15–19.

15. *the second son.* Apparently the second son of Manasseh.

27. *Non.* Elsewhere "Nun."

33. *Bimhal.* "Bi(n)-Mehala," which may be the source of the name of an Arab village, ʿEyn Mahl, in Zebulun. See Yeivin in *Mélanges bibliques rédigés en l'honneur de André Robert*, p. 101, n. 2.

COMMENT

The preceding chapters, i–vi, dealt with Judah, Simeon, Reuben, Gad, the half-tribe of Manasseh and Levi, and with the priestly and Levitical families and their possessions. Here the genealogies of Issachar, Benjamin, Naphtali, Ephraim, and Asher are given. As usual, the chapter is fraught with problems of various types as will appear.

[The line of Issachar, vii 1–5]: The main list follows, in general, that of Gen xlvi 13 and Num xxvi 23–25. But in the former passage there is a different spelling for Puah and it has Job for Jashub. The names Tola and Puah occur also in Judg x 1 where Tola is referred to as a son of (perhaps belonging to the family of) Puah. There is some connection, possibly, with the genealogy but it escapes us (see

M. Noth in FAB, pp. 409 f.). The list is composed of two elements, or perhaps an original and an addition, as shown by the two summations. The first list includes the register of the sons of Tola which in the time of David numbered 22,600 fighting men. The second list takes in the descendants of Uzzi who, because of their expanded progeny, numbered 36,000. Each list represents the available manpower of the specified families at a given time. While the total given for Issachar is certainly not the sum of the preceding numbers, it could refer to that of all the families of the tribe at another time. Cf. the totals in Num i 29, 54,400; Num xxvi 25, 64,300. The final editor of the section may have drawn from a number of census lists whose import he no longer understood. For an excellent treatment of the problem of numbers in the census lists, see G. E. Mendenhall, "The Census Lists of Numbers 1 and 26," JBL 77 (1958), 52–66.

[Benjamin, 6–12a]: This is a quite orderly list naming the three sons of Benjamin, and the sons of each of them in order, with the line of Jediel followed through his son Bilhan. It is generally thought that the writer followed the source in Gen xlvi 21 rather than in Num xxvi 38–40, which he appears to copy pretty closely elsewhere, but there are only two names, Bela and Becher, alike in Genesis and here. Moreover, Shuppim and Huppim (may be an Arabic name) appear to come from the Numbers source, since Genesis has Muppim and Huppim (supported by LXX). The numbers are much higher than those of Num i 37 (35,400) and Num xxvi 41 (45,600). Here there is a total of 59,434, which is not a round number. It appears that the list reflects both genealogical and census lists, as do most of the others. It is probably built up out of old and new materials and as it stands reflects a time when the Benjaminite genealogy was reckoned through the three families name. The names of Benjamin and Ehud (vs. 10) point to papponymy which is absent almost entirely before the postexilic period (see Noth, IPN, pp. 60 f.). Verse 15 points to an old intermarriage relationship between Benjamin and Machir (Gilead) which may account for the latter's refusal to participate in the primitive expedition against Benjamin (Judg xxi 8 ff.) and why Jabesh-gilead appealed to Benjamin when under severe pressure from Ammon (I Sam xi). Then too the connection of personal names with places is significant (as Anathoth, cf. Ezra ii 23; Neh x 19). The name of Elioenai (vs. 8) does not occur before the age of Hezekiah, but mostly later, in postexilic times. The names Bilhan and Jeush appear in i 42, 35, the Esau genealogy, which may point to the population movements in exilic and postexilic times.

[Dan, 12b]: In the list of Gen xlvi 23 and Num xxvi 42 Dan follows Benjamin with only one son (Hushim or Shuham). For some reason the name of Dan dropped out, but that Hushim is to be reckoned as referring to him is indicated by the reference to Bilhah in the next verse; Bilhah was the mother of Dan and Naphtali. The problem of Aher is difficult but E. Klostermann's suggestions (*Realenzyklopädie für protestantische Theologie u. Kirche,* IV, 1898, p. 94) that it be read *'eḥād* ("one") and "his son" be read for "sons of" may be correct. The verse would then read: "[The sons of Dan] were Hushim, his son, one." Otherwise Dan would not be included in the tribal list here. For other suggestions see Rudolph, pp. 68 f.

[Naphtali, 13]: The sons of Naphtali are exactly the same as those in Gen xlvi 24 and Num xxvi 48, but that the Genesis list was followed is evident from the quotation of the parenthetical statement, "these were the sons of Bilhah."

[Manasseh, 14–19]: Much of the genealogy deals with the Transjordan situation, to which has been added a reference to that of Cisjordan. The list is extremely complicated and somewhat corrupt. It is drawn from various sources but mostly from the Davidic census list of Num xxvi 29–33; Josh xvii 1 ff. is more orderly: "To Machir the first-born of Manasseh, the father of Gilead, were allotted Gilead and Bashan. . . . And the allotments were made to the rest of the tribe of Manasseh, by their families, Abiezer, Helek, Asriel, Shechem, Hepher, and Shemida." Here there can be no question that the allotments made to the remainder of Manasseh were in Cisjordan, while those of Machir's were in Transjordan. (For the situation in the time of Solomon see Albright, JPOS 5 [1925], 28–31; but cf. Alt's caveat in KS, II, p. 85, n. 2.) The relation between Machir and Huppim and Shuppim is obscure, especially in view of the fact that Maachah here is said to be the sister of Machir while in vs. 16 she is referred to as his wife. The strong position of Machir is supported by Judg v 14. Gilead, as we know, was always under the influence of Aramaeans. Interestingly enough, the names of Shemida, Abiezer, and Helek occur as names of persons, tribes, or places in the ostraca of Samaria (*Harvard Excavations at Samaria,* G. A. Reisner et al., I, 1924, pp. 229 f.). Other names from the

Joshua and Numbers lists occurring in the ostraca are Shechem, Hoglah, and Noah.

[Ephraim, 20–29]: This passage is composed of three constituents: the location of Ephraim and Manasseh (Joseph), the line of Joshua, and some old traditions. The list of descendants of Ephraim is difficult and has been treated in numerous ways. The notices from "whom the men of Gath" in vs. 21 to the end of vs. 25 have separated the list. The names of Ephraim's sons, Shutelah, Bered (Becher), and Tahath (Tahan), may be said to follow Num xxvi 35, where a son of Shutelah, Eran, is included. Not much can be made of the other names except those of Ammihud, Elishama, Non, and Joshua. Elishama appears as the Ephraimite chief, the son of Ammihud, in Num i 10, ii 18, vii 48, x 22. There may be some duplication; some of the persons listed may have been brothers. Two lists may have been brought together. In the first one (vss. 20, 21) there is a series of ten names, including that of Ephraim; in the second one (vss. 22–27), a series of ten male names (excluding Ephraim). How they can be reconciled is not clear. In any case, there appear to have been at least ten generations between Ephraim and Joshua, which fits in fairly well with the chronological situation (a period of about 250 years). The list, therefore, seems more plausible than any other extant. There can hardly be any doubt that vs. 21b (beginning "whom the men of Gath") reflects the conflicts between Israel and Canaan in the patriarchal period when the sons of Jacob occupied the central highland and made forays into low hills, possibly the plains, to the west. Because of the location of Ephraim these exploits were connected with him, though anachronistically (cf. Gen xxxiv, xlviii 22 and Jubilees xxxiv). See Albright, FSAC, p. 211; BASOR 35 (October 1929), 6; ZAW 47 (1929), 4–13. One problem is the location of Gath, which has lately been associated with Gittaim (cf. II Sam iv 3; Neh xi 33), nearly midway between Gezer and Lod, and much more in line with historical probability than the Gath of the Philistines about twenty-five miles farther south (see B. Mazar, "Gath and Gittaim," IEJ 4 [1954], 227–35; cf. also A. Alt, "Gittaim," PJB 35 [1939], 100–4, especially pp. 102 f.). The failure of this expansionist movement led to the settling of upper and lower Beth-horon, farther to the east. Nothing further is known of Uzzen-sheerah, though Sheerah may refer to an individual or to a kind of central encampment of the clans of western Ephraim. The location of the territory of Ephraim and

Manasseh (so?) is subsumed under the name of Joseph. In general (except for Shechem and Aijah, whose locations are uncertain) the list represents the southern and northern boundaries of the combined Ephraim-Manasseh territory (cf. the possession and boundary lists in Josh xvi–xviii). Bethel was conquered by Joseph tribes (Judg i 22); it was regarded as a boundary city in Josh xvi 1 f., xviii 13, and as belonging to Benjamin in Josh xviii 22. Shechem is clearly within the limits of Manasseh (Josh xvii 7 ff.) but apparently assigned to Ephraim (Josh xx 7, xxi 21), perhaps on the basis of Josh xvi 9 (cf. xvii 8 f.). It must be remembered that Shechem was a city of refuge for the central tribes and thus was shared between Ephraim and Manasseh and Benjamin. The line from Naaran (Naarath) to Gezer running near or through Bethel is clear, as is that on the north from Beth-shean by Taanach and Megiddo to Dor. On the north boundary of Benjamin see Albright, AASOR 4 (1924), Appendix vi.

[Asher, 30–40]: The first portion of the list—to Malchiel—follows Gen xlvi 17 and not Num xxvi 44–46 as the name Ishvah does not occur in the latter. There is no parallel elsewhere to the remainder of the genealogy, which is extraordinarily full considering the peripheral character of the tribe of Asher (son of Zilpah, Leah's handmaid). The writer evidently had a special source which he utilized. It is to be noted that even the number of the men of war is extremely low compared to those of Numbers (i 40 and ii 27 f., 41,500; xxvi 47, 53,400), a fact which runs counter to the Chronicler's passion for high numbers, and may indicate a later situation. The only certain place name is that of Birzvaith, of unknown location.

8. THE BENJAMINITES
(viii 1–40, ix 1)†

The descendants of Benjamin

VIII 1 Benjamin fathered Bela his first-born son, Ashbel the second, Aharah the third, 2 Nohah the fourth, and Rapha the fifth. 3 The sons of Bela were Addar, Gera, Abihud, 4 Abishua, Naaman, Ahoah, 5 Gera, Shephuphan, and Huram.

Those at Geba

6 These were the sons of Ehud—these were the chiefs of families who lived at Geba when they exiled them to Manahath—7 Naaman, Ahijah, and Gera. *He exiled them; he fathered*ª Uzza and Ahihud.

Those in Moab and the west

8 Shaharaim fathered children in the land of Moab after he had sent away Hushim and Baara his wives. 9 He fathered also from *ᵇHodesh his wifeᵇ, Jobab, Zibia, Mesha, Malcam, 10 Jeuz, Sachiah, and Mirmah. These were his sons, chiefs of families. 11 From Hushim he fathered Abitub and Elpaal. 12 The sons of Elpaal were Eber, Misham and Shemed who built Ono and Lodᶜ and its dependencies.

Those in Gath, Aijalon, and Jerusalem

13 Beriah and Shema were the chiefs of the families who lived at Aijalon; they routed the inhabitants of Gath. 14 ᵈTheir

† I Chron viii 1–5 ‖ Gen xlvi 21, Num xxvi 38–40; 33–40 ‖ I Sam xiv 49–51.

ª–ª Could also be read "that is Heglam who fathered." Cf. LXXᴬ and RSV.
ᵇ–ᵇ Might be read "his new wife."
ᶜ Omitted by LXXᴬᴮ.

brothers[d] were Shashak and Jeremoth. 15 Zebadiah, Arad, Eder, 16 Michael, Ishpah, and Joha were the sons of Beriah. 17 Zebadiah, Meshullam, Hizki, Heber, 18 Ishmerai, Izliah, and Jobab were the sons of Elpaal. 19 Jakim, Zichri, Zabdi, 20 Elienai, Zillethai, Eliel, 21 Adaiah, Beraiah, and Shimrath were the sons of Shimei. 22 Ishpan, Eber, Eliel, 23 Abdon, Zichri, Hanan, 24 Hananiah, Elam, Anthothijah, 25 Iphdeiah, and Penuel were the sons of Shashak. 26 Shamsherai, Shehariah, Athaliah, 27 Jareshiah, Eliah, and Zichri were the sons of Jeroham. 28 These were chiefs of families according to their descendants[e]; they lived at Jerusalem.

Those in Gibeon and Jerusalem

29 At Gibeon lived Jeiel the father of Gibeon the name of whose wife was Maacah. 30 His first-born son was Abdon, then Zur, Kish, Baal, Nadab, 31 Gedor, Ahio, Zecher, and Mikloth[f]. 32 Mikloth fathered Shimeah. They also lived near their brothers at Jerusalem, in conjunction with their brothers.

The family of Saul

33 Ner fathered Kish, Kish fathered Saul, Saul fathered Jehonathan, Malchishua, Abinadad, and Eshbaal. 34 The son of Jehonathan was Meribbaal, and Meribbaal fathered Micah. 35 The sons of Micah were Pithon, Melech, Tarea, and Ahaz. 36 Ahaz fathered Jehoaddah and Jehoaddah fathered Alemeth, Azmaveth, and Zimri. Zimri fathered Moza, 37 Moza fathered Binea, Raphah his son, Eleasah his son, and Azel his son. 38 Azel had six sons, and these are their names: Azrikam, Bocheru[g], Ishmael, Sheariah, Obadiah, and Hanan—all these were sons of Azel. 39 The sons of Eshek his brother were Ulam his first-born son, Jeush the second, and Eliphelet the third. 40 The sons of Ulam were warriors who could draw the bow. They had as many

d-d So with LXX[L] for Heb. "his brother" or "his brothers." Some read "and Ahio."
e-e Omit "chiefs," "leaders," after "descendants" in MT. Redundant.
f Add with LXX[AB] and ix 37; the name fell out by haplography.
g LXX "first-born son."

as a hundred and fifty sons and grandsons. All these belonged
to the sons of Benjamin.

Conclusion to preceding chapter

IX 1 Now all Israel had been officially registered and recorded
in the chronicle of the kings of Israel and Judah [when] they
were exiled because of their defection.

NOTES

viii 1. *Bela his first-born son.* I Chron vii 6; Gen xlvi 21 have "Becher,"
the same consonants but with suffix, and which has probably fallen out
by haplography.

3. *Addar.* On "Addar," see W. F. Albright's review of Abel, *Géographie de la Palestine*, II, in JBL 58 (1939), 179 f.

8. *Hushim.* One could read the sign of the accusative and take the
m with the proper name "Mehushim." The suffixed accusative is mascu-
line as it stands and ordinarily could not refer to the two wives, but the
verse may be based on a popular tradition where the genders were confused, examples of which occur in Ruth and elsewhere. Yet it is difficult to conceive "Mehushim" here when "Hushim" is mentioned below
(vs. 11) as the mother of Shaharaim's children.

24. See W. F. Albright in AJSL 41 (1924), 73–101, 283–85.

29. *Jeiel.* Insert with ix 35.

31. *Gedor.* On Gedor see NOTE on ix 37.

33. See W. F. Albright, BASOR 80 (December 1940), 7, n. 8a.

36. *Azmaveth.* On name see AASOR 4 (1924), 156 f.

COMMENT

Chapter viii is devoted entirely to another Benjaminite list, rather
unexpectedly since Benjamin was treated in the preceding chapter
in the proper place (vss. 6–12). It represents another tradition as
may be seen from the style which is like that of *P,* for example,
"Benjamin fathered" as over against the usual formula "the sons of
Benjamin [were]." Moreover it follows at the beginning the list in
Num xxvi 38–40 whereas the previous one appears to have had in
mind Gen xlvi 21. In Numbers and here Benjamin is credited with
five sons; in vii 6 with three. Rudolph, p. 77, is probably right in

seeing here lists of Benjaminite families and their dwelling places at a particular period; but what that period was escapes us at present.

[Benjaminites in Geba, 1–7]: The Benjaminites are frequently presented in conjunction with other tribal groups (e.g., with Ephraim and Manasseh, the Joseph tribes, Num ii 18–24; cf. Num i 32–37, and the border between Benjamin and Ephraim fluctuates between the two, as noted above, and later with Judah, I Kings xii 23; II Chron xi 1, 3, 10, 12, 23, xiv 8, xv 2, 8, 9, xxv 5, etc.). At least seven of the names in this passage occur also in Genesis and Numbers genealogies. The piece is woven about the Benjaminite family of Ehud at Geba, present-day Jiba, about six miles north of Jerusalem. According to Judg iii 15, Ehud was the son of Gera. The deportation of the sons of Ehud to Mahanath defies all efforts at explanation, though it may be a garbled version of a tradition growing out of the Geba situation depicted in Judg xx.

[Benjaminites in Moab and the west, 8–12]: Once again there is no hint elsewhere of the material used by the writer for his statement as to the Benjaminite relationship with Moab, though there is evidence of Israelites living in Moab, at least for a time (cf. Ruth i; I Sam xxii 3, 4) and that must have been the case so long as that land remained under the control of Israel. Nor are we any better off with reference to Lod and Ono, but the tradition is well preserved in the Chronicler's work (cf. Ezra ii 33; Neh vii 37, xi 35). It is possible that the location was settled by Benjaminites in the time of Rehoboam (cf. II Chron xi 10). The names occur as early as the time of Thutmose III's list but not in the Bible before Chronicles, Ezra and Nehemiah (for Ono, see Abel, *Géographie de la Palestine*, II, p. 401; W. F. Albright, *The Vocalization of the Egyptian Syllabic Orthography*, 1934, p. 35). The problem is how locations so far west could have come into the hands of Benjamin. After the removal of Dan, they fell within the territory of Ephraim and later in that of the Philistine states. They must have been included in the Ashdod province of Assyria and in the Persian period were in the Fifth Satrapy. In Josh xix 40–46, the allotment of Dan is said to have run "opposite Joppa," and since Dan is mentioned only twice in Chronicles (I Chron ii 2, xxvii 22), his inheritance can most naturally be assumed to have been absorbed by Judah and Ephraim. But Judah and Benjamin more or less coalesced from the time of the division of the kingdom and the Benjaminites, because of their close relationship earlier with the Joseph tribes, probably occupied some of the more questionable territory, particularly in the west where the situation was less stable. Moreover, according to Neh xi 35, Benjaminites lived at Ono and Lod, which was then in Persian hands, and they would have encountered no difficulty although they were not in the province of Judah. Ezra ii 1 speaks of the returnees settling in their home towns and if that statement is to be taken seriously then these places were occupied by Judah-Benjamin before the Exile, and may have been so, at least intermittently, from the time of Rehoboam, especially during the reigns of Jehoshaphat and Uzziah. Not much can be made of the names, though they occur elsewhere, some in late documents.

On the Josh xv 21–62 list of the cities of Judah, see Cross and Wright, JBL 75 (1956), 202–26. They think it is a revised list of Judahite cities "revised and brought up to date" by the officials of Jehoshaphat in the ninth century. In that list occur the names of cities and territories all around to the south and west of Lod and Ono which, in any case, must have been on the periphery, perhaps no more than straggling outposts of a few families at the time. But cf. Alt's view in KS, II, p. 283.

[Those in Gath, Aijalon, and Jerusalem, 13–28]: Another indication of mixture of peoples and places is the reckoning of Aijalon as referring to Benjamin. In II Chronicles, xi 10 says it belongs to Judah and/or Benjamin, xxviii 18 gives it to the former. I Chron vi 69 lists it among the possessions of Ephraim which it took over from Dan (cf. Josh xix 42). Gath here may be Gittaim (see Mazar, IEJ 4 [1954], 227–35). Nothing of historical importance can be wrung from the names themselves, but the fact that these Benjaminites lived at Jerusalem is a further illustration of the tendency of Judahites and Benjaminites to mix in the same location after the division of the kingdom, due perhaps to pressures exerted on border cities of the latter and the emphasis on the continuity of district administration.

[Those living at Gibeon and Jerusalem, 29–32]: Joshua in xviii 25 lists Gibeon as one of the cities of Benjamin and in xxi 17 allots it to Aaron's descendants as a priestly residence, with Geba, Anathoth, and Almon. It was resettled by the returnees in the time of Nehemiah (vii 25). It is the modern el-Jib, about eight miles north of Jerusalem and about five miles south of Bethel, just west of the main road between the two (see J. B. Pritchard, *University Museum Bulletin* 21 [March 1957], 3 f., and *Hebrew Inscriptions and*

Stamps from Gibeon, p. 17. But see the opposing views of A. Alt, ZDPV 69 [1953], 25 f., and K. Elliger, ZDPV 73 [1957], 129–32, who place it in the region of el-Bire.). Jeiel was the founder of the new Israelite population, either after the conquest or after the Exile. The use of the name Baal points to early sources or to a very late postexilic period when its associations were forgotten. The name of the wife of Jeiel, Maacah, may conceal a connubium with outside elements and the statement that they lived with their brothers in Jerusalem reflects a situation that persisted from the period of the Judges (i 21) to that of Nehemiah (xi 4).

[The family of Saul, 33–40]: Up to the end of vs. 34 the genealogy of Saul, doubtless inspired by the mention of Kish in vs. 30, is based on the records of Samuel (I Sam xiv 49, xxxi 2; II Sam ix 12). The Saulite ancestors (I Sam ix 1) do not correspond to the Chronicler's scheme here. According to I Sam xiv 51, Ner and Kish were brothers, not father and son. Rudolph and Goettsberger each suggest that "the son of Ner" has dropped out after Kish in I Sam ix 1 by homoioarkton so that both Kish and Abner were the sons of Ner, grandsons of Abiel. Hence "Saul's uncle" in I Sam xiv 50b refers not to Ner but to Abner, and the Chronicler's genealogy is correct. Otherwise Saul and Abner are cousins, which must be the case if the references to Saul, son of Kish and Abner son of Ner are to be taken literally (I Sam xiv 51; I Chron xxvi 28). On the other hand Abner may have been regarded as a descendant of Ner rather than a direct son. The list from vs. 35 on does not appear elsewhere (except in the duplicate, ix 35–44) but is drawn from a special source whose intent is to bring the genealogy down to a time referred to by the writer (possibly the Exile; cf. vi 15, ix 1). It is to be noted that there is no offense in the retention of the Baal names— Baal (vs. 30), Eshbaal (vs. 33) and Meribbaal (vs. 34)—a retention which stresses the fact that the sources were accurately transmitted, though the feeling against Baalism had not diminished.

[The conclusion to the preceding portion, ix 1]: The first verse of chapter ix limits itself to the plain announcement that what has gone before pertains only to the official register of the families and situations already considered. "[When] they were exiled" separates the foregoing from what follows.

9. THE CITIZENS OF JERUSALEM AND ITS ENVIRONS
(ix 2–44)†

First returnees

IX 2 The first citizens who returned to their property in their cities were Israelites, the priests, the Levites, and the temple slaves. 3 Of those of the sons of Judah, of the sons of Benjamin and of the sons of Ephraim and Manasseh who took up residence in Jerusalem were:

From Judah

4 Uthai the son of Ammihud, the son of Omri, the son of Imri, the son of Bani; of the sons of Perez, the son of Judah. 5 Of the Shilonites there were Asaiah the first-born and his sons. 6 Of the sons of Zerah there was Jeuel. Their brothers numbered six hundred ninety.

From Benjamin

7 Of the sons of Benjamin there were Sallu, the son of Meshullam, the of Hodaviah, the son of Hassenuah; 8 and Ibneiah the son of Jeroham; and Elah the son of Uzzi, the son of Michri; and Meshullam the son of Shephatiah, the son of Reuel, the son of Ibnijah. 9 Their brothers according to their descendants numbered nine hundred fifty-six. All of these men were family chiefs of their families.

The priests

10 Of the priests there were Jedaiah, Jehoiarib, Jachin, 11 Azariah the son of Hilkiah, the son of Meshullam, the son of

† I Chron ix 2–3: cf. Neh xi 4a; 4–6: cf. Neh xi 4b–6; 7–9: cf. Neh xi 7–9; 10–13: cf. Neh xi 10–14; 14–16: cf. Neh xi 15–18; 17–18: cf. Neh xi 19; 35–44 ‖ Chron viii 29–38.

Zadok, the son of Meraioth, the son of Ahitub, the chief custodian of the house of God; 12 Adaiah the son of Jeroham, the son of Pashhur, the son of Malchijah; and Maasai the son of Adiel, the son of Jahzerah, the son of Meshullam, the son of Meshillemith, the son of Immer. 13 Their brothers, chiefs of their families, numbered seventeen hundred sixty—experts in the ministerial service of the house of God.

The Levites

14 Of the Levites there were Shemaiah the son of Hashshub, the son of Azrikam, the son of Hashabiah, of the sons of Merari: 15 Bakbakkar, ªHeresh, ªGalal, ªMattaniah the son of Mica, the son of Zichri, the son of Asaph; 16 Obadiah the son of Shemaiah, the son of Galal, the son of Jeduthun; and Berechiah the son of Asa, the son of Elkanah who lived in the dependencies of the Netophathites.

The gatekeepers

17 The gatekeepers were Shallum, Akkub, Talmon, and Ahiman; their brother Shallum was the chief 18 and until now the gatekeeper of the king's gate to the east. They were the gatekeepers of the camps of the sons of Levi.

Status and function of gatekeepers

19 Shallum the son of Kore, the son of Ebiasaph, the son of Korah and his brothers belonging to his family, the Korahites, were also in charge of the ministerial service as doorkeepers of the tabernacle, as their fathers were keepers of the entrance to the camp of Yahweh. 20 Formerly Phinehas the son of Eleazar had been their superintendent—Yahweh be with him! 21 Zechariah the son of Meshelemiah was the gatekeeper at the door of the tent of meeting. 22 All those selected as doorkeepers numbered two hundred and twelve and they were officially registered in their own compounds. David and Samuel the seer had appointed them because of their dependability, 23 so that they and

ª As vs. 14 probably is meant to follow the line of Bakbakkar, "son of" ought to be inserted in these places to show the connection, though LXX follows MT.

their sons continued in charge as guards of the gates of Yahweh's house, the house of the tent; 24 the [chief] gatekeepers were [assigned] to the four sides, east, west, north, and south, 25 and their brothers in their compounds were required to assist them from time to time for seven days, 26 because the four chief gatekeepers were on duty constantly.

Levitical functions

They were Levites and had charge of the chambers and the supplies of the house of God. 27 They spent the night round about the house of God because they were responsible for the guard and for opening it morning by morning. 28 Some of them were in charge of cultic implements, for they had to count them when they brought them in and when they took them out. 29 Others of them were placed in charge of the implements, of all the objects of the sanctuary and of the flour, the wine, the oil, the incense, and the spices. 30 But some of the priestly caste mixed the ointment for the perfume. 31 Mattithiah, of the Levites—he was the first-born son of Shallum, the Korahite—regularly had charge of baking operations. 32 ᵇSome of their brothers, of the sonsᵇ of the Kehathites, had charge of preparing the layer bread for each Sabbath.

The musicians

33 In addition there were the singers, the chiefs of the Levitical families, who lived in the chambers free from other responsibilities because they were on duty day and night. 34 These were the chiefs of the Levitical families according to their descendantsᶜ; these lived in Jerusalem.

Ancestors and descendants of Saul

35 Jeiel the father of Gibeon lived at Gibeon and the name of his wife was Maacah. 36 His first-born son was Abdon, then Zur, Kish, Baal, Ner, Nadab, 37 Gedor, Ahio, Zechariah, and Mikloth. 38 Mikloth fathered Shimeam; they too lived near their

ᵇ⁻ᵇ LXX reads "the Qehathite Benaiah of their brothers."
ᶜ Omit "chiefs" here. See textual note ᵉ in Sec. 8.

brothers in Jerusalem, in conjunction with their brothers. 39 Ner fathered Kish, Kish fathered Saul, Saul fathered Jehonathan, Malchishua, Abinadab, and Eshbaal. 40 Meribbaal was the son of Jehonathan and Meribbaal fathered Micah. 41 The sons of Micah were Pithon, Melech, and Tahrea. 42 Ahaz fathered Jarah, Jarah fathered Alemeth, Azmaveth and Zimri; Zimri fathered Moza, 43 Moza fathered Binea, Rephaiah his son, Eleasah his son, and Azel his son. 44 Azel had six sons who were named Azrikam, Bocheru*d*, Ishmael, Sheariah, Obadiah, and Hanan; these were the sons of Azel.

d LXX has "first-born son," as in viii 38.

NOTES

ix 2. *The first citizens who returned.* Those returning from exile.
Israelites. The lay returnees (cf. Ezra x 25).

the temple slaves. Occur in Ugaritic as a class. Cf. *spr ytnm* in Text 301 of C. H. Gordon's *Ugaritic Handbook*, II, 1947, p. 169. For a recent discussion of the *nethinim* (temple slaves), see E. A. Speiser, IEJ 13 (1963), 70 ff.

4. *the son of Bani.* Separating the word *Banimin.*

5. *Shilonites.* Num xxvi 20 has Shelanites (descendants of Shelah).

11. *Azariah.* See Neh xi 11; line may have been originally Seraiah son of Azariah son of Seraiah son of Azariah son of Hilkiah.

12. *Adaiah.* This Adaiah (cf. Neh xi 12) is probably the Adaiah whose name occurs on postexilic jar-handle stamps. He must have been connected with administrative duties pertaining to the treasury. See Albright, JPOS 6 (1926), 96 ff.

13. *experts.* For another possible translation, see Albright, *ibid.*, p. 97.

25. *from time to time for seven days.* So for "had to come for seven days, from time to time, with these."

27. *leböqer leböqer,* "around the clock," as a Ugaritic idiom, *lymm lyrḫm lyrḫm lsnt,* in I Aqht 175–76. See C. H. Gordon, "North Israelite and Postexilic Hebrew," IEJ 5 (1955), 88.

37. *Gedor.* On Gedor see BA 23 (February 1960), 25; Pritchard, *Hebrew Inscriptions and Stamps from Gibeon,* pp. 9 f.; the Gedor of Chronicles may be the one which appears on the jar handles (19 times) and seems to be located near Gibeon. Place names and those of persons occur together frequently in Chronicles.

41. *Tahrea.* viii 35 adds Ahaz.

42. Verse ‖ viii 36; see Albright, AASOR 4 (1924), 157.

COMMENT

There has always been a serious question of the relation of this
chapter to Neh xi, which is a list of family heads who lived in
Jerusalem in the time of Nehemiah, with reference also to those
who remained outside in their own towns. (For a discussion of the
position of Neh xi, see J. M. Myers, *Ezra and Nehemia,* 1965, Introduction and the COMMENT on the chapter there. For the significance of these chapters, Neh xi and I Chron ix, see Ginsberg's
quotation from Albright's letter in AMJV, p. 364, n. 47a.) The list
here was doubtless inspired by the several references in chapter
viii to the Benjaminites who lived at Jerusalem (vss. 28, 32). It
is another recension of the Nehemiah list (Goettsberger), though
the two lists are not so nearly alike as sometimes supposed; they
correspond most closely in the priestly and Levitical names, as might
be expected. Interestingly enough, LXX^{AB} omit about a score of
names from the Nehemiah list but only three or four from the
Chronicles list. MT has about eighty-one names for Neh xi and
about seventy-one for Chronicles of which only about thirty-five are
the same or nearly so, as the text now stands. That means that the
compiler of our list either had another purpose in mind and deliberately excluded some of the names or had other information at
hand.

[The first returnees, ix 2–3]: These verses are introductory to
the list of the names of those who returned and took up residence
in Jerusalem. Four classes are mentioned: the laity, priests, Levites,
and temple slaves. In line with the main emphasis of Chronicles on
"all Israel," Judah and Benjamin—which often occur together—
and Ephraim and Manasseh—which stand for the Joseph tribes and
are representative of the north—are specified, though there is no
follow-up in the list below.

[From Judah, 4–6]: The returnees of Judah are listed in line
with the families of Judah (ii 3 f.): Perez, Shelah, and Zerah; the
last-named is not included in the Nehemiah list, though a descendant
of Zerah is mentioned in Neh xi 24 (for F. X. Kugler's speculation
on the periods of the two lists see *Von Moses bis Paulus,* pp. 289–
300 [Selected Bibliography]). The list here is considerably curtailed
and only the Perez line is extended, with some variations from that

in Nehemiah, and there is some difference between LXX and MT and between LXX^A and ^{B} which can be explained on other grounds. The writer maintained the general line of Judah but did not elaborate, as did Nehemiah, on the Perez and Shelah line, though he did include Zerah. As to the numbers, 690 here appears to refer to the brothers of Zerah, that is, the sons of Perez and Shelah; while the 468 of Neh xi 6 is attributed to the sons of Perez.

COMPARISON OF NAMES IN MT AND LXX

1 Chron ix 4–6		*Neh xi 4–6*	
MT	LXX	MT	LXX
(1) Uthai	Gothi	(1) Ataiah	Athaia
Ammihud	Ammioud	Uzziah	Azaia
Omri	Amri	Zechariah	Zacharia
Imri	Phares	Amariah	Amaria
Bani (Benjamin)	Judah	Shephatiah	Saphatia
Perez		Mahalalel	Malelel
Judah		Perez	Phares
		Judah	
(2) Asaiah	Asaia	(2) Maaseiah	Maasia
Shelah	Shelomites	Baruch	Barouch
		Colhozeh	Chalaza
(3) Jeuel	Iiel	Haziah	Ozia
Zera	Zara	Adaiah	Adaia
		Joiarib	Iorib
		Zechariah	Thezia
		Shelah	Seloni (?)

[From Benjamin, 7–9]: If the text has been read correctly there were four branches of the Benjaminite line—Sallu, Ibneiah, Elah, and Meshullam—who were among the first of those to return to Jerusalem. LXX^{AB} obviously had the same text though they read "these" for Elah and then took Uzzi as the son of Michri and the representative of the third group. The only close correspondence with Neh xi 7–9 is Sallu with one of his sons, Meshullam; in Neh vii 9 Hassenuah is mentioned as the father of Judah. A private seal from Ramat Rahel has the name Yhwbnh/Ybnh (?) and comes from Iron Age II (see Y. Aharoni, "Excavations at Ramat Rahel," IEJ 6 [1956], 145. A similar stamp was also found at Beth-shemesh: see E. Grant and G. E. Wright, *Ain Shems Excavations* [Haverford, 1939], Pt. v, pp. 81 f. and Figs. 5, 10a).

COMPARISON OF NAMES IN MT AND LXX

I Chron ix 7–9		Neh xi 7–9	
MT	LXX	MT	LXX
(1) Sallu	Salo	(1) Sallu	Selo
Meshullam	Mosollum	Meshullam	Messoulam
Hodaviah	Odouia	Joed	Ioad
Hassenuah	Sanaa	Pedaiah	Phadaia
		Kolaiah	Kolia
		Masseiah	Masaia
		Ithiel	Aithiel
		Jeshaiah	Iesai
(2) Ibneiah	Ibanaa		
Jeroham	Iraam	(2) Gabbai	Gebi
		(3) Sallai	Seli
(3) Elah			
Uzzi	Ozi	(?) Joel	Joel
Michri	Machir	Zichri	Zechri
(4) Meshullam	Massalem	(?) Judah	Ioudas
Shephatiah	Saphatia	Hassenuah	Asana
Reuel	Ragouel		
Ibniyah	Banaia		

[The priests, 10–13]: Apparently six families of priests are named, but Jedaiah, Jehioarib, and Jachin are progenitors of Azariah, thus making in reality only three (Rudolph, pp. 84 f. Möhlenbrink [ZAW 52 (1934), 204 f.] regards this as the oldest list of the Zadokites. For a reconstruction of part of the list, see Albright, [JPOS 6 (1926), 96 f.]). The family list does not differ substantially from that of Neh xi, except that Seraiah is found there in place of Azariah. The family of Harim is not listed (cf. I Chron xxiv 8; Ezra ii 39, x 21). Note the lack of genealogical connection between the first three persons named but there can be no doubt that Jedaiah was the leader of Jeshuaites (Neh vii 39), Adaiah of the Pashhurites, and Maasai of the Immerites. Of the first family, Merioth is an intrusion, as in Neh xi 11. From the Adaiah line the names of Pelaliah, Amzi, and Zechariah are not given (cf. Neh xi 12) and in that of Maasai there is Adiel for Azarel, Jahzerah for Ahzai, Meshillemith for Meshillemoth, with the addition of Meshullam (cf. Neh xi 13). LXX follows MT, vs. 11, "chief custodian"; the Hebrew was descriptive of both civil and religious officials, especially of the high priest (cf. Jer xx 1; II Chron xxxi 13, et al.). Cf. Ar. *Imam,* vs. 13, "experts"; Heb. "men of standing," "landed proprietors," that is, people of importance.

COMPARISON OF NAMES IN MT AND LXX

	1 Chron ix 10–13			*Neh xi 10–14*	
	MT	*LXX*		*MT*	*LXX*
(1)	Jedaiah	Iodae	(1)	Jedaiah	Iadia (A)
(2)	Jehoiarib	Ioarim		Joiarib	Iorib
(3)	Jachin	Iachin	(2)	Jachin	Iachin
(4)	Azariah	Azaria	(3)	Seraiah	Saraiah
	Hilkiah	Chelkia		Hilkiah	Elkia
	Meshullam	Mosollam		Meshullam	Mesoulam
	Zadok	Sadok		Zadok	Saddouk
	Meraioth	Maraioth		Meraioth	Marioth
	Ahitub	Achitob		Ahitub	Aitob
(5)	Adaiah	Adaiah	(4)	Adaiah	Amasi
	Jeroham	Iraam		Jeroham	Zacharia
	Pashhur	Paschor		Pelaliah	Phassour
	Malchijah	Malchia		Amzi	Melchia
				Zechariah	
				Pashhur	Amessai
				Malchijah	Esdriel
(6)	Maasai	Maasaia	(5)	Amashsai	?
	Adiel	Adiel		Azarel	
	Jahzerah	Iediou		Ahzi	
	Meshullam	Mosollam		Meshillemoth	
	Immer	Emmer		Immer	
			(?)	Zabdiel	
				(Haggedolim)	

[The Levites, 14–16]: According to MT, seven Levitical families are included in the list. Neh xi 15–18 parallels Chronicles for the first family with the exception of its addition of Bunni, which is perhaps not to be taken as a personal name but as "sons of," Merari having fallen out. Bakbakkar as a family name occurs only here; it may be represented by Bakbukiah in Neh xi 17. The Jeduthun family is the same in both recensions, though the name forms are spelled differently; the Berechiah-Elkanah family is wanting in Nehemiah. The omission of the names Shabbethai and Jozabad (Neh xi 16) may indicate that the compiler meant his list to refer to another time, since both these men were active in the time of Ezra (cf. Ezra viii 33, x 15; Neh viii 7). The name Hashshub occurs on an inscription on a sherd found at Tell Abu Zeitun in the Yarkon Valley dating from the Persian period (see IEJ 8 [1958],

133 f.). The name Galal occurs in Persian administrative documents (cf. R. A. Bowman, "Nehemiah," IB, III, p. 777). Netophah was somewhere near Jerusalem, perhaps between there and Bethlehem. Ramat Rahel has been suggested. See Aharoni, IEJ 6 (1956), 102–11, 137–55.

COMPARISON OF NAMES IN MT AND LXX

I Chron ix 14–16		*Neh xi 15–18*	
MT	*LXX*	*MT*	*LXX*
(1) Shemaiah	Samaia	(1) Shemaiah	Samaia
Haššub	Asob	Haššub	Asoub
Azrikam	Esrikam	Azrikam	Ezri
Hashabiah	Asabia	Hashabiah	
Merari	Merari	Bunni	
(2) Bakbakkar	Bakbakar	(2) Shabbethai	
(3) Heresh	Ares	(3) Jozabad	
(4) Galal	Galal	(4) Bakbukiah	
(5) Mattaniah	Manthanias	(5) Mattaniah	Mathania
Mica	Micha	Micah	Micha
Zichri	Zechri	Zabdi	Obed
Asaph	Asaph	Asaph	Samoui
(6) Obadiah	Abdia	(6) Abda	
Shemaiah	Samia	Shammua	
Galal	Galal	Galal	
Jeduthun	Idithon	Jeduthun	
(7) Berechiah	Barachia		
Asa	Ossa		
Elkanah	Elkana		

[The gatekeepers, 17–18]: Neh xi 19 gives only two names; here four are listed (cf. vs. 26). Shallum was the chief and occupied an especially honored position as the gatekeeper of the east gate through which the king usually entered (cf. Ezek xlvi 1 ff.) and was the one which faced the entrance to the sanctuary. Three of the family names appear also in Ezra ii 42.

COMPARISON OF NAMES IN MT AND LXX

I Chron ix 17		*Neh xi 19*	
MT	*LXX*	*MT*	*LXX*
Shallum	Salom		
Akkub	Akoub	Akkub	Akoub
Talmon	Talman	Talmon	Talamin
Ahiman	Aiman		

The gatekeepers were reckoned with the Levites (vs. 26; I Chron xxiii 3 ff.) though they were held apart somewhat as may be seen from the mention of priests, Levites, gatekeepers, and temple slaves in many places. The Chronicler traces the tradition of the organization of the temple service to David; it may go further back since Samuel was employed at Shiloh in typical Levitic service and it is hard to see how one can deny some Levitical functions even in the time of Moses (cf. Exod xxxii 26–29; Num i 50–53) though they were not so highly organized or specialized. Perhaps something of an attempt to separate the gatekeepers from the Levites is reflected in 18b although it is difficult to understand how they could have performed their duties without Levitical status (cf. vs. 26).

[Status and function of gatekeepers, 19–26a]: Verse 19 identifies the gatekeepers with the family of Korah of the family of Kehath, the second son of Levi (vi 1, 22, 23). Kore is elsewhere identified with the gatekeepers (xxvi 1). In II Chron xxxi 14 a Levite by the same name is said to have had charge of the east gate in the time of Hezekiah; he was doubtless a descendant of the Levitical line of gatekeepers as was Shallum. Their importance is further stressed by the fact that the priest Phinehas was their superintendent, as his father Eleazar had been (Num iii 32), because he was the overseer of the sanctuary. Zechariah and Meshelemiah are mentioned again in xxvi 2, 14, where the former's lot fell at the north gate and the latter's at the east; Zechariah doubtless succeeded his father. Their official register in their compounds in the local towns did not detract from their position because they owed their office to David (ch. xxvi) and that by virtue of their dependability. The chief gatekeepers had charge of the gates on the four sides and apparently lived in Jerusalem while their brothers (i.e., their assistants), who lived in their compounds in the towns in the outlying districts, were required to serve in relays of a week. Chapter xxvi 12–18 says there were a total of twenty-four guard posts to be manned around the clock, thus requiring at least seventy-two watchmen for each day. That meant service for each of the 212 gatekeepers, if the number is to be taken seriously, every third week.

[Levitical functions, 26b–32]: Once more the writer stresses the fact that the gatekeepers and other temple functionaries were Levites—whom he is at pains to upgrade at every opportunity—so that 26b actually faces both directions. Rudolph, p. 91, has rightly emphasized that the Levites were responsible for four types of service. (a) They were in charge of the chambers around the temple and the supply rooms (cf. xxiii 28, xxvi 20 f.). (b) It was their duty to maintain guard over the sacred precincts night and day and to open its gates at the proper times every morning (cf. Exod xxxii 26–29). (c) They were responsible for the implements used in the performance of janitorial service, to see that they were all accounted for, and to bring them in and out of the sacred place; a duty that indicates special consecration because of the necessity for access thereto (cf. vs. 32, xxviii 13 ff. and Ezra i 9–11). (d) The vessels used in actual offerings, as well as the materials used, were in their custody. But the writer or an editor observes that the preparation of the perfume was the function of the priests themselves, probably a reminder of the regulations given in Exod xxx 23–33, especially the latter verse. Baking operations and the preparation of the layer bread were also handled by the Levites. The Shallum mentioned here as the father of Mattithiah was not the same one mentioned above as the ancestor of the gatekeepers since the latter's first-born son was Zechariah (xxvi 2). On the preparation of baked goods see Lev ii 5–7, vii 9.

[The musicians, 33–34]: Like vs. 30, vs. 33 may be the comment of a Levitical chorister who wanted to point out that the musicians too belonged to the favored group and as a matter of fact were free from menial responsibilities. One should expect some definite references such as those given in xv 16–22. Perhaps it was enough that at least two of the heads of musical guilds—Asaph and Jeduthun— were mentioned above (vss. 15, 16). The singers were not to be outdone by the gatekeepers, for they too ministered day and night (cf. Ps cxxxiv; Isa xxx 29). Vs. 34 is almost identical with viii 28— only the Levites are added here—and is transitional here, as there, between the Levitical musicians and the genealogy of Saul. It is preparatory to the story of the death of Saul related in the next chapter. This may be an indication that the preceding portion of ix is an insertion not present in the original compilation of chapters i–viii, x.

[The ancestry of Saul, 35–44]: Verses 35–44 are nearly an exact duplicate of viii 29–38. It has Ner between Baal and Nadab in vs. 36; it includes the name of Mikloth in vs. 37; has Shimeam for Shimeah in vs. 38; and adds Ahaz to the sons of Micah. The spellings too are different in a few instances: Tahrea for Tarea, Jarah for Jehoaddah, Rephaiah for Raphah, Zechariah for Zecher.

II. DAVID AND
THE FOUNDING OF THE TEMPLE

10. THE DEATH OF SAUL
(x 1–14)†

X 1 When the Philistines made war on Israel, the men of Israel fled before the Philistines and the slain fell on Mount Gilboa. 2 But the Philistines hotly pursued Saul and his sons and*a* slew Jonathan, Abinadab, and Malchishua, the sons of Saul. 3 When the battle bore down heavily against Saul, the bowmen discovered him and he was wounded by the archers. 4 Then Saul said to his armor-bearer, "Draw your sword and pierce me with it, lest these uncircumcised men come and amuse themselves with me." But the armor-bearer was unwilling to do it because he was very much afraid. So Saul himself took the sword and fell upon it. 5 When the armor-bearer saw that Saul was dead, he too fell upon the sword and died. 6 So Saul and his three sons died; and thus his whole house perished at one stroke. 7 When all the Israelites in the valley saw that they fled and that Saul and his sons were dead, they forsook their cities and fled and the Philistines entered and occupied them. 8 The next day when the Philistines came to strip the slain, they found Saul and his sons fallen on Mount Gilboa. 9 When they had stripped him, they took his head and his armor and sent them around through the land of the Philistines as an announcement of the good news of victory to their idols and the people. 10 They placed his armor in the house of their god and they exposed*b* his skull in the house of Dagon. 11 When all the citizens of Jabesh-gilead heard about everything that the Philistines did to Saul, 12 every warrior arose, took the corpse of Saul and the corpses of his sons, brought them to Jabesh and buried

† **I Chron x 1–14** ‖ I Sam xxxi.

a MT repeats "the Philistines." Omitted as unnecessary and redundant.
b So for Heb. "blow," of a trumpet. For the whole verse see I Sam xxxi 10.

their bones under the oak at Jabesh; afterward they fasted for seven days. ¹³ So Saul died in his unfaithfulness of which he was guilty before Yahweh, in that he did not obey the word of Yahweh and because he consulted the necromancer for guidance. ¹⁴ Because he did not consult Yahweh, he slew him and transferred the kingdom to David the son of Jesse.

NOTES

x 3. *was wounded.* Pointing the verb as niphal.

4. *lest these . . . with me.* Refers to torture and mutilation, but also to abuse and sexual humiliation. The prospect was so horrifying and humiliating that suicide was not regarded as reprehensible under the circumstances. The fact that suicide is otherwise practically unknown in the whole of biblical history throws into stark relief the frightful prospects facing Saul should he fall into the hands of the Philistines alive. The Chronicler has thus chosen the suicide tradition of I Sam xxxi in preference to that of death at the hands of one of his own men reported in II Sam i.

7. *all the Israelites in the valley.* Those living in the valley of Jezreel.

they. I.e., the men of the army.

COMMENT

The preceding chapters are, for the most part, secondary to the Chronicler's work. Perhaps it was simply because the material just happened to be available at the time in the archival records which had been assembled for other purposes and which embodied information the editor thought ought not be lost. On the other hand, it may have provided, to his way of thinking, indirect authentication of the method for establishing membership in the community of Israel in use in the period of Ezra-Nehemiah. While these lists can hardly be regarded as a satisfactory substitute for the history of Israel before David, they are certainly meant, by the editor of the whole work, to be an introduction to the book or history as we now have it.

It is almost axiomatic among biblical scholars to affirm that the real work of the Chronicler begins here. If that is so, then why does he begin his story with the death of Saul? Since David is the central figure in the pre-exilic history of Israel (Judah), it could be said that he introduces it with the demise of the nation's first king. But, as Freedman points out (CBQ 23 [1961], 436–42), that doesn't fully explain the situation. He thinks the present narrative of the Chronicler was intended to supplement the accepted and more or less official history of the nation. Hence the author must have been satisfied with the Deuteronomic portrait of the earlier period. He did not believe that Israel began with Saul and David as may be seen from the sources of references to "the God of the fathers" (a technical term referring to the God of the patriarchs and their successors. Cf. I Chron xii 18, xxix 20; II Chron xi 17, xiii 12, 18, xiv 3, xv 12, etc., none of which are from the Samuel-Kings source), the patriarchs (non-parallel passages are I Chron xxix 18; II Chron xx 7, xxx 6; Neh ix 7), Moses, Aaron and his sons. All of this could only mean that he looked upon the history of his people as authentic up until the time of David, after which he tells the story in his own way. Whether he wanted to replace the earlier Deuteronomic history is another matter; that was already fixed and canonical. It may be that he did intend his treatise to be the official history of Judah and the subsequent commonwealth of Israel. That might account for his "correction" of the earlier history and the addition of important details, though on the former point one must not draw unwarranted conclusions; the writer may have utilized a different manuscript than that represented in the MT of Samuel and Kings (see penultimate paragraph below, sentence beginning "Rudolph, p. 92, suggests . . .").

In the last analysis, one's conception depends on his theory of authorship and date. If the work of the original Chronicler was written in the time of Haggai and Zechariah, then a second Chronicler who lived in the time of Ezra must have been responsible for the present complex of Chronicles-Ezra-Nehemiah (with the possible exception of a few later additions), including the prefixing of I Chron i–ix as an introduction to this production. This later writer revived the work of the first Chronicler to which he joined the memoirs of Ezra and Nehemiah together with some observations of his own by which he intended to make the whole thing a tract for the times. That, if I understand it correctly, is in substance the view of Freedman.

If, however, one takes the view that the Chronicler was the same

person who wrote the memoirs of Ezra (see Introduction, footnote
[106]), the outlook is substantially different and somewhat as outlined
in the Introduction. The writer was, then, conceivably motivated by
the historical situation. That is why he drew attention primarily to
the cult relationships of David—Jerusalem, the temple, and cult
arrangements and personnel. He could not ignore the facts of history
but he did play some of them down somewhat. Thus he did not deal
with the family involvements of the great king, since that might have
reflected on the latter's cultic status. He stressed reform elements
(Jehoshaphat, Hezekiah, Josiah) because that was the need of his
time. The Chronicler, then, composed the complex noted in the
preceding paragraph from the sources available to him, as has been
discussed in the Introduction. He rewrote the history of Judah from
his own viewpoint, for his own purposes. To that history he appended his own memoirs and those of Nehemiah, with some related
material, to bring it up to date. To introduce his composition he
prefixed the archival lists of I Chron i–ix. Both views have their
difficulties and neither can be regarded as definitive.

The story begins here in ch. x with a retelling of the end of the first
king of Israel in his final struggle against his lifelong opponents, the
Philistines. In so doing, the writer borrows almost verbally the story
of the battle at Mount Gilboa, some dozen miles southeast of Megiddo, from I Sam xxxi 1–13. He apparently takes for granted his
reader's knowledge of the events of Saul's life and the movements of
his day. Comments are required here only where there are differences between the Chronicler's account and that in Samuel. It should
be observed that the Philistine movement against Saul was due to his
cutting off the trade routes and that though they won the battle at
Mount Gilboa, they had really been fought to a standstill and never
advanced any farther. In fact, the forces of David were already
making quiet but effective progress against them in the south. See
article on David in IDB, I, pp. 771–82.

In vs. 6, Saul and all his house are said to have perished. The
corresponding vs. in I Samuel (xxxi 6) omits "his house" but has
instead "his armor-bearer and all his men." Thus the Chronicler
ignores the survival of Ishbaal who continued the kingdom for a
time from Transjordan (cf. II Sam ii–iv). He dropped Saul completely after Yahweh had rejected him and never mentions any of
his descendants. Unless the Saul sections of chapters viii and ix are
later additions, he may have thought that was all that was required

in view of his over-all purpose. The sending around of the head
and armor of Saul to announce the good news of victory to gods
and people may have been a symbolic offering of the fruits of tri-
umph to their deities.

A significant point is the omission of Ashtaroth and the substi-
tution of "their god[s]" in vs. 10, though the name of Dagon is
used. This may have been due, as Rudolph suggests, p. 95, to the
abhorrence of pagan sexual orgies which centered about their cults,
and especially because Chronicles seems to be strongly influenced
by the prophets who condemned them severely. Dagon, referred to
some thirteen times (Judg xvi 23; I Sam v; here) in the Bible, was
an old Akkadian deity dating back to the twenty-fifth century B.C.
At Ugarit he was said to be the father of Baal and had a temple
there. (See C. F. A. Schaeffer, *The Cuneiform Texts of Ras-
Shamra—Ugarit,* 1939, p. 8, and *Ugaritica* I [1939], p. 14, Fig.
9; Albright, ARI, pp. 74 f., 106, 220, n. 115; J. Bottéro and A.
Finet, *Archives royales de Mari XV: Répertoire analytique des
tomes I à V,* 1954, p. 161 [for references].) He was a vegetation
deity. It should be noted that Samuel says nothing about the exposition of the skull; it does speak of the impaling of his corpse on
the walls of Bethshan. Rudolph, p. 92, suggests the possibility of
the Chronicles reference having been present originally in the Samuel text and falling out because of the graphic similarity of the two
expressions—the hanging of the skull in the house of Dagon and the
hanging of the corpse on the walls of Bethshan. The Qumran evidence now makes it clear that Chronicles was based upon a different
Hebrew version of Samuel than MT, and much closer to LXX. This
supports Rudolph's suggestion. In general Chronicles must be regarded, where it follows Samuel, as a faithful witness to a Hebrew
Vorlage (archetype), differing from MT in certain particulars, but
attested at Qumran in its Samuel documents. See Introduction. The
citizens of Jabesh-gilead expressed their loyalty to the house of
Saul by attending to funeral rites—and later by supporting Saul's
son Ishbaal. Our text says nothing of the burning of the corpses, a
practice that may have offended the writer since it applied only in
the case of certain criminals (Lev xx 14, xxi 9; Josh vii 25). The
seven-day fast points to the respect they had for the king (cf. the
one-day fast of David, II Sam i 12).

The last verses of the chapter are the writer's comment on the
reasons for the misfortune of Saul, which he uses to illustrate (or

demonstrate) his theology. Three charges are laid against him: (a)
he did not obey the word of God, by which may be meant Saul's
failure to await the coming of Samuel to offer sacrifices (I Sam xiii)
and to carry out his orders with respect to the Amalekites (I Sam
xv); (b) he summoned the spirit of Samuel from the grave (nec-
romancy; I Sam xxviii); (c) he did not consult Yahweh, which is
not quite in accord with other aspects of the story as told in Samuel.
Saul is specifically said to have consulted Yahweh (I Sam xxviii 6)
but got no response because he had already separated himself from
Yahweh. In the wake of the rejection of Saul, David received the
kingdom.

11. DAVID'S RISE TO POWER
(xi 1–9)†

David made king of Israel

XI ¹ Then all Israel came together to David at Hebron and said, "Behold, we are of your bone and your flesh! ² Formerly, even while Saul was king, you were the one who led out and brought back Israel. Moreover, Yahweh your God has said to you, you shall shepherd my people Israel and you shall be a prince over my people Israel." ³ So when all the elders of Israel had come to the king at Hebron and David had made a covenant with them at Hebron before Yahweh, they anointed David king over Israel in accordance with the word of Yahweh by Samuel.

The capture of Jerusalem

⁴ Then David and all Israel went to Jerusalem—that is Jebus where the Jebusites, the inhabitants of the land, lived. ⁵ But the inhabitants of Jebus said to David, "You cannot come here." However, David captured the fortress of Zion which is the city of David. ⁶ David said, "Whoever kills a Jebusite first will be chief and commander." Joab the son of Zeruiah went up first and so he became chief. ⁷ Because David took up residence in the fortress they called it the city of David. ⁸ He built the city from around the Millo to the surrounding wall, while Joab restored the remainder of the city. ⁹ David kept growing stronger and stronger because Yahweh of hosts was with him.

† I Chron xi 1–3 ‖ II Sam v 1–3; 4–9 ‖ II Sam v 4–10.

NOTES

xi 6. *Joab the son of Zeruiah went up first.* Amenemheb, a valiant man, was the first to breach the wall of Kadesh during the campaign of Thutmose III, a heroic exploit comparable to that of Joab. Cf. ANET, p. 241. The sense of the clause is that Joab was the first to kill a Jebusite, which required getting into the fortress.

7. *the city of David.* Capital cities were often named after conquerors. Cf. in Egypt the city of Akhetaton named after Akhnaton; the city Raamses in the eastern Nile Delta; in Assyria Dur-Sharrukin (Sargon's-burg), the city of Sargon; Alexandria named for Alexander the Great.

8. *the surrounding wall.* Wall must be added since the term "surrounding" is not used elsewhere as a noun. Possibly, on the basis of II Sam v 19, the Chronicler meant to interpret the difficult "inward" as "to the house." Under the influence of the preceding "around," "to the house" was altered. For translation of the whole verse see K. Galling, BRL, col. 303.

remainder. Galling (BRL and *Die Bücher der Chronik* . . . , p. 40) reads: "and Joab rebuilt the gates of the city."

COMMENT

After the introductory notice (ch. x) on the end of the kingdom of Saul, together with the death of the king and the reasons for both, the writer plunges to the very center of his theological ideal: David and the Davidic kingdom. It is not to be expected that he should be deflected from his purpose by what he considered irrelevant episodes in the history of his people. That does not mean that he denied them validity, but that they did not enhance his religious purpose for the people of his day.

The source for this material is II Sam v 1–10. As was observed above, the struggle of David with Saul (I Sam xvi–xxvi) and the remnants of his kingdom are completely ignored (II Sam ii–iv), probably because the writer was interested only in the legitimate line of Israel, which was represented by David and his successors (after Solomon in the kingdom of Judah) and which alone survived the Exile. Hence he stresses the unity of the kingdom under the term "all Israel" and begins his narrative of David with his anointing as king by the elders of Israel. He says nothing about the Hebron period of David's rule over Judah, though there is a hint of it in the retention of the statement that they came "to the king at Hebron," as if to say he was already king. His reference to "the word of Yahweh by Samuel" takes in a pretty large area and assumes the reader's knowledge of the details underlying David's anointing by the seer (I Sam xvi). The declaration in vs. 2b, copied directly from II Sam v 2b, refers to II Sam iii 10. Omitted also is the notice of the length of David's reign (II Sam v 4–5) which does not come until I Chron xxix 27 and then without reference to his reign over Judah alone (but cf. I Chron iii 4). The important point stressed is the fact that "all Israel came together" to anoint David in accordance with Yahweh's promise; which means that the Chronicler puts forth a different point of view from that expressed in his source where "all the tribes of Israel" means those who had followed Saul and excludes Judah by virtue of what transpired before.

The conquest of Jebus (Jerusalem) fits into his scheme. For him "David and all Israel went to Jerusalem," whereas II Sam v 6 says "the king and his men went to Jerusalem." By this slight twist he indicates that "all Israel" had a share in the capture of the city which became the holy city and the place of the temple, the religious as well as political focus of the kingdom. Left out is the obscure reference to the lame and the blind. The fortress of Zion then became the city of David by right of conquest; it was so called because David took up residence there (vs. 7). Another emphasis developed here has to do with Joab, whose position was due to the fact that he was the first to slay a Jebusite. For the Chronicler Joab was always David's right-hand man and nowhere does he refer to the curse resting upon him (I Kings ii 5) which demanded action by Solomon. David himself handled the construction of the acropolis around the Millo while Joab restored the remainder of the city. (On the Millo see Galling, BRL 7, 300; L. H. Vincent and A. M. Steve, *Jerusalem de l'Ancien Testament*, 1954, 1956, pp. 635 ff.; M. Avi-Yonah in *Sepher Yerushalayim* [in Hebrew], 1956, pp. 156 f., who thinks the Millo joined the city of David with the mountain of the house to the north.) The reference to Joab's activities is doubtless another attempt to glorify him since it is missing in II Samuel. This section concludes with the Chronicler's assertion that David kept increasing in power because "Yahweh of hosts was with him," of special interest to him because it fit into his scheme. This phrase occurs only here and in xvii 24 in his writings.

12. DAVID'S MIGHTY MEN
(xi 10–47)†

XI ¹⁰ These are the chiefs of David's mighty—men who joined forces with him in his kindgom and, with all Israel, helped to make him king in accordance with the word of Yahweh concerning Israel. ¹¹ This*a* is the list of David's mighty men: *b*Jashobeam the son of Hachmoni*b* was chief of the thirty*c*; he brandished his spear over three hundred men slain at one time. ¹² After him among the three mighty men came Eleazar the son of Dodo, the Ahohite. ¹³ He was with David at Pasdammim where the Philistines had mobilized for the battle and where there was part of a field of barley. When the people fled before the Philistines, ¹⁴ they*d* took their stand in the midst of that part [of the field], held it, and defeated the Philistines. So Yahweh helped [them] achieve a great victory. ¹⁵ *e*Three of the thirty chiefs*e* went down among the crags to David, to the cave of Adullam, while a division of Philistines was encamped in the valley of Rephaim. ¹⁶ At the time David was in the fortress and a Philistine garrison was stationed at Bethlehem. ¹⁷ Faint with longing, David said, "Oh that I had water to drink from the cistern at Bethlehem—the one at the gate." ¹⁸ Then the three broke into the Philistine garrison, drew water from the cistern at the gate of Bethlehem, took it up, and brought it to

† I Chron xi 10–47 ‖ II Sam xxiii 8–35.

a For Heb. "these."
b–b Some manuscripts of LXX*L* read "Ishbaal"; LXX*AB* of II Sam xxiii 8 read "Ishbosheth the Canaanite"; but cf. I Chron xxvii 2.
c So Kings, but LXX*L* has "three," which appears to be preferred by many commentators; also by L. Koehler and W. Baumgartner, *Lexicon in Veteris Testamenti Libros*, 1953, p. 977.
d The reference is apparently to David and his mighty men. LXX here and II Sam xxiii 12 are singular and refer to David.
e–e With LXX.

David; however, David would not drink it but poured it out to
Yahweh, 19 saying, "May I be damned by my God if I should
do this! Shall I drink the very life blood of these men? For at
the risk of their lives they brought it." And so he would not
drink it. The three mighty men did these things. 20 ʼAbishai
the brother of Joab was the chief of the thirtyʼ—he is the one
who brandished his spear over three hundred slain men—but he
was not reckoned among the three. 21 ᵍHe was a most illustrious
one of the thirtyᵍ and was their commander; but he did not
come up to the three. 22 Benaiah the son of Jehoiada from
Kabzeel wasʰ a mighty man with many achievements; he is
the one who slew two Moabite heroes and he also went down
and killed the lion in the pit on a snowy day. 23 In addition he
slew an Egyptian, a man who was seven and a half feet tall;
though the Egyptian had a spear like a weaver's beam, he went
to him with a staff, tore away the spear from the hand of the
Egyptian, and slew him with his own spear. 24 These things
Benaiah the son of Jehoiada did, but he was not reckoned with
the three mighty men. 25 Though he was a most illustrious one
of the thirty, he did not come up to the three; so David put
him in command of his bodyguard. 26 The mighty men of the
army were Asahel the brother of Joab, Elhanan son of Dodo
from Bethlehem, 27 Shammoth the Harorite, Helez the Pelonite, 28 Ira the son of Ikkesh the Tekoite, Abiezer the Anathothite, 29 Sibbecai the Hushathite, Ilai the Ahohite, 30 Maharai
the Netophathite, Heled the son of Baanah the Netophathite,
31 Ithai the son of Ribai from Gibeah of the Benjaminites,
Benaiah the Pirathonite, 32 Hurai from the wadis of Gaash,
Abiel the Arbathite, 33 Azmaveth the Bahrumite, Eliahba the
Shaalbonite, 34 ⁱthe sons of Hashem the Gizonite,ⁱ Jonathan the
son of Shageh the Hararite, 35 Ahiam the son of Sachar the

ᶠ⁻ᶠ So with Syr.; MT has "three." Verse 21 says explicitly he was not one of
the three.
ᵍ⁻ᵍ So with Syr. and omitting "among the two." Hebrew reads "Of the three he
was honored among the two."
ʰ Omitting "son of" with LXX.
ⁱ⁻ⁱ II Sam xxiii 32 and LXXᴬ have "Jashen." Perhaps omit "sons of" as
dittography from Shaalbonite, to make phrase read "Hashem the Gizonite."

Hararite, Eliphal the son of Ur, 36 Hepher the Mecherathite, Ahijah the Pelonite, 37 Hezro the Carmelite, Naarai the son of Ezbai, 38 Joel the brother of Nathan, Mibhar the son of Hagri, 39 Zelek the Ammonite, Naharai the Berothite the armor-bearer of Joab the son of Zeruiah, 40 Ira the Ithrite, Gareb the Ithrite, 41 Uriah the Hittite, Zabad the son of Ahlai, 42 Adina the son of Shiza the Reubenite, ʲthe Reubenite chief of thirty,ʲ 43 Hanan the son of Maacah, Joshaphat the Mithnite, 44 Uzzia the Ashterathite, Shama and Jeiel the sons of Hotham the Aroerite, 45 Jediael the son of Shimri, Joha his brother the Tizite, 46 Eliel the Mahavite, Jeribai and Joshaviah the sons of Elnaam, Ithmah the Moabite, 47 Eliel, Obed, and Jaasiel the Mezobaite.

ʲ⁻ʲ So with Syriac. Heb. "and over him thirty."

NOTES

xi 11. *the list.* So for "number" (cf. Ezra i 9).
19. *"May I be damned . . . do this!"* I.e., declared tabu or put under the ban. A solemn oath with a self-curse.

COMMENT

Verses 11 to 41a were taken from II Sam xxiii 8–39, with some variations. The Samuel passage forms part of a secondary addition to that book but is undoubtedly genuine. See O. Eissfeldt, *Einleitung in das Alte Testament,* 3d ed., 1964, pp. 370 ff., and especially the excellent treatment by Elliger, PJB 31 (1935), 29–75. Here it is wrought into the framework of the narrative to magnify David and to accentuate the support he received from the mighty men to carry out the word of God. That appears to be the intent of vs. 10 which emphasizes the unity of "all Israel" in the achievement of the divine will. Before listing the thirty, the Chronicler takes up the heroic exploits of two (of the thirty) and of Abishai and Benaiah. Jashobeam is said to have been the chief of the thirty (II Sam xxiii 8 "of the three") though he is not included in the list given below. It may be that thirty here is an error for three, since in both accounts he stands at the head of the three. It is interesting to observe that, contrary to his custom, the Chronicler reduces the number of his victims from eight hundred to three hundred. Eleazar, who was responsible for a classic victory over the Philistines, was the second of the three. His exploit was in the locality of Pas-dammim (cf. I Sam xvii 1), probably between Socoh and Azekah, and may refer to the time of Saul. The name has dropped out of the II Samuel passage. The third of the three, Shammah, is omitted here, perhaps through a copyist's error. It appears that the writer has attributed some of the circumstances surrounding Shammah's stand to Eleazar (cf. II Sam xxiii 10–12 with vss. 13–14).

The little pericope (15–19) is somewhat loosely connected with the preceding verses dealing with the three, which offers the link between them. David had two brushes with the Philistines in the valley of Rephaim (II Sam v 17–25) but this episode may belong to an earlier period, during his outlaw days. The passage indicates hostility between David and the Philistines. In any case, the three heroes broke through the lines of the enemy and brought David water from the well at Bethlehem which he refused to drink but poured out as a libation before Yahweh (cf. I Sam vii 6), since they had risked their lives to procure it.

Though Abishai is not mentioned in the list below, he is here described as the chief of the thirty and is credited with slaying three hundred men. While he was thus a valiant man, he did not quite attain the status of the three. The fact that he is referred to as the commander of the thirty points to the probability of a shifting roster that was kept up to date from time to time until it was committed to the record as we have it later on. It may be that Abishai took the place of Asahel after the latter was slain by Abner, in which case the list would have to date pretty early in the Davidic period—during the Hebron period or earlier. Abishai's exploit is not otherwise known but may be a reflection of his campaign against Edom (I Chron xviii 12). It is significant that Joab does not appear among either the three or the thirty. Benaiah figures prominently in the Davidic organization (he is not the one mentioned in the list who was a Pirathonite, from Ephraim). He was a Southerner from Kabzeel (possibly Khirbet Hura) in the region of Beer-sheba. He had many achievements to his credit and therefore was included among the famous men of David. Though he was a valiant man and among the thirty (cf. II Sam xxiii 23; I Chron xxvii 6), and a man of renown, he was not quite up to the three. He became the head of the king's bodyguard (II Sam viii 18, xx 23; I Chron xviii 17).

The main list (vss. 26–41a) contains thirty-one names, that of II Sam xxiii 24–39 has thirty (see Elliger, PJB 31 [1935], 30–36). Naturally there are a few variations in names and spelling. The following table will illustrate both points:

II Sam xxiii		*I Chron xi*	
Asahel	Eliahba	Asahel	Hashem
Elhanan	Jashen	Elhanan	Jonathan
Shammah	Jonathan	Shammoth	Ahiam
Elika	Ahiam	Helez	Eliphal
Helez	Eliphelet	Ira	Hepher
Ira	Eliam	Abiezer	Ahijah
Abiezer	Hezro	Sibbecai	Hezro
(Sibbecai) *	Paarai	Ilai	Naarai
Zalmon	Igal	Maharai	Joel
Maharai	Bani	Heled	Mibhar
Heleb	Zelek	Ithai	Zelek
Ittai	Naharai	Benaiah	Naharai
Benaiah	Ira	Hurai	Ira
Hiddai	Gareb	Abiel	Gareb
Abialbon	Uriah	Azmaveth	Uriah
Azmaveth		Eliahba	

* So for "Mebunnai" of MT, cf. LXX^L.

As Elliger has shown (*op. cit.,* pp. 63 f.) the great majority of the thirty came from the Judah-Simeon and old Dan areas, and two from Mount Ephraim, one from the Jordan Valley, one from Benjamin, and three from Transjordan. This is just what might be expected—strong and alert personalities from his own area and a few from elsewhere gathering about David because they recognized in him the qualities necessary for effective leadership during the decline of the kingdom of Saul and the rise of his own. The idea of the thirty probably comes from Egypt from whose administrative machinery David borrowed more than one feature. See R. de Vaux, "Titres et fonctionnaires égyptiens a la cour de David et de Salomon," RB 48 (July 1939), 394–405.

The Chronicler's expansion of the list (vss. 41b–47) may have been inspired by the following chapter (cf. Cazelles, p. 74, n. a.). He may have had a further list of men who were associated in some way with David which he added here, thus paying little attention to the idea of the thirty, or because he wanted to magnify his hero still further by increasing his coterie of followers. The fact that most of the sixteen probably came from Transjordan appears to weigh against Noth's argument (ÜS, p. 136, n. 8 and Rudolph, p. 101) that the list is postexilic on the basis of some late names (doubtless of persons who traced their ancestry back to early followers of David), since by that time there was an attempt to minimize connections with that region because of the heterodox elements involved. B. Mazar ("David's Mighty Men," VT 13 [1963], 311–320) thinks the addition of fifteen (vss. 42–47) does not belong to the original list but represents a later addition.

13. FOLLOWERS OF DAVID. HIS SUPPORTERS AT HEBRON
(xii 1–41 [xii 1–40E])

Defections to David

XII ¹ These are the ones who joined David at Ziklag while he was still held in check by Saul the son of Kish: they were among the mighty men, the warriors. ² They were equipped with bow and could use either right or left hand to sling stones or shoot arrows with the bow; they were Saul's compatriots from Benjamin. ³ The first was Ahiezer, then Joash the son*ᵃ* of Shemaah the Gibeathite, Jeziel and Pelet the sons of Azmaveth, Berachah, Jehu the Anathothite, ⁴ Ishmaiah the Gibeonite, mighty man of the thirty and also over the thirty, ⁵ Jeremiah, Jahaziel, Johanan, Jozabad the Gederathite, ⁶ Eluzai, Jerimoth, Bealiah, Shemariah, Shephatiah the Haruphite, ⁷ Elkanah, Isshiah, Azarel, Joezer, Jashobeam, the Korahites, ⁸ and Joelah and Zebadiah, the sons of Jeroham from Gedor. ⁹ Of the Gadites there defected to David, at the fortress in the wilderness, capable men ready for combat, who could wield shield and spear, like lions in appearance and as nimble as gazelles upon the mountains. ¹⁰ Ezer was the first, Obadiah the second, Eliab the third, ¹¹ Mishmannah the fourth, Jeremiah the fifth, ¹² Attai the sixth, Eliel the seventh, ¹³ Johanan the eighth, Elzabad the ninth, ¹⁴ Jeremiah the tenth, and Machbannai the eleventh. ¹⁵ These of the Gadites were chiefs of the host; each one could match a hundred lesser ones, the greatest a thousand. ¹⁶ These were the ones who once crossed the Jordan in the first month when it had overflowed all its banks and made impassable*ᵇ* all the lowlands to the east and to the west. ¹⁷ Some of the Benjaminites

---

ᵃ So for MT "sons."
ᵇ Reading the verb as a denominative of *beriaḥ*, "bar" (of a gate).

and Judahites also joined David at the fortress. 18 When David came forward to meet them, he responded by saying to them, "If you have come to me with peaceful intent, °to help me,° I am eager for an alliance with you, but if you have come to betray me to my enemies though my hands have done no wrong, may the God of our fathers look upon it and condemn you." 19 Then a spirit clothed Amasai the chief of the thirty:

O David we*d* are yours,   *e*with you,*e* O son of Jesse
Success, success to you;   *e*success*e* to your helper
For your God has helped you . . . .

So David accepted them and placed them under the chiefs of the troop. 20 Some from Manasseh also defected to David when he was to go to battle with the Philistines against Saul, though *f*he did not actually help*f* them because the Philistine tyrants had sent him away on purpose, saying, "By our heads, he will defect to his master Saul." 21 When he went to Ziklag there defected to him from Manasseh Adnah, Jozabad, Jediael, Michael, Jozabad, Elihu, and Zillethai, chiefs of the families of Manasseh. 22 They aided David against the marauders, for all of them were men of standing and commanders of the host. 23 At that time people came to David day after day to assist him until the camp became as large as the largest camp.

List of David's forces

24 These are the numbers of the persons with military training who joined David at Hebron to deliver the kingdom of Saul to him in accordance with the word of Yahweh. 25 The sons of Judah who bore shield and spear numbered sixty-eight hundred men with military training. 26 Of the sons of Simeon, men of standing for the army, there were seventy-one hundred men. 27 Of the Levites there were forty-six hundred men, 28 and in addition the thirty-seven hundred with Jehoiada the Aaronite 29 and Zadok, a young man of standing, and his family with

o-o Omitted by LXX.
d Insert "we" with Vulg.
e-e Omitting the conjunctions of MT.
f-f Singular with LXX*AL*.

twenty-two commanders. 30 Of the Benjaminites, the brothers of Saul, the greater part of whom had maintained their allegiance to the house of Saul until now, there were three thousand. 31 Of the Ephraimites there were twenty thousand eight hundred men of standing, men of renown in the families. 32 Of the half-tribe of Manasseh there were eighteen thousand who had been designated by name to come to make David king. 33 Of the sons of Issachar who understood the times and recognized what Israel ought to do, there were their two hundred chiefs together with all their brothers under their direction. 34 Of Zebulun there were fifty thousand men, capable and prepared for battle, with all kinds of weapons for war to assist[g] David with undivided heart. 35 Of Naphtali there were a thousand commanders together with thirty-seven thousand men with shield and spear. 36 Of the Danites there were twenty-eight thousand six hundred men prepared for war. 37 Of Asher there were forty thousand men capable and prepared for war. 38 Of those on the other side of the Jordan, of the Reubenites, the Gadites, and the half-tribe of Manasseh there were one hundred twenty thousand men equipped with all kinds of weapons for war. 39 All these were warriors in battle array who came to David at Hebron with singleness of purpose, to make David king over all Israel; also all the rest of Israel was unanimous in wanting to make David king. 40 They remained there with David for three days eating and drinking, for their brothers had prepared for them. 41 Their neighbors too, from as far as Issachar, Zebulun, and Naphtali brought food on asses, camels, mules, and oxen—supplies of flour, fig cakes, raisins, wine, oil, cattle, and sheep in quantity— for joy prevailed in Israel.

[g] So in place of Heb. "to flock together"; with LXX, Vulg. An Aramaic form.

NOTES

xii 1. *while . . . Kish.* Rudolph suggests reading "while he was still excluded from Israel on account of Saul the son of Qish"; the "from Israel" has fallen out because of its similarity, in Hebrew, to "from before Saul." Cf. I Sam xxvii 1.

the mighty men, the warriors. On the translation see Gordon, IEJ 5 (1955), 88. Also J. Gray, *The Legacy of Canaan,* 1957, p. 34, n. 10.

20. *"By our heads".* An oath formula. See V. Rogers, JBL 74 (1955), 272.

21. *chiefs of the families.* So for thousands. See Mendenhall, JBL 77 (1958), 52–66.

23. See VT 3 (1953), 213 ff.

the largest camp. Literally "camp of God." Behind the expression could possibly be the idea of the heavenly host.

24. *the persons.* For the use of *rōš* as "person" or "each one," see Judg v 30; I Sam xxviii 2.

35. *a thousand commanders.* Mendenhall (JBL 77 [1958], 62, n. 51) suggests an original reading, "officers of thousands" followed by the number 37.

COMMENT

Chapter xii falls naturally into two parts, vss. 1–23 and 24–41. The first part is apparently an insert dealing with the pre-Hebron period of David which should logically follow xi 9. The whole of chapter xi is concerned with the glorification of David during and after the assumption of power as king of all Israel, while the Ziklag and outlaw periods are brought in here. Obviously two periods are involved as is indicated by the references to Ziklag in vs. 1 and to the "fortress" in vss. 9 and 17. Whether the whole chapter is a unit or composed of smaller segments is not quite clear. Rudolph, p. 103 ff., thinks there are independent pieces held together by the general theme of Davidic helpers. Rothstein holds the opposing view, i.e., that it is all one piece (Rothstein and Hänel, pp. 227 f.). But most recent commentators regard the list as old and coming from sources not otherwise utilized (Rudolph, p. 105; Welch, *The Work of the Chronicler,* pp. 14 f.; Rothstein and Hänel, p. 244; Goettsberger, p. 107).

Noth (ÜS, pp. 115 f.) believes that vss. 24–41 are a secondary addition and vss. 1–23 a still later insertion because they do not fit into the Chronicler's scheme, which was to treat the kingdom of David and not its antecedents. But while, from our point of view, vss. 24–41 drawn from a census list represent a later attempt to draw out and complete the early notices in chapter xi, and vss. 1–23 found a place in the work of the Chronicler still later does not ipso

facto make them pure postexilic fabrications. Both portions throw
welcome light on the way David's followers joined themselves to his
efforts and rendered his accession to power possible. The writer's
conception of the whole process with its consummation is clearly
expressed in the words of Amasai—"For your God has helped you."

[Followers from Benjamin, xii 1–8]: The twenty-three men from
Benjamin who joined David at Ziklag are probably placed first
because of the special honor their support bestowed upon David
since they defected from Saul, who was a Benjaminite. Moreover
they were valued men by virtue of their skill in warfare and made
up in that way what they lacked in numbers. They are associated
with eight localities in Benjamin. Two of them came from Gibeah
itself, the center of Saul's kingdom, *tell el-ful*. Azmaveth is both a
personal and place name (see Albright, AASOR 4 [1924], 157);
Hizmeh is about six miles northeast of Jerusalem. Anathoth, *Ras
el-Karrubeh,* is about three miles east-northeast of Jerusalem;
Gibeon, *el-Jib,* is some eight miles north of Jerusalem; Gederah is
probably *Jedireh* near Gibeon; Gedor, Haruph, and Korah (if a
place name) are unknown. Since this is a Benjaminite list Korah
here has nothing to do with the Levitical Korah, nor with the
Calebite Korah in ii 43. Ishmaiah is referred to here as "over the
thirty," a place attributed to Abishai in xi 20 and Amasa in xii 19;
but since the list doubtless shifted from time to time, the change in
command need cause no difficulty (cf. Elliger, PJB 31 [1935], 67 ff.
and 74 f.) and reflects another stage in their history. The name
Jashobeam occurs also in xi 11 and xxvii 2, but whether the same
person is involved is a question.

[Followers from Gad, 9–16]: Before taking refuge with the
Philistines, with Ziklag as his center of operations (I Sam xxvii 6 f.),
David hid from Saul in the wilderness (I Sam xxiii 14, xxiv 1, xxv 1,
xxvi 1). It was during that period that the men of Gad "defected to
David." It has been assumed that the most appropriate time for
this episode was when David roamed the hills around Engedi (I Sam
xxiv 1), since it would have been most convenient for contact with
him there. In any case, the eleven men were extraordinary warriors
who were adept at hand-to-hand combat, fierce looking, and "nimble
as gazelles." They were of such high quality that they became leaders
who could hold off a multitude of opponents. Especially stressed is
their exploit of crossing the Jordan at flood stage in the spring of
the year. The author, by calling attention to the peculiar qualities of

those who joined David, seems to have as his main purpose the enhancement of his hero's reputation—the best and most capable men became his followers because they recognized in him the chosen vessel of Yahweh.

[Followers from Benjamin and Judah, 17–19]: Since only one person is named, the offer of those from Judah and Benjamin was in all probability recalled because of the declaration of Amasai (vs. 19). That the occurrence must be placed in "the fortress period" is shown not only by that specification but by the suspicion aroused in the mind of the outlaw chief. It may be attention is here directed to lesser individuals or families who sought to join the growing ranks of David; the suspicion of the future king would naturally be aroused because he was betrayed on three previous occasions—by Doeg the Edomite (I Sam xxi, xxii), by the people of Keilah (I Sam xxiii), and by the Ziphites (I Sam xxvi). The inspired reply of Amasai reassured David but he placed the men of Benjamin and Judah under the heads of his troops. "A spirit clothed Amasai" is a most significant conception of inspiration and revelation in the Old Testament (cf. Judg vi 34; II Chron xxiv 20; Job xxix 14) and may be a forerunner of the idea of incarnation. If "we" is inserted in the first line of the poem (with Vulg.) there is a regular 3+2, 3+2, 3, the last colon of the third line having dropped out. Rudolph, p. 107, thinks it is 3+2+3+2+2 forming a stanza of five half-lines as in Song of Solomon. It is a powerful confession of faith in David as the chosen of Yahweh.

[Followers from Manasseh, 20–23]: The defection of the seven chiefs from Manasseh occurred just before the battle of Gilboa when David was sent away by the Philistines because the other tyrants mistrusted him, though Achish did not (cf. I Sam xxix). Apparently David and his host had accompanied them to the rendezvous of the opponents of Israel, for we read that he was sent back. Thus he would have been in the territory of Manasseh, where it was possible for these men to have come in contact with him. From Samuel we learn that David made good use of his position to consolidate his authority over the area around Ziklag and secure provisions for his followers (I Sam xxx). In this the Manassites assisted him. His leadership, genius, and far-reaching vision won over many of the dissidents so that his forces grew by leaps and bounds.

[List of units supporting the kingship of David at Hebron, 24–41]: Here the writer catalogues those units that came to David at

Hebron to proclaim him king and so the list is a further expansion of xi 1. Mendenhall's study (JBL 77 [1958], 52–66) of the census lists points toward a solution of the vexing problem of the large numbers for military units. He thinks the word *eleph* stands for tribe, part of a tribe, or a unit, and is based on social structure. His theory would necessitate a radical retranslation of the whole passage somewhat as follows:

25 The sons of Judah who bore shield and spear numbered six units with eight hundred men with military training.

26 Of the sons of Simeon, men of standing for the army there were seven units with one hundred men,

27 Of the Levites there were four units with six hundred men,

28 And in addition the three units with seven hundred men with Jehoiada the Aaronite

29 and Zadok, a young man of standing, and his family with twenty-two commanders.

30 Of the Benjaminites, the brothers of Saul, the greatest part of whom had maintained their allegiance to the house of Saul until now, there were three units.

31 Of the Ephraimites there were twenty units with eight hundred men of standing, men of renown in their families.

32 Of the half-tribe of Manasseh there were eighteen units who had been designated by name to come to make David king.

33 Of the sons of Issachar who understood the times and recognized what Israel ought to do, there were their two hundred chiefs and all their brothers under their direction.

34 Of Zebulun there were fifty units, capable and prepared for battle, with all kinds of weapons for war, to assist David with undivided heart.

35 Of Naphtali there were officers of thousands to the number of thirty-seven, with shield and spear.

36 Of the Danites there were twenty-eight units with six hundred men prepared for war.

37 Of Asher there were forty units, capable and prepared for war.

38 Of those on the other side of the Jordan, of the Reubenites, the Gadites and the half-tribe of Manasseh, there were one hundred and twenty units equipped with all kinds of weapons for war.

The ratio between units and numbers is unsatisfactory but the plan does offer a workable basis for a realistic view of the otherwise astronomical figures. The numbers are missing in some cases, though the units are specified.

The best indication of the age of the lists is that the term *eleph* was no longer understood by later writers. An interesting point which tends to confirm that view here is vs. 33, which mentions only the two hundred chiefs with no specified number of their troops. If that scheme is followed, units are specified for all of the tribes (the Transjordan ones together) except for Issachar where the two hundred heads are listed, and actual numbers of men only for four tribes (Simeon, Judah, Ephraim, Dan), while those for the others remain unspecified. But since the crowning of David was not a military operation, such designation was not deemed essential as in the lists of Numbers i, xxvi. That fact is emphasized by the inclusion of the Levites and priests. However one may interpret the numbers, the writer was careful to include all the tribes and religious officials in his list of those who came to make David king over Israel. He was at pains to stress those elements which subsequently constituted the Northern Kingdom. The coronation was an occasion for a great feast, probably including religious ceremonies because it was "in accordance with the word of Yahweh." That may be a reason for the presence of Levites and priests in the list, doubtless an insertion by the author and not part of the original one. Who Jehoiada was is unknown at present.

14. THE FIRST ATTEMPT TO MOVE THE ARK
(xiii 1–14)†

XIII 1 David took counsel with the commanders of the thousands and the hundreds; in fact with every chief. 2 Then David said to the whole convocation of Israel, "If it appears right to you and if Yahweh our God is agreed, let us issue an order and invite our brothers who remain in all the regions of Israel together with their brothers, the priests and the Levites, in cities with their pasture ground to assemble to us, 3 and let us restore for ourselves the ark of our God to which we paid no attention in the days of Saul." 4 The whole convocation of Israel consented to do so because the matter appeared right in the sight of all the people. 5 So David summoned all Israel from the river of Egypt to the entrance of Hamath to bring the ark of God from Kiriath-jearim. 6 Then David and all Israel went up to Baalath, to Kiriath-jearim, of Judah to bring up from there the ark of God, whose legend reads: "Yahweh who is enthroned above the cherubs." 7 They transported the ark of God from the house of Abinadab on a new cart and Uzza and Ahio*ᵃ* drove the cart. 8 David and all Israel danced before God with all their might, to the accompaniment of songs, zithers, harps, tambourines, cymbals, and trumpets. 9 When they came to the threshing floor of Chidon*ᵇ*, Uzza put out his hand to keep the ark steady because the oxen nearly upset it. 10 The anger of Yahweh flared up against Uzza so that he struck him down because he put out his hand upon the ark; and he died right there

† I Chron xiii 1–14 ‖ II Sam vi 2–11.

ᵃ Could be vocalized also as "his brother" or "his brothers." (Cf. LXX and Vulg.)
ᵇ II Sam vi 6 has "Nacon." Vulg. and Josephus have "Chidon" but some Greek manuscripts have *cheilo, cheidon,* etc. Cf. A. W. Marget, JBL 39 (1920), 70–76.

before God. 11 David became angry because Yahweh had rent asunder Uzza and that place is called Perez-uzza until this day. 12 David was afraid of God that day and said, "How can I bring the ark of God to me?" 13 But David did not remove the ark to himself in the city of David; he had it put in the house of Obed-edom the Gittite. 14 The ark of God remained for three months with° Obed-edom, in his house, and Yahweh blessed the house of Obed-edom and all that he had.

° Omitting *byt*, "house" with Targ. LXX reads "in the house of" Obededom.

NOTES

xiii 5. *river*. Egyptian word meaning pond or pool of Horus, Si-hor. Found only in Josh xiii 3; Isa xxiii 3; Jer ii 18 and here. See A. Erman and H. Grapow, *Wörterbuch der ägyptischen Sprache*, IV, 1930, p. 397.

6. See AASOR 5 (1925), 106.

8. On musical instruments see C. Sachs, *The History of Musical Instruments*, 1940, Ch. 5; O. R. Sellers, "Musical Instruments of Israel," BA 4 (1941), 33–47; M. Wegner, *Die Musikinstrumente des alten Orients*, 1950, pp. 38 ff.; Galling, BRL, cols. 389 ff.

11. *Perez-uzza*. I.e., the rending asunder of Uzza.

12. *to me?*. As the Fr. *chez moi* "to my house, to myself, to my dwelling place."

COMMENT

The story of the adventures of the ark is very complex (see N. H. Tur-Sinai, "The Ark of God at Beit Shemesh," VT 1 [1951], 275–86). It was taken by the Philistines in the battle of Ebenezer (I Sam v) and caused them no end of trouble. So they resolved to send it back to Israel with a guilt offering (I Sam vi 1–9). When it arrived at Beth-shemesh, the men there "looked into it" and in consequence suffered death (I Sam vi 10–20). Messengers were dispatched to Kiriath-jearim requesting the people of that town to take it away, which they did (I Sam vi 21–vii 1). There it was placed in the house of Abinadab where it remained for a long time, in fact until the time of David as related in this chapter and its parallel in II Sam vi. Thus during the lifetime of Saul it remained in obscurity, from which David rescued it. The implication is clear that the reason for Saul's misfortune was due to the neglect of the sacred symbol of the presence of Yahweh. On the significance of the Ark, cf. de Vaux, *Les Institutions de l'Ancien Testament,* II, pp. 127–33.

The most striking feature of the story is that the attempted removal of the ark to the place where David was (vs. 12) was a religious matter and not a semimilitary ceremony as in Samuel. While the officials were consulted, it was "the whole convocation of Israel," together with the priests and Levites, that was directly involved. Moreover, Yahweh was invoked too. Because it seemed right in the sight of all, the venture was made so as to remedy the defect in Saul's attitude toward the ark. Ostensibly this had to be the first move of the new king to prevent the same debacle befalling him as had befallen Saul. That is why the passage stands before the Philistine raids here whereas it follows them in Samuel. It must be remembered that the Chronicler's story is primarily religious and he arranges his material accordingly. That he idealized frequently is thus understandable. The reference to "our brothers who remain in all the regions of Israel" and the summoning of "all Israel from the river of Egypt to the entrance at Hamath" could not have applied before the capitulation of the remnants of Saul's kingdom, as the Samuel order has it.

While the intention of David and Israel was commendable, the method chosen for the removal of the ark from the house of Abinadab was not. Perhaps the story was related, in part, to call attention to the misfortune attendant upon the failure to act in accordance with the commandments of God (cf. xv 13). The catastrophe that overtook Uzza was thus due to the violation of some kind of taboo to which the ark was subject. And however noble the motive of Uzza, the sanctity of the sacred symbol of Yahweh's presence could not be taken lightly. The Chronicler wanted to show that Uzza and Ahio were not "legally" qualified to handle it.

Kiriath-jearim (city of forests), present-day Tell el-Azhar about eight miles west of Jerusalem, was part of the Gibeonite tetrapolis (Josh ix 17) and located on the Judahite-Benjaminite border (Josh xviii 15). In Josh xviii 14 it is called Kiriath-baal and in xv 9 Baalah, as in vs. 6 (Baalath). In II Sam vi 2 it is referred to as Baale-judah. It was the home of Uriah, the prophet (Jer xxvi 20) and figured in postexilic history (Neh vii 29). Of Chidon and Perez-uzza nothing is known beyond the passage here and II Sam vi. Nearby was

the house of Obed-edom the Gittite (which indicates that he came
from Gath), in which the ark was placed. Kugler (*Von Moses bis
Paulus*, p. 263) suggests Gath-rimmon mentioned in Josh xix 45, xxi
24 and I Chron vi 69 may be a Danite Levitical city. Josephus
(*Antiquities* VII.iv) makes Obed-edom a Levite, in which case he
could be associated with the man of the same name in ch. xv who was
one of the gatekeepers for the ark. Josephus obviously did so, perhaps
also on the grounds of the blessing Obed-edom received undoubtedly
because the proper care of the ark was given by a proper person.
David was disappointd by the unexpected turn of events and so the
ark remained with Obed-edom for three months, that is, probably
until he saw the results of the right handling of the palladium.

15. HIRAM'S MISSION. THE PHILISTINE WARS
(xiv 1–17)†

The activity of David at Jerusalem

XIV 1 Meanwhile Hiram king of Tyre sent representatives to David, together with cedar lumber, masons, and carpenters to build a house for him. 2 So David realized that Yahweh had confirmed him as king over Israel because his kingdom was so highly exalted for the sake of his people Israel. 3 David also married more wives at Jerusalem and fathered more sons and daughters. 4 These are the names of the children born to him at Jerusalem: Shammua, Shobab, Nathan, Solomon, 5 Ibhar, Elishua, Elpelet, 6 Nogah, Nepheg, Japhia, 7 Elishama, Beeliada, and Eliphelet.

The Philistine wars

8 When the Philistines heard that David had been anointed king over all Israel, all the Philistines came up to seize David. When David heard about it, he marched out in their direction. 9 Meanwhile the Philistines had come and engaged in plundering in the valley of Rephaim. 10 Then David consulted God, saying, "Shall I attack the Philistines and will you deliver them into my hand?" Yahweh said to him, "Attack, for I will deliver them into your hands." 11 So David attacked at Baal-perazim where he vanquished them. David said, "God has broken through my enemies by my hand as water breaks through [a dam]." Therefore they called the name of that place Baal-perazim. 12 When they abandoned their gods there, David ordered that they be burned in the fire. 13 Then the Philistines engaged again in plundering in the valley. 14 So David consulted God again. God said to him, "Do not attack them directly, but

† I Chron xiv 1–7 ‖ II Sam v 11–16; 8–17 ‖ II Sam v 17–25.

turn away from them and come at them in front of the Baka-bushes; 15 and when you hear the sound of steps in the tops of the Baka-bushes, then proceed to battle for God has gone out before you to destroy the Philistine army." 16 David did as God had commanded him and vanquished[a] the Philistine army from Gibeon[b] to Gezer. 17 Then David's fame spread to all countries and Yahweh made all nations fear him.

[a] Singular with LXX. Subject is David.
[b] II Sam v 25 has "Geba," but cf. LXX.

NOTES

xiv 8. *he marched out in their direction.* Cf. II Sam v 17 which has the enigmatic "he went down to the fortress." On the problem involved see Noth, *The History of Israel,* p. 187, n. 2; Alt, KS, II, p. 48, n. 3. If the Samuel text is in order, the Philistines attacked before the capture of Jerusalem or before David had time to fortify it. He was crowned king of Israel before the end of the Hebron period (II Sam ii 8 ff.). Ishbaal ruled for only two years and David reigned over Judah (and Israel for part of the time) for seven and a half years. That would appear to indicate he was king of all Israel for at least five years during his residence at Hebron and before coming to Jerusalem.

9. *plundering.* II Sam v 18 has "spread themselves out." The verb *pāšaṭ* could be influenced by Aramaic meaning to "stretch out," "spread out," though it is doubtless better to retain the Hebrew meaning "plundering, making a raid." Cf. Akk. *pašāṭu* "to destroy, wipe out."

11. *David . . . he.* Reversing the noun and pronoun for the sake of the English.

COMMENT

Here the Chronicler backtracks on his sources. II Sam vi 1–11 tells the story of the attempted transfer of the ark to Jerusalem which the Chronicler took up in ch. xiii for his own purpose as explained above. Both II Sam vi 11 and I Chron xiii 14 speak of a three months' interval between the first and second attempt. Now he reverts to II Sam v, as if to suggest that this is what went on during that period. But on closer inspection of the material itself it is obvious that that was not his purpose. It was rather to show further how

Yahweh was with David in his undertakings as shown by the progress on his building enterprises, the expansion of his family and his defeat of the Philistines, and so partially offsets the disconcerting failure to deal with the ark.

[Hiram's mission, xiv 1–2]: If current synchronisms are correct cf. W. F. Albright, "The New Assyro-Tyrian Synchronism and the Chronology of Tyre," *Mélanges Isidore Lévy,* 1955, pp. 1–9; Hiram reigned ca. 969–936 B.C.), Hiram's reign over Tyre began in the last decade of David's rule over Israel which means that II Sam v is chronologically almost as far out of place as the Chronicler's, since he too places it at the beginning of the reign of David. In any case, it is difficult to see how all of his building activity could have taken place at the early stages of his reign when he was occupied with wars on many sides. Hiram's friendship for David was the basis for the continuance of his relationship with Israel after the latter's death.

David was led to the realization that Yahweh had chosen him "for the sake of his people Israel"—an excellent illustration of the blessing of Yahweh—by his success within the kingdom and the support of the Tyrian king. This backing from Hiram could not have come before substantial progress had been made in the political aspects of the empire (Bright, *A History of Israel,* p. 183). It is not impossible that David had entered into some kind of relationship with Hiram's father Abibaal which was renegotiated with Hiram and continued into the reign of Solomon, but that cannot be proved at present. It is preferable to regard this situation as falling late in David's reign, after his various conquests, particularly after his subjugation of the Philistines, who were also Hiram's enemies, and of the Aramaean states which may have opened new trade possibilities.

[David's family expansion at Jerusalem, 3–7]: This passage also presupposes a lengthy occupation of Jerusalem, though of course considering his "many wives" the sons could have been born relatively close together. However, Solomon is listed among them and he was born during or shortly after the Ammonite campaign (II Sam xii 24). It is interesting to note that the list of thirteen sons follows substantially that of ch. iii and deviates somewhat from that in II Sam v 14–16. The situation is clear from the following lists:

II Sam v 14–16	I Chron xiv 4–7	I Chron iii 5–8
Shammua	Shammua	Shimea
Shobab	Shobab	Shobab
Nathan	Nathan	Nathan
Solomon	Solomon	Solomon
Ibhar	Ibhar	Ibhar
Elishua	Elishua	Elishama
	Elpelet	Eliphelet
	Nogah	Nogah
Nepheg	Nepheg	Nepheg
Japhia	Japhia	Japhia
Elishama	Elishama	Elishama
Eliada	Beeliada	Eliada
Eliphelet	Eliphelet	Eliphelet

The author of this chapter copied the list of II Samuel, inserted the two extra names from that in chapter iii and doubtless gave the original name of Eliada (Beeliada). Family growth was important for his purpose, to show the blessing of Yahweh upon his hero.

[The Philistine wars, 8–17]: The writer makes a point of the Philistine attack coming after they learned that David had been made king "over all Israel," a favorite expression of the Chronicler. The place they struck was in the valley of Rephaim, southwest of Jerusalem on the old boundary between Judah and Benjamin (Josh xv 8; cf. *Sepher Yerushalayim*, I, Map 5 between pp. 40–41 and Pl. 2 following p. 32. For another view see L. H. Grollenberg, *Atlas of the Bible*, 1956, Map 24A). The place of attack was at Baal-perazim somewhere in the valley of Rephaim near Jerusalem and which received its name from the event (vs. 11). The defeat of the enemy caused such consternation that they left their gods behind as they fled. David consigned them to the fire. The second attack apparently followed as soon as they recovered; this time they suffered a worse defeat, for David pursued them into their own country, clearing them out "from Gibeon to Gezer." The effect of David's conquest of the Philistines had repercussions and it may be that the Chronicler is right in his observation that "his fame spread to all countries." On the other hand, it may be just another of the writer's efforts to glorify David.

16. DAVID'S PLAN FOR A SECOND ATTEMPT TO MOVE THE ARK TO JERUSALEM
(xv 1–24)

Preparations for the bringing of the ark to Jerusalem

XV 1 After he had constructed houses for himself in the city of David, he arranged for a place for the ark of God and set up a tent for it. 2 Then David said "No one but the Levites must carry the ark of God because Yahweh has chosen them to carry the ark of Yahweh and to minister to him forever." 3 David convened all Israel at Jerusalem to transport the ark of Yahweh to its place which he had arranged for it. 4 David also summoned the sons of Aaron and the Levites. 5 Of the sons of Kehath there was Uriel the chief together with his one hundred twenty brothers. 6 Of the sons of Merari there was Asaiah the chief together with his two hundred twenty brothers. 7 Of the sons of Gershom there was Joel the chief together with his one hundred thirty brothers. 8 Of the sons of Elizaphan there was Shemaiah the chief together with his two hundred brothers. 9 Of the sons of Hebron there was Eliel the chief together with his eighty brothers. 10 Of the sons of Uzziel there was Amminadab the chief together with his one hundred twelve brothers. 11 So David called Zadok and Abiathar the priests and of the Levites, Uriel, Asaiah, Joel, Shemaiah, Eliel, and Amminadab, 12 and said to them, "You are the chiefs of the Levitical families: sanctify yourselves, you and your brothers that you may transfer the ark of Yahweh God of Israel to the place*a* that I have arranged for it. 13 In as much as you were not present with us the first time, Yahweh our God thwarted us because we did not handle it properly." 14 Then the priests and Levites sanctified themselves to transfer the ark of Yahweh God of Israel. 15 The

---

a So with several manuscripts, Vulg. and Targ. Others read "tent," which may be correct but more likely is based on xvi 1.

Levites carried the ark of God on their shoulders with the carrying poles, as Moses, in accordance with the word of Yahweh,
had commanded. 16 David also requested the Levitical chiefs
to appoint their brothers as singers to lift up their voices in joy-
ful acclaim, accompanied by musical instruments, harps, zithers, and cymbals. 17 So the Levites appointed Heman the son
of Joel and from his brothers Asaph, the son of Berechiah, from
the sons of Merari their brothers, Ethan the son of Kushaiah[b],
18 and with them their brothers who were second in rank:
Zechariah,[c] Jaaziel[d], Shemiramoth, Jehiel, Unni, Eliab, Benaiah,
Maaseiah, Mattithiah, Eliphelehu, Mikneiah, and Obed-edom
and Jeiel the porters. 19 The singers were Heman, Asaph, and
Ethan [each] with two brass cymbals for making music. 20 But
Zechariah, Aziel, Shemiramoth, Jehiel, Unni, Eliab, Maaseiah,
and Benaiah had harps to play according to Alamoth. 21 Mattithiah, Eliphelehu, Mikneiah, Obed-edom, Jeiel, and Azaziah
had zithers to lead according to Sheminith. 22 Chenaniah[e], the
Levitical chief of music, was music director because he was
skilled in music. 23 Berechiah and Elkanah were porters for the
ark. 24 Shebaniah, Joshaphat, Nethanel, Amasai, Zechariah,
Benaiah, and Eliezer the priests blew the trumpets before the
ark of God, while Obed-edom and Jehiah also were gatekeepers
for the ark.

[b] Ch. vi 44 reads "Kishi" (LXX "Qushi"); cf. H. Bauer, ZAW 48 (1930),
74, n. 4, and p. 79.
[c] Omitting "son," before "and Jaaziel" in MT, with some manuscripts and
LXX.
[d] LXX[B] has "Uzziel."
[e] LXX[BA] have "Koneniah."

NOTES

xv 13. *the first time.* So in accordance with context and with slightly
different pointing.

16. *harps, zithers, and cymbals.* For a description of the musical instruments see Sachs, *The History of Musical Instruments,* Ch. 5; Sellers,
BA 4 (1941), 33–47.

20. *Alamoth.* Uncertain term; also in title of Ps xlvi. Sometimes interpreted as soprano. See H. Gunkel and J. Begrich, *Einleitung in die*

Psalmen, 1933, pp. 456 f.; S. Mowinckel, *Psalmenstudien*, IV, 1923, pp. 35 f., who thinks it refers to a cultic occasion in which harps are used.

21. *Sheminith.* Also uncertain. Term appears in title of Pss vi, xii. Usually interpreted as having something to do with the octave, the bass in contrast to soprano above. Cf. Gunkel and Begrich, *op. cit.*, p. 457; Mowinckel, *loc. cit.*—a cult occasion in which zithers are used.

22. Could be rendered: "Chenaniah, the Levitical chief of transport was transportation director because he was skilled in it." Perhaps the word *maśśā'* ("music leader" or "transport") was chosen intentionally to show that Chenaniah was regarded the leader (starter) of the whole ceremony. Cf. von Rad, *Das Geschichtsbild . . . ,* p. 110.

COMMENT

It has been pointed out (Noth, *US*, p. 116) that chapter xv contains two insertions in line with the more specific cultic interests of the period of Chronicles. They are (a) vss. 4–10 with their details on the family and number of the participants in the ceremony of removing the ark to Jerusalem; and (b) vss. 16–24 which have to do with ceremonial directions dealing with music and transport, together with those appointed for those responsibilities. The literary aspects of the chapter are easily apparent when it is compared with its parallel in II Sam vi 12–20. There are variants in the basic materials, but they are not momentous; they only have to do with certain aspects that were manifestly obnoxious to the Chronicler.

[David's plan for another attempt to move the ark to Jerusalem, xv 1–3]: According to II Sam vi 17 the simple fact is that the ark was placed in "the tent" that David had set up for it. Here there is emphasis upon special preparation of "the tent" as "a place arranged for the ark of God," which followed upon the construction of "houses for himself in the city of David." This presupposes a lengthy interval between the first and second attempts to bring the ark to Jerusalem, far beyond the three months during which it is said to have remained in the house of Obed-edom (II Sam vi 11; I Chron xiii 14). The observation here may be due to the writer's accentuation of proper preparation and care in both transportation and reception for it. Or it could be a reflection of the preparation for the temple that was to become the permanent resting place of the ark (I Chron xvii 1; II Sam vii 2). While chapter xiii speaks of the blessing that came to Obed-edom by virtue of the presence of the ark, nothing is said about it here (but cf. II Sam vi 12 which infers that because of it, David decided the danger was past and determined to bring it to Jerusalem at once). Meticulous care must be taken that the proper personnel alone should "carry the ark of God" as the law of Moses required (cf. Deut x 8; Exod xxv 13–14, xxxvii 4–5); it must not be handled improperly as chapter xiii suggests was done. It was solely David's decision and not the suggestion of others.

[The list of priests and Levites summoned to assist in the ceremony, 4–10]: This later addition is intended to supply specific information on priestly and Levitical participation; it is a commentary on vs. 11 and probably owes its position to the statement in vs. 3 to the effect that David convened all Israel at Jerusalem to help him carry out his plan, which could not be done without the religious officials. Furthermore it specifies the family connections of the Levites mentioned in vs. 11 together with their numbers. In addition to the three regular branches of the Levites—Kehath, Merari, and Gershom—three others are added—Elizaphan, Hebron, and Uzziel—who must have attained sufficient numbers or prestige to gain independent status. The three latter ones were originally offshoots of the Kehathite family (Elizaphan, a grandson [Exod vi 22; Lev x 4], Hebron and Uzziel, sons [I Chron vi 18]).

[Summons to the religious leaders, 11–15]: Despite his special interest in the Levites and their functions, the Chronicler specifically includes the priests and names them first, though the summons to preparation for the event appears to be directed chiefly to the Levites. They were to sanctify themselves and their families and, in effect, take charge of the transfer. They were reminded of what happened in the course of the first attempt because the ark was improperly handled. There was ready response by both groups but the Levites assumed their function in accordance with the command of Moses. How different from the simple events recorded in II Sam vi 12! There is no indication that the Levites bore the ark, though an elaborate ceremony of sacrifice is mentioned (vss. 25–29, xvi 1–3). Here David acts through the proper ecclesiastical officials.

[Provision for musicians and other helpers, 16–24]: That David was an originator of musical guilds and services in connection with worship at Jerusalem is pretty well established in the tradition (cf. Albright, ARI, pp. 125 f.). This passage is, however, a secondary addition which connects the appointing of musicians with the transfer of the ark, while xvi 4 ff. has the appointments taking place only after the ark had been moved to Jerusalem. It simply accentuates the tradition by pushing it backward to the first great religious ceremony connected with the establishment of the new capital. The musicians were of two kinds: vocalists and instrumentalists, both being connected with the Levites. The instrumentalists included those who played cymbals, harps, and zithers. The priests were the trumpeters. The three Levitical families were represented—Heman from the Kehathites, Asaph from the Gershunnites, and Ethan from the Merarites. In addition there were thirteen others of second rank (LXX has fourteen, adding the name of Azaziah, probably from vs. 21), two of whom function in the dual capacity of porters and musicians. Ethan appears as a singer only in I Chron vi 44 and xv 17, his place being taken by Jeduthun (cf. xvi 41, 42). Certain classes of singers were obviously not Levites (cf. II Chron xxxv 25; Ezra ii 65b) but whether one can go as far as Rudolph (p. 121) and say that the cult musicians in the time of David were not Levites and that the Chronicler was the first to regard them as such is a question. Ezra ii 41 specifically makes the singers sons of Asaph, who is reckoned as a Levite in Chronicles. Heman and Ethan are also referred to as wise men (I Kings iv 31; I Chron ii 6) and hence were of a select group. There is no reason, therefore, to suspect the Chronicler of fabrication, for Levites were just such a group in the widest meaning of the term (cf. ARI, pp. 109 f.). To be summoned by the king for service in connection with the cult was enough to bring them under such classification and it is at least questionable whether we can say that the singers were first brought together with the Levites in Neh xi 17, xii 24. The schematic arrangement may be later, but the over-all tradition seems to be authentic (cf. Möhlenbrink, ZAW 52 [1934], 184–231, especially 202–3 and 229–30).

The procession was composed of four groups of musicians of Levitical and priestly rank: the cymbalists, those who played the harps and zithers, and the priests who blew the trumpets. Besides there were four porters and a director (of music or transport), together with David and the other officials. The word for trumpets (ḥaṣoṣeroth) is used almost entirely in connection with sacred matters; only twice pertaining to the secular (Hos v 8; II Kings xi 14). It occurs in late writings particularly (Numbers, II Kings, Chronicles, Ezra, Nehemiah, and Psalms) but doubtless reflects earlier practices. On the basis of Num x 1 ff., Josephus (*Antiquities*

III.xii) says Moses invented silver trumpets. But there also are Egyptian representations of them: Cf. *Medinet Habu Reports,* OIC 10 (1931), 30 f. and Fig. 19, which depicts the siege of Tunip in Syria by Ramses III (1198–1167 B.C.), a detail of which shows a trumpeter sounding the trumpet of victory from the walls of the city. There is another from the reign of Amenhotep IV (1387–1366 B.C.)—see *Views of the Biblical World,* eds. M. Avi-Yonah and others, I (Jerusalem, 1959), pp. 206 f. For later reproductions see Sellers, BA 4 (1941), 42 f. and Figs. 10b, c; and for their use cf. 1QM, cols. 3, 7–9, 16 f.

17. SUCCESSFUL REMOVAL OF THE ARK AND PROVISIONS FOR ITS CARE
(xv 25–29, xvi 1–43)†

XV 25 Then David, the elders of Israel, and the commanders of the thousands who went to transport the ark of the covenant of Yahweh from the house of Obed-edom were jubilant and, 26 because God assisted the Levites who carried the ark of the covenant of Yahweh, they slaughtered seven bulls and seven rams for sacrifice. 27 David and all the Levites who carried the ark wore a mantle of byssus as did the singers and Chenaniah the chief director of the singers. David also had on a linen ephod. 28 So all Israel transported the ark of the covenant of Yahweh with shouts of joy accompanying the sounding of the horn, the trumpets and the cymbals, and the music of the harps and zithers. 29 As the ark of the covenant of Yahweh arrived at the city of David, Michal the daughter of Saul looked out through the window and when she saw King David dancing merrily, she felt contempt*a* for him in her heart.

XVI 1 So they brought the ark of God, placed it within the tent which David had set up for it, and offered burnt offerings and peace offerings before God. 2 When David was finished offering the burnt offering and the peace offerings, he blessed the people in the name of Yahweh, 3 and parceled out to all the Israelites, both men and women, to each one a loaf of bread, *b*a piece of meat,*b* and a raisin cake.

† I Chron xv 25–29 ‖ II Sam vi 12–19; I Chron xvi 1–3 ‖ II Sam vi 17–19; 4–43 ‖ Ps cv 1–15, xcvi, cvi 1, 47–48, II Sam vi 19, 20.

a From *būz* rather than *bāzāh*.
b–b Word occurs only here and in its parallel in II Sam vi 19. Meaning is uncertain. LXX of Samuel has "bread baked over a fire"; here simply a product of baking. Targ. "a portion"; Vulg. "part of a roast ox"; Syr. "portion." Koehler (Koehler and Baumgartner, *Lexicon* . . . , *in loco*) thinks it means "date cake," but inasmuch as peace offerings were involved, it is better to render "a portion" (of meat).

The Levitical ministrations

⁴ He commissioned some of the Levites as ministers before the ark of Yahweh to extol, to give thanks to and to praise Yahweh God of Israel. ⁵ Asaph was the chief and next to him were Zechariah, Jeiel, Shemiramoth, Jehiel, Mattithiah, Eliab, Benaiah, Obed-edom and Jeiel who played harps and zithers; Asaph was the cymbalist. ⁶ Benaiah and Jahaziel the priests blew the trumpets continually before the ark of the covenant of God. ⁷ Then David^c for the first time assigned to Asaph and his brothers the giving of thanks to Yahweh.

8   Give thanks to Yahweh,
    Call upon his name,
    Publicize among the peoples his deeds.

9   Sing to him,
    Sing praise to him,
    Proclaim all his wonders.

10 Take pride in his holy name,
    Let those who seek Yahweh be glad.

11 Consider Yahweh and his might,
    Call upon him continually.

12 Remember the wonders which he has performed,
    His miracles^d, and the judgments he has delivered.

13 O seed of Israel, his servant,
    O sons of Jacob, his chosen!

14 Yahweh is our God,
    Everywhere in the earth are his judgments.

15 He remembers^e forever his covenant—
    The word he decreed for a thousand generations—

^c Omitting "on that day," which is in MT, unnecessary when Heb. 'z ("then") follows.
^d So with LXX. Heb. "tokens," "signs."
^e So for Heb. "remember" (imperative plural); required by the context.

16   which he made with Abraham.
       And his oath to Isaac.

17   He confirmed it to Jacob as a statute,
       To Israel as an everlasting covenant,

18   saying,
     "To you I am giving
       The land of Canaan
       As your allotted inheritance,

19   Though you are only a handful,
       Just a few strangers in it."

20   When they wandered about from nation to nation
       And from one kingdom to another people,

21   He did not allow anyone to oppress them,
       And on their behalf he reproved kings.

22   "Do not touch my anointed ones,
       My prophets do not hurt."

23   Let the whole earth sing to Yahweh,
       Proclaim his salvation from day to day!

24   Broadcast his glory among the nations,
       His wonders among all the peoples.

25   For Yahweh is great and abundantly to be praised,
       He is to be revered above all gods.

26   For all the gods of the peoples are idols,
       But Yahweh made the heavens.

27   Splendor and majesty are before him,
       Strength and joy*f* in his place.

28   Give to Yahweh, O families of peoples,
       Give to Yahweh glory and strength;

29   Give to Yahweh the glory belonging to his name,
       Take an offering and come before him;
       Worship Yahweh in holy grandeur!

f Hebrew only here and Neh viii 10; Ps xcvi 6 "splendor."

30 Tremble before him, all the earth!
   Verily the world is fixed, not to be moved.

31 Let the heavens rejoice and the earth be glad,
   Let them say among the nations, "Yahweh is king."

32 Let the sea in its fullness roar,
   Let the country[side] rejoice and all that is in it.

33 Then shall the trees of the forest shout with joy
      before Yahweh,
   When he comes to judge the earth.

34 Give thanks to Yahweh for he is good,
   For his devotion continues forever.

35 Say, "Save us, O God of our salvation,
   Gather us and deliver us from the heathen,
   That we may give thanks to your holy name,
   And glory in your praise."

36 Blessed be Yahweh God of Israel,
   From everlasting to everlasting.

Then all the people said "Amen; praise Yahweh!"

37 So he left Asaph and his brothers there before the ark of
the covenant of Yahweh to minister before the ark continually*g* according to the daily requirements, 38 together with Obed-
edom and his*h* sixty-eight brothers. Obed-edom the son of Jeduthun and Hosah were gatekeepers. 39 But [he ordered] Zadok
the priest and his brothers, the priests, [to remain] before the
tabernacle of Yahweh at the high place at Gibeon 40 to offer
burnt offerings regularly, morning and evening, to Yahweh
upon the altar of burnt offering in accordance with everything
prescribed in the law of Yahweh which he decreed for Israel.
41 With them were Heman, Jeduthun and the rest of those
selected and designated by name to render "Give thanks to
Yahweh for his devotion is everlasting." 42 They also, ʿthat is
Heman and Jeduthunʾ, had trumpets and cymbals to play as

g Cf. 1QM 2:2.
h So with LXX, Vulgate. Heb. "their brothers," which may indicate an omission in the text of the name Jehiah (cf. xv 24).
ʿ⁻ʾ Omitted by LXX^{AB}.

well as instruments for [the accompaniment of] sacred songs. The sons of Jeduthun were in charge of the gates. 43 Then all the people departed each to his home and David returned to salute his household.

NOTES

xv 27. *a mantle*. On meaning of *mkrbl* see C. Rabin, *Orientalia* 32 (1963), 123 f.

a linen ephod. See Exod xxviii 4 ff.; Lev viii 7 where it is the vestment of the high priest.

xvi 7. Rothstein (Rothstein and Hänel, *in loco*) translates: ". . . then at the beginning of [the service] of singing thanks to Yahweh, David committed to Asaph and his brethren [the thanksgiving hymn]." The meaning presumably is that David gave this hymn to inaugurate the service centering about the ark.

13. *seed of Israel*. Ps cv 6 "seed of Abraham."

16. *Isaac*. Sibilant variant in spelling in Ps cv 9 (*yiṣḥaq* for *yiśḥaq*).

18. *To you*. Singular suffix for plural in last stich; so also Ps cv 11.

19. *you*. Ps cv 12 "they."

21. *anyone*. '*iš* for '*ādām* in Ps cv 14.

27. *In his place*. So for sanctuary in Ps xlvi 6.

29. *before him*. Ps xlvi 8 "his courts."

32. *rejoice*. Sibilant variant in spelling in Ps xcvi 12 (*ya'alōṣ* for *ya'alōz*).

35. *God*. Ps cvi 47 "Lord (Yahweh)."

our salvation. Ps cvi 47 "our God."

Gather us and deliver us. Chronicles inserts "save us."

36. *said*. Plural for singular in Ps cvi 48.

praise Yahweh. So for Hallelujah (compound meaning same thing) in Ps cvi 48.

38. *sixty-eight*. xxvi 8 has sixty-two.

Obed-edom. xvi 5 records him among the musicians.

38a. This may be an explanatory note.

39. *high place*. On the significance of the term high place see W. F. Albright, "The High Place in Ancient Palestine," *Volume du Congrès: Strasbourg, 1956*, VTS, iv (Leiden, 1957), pp. 242–58.

43. *to salute his household*. I.e., to his family.

COMMENT

[The moving of the ark to the city of David, xv 25–29, xvi 1–3]:
The main facts of the story are recorded in II Sam vi 12–19. The
author views the transaction under three heads: (a) procession to
the house of Obed-edom, with a description of the sacrifices offered
and the regalia worn by the chief participants (25–27); (b) the
transportation of the ark to Jerusalem with its ceremonial accom-
paniments, the rejoicing of the king and Michal's attitude (28–29);
(c) its deposit in the tent prepared for it, the ceremonial offerings
and popular feast (xvi 1–3).

Along with the Levites and other religious officials who participated in the ceremonies, were the king, "the elders of Israel and
the commanders of the thousands." II Sam vi 15 simply says, "David
and all the house of Israel." Here the emphasis falls on the tribal
(family; on the elders and śārīm see De Vaux, Les Institutions de
l'Ancien Testament, I, pp. 108 ff., 212 f.) and military chiefs who
act in an official capacity. The writer does not follow the story of
II Samuel which says they offered sacrifices every six paces but
apparently thinks of only one sacrifice to Yahweh in thanksgiving
for his assistance of the Levites, who must have trembled for fear
because of what had happened to Uzza before (cf. Num iv 15, 20).
It is probable that a later editor added the last sentence of vs. 27
on the basis of II Sam vi 14 (see Rudolph, p. 119), though it ought
to be noted that our text has "David had on a linen ephod," while
the former text has "David was girded with a linen ephod." The
wearing of the ephod was restricted to the high priest in the Chronicler's day (Exod xxviii 4 ff.) and so he has the king clothed in
ordinary priestly vestments of linen.

When things went well the ceremony proceeded in glad acclaim
to the accompaniment of the musical instruments. David's emotional
display is toned down somewhat. Michal's reaction is repeated because it portrays the different attitudes toward the ark taken by
Saul and David which had already been contrasted in x 13–14.

The arrival of the ark and its being placed in the tent pitched
for it was the signal for rejoicing which took the form of the offering
of burnt and peace offerings. Apparently the Chronicler has the
priests offering the sacrifices rather than David (II Sam vi 17),

though it was done on behalf of the king and people. The parceling out of food may be connected with the peace offering in which the worshipers always shared (Lev vii 11 ff.) and which marked the reconciliation of the worshiper with God (see Rothstein and Hänel, p. 285). Verse 2 follows II Sam vi 18 almost exactly; David performed the priestly rites himself—an act specifically toned down in the preceding verse. Furthermore, he blessed the people—another priestly function, attributed also to Solomon in I Kings viii 55 but avoided by the Chronicler in the parallel passage (II Chron vii 1 ff.).

[Appointment of Levites to minister before the ark, 4–6]: This little pericope is significant because it reveals the Chronicler's continued concern for the Levites, who had been pretty much neglected by the Deuteronomist or consigned to menial service. The appointment of the Levites and priests in the preceding chapter was regarded as a temporary measure for the occasion of the removal of the ark to Jerusalem. That arrangement proved so satisfactory that it was continued on a permanent basis, though for the time being there had to be a division of personnel between Gibeon and Jerusalem. Whether the Chronicler's account is true in detail is beyond proof, but he certainly does follow the Deuteronomist in recognizing two great centers of religion in the time of David— Gibeon (I Kings iii 4–5) and Jerusalem, the latter sharing honors with the former before the construction of the temple with its altar. Reference to the care of the ark is doubtless due to the writer's interest in the Levites, whose chief duty was its transportation. But since there was no longer need for such service, other duties were assigned to them, that is, that of singers and caretakers. The ark played a significant role in the organization and administration of the kingdom of David; indeed the Chronicler may be right in his assertion that some kind of worship centered about it even though sacrifices were still carried on at Gibeon. And those who ministered in connection with the ark were obviously dedicated persons of some sort—Levites for the Chronicler. See COMMENT on Sec. 16, xv 16 ff. Whether the singers were first connected with the Levites by the Chronicler himself is uncertain. Some think they were still regarded as a separate class in Ezra ii 41 but obviously not in Ezra iii 10; Neh ix 5, xi 22, xii 8, 24 (cf. Rudolph, p. 121; H. Schneider, *Die Bücher Esra und Nehemia*, 1959, p. 98). In the final analysis, the matter is probably one of terminology and rests on the definition of "Le-

vites." In the narrow construction of the term, the singers and doorkeepers were doubtless not Levites, but in its widest meaning as
vowed or dedicated persons serving the cult they could be regarded
as such. The contention of the Chronicler is that David introduced
the musical guilds in connection with the cult service centering about
both ark and tabernacle and he is doubtless right, but whether the
members of those guilds were Levites is another question. The reason for the avoidance of cult service of sacrifice is due to the fact
that the cultus as such was not yet legitimatized as we know from
chapters xxi and xxii (cf. Noth, ÜS, p. 137, n. 6). It should not be
overlooked that singers were, in all probability, attached to Canaanite temples and hence were cult officials—a precedent for the
practice of the Hebrews at Jerusalem.

The writer's concern for the ark and the cult center at Jerusalem
is expressed by the position in which he places them over against
the high place at Gibeon. Also direction for service before the ark
is given first to the Levites, then to the priests (cf. xv 16–24). Cf.
the reversal of the order of the cultic personnel at Gibeon (vss.
39–43) later. Nine Levites plus Asaph and two priests are listed by
name. All of the names of the Levites occur in chapter xv, though
not in the same order; of the two priests named here, only Benaiah
is included in the list there.

[Asaph's hymn of thanksgiving, 7–36]: Asaph's hymn of thanks-
giving is composed of portions of several Psalms. Verses 8–22 || Ps
cv 1–15; vss. 23–33 || Ps xcvi 1b–13; vss. 34–36 || Ps cvi 1, 47–48.
Commentators are agreed that the Chronicler utilized the Psalms
and that they are therefore older than his work. There are no really
significant differences between the two versions (see textual note[f]
and NOTES). For the interpretation of the hymn see commentaries on
Pss xcvi, cv, cvi. It is possible that Pss xxiv 7–10, cxxxii 6–9 were
parts of martial hymns used in the bringing of the ark to Jerusalem.
See O. Eissfeldt, WO 2 (1959), 480–83. The Chronicler here illus-
trates what he believed was the origin and practice in the time of
David, by a concrete example from his own time and in so doing gives
us an insight into certain liturgical usages in postexilic times. He thus
offers precedent for cultic ceremonies, apart from sacrifices, which
were held in both temple and synagogue in his period (cf. Rothstein
and Hänel, pp. 295, 316. Also Van Selms, *I Kronieken,* p. 144 [for
complete reference see Selected Bibliography, Commentaries]).

[Provision for service at Jerusalem (in connection with the ark)

and at Gibeon (the high place), 37–43]: The fact that cultic service
with the ark is placed first here may be of some significance since
it appears to stress the importance of worship without sacrifice. Just
as Aaron was the recipient of a commission from Moses to offer
sacrifices (Lev ix), so Asaph is here said to have been commissioned by David to carry out the service "before the ark continually."
In Chronicles David virtually displaces Moses. The name of Moses
occurs only 31 times in Chronicles, Ezra, Nehemiah whereas that of
David occurs there more than 250 times. While statistics cannot be
regarded as proof, they do indicate certain trends that cannot be
ignored, especially in view of the writer's inclinations. There was
surely some reason for this emphasis. For the Chronicler, the temple
and its services were central, and for this David was the key person
since, in the Chronicler's theory, he was responsible for the whole
of temple worship. He connected Moses with the tabernacle, which
was only of antiquarian interest, because the temple had inherited its
tradition. Only here is Obed-edom associated with Jeduthun. He and
Hosah are listed as gatekeepers also in xxvi.

Verses 39–42 are devoted to the ministrations before the tabernacle at Gibeon. Nothing is known of the circumstances under which
Gibeon became the cultic center of Israel, since it was originally a
member of the famous Gibeonite league (Josh ix 17) and hence a
Canaanite city. It may be no accident that Zadok alone is mentioned
as the priest who was sent by David to officiate there. On the whole
problem of Zadok see Rowley, FAB, pp. 461–72, especially literature referred to on p. 464, n. 8. For the argument of E. Sellin that
Zadok was originally connected with Gibeon, see *Geschichte der
israelitish-jüdischen Volkes*, I, 1924, pp. 167, 169 f. Y. Kaufmann,
The Religion of Israel, 1960, p. 197, thinks the Zadokites did not
claim affiliation with the old Aaronite line but first served with them
as Levitical priests in the time of David. The whole matter is too
involved and complex for discussion at this point but it is interesting
to observe that the line of Zadok assumed increasing importance
as the institutional aspect of Israelite religion developed, whereas the
Aaronites (Abiathar) were squeezed out. With Zadok were Heman
and Jeduthun, the other representatives of the singers, appointed by
David for the purpose giving "thanks to Yahweh." Verse 42 is
difficult. It may be intended to apply to both groups, that is, the one
at Gibeon and the one with the ark, since LXX omits the names of
Jeduthun and Heman. In that case it simply reiterates what was said

in vss. 5, 6 about the instruments used in the conduct of the service. Verse 43 is drawn from II Sam vi 19, 20. The Chronicler leaves out entirely the story of Michal's altercation with the king because he considered his extravagant behavior unbecoming.

18. DAVID'S DESIRE TO BUILD THE TEMPLE MEETS WITH YAHWEH'S DISAPPROVAL
(xvii 1–15)†

David's desire to build a temple

XVII 1 Now it happened when David was occupying his house that David said to Nathan the prophet, "See, I am living in a house of cedar while the ark of the covenant of Yahweh is under tent curtains." 2 Nathan replied to David, "Do everything you have in mind, for God is with you." 3 That very night the word of God came to Nathan saying, 4 "Go tell David my servant: thus has Yahweh said, you yourself shall not build the house for me to live in! 5 For I have not lived in a house from the time I brought Israel up until this very day, but I have been going around from tent to tent and from *habitation to habitation*. 6 At any time when I accompanied all Israel, did I ever *say anything like this* to any of the judges* whom I commanded to shepherd my people: why have you not built me a house of cedar? 7 Now, you must tell my servant David: Thus has Yahweh of hosts said: I took you from following the sheep in the pasture to be a leader for my people Israel, 8 I have been with you wherever you went and I have destroyed all your enemies before you. Now I am going to make for you a name like that of the greatest men in the earth. 9 I am going to provide a place for my people Israel and plant them so that they may live in their own place and no more be perturbed, nor shall villains again oppress them as formerly, 10 at the time when I appointed judges over my people Israel. I will also subdue all your

† I Chron xvii 1–15 ‖ II Sam vii 1–17.

a–a So to harmonize with preceding expression; LXX^A reads "in tent and inn."
b–b For Heb. "saying."
c II Sam vii 7 has "tribes"; so also LXX here but MT is probably correct in view of vs. 10.

enemies. And I told you that Yahweh will build a house for you. 11 When your days have been completed and you go the way of your fathers, then I will commission your heir, who shall be one of your sons, to succeed you and I will maintain his kingdom. 12 He shall build a house for me and I will maintain his throne forever. 13 I will be his father and he shall be my son; I will not deprive him of my devotion as I deprived him who preceded you. 14 I will set him over my house and my kingdom forever and his throne shall be maintained forever." 15 Nathan relayed to David precisely these words and this vision.

NOTES

xvii 5. *up.* II Sam vii 6 adds "from Egypt."

I have been going around. So with II Sam vii 6.

9–10. These verses connect David specifically with Israel, though they are actually a digression from the main topic which is David and his succession.

10. *And I told you.* Yahweh is the speaker.

11. *you . . . your fathers.* Literally "to go with your fathers." II Sam vii 12 "you sleep with your fathers."

heir. Literally "seed."

14. *his throne.* Cf. xxviii 5, xxix 23; II Chron ix 8, xiii 8—the throne and kingdom of the Davidides are portrayed as belonging to Yahweh himself. Following Isaiah, the Chronicler holds that the king is an official (II Chron ix 5 f.) and that Yahweh is king (II Chron vi 5). See A. Alt, VT 1 (1951), 2–22.

COMMENT

Here the interest of the Chronicler makes itself apparent—his concern for worship with all its accoutrements. In the preceding chapter he dealt with the successful transfer of the ark to Jerusalem and the provision for worship. It is not accidental that in vs. 1 the statement "when Yahweh had given him rest from all his enemies round about" from II Sam vii 1 was omitted. That implied the lapse of some time between the bringing of the ark to Jerusalem and the desire to build a temple. Both stories assert the initial assent of Nathan to the ambition of David, but the word of Yahweh to the former changed all that. In some respects the writer has toned down the language employed in II Sam vii, in others strengthened it, in accordance with his views. In vs. 4 he has considerably sharpened the prohibition against David's building of "the house." In the parallel passage it is put in the form of a question and not in that of a strong command as here. Note also the use of the article with house which emphasizes the fact that Yahweh did not question the building of the temple but that David was not the person to do it. Verses 5–6 doubtless refer to both the wilderness wanderings (Num xxxiii) and the early localizations of the shrine in the land at Gibeon, Shiloh, and Nob; there may also be a hint as to its fortunes after the fall of Shiloh or even the situation at the time when it was localized at Gibeon while the ark itself was at Jerusalem (cf. vs. 1).

In lieu of the honor of building a temple for Yahweh, Yahweh himself "will build a house for you," that is, provide a line of descent. What is involved is the nation of Israel (cf. Noth, ÚS, p. 179), Yahweh's people for whom David and his line are to be the shepherd as the judges had been earlier. David himself had been a man of war, subduing enemies so that Israel might have peace and be free from molestation. The writer clearly views all that as not having taken place yet so that the shepherd's time and energy will be occupied with the establishment of the nation and the consolidation of its position in the land. In the background is the unsettled situation under Saul, who is almost entirely ignored. The Chronicler, like his source, thus faces the reality of the situation which both attribute to the will and purpose of Yahweh. Verse 11 must not be made to bear too much weight; while it doubtless reflects messianic overtones, it seems to refer only to Solomon as the explanatory addition "one of your sons" indicates. David's heir has a twofold significance: (a) a demonstration of the continuity of the throne and (b) the verification of the presence of Yahweh by the fulfillment of the promise to "build a house for me." The crucial verses are 13 and 14, for both the Deuteronomist, in II Sam vii 14–16, and the Chronicler, each interpreting in line with his theology as shown by the specific textual nuances. Both writers believed in the persistence of the Davidic kingdom, after a period of trials (II Sam vii 14; Ezra ix 7–9; Neh ix 32–37). The same idea is present to a more pronounced degree in the royal psalms (ii, lxxxix, cxxxii) which stress the close relationship between Yahweh and his anointed one. Both of these verses and the royal psalms are surely messianic in outlook, if not in intent, though that idea ought not be pressed too far. On the Chronicler's messianism, see Introduction. The royal psalms, with their rich poetic imagery and cosmic outlook, which can be interpreted universally and eschatologically, present a more vivid portrait than the prosaic account here, which is more narrowly dynastic and national. The whole vision of Nathan connects the Davidic throne with the religious institution of the nation, which is characteristic of much of Old Testament theology.

19. DAVID'S PRAYER IN REPLY
(xvii 16–27)†

David's prayer before Yahweh

XVII 16 Then King David came in and took his seat before [in the presence of] Yahweh; he said, "Who am I, O Yahweh God, and what is my house that you have brought me hither? 17 Because this was too little in your sight, O God, you have spoken concerning the house of your servant for the distant future and you have regarded me as [having] the rank of the highly exalted man. O Yahweh God 18 what further can David say to you *for honoring* your servant, since you know your servant, 19 O Yahweh; for *your servant, your dog*, you have done this* great thing, to reveal all the great achievements. 20 O Yahweh, there is none like you and apart from you there is no God, according to everything we have heard with our own ears. 21 And who is like your people Israel, one nation in the earth, whom God proceeded to redeem for himself as a people; you made a name for yourself, by great and fearful deeds, when you drove out nations before your people whom you redeemed from Egypt. 22 At the same time you made your people Israel your own people forever and you, O Yahweh, became their God. 23 Now, O Yahweh, let the promise you made concerning your servant and his house remain valid forever, and do as you have promised. 24 May your fame be sure and great forever so that people will say, 'Yahweh of hosts, the God of Israel is Israel's God.' Let the house of David your servant endure before you, 25 for you, O my God, have disclosed to your servant tht you will build a house for him.

† I Chron xvii 16–27 ‖ II Sam vii 18–29.

a–a With LXX.
b–b So for MT and LXX "according to your heart."
c Omitting the *kl* ("all") of MT.

Therefore your servant has ventured to pray before you. 26 Now,
O Yahweh, you are God and have made this precious promise
concerning your servant. 27 What is more, you have deigned to
bless the house of your servant that it may remain before you
forever, and since you, O Yahweh, have blessed it, therefore it
is blessed forever."

NOTES

xvii 17. *the rank . . . man.* Hebrew is uncertain and no suggestion is
fully satisfactory. II Sam vii 19 "and this is the law of man." For possibilities and suggestions see Rothstein and Hänel, pp. 327–30; Bewer,
FAB, pp. 74 f.; Rudolph, p. 131.

O Yahweh God. Phrase is to be connected with the following verse
rather than with this one.

18. *what . . . say.* With II Sam vii 20.

19. *for . . . dog.* Cf. Lachish Letter 2 for parallel to "your dog"; see
discussion by H. Torczyner, *Te'udoth Lakish,* 1940, pp. 26, 31–33, and
J. Hempel, "Die Ostraka von Lakis," ZAW 56 (1938), 129, n. d.

21. *one . . . earth.* On basis of Ezek xxxvii 22.

COMMENT

David's response to the announcement of Nathan takes the form
of a prayer to Yahweh at the local shrine, that is, in the newly
established sanctuary for the ark at Jerusalem. While there are some
alterations and omissions, the text is substantially that of II Sam vii.
The prayer breathes a sort of confessional spirit, acknowledging the
humble state of the king's origins and crediting Yahweh with his
exaltation far beyond his deserts. Three things stand out quite con-
spicuously: (a) the greatness and aloneness of God, (b) the election
and deliverance of Israel, and (c) the continuity of the throne.
Stress is laid on faith in the validity of the promises of Yahweh and
the hope that they will persist despite the vicissitudes of time—the
terms "forever," "valid forever," "endure before you" are evidences of that faith and hope which become a certainty in the last
clause of vs. 27. In taking over this remarkable chapter from II Sam
vii, the Chronicler gives expression to his theology, especially in view

of the fact that he has omitted from his work everything that militated against his conception of the Davidic line or that might detract from the weight he attributed to it.

The obvious source for chapter xvii (Secs. 18 and 19) was II Sam vii. For a discussion of the details, see Rudolph and Rothstein and Hänel. The former rightly points out that the writer followed his source fairly closely, with insignificant variations; the latter thinks he followed a proto-Samuel source. See also H. van den Bussche, *Le Texte de la Prophétie de Nathan sur la Dynastie Davidique,* 1948, pp. 10, 31. As has been remarked in the Introduction, Qumran evidence renders it imperative to take into account the fact that Chronicles reflects a somewhat different Vorlage (archetype) than MT and conforms more closely to the Samuel MSS found at Qumran which are more Septuagintal in character. Still to be evaluated are the LXX of Chronicles, and the weight to be given to peculiar readings in Chronicles in determining between original readings common to Samuel and Chronicles, and harmonizing tendencies which are inevitable in parallel documents. Care must be taken not to attribute variants to the deliberate purpose of the Chronicler, who may simply have been following a different text, which may be attested by LXX of Samuel or the Qumran MSS, especially 4Q Sam[a], only a small part of which has so far been published (see Introduction). On the relationship between David and Israel according to II Sam vii see M. Noth's, "David und Israel in II Samuel 7," in *Mélanges Bibliques rédiqués en l'honneur de André Robert,* pp. 122–30.

20. DAVID'S CAMPAIGNS
(xviii 1–17, xix 1–19, xx 1–8)†

XVIII 1 Afterwards David attacked and subdued the Philistines; he also captured Gath with its dependencies from the Philistines. 2 He conquered Moab, and the Moabites became David's tribute-paying subjects. 3 He attacked Hadadezer*a* the king of Zobah, which lies in the direction of Hamath, when he set out to establish his dominion on the Euphrates River. 4 David captured from him one thousand chariots, seven thousand horsemen and twenty thousand infantrymen; but David hamstrung all the chariot teams except a hundred of them which he kept. 5 When the Aramaeans of Damascus*b* came to assist Hadadezer the king of Zobah, David slew twenty-two thousand men. 6 David then put garrisons among the Aramaeans at Damascus and the Aramaeans also became David's tribute-paying subjects. Moreover, Yahweh gave victory to David wherever he went. 7 David took the golden shields borne by the servants of Hadadezer and brought them to Jerusalem. 8 From Tibhath and Cun, cities of Hadadezer, David captured a huge quantity of bronze with which Solomon made the bronze sea, the pillars, and the bronze instruments. 9 When Tou the king of Hamath heard that David had completely defeated the army of Hadadezer the king of Zobah, 10 he sent his son Hadoram*c* to King David to greet him and to congratulate him because he had fought Hadadezer and completely defeated him [for Hadad-

† I Chron xviii 1–13 ‖ Sam viii 1=14; 14–17 ‖ II Sam viii 15–18; I Chron xix 1–19 ‖ II Sam x 1–19; I Chron xx 1–8 ‖ II Sam xi 1, xii 26, 30–31, xxi 18–22.

a So with BH³ for "Hadarezer" of the MT. Also in vss. 5, 7–10. See NOTE.
b MT reads "Darmesek," late Aramaic for "Damesek" of the Samuel parallel. See NOTE.
c II Sam viii 10 reads "Joram" where LXX reads "Ieddouran." Perhaps the name is a contraction of *hdd-rm* "Hadad is exalted."

ezer had been at war with Tou]. [He also sent] all sorts of gold, silver, and bronze objects 11 which King David dedicated to Yahweh together with the silver and gold which he had taken away as booty from all the nations, from Edom, Moab, the Ammonites, the Philistines, and Amalek. 12 Abishai the son of Zeruiah defeated eighteen thousand men of Edom in the valley of Salt. 13 He*d* stationed garrisons in Edom and all Edom became subjects of David. Yahweh gave victory to David wherever he went.

Organization of the kingdom

14 David was then king over all Israel and governed all his people with justice and rectitude. 15 Joab the son of Zeruiah commanded the army, Jehoshaphat the son of Ahilud was spokesman [for the king], 16 Zadok the son of Ahitub and Abimelech*e* the son of Abiathar were priests, Shavsha was secretary, 17 Benaiah the son of Jehoiada was in charge of the Cherethites and the Pelethites and the sons of David were chiefs next to the king.

The Ammonite campaign

XIX 1 Later when Nahash, the king of the Ammonites, died and his son*f* became king in his place, 2 David said, "I will show my respect to Hanun the son of Nahash as his father showed respect to me." So David sent representatives to console him concerning his father. When David's servants went to Hanun in the country of the Ammonites to console him, 3 the Ammonite princes said to Hanun, "Do you really believe that David wants to honor your father by sending consolers to you? Have not his servants come to you to search out, to overthrow*g*, and to spy on the country?" 4 So Hanun seized the servants of David, clipped them, cut off their garments in the middle, just at

d Obviously David, with Syr.
e II Sam viii 17 reads "Ahimelech"; so also LXX in both passages.
f LXX adds "Hanun."
g Omitted by LXX; perhaps *ḥāpar*, "explore," ought to be read. Latter part of verse is quite awkward but in view of LXX and Vulg. reading, no easy solution is apparent. LXX adds "the city" after "search out," which may have dropped out by haplography.

the point they were intended to cover, and sent them away.
5 When they came and informed David about the men, he sent
someone to meet them—for the men felt very greatly humiliated.
The king said, "Remain at Jericho until your beards grow out,
then you can return." 6 When the Ammonites saw that they
had made themselves repulsive to David, Hanun and the Ammonites dispatched a thousand talents of silver to hire for themselves chariots and horsemen from the Aramaeans of Naharaim,
of Maacah, and of Zobah. 7 They hired for themselves thirty-
two thousand chariots together with the king of Maacah and
his people who came and encamped before Medeba. The Ammonites too assembled from their cities and came out for battle.
8 When David heard about it, he sent out Joab and the whole
army of warriors. 9 The Ammonites came out and prepared for
battle at the city gate while the kings who had come were alone
in the open field. 10 When Joab saw that the battle threatened
him from front and rear, he chose some of the select men of
Israel and arrayed them in front of the Aramaeans; 11 the rest
of the people he put under Abishai his brother, and they drew
up for battle before the Ammonites. 12 Then he said, "If the
Aramaeans are too powerful for me, you must come to assist
me, and if the Ammonites are too powerful for you, I will assist you. 13 Be brave! let us show ourselves courageous for the
sake of our people and the cities of our God and may Yahweh
do what is pleasing to him." 14 But when Joab and the people
with him approached the Aramaeans for battle, they fled before
him. 15 The Ammonites, seeing that the Aramaeans had fled,
also fled before Abishai his brother and entered the city. Then
Joab returned to Jerusalem. 16 When the Aramaeans saw that
they were overpowered by Israel, they sent messengers who
brought the Aramaeans from the other side of the river; at their
head was Shophach, the general of Hadadezer's army. 17 When
it was reported to David, he mobilized all Israel, crossed the
Jordan, came toward them and prepared for battle against them.
Then the *Aramaeans* prepared to meet *David* in battle and
fought with him. 18 The Aramaeans fled before Israel and Da-

h–h Interchange with LXX and II Sam x 17.

vid slew seven thousand Aramaean charioteers and forty thousand infantrymen; he also put to death Shophach the general of the army. 19 When the servants of Hadadezer observed that Israel had prevailed over them they made peace with David and served him. The Aramaeans were no longer willing to support the Ammonites.

Further activities of David

XX 1 Now at[i] the turn of the year when the kings customarily went out to battle, Joab led out the army, devastated the land of the Ammonites and then came and besieged Rabbah, while David remained at Jerusalem. Joab conquered Rabbah and overthrew it. 2 Then David took the crown off the head of their king[j] and discovered that it weighed about a talent of gold and in it was a precious stone; it was put on David's head. He also brought away from the city a very great quantity of booty. 3 He brought out the people who were in it, [k]put them to work with the saw,[k] with iron picks and with axes, just as he did with all the cities of the Ammonites. Then David and all the people returned to Jerusalem. 4 Afterwards war arose with the Philistines at Gezer. At the time Sibbecai the Hushathite killed Sippai one of the family of giants, and [l]they were subdued[l]. 5 Again there was war with the Philistines and Elhanan the son of Jair killed Lahmi, the brother of Goliath the Gittite, the shaft of whose spear was like a weaver's beam. 6 There was yet another war at Gath where there was a man of extraordinary stature who had twenty-four fingers [and toes], six on each hand and foot; he too was a son of the giants. 7 When he taunted Israel, Jehonathan the son of Shimea, David's brother, killed him. 8 These were descended from the giants of Gath and fell by the hand of David and his servants.

---

[i] Omitting "time" with II Sam xi 1 and LXX. See NOTE.
[j] Possibly Milkom, the god of Ammon, with LXX in Samuel and Chronicles, and Vulg. here.
[k-k] For Heb. "he conducted them to the saw," i.e., sawed them to pieces. Read *śīm* for *śrr*. Cf. II Sam xii 31.
[l-l] LXX "he humbled him."

NOTES

xviii 1. *Gath with its dependencies*. The Chronicler so renders the difficult Methegh-ammah of II Sam viii 1. For interpretation see A. Alt,
ZAW 54 (1936), 149–52; W. F. Albright, IEJ 4 (1954), 3 f., thinks the
latter is an abbreviation of *mtg <b'ny> 'mh* "horse's bit of the dwarfs."
But see Rudolph's caveat, p. 134. Cf. Noth, *The History of Israel*, p. 193,
n. 2.

3. *Hadadezer*. For a possible explanation of the form, see R. T.
O'Callaghan, *Aram Naharaim*, 1948, p. 128, n. 2.

when he . . . his dominion. Aramaean expansionist movements began
early in the reign of Ashurrabi II (1012–972) from whom Hadadezer
had apparently taken some Assyrian territory in the Euphrates district
before he came into collision with David. See A. Malamat, BA 21
(1958), 100–2.

5. *Damascus*. The spelling "Darmesek" for "Damascus" occurs only
in Chronicles, which is so far the earliest known document with that
spelling. See O'Callaghan, *Aram Naharaim*, and F. Rosenthal, *Die
aramaistische Forschung*, 1939, pp. 15–18.

6. *David . . . garrisons*. Added on basis of II Sam viii 6.
Damascus. See NOTE on vs. 5.

7. *shields*. Not certain. Some suggest "armor."

8. *Tibhath and Cun*. Cities in the Beka Valley between Lebanon and
Antilebanon mountains, northeast of Baalbek.

10. *[for . . . Tou]*. Literally "for the man of wars of Tou was Hadadezer."

12. *Abishai . . . defeated*. See II Sam viii 13.

15. *spokesman*. Usually rendered "recorder" but see COMMENT.

16. *Shavsha*. II Sam viii 17 has "Seraiah." Some scholars think
Shavsha is equivalent to Babylonian Samsu but, as De Vaux suggests, it
is better to look for an Egyptian name here. The fathers of all the other
officials are given but not that of Shavsha, a pretty good sign that he
was a foreigner.

17. *the Cherethites and the Pelethites*. Mercenary bodyguard of the
king, apparently non-Israelite. Marks a departure from Israelite practice
and indicates that David had profited from his experience as a Philistine
mercenary. Cf. W. F. Albright, JPOS 1 (1921), 189 f.

xix 2. *"I . . . me."* Literally "I will do *hesed* with Hanun . . . as his
father did *hesed* with me." The term *hesed* means "loyalty," "devotion
(to an obligation)." Behind the term lies the deep Israelite feeling for
mutual devotion to an obligation assumed in a common cause. Apparently there was a treaty of friendship between David and Nahash by

virtue of the fact that they had joined hands against Saul. Cf. W. F. Albright, "Notes on Ammonite History," *Miscellanea Biblica B. Ubach*, 1953, p. 132 f.

4. *cut off their garments.* II Sam x 4 "half their beards."

just . . . cover. II Sam x 4 "to their buttocks."

6. *a thousand talents.* About 37½ tons.

of Naharaim, of Maacah, and of Zobah. I.e., the two rivers, north Mesopotamia. II Sam x 6 has "Beth-rehob." On LXX rendering of Syria of Mesopotamia, Syria of Moocha, and Syria of Sobal, see O'Callaghan, *Aram Naharaim*, p. 142.

7. *encamped before Medeba.* Not in Samuel source. Rothstein and Hänel, pp. 351 f., read "waters of Rabbah." The Medeba known is too far south and is in the territory of Moab (cf. II Sam xii 27).

13. *and may . . . him.* The last clause is really indicative: "Yahweh will do as he pleases" or "Yahweh will do what he thinks best." The meaning is: once we have done our utmost and shown courage, the matter is in God's hands.

15. *Then Joab returned.* Cf. II Sam x 14. "Came" here under the influence of "entered."

16. *the river.* I.e., the Euphrates. BA 21 (1958), 102.

17. *toward them.* Words may conceal the Helam of II Sam x 17. A *Hl'm*, presumably north of Gilead occurs in the Brussels figurine lists (cf. W. F. Albright, BASOR 83 [October 1941], 33).

xx 1. *Now at.* The turn of the year probably refers to the spring. It appears that we have to reckon with the probability that two calendars operated at the same time: the one beginning in the spring and the other in the autumn.

Joab . . . it. Cf. II Sam xii 26 ff. Several Greek minuscules add from II Sam xii 27–29: "And Joab sent messengers to David saying, 'You capture Rabbah, lest I capture it and my name be called upon it' [I get credit for it]. So David gathered the people and went to Rabbah and captured it."

2. *about a talent of gold.* Some 75½ lbs., much too heavy for one human head.

3. *with axes.* So with II Sam xii 31, for "saws" here.

4. *at Gezer.* II Sam xxi 18 "in Gob."

Sippai. II Sam xxi 18 "Saph."

5. *war with the Philistines.* II Sam xxi 19 adds "in Gob."

Lahmi. Laḥmī is a corruption of *bēt-laḥmī* (for *bēt-(hal)-laḥmī* in II Sam xxi 19). The creation of a brother of Goliath eases the problem raised by the Samuel verse which goes against the tradition that David slew Goliath. On the other hand, El hanan has been taken as the personal name of David. Cf. L. M. von Pákozdy, ZAW 68 (1956), 257–59.

6. *a man . . . [and toes].* Cf. II Sam xxi 20.

COMMENT

Chapters xviii–xx deal with the wars of David. They owe their position largely to the arrangement found in the writer's sources (xviii 1–17 ‖ II Sam viii 1–18; xix 1–xx 3 ‖ II Sam x 1–xi 1 and xii 26–31; xx 4–8 ‖ II Sam xxi 18–22), but it is obvious that the Chronicler had another reason for grouping the whole series of wars together, while at the same time omitting from his account the interspersed chapters of II Samuel having to do with domestic matters. The chief reason why David was not to build the temple was that he was a man of war (xxii 8, xxviii 3) and hence the author immediately plunges into an account of the wars of his hero after the restraining prophecy of Nathan. But it should not be overlooked that the war booty was in part dedicated to Yahweh for later use in the temple.

[The wars of David, xviii 1–13]: The defensive war with the Philistines was not enough to provide Israelite security against their ancient foes and so David took offensive action against them. So much is certain from both II Sam viii 1 and vs. 1 here, though the details escape us. But Gath may well have been taken since it was the Philistine center nearest to David's base of operations. Moab too was conquered but our author omits the gruesome treatment of the Moabites related in II Sam viii 2 because it does not fit the portraiture of his hero. Collision with the Aramaean state of Zobah is noted but in what connection is not stated; it is doubtless to be associated in some way with the campaign against Ammon (ch. xix). Zobah was the strongest of the Aramaean states at the time and was located in the Antilibanus around Homs, "in the direction of Hamath." For discussion of the location and of David's wars with the Aramaeans see O'Callaghan, *Aram Naharaim,* pp. 125–30. The cities of Zobah were Cun, Tibhath (Betah), and Berothai. The land was apparently rich in copper, for David derived thence the metal from which Solomon made numerous articles for the temple. The number of captured horsemen is exaggerated from seventeen hundred to seven thousand. Hadadezer had been in an expansionist war with the king of Hamath, Tou, who was so delighted by the success of David that he sent his son with a message of congratulation together with a large quantity of presents. All the tribute and presents gained were carried to Jerusalem, where they were solemnly dedicated to Yahweh. Notice is also taken of Abishai's conquest of Edom and its occupation by the forces of David. David's empire was thus expanding by leaps and bounds. He added to his realm the Philistine territory, Zobah, Damascus, Edom, Moab, Amalek, and Ammon, though none of them were incorporated into Israel to form an organized empire (cf. Alt, "Die Staatenbildung der Israeliten in Palästina" and "Das Grossreich Davids" in KS, II, pp. 1–75). Naturally his success was due to the presence and blessing of Yahweh.

[Brief note on the organization of the kingdom, 14–17]: The growth of David's dominions necessitated some organization to take care of their administration. David himself was of course the king and, being the kind of king he was, he ruled with judgment and justice. To assist him he had certain officials whose duties are specified by the terms applied to them. Joab was the commander of the militia; Jehoshaphat was the *mazkīr*, that is, the spokesman or chief of protocol. For this reading see J. Bergrich, "Sofer und Mazkir," ZAW 58 (1940/41), 1–29; De Vaux, RB 48 (1939), 394–405; cf. H. G. Reventlow, "Das Amt des Mazkir," TZ 15 (1949), 161–75. It is now certain that David's administrative machinery was modeled after that of Egypt. The Mazkir corresponds to the Eg. *whm nśw. t,* that is, the royal herald attested in both the old and new kingdoms. As De Vaux points out, the stele of Intef, the royal herald of Thutmose III, indicates that his duties included regulation of the palace ceremonies, admission to royal audience, reporting to the king the matters concerning the people and the country and reporting to them the orders of the king of which he is the official interpreter; he accompanied the king in travel, served as his personal secretary, arranged for the stages of his itinerary in travel and acted as the police chief for the pharaoh. Perhaps the best description of him is the chief of protocol. In any event he was a very important official. Cf. J. H. Breasted, *Ancient Records of Egypt,* II, 1906–7, pp. 763–71.

Zadok and Abimelech were the priests and Shavsha was the secretary. In Egypt the duties of the secretary or royal scribe cannot be clearly distinguished from those of the speaker. He was in charge of the royal correspondence. He was also the personal secretary of the pharaoh, the writer of the royal decrees in accordance with the order of the king, the publisher of those decrees and laws,

the bearer of diplomatic correspondence, ambassador, a kind of
intercessor for the king, a bodyguard, and the officer who listed the
captives in campaigns. For illustration from period of Amenophis
III see Breasted, *op. cit.*, 913 ff.

The head of the professional military corps was Benaiah. The
Chronicler deliberately alters the statement of his source to the
effect that the sons of David were priests; in his view they could
not officiate as priests because they were laymen. Thus he makes
them lieutenants of David.

[The Ammonite campaign, xix 1–19]: Just at what period in
David's reign the Aramaean wars took place is not certain, though
it must have been some time after his position in Israel and the
west was secure. In the preceding chapter there is a reference to his
dealings with the Philistines, notably the taking of Gath. There was
manifestly more to it than simple subjugation. Provisions were made
for the consolidation of his gains and for the retention of the territory thus falling under his control. There is evidence at Beth-
shemesh and Tell Beit Mirsim that casemated walls had been constructed in the early part of the tenth century, the Davidic period. See
Albright, "The Excavation of Tell Beit Mirsim, Vol. III: The Iron
Age," AASOR 21–22 (1943), 37. He attributes the fortifications
to the early Davidic period, between ca. 1000 and 990 B.C. But
see now Y. Aharoni, BASOR 154 (April 1959), 35–39. There is
some indication that David had already taken care of Moab and
Edom before the time of the incident related in chapter xix. It appears that he came into conflict with the Aramaeans indirectly and
that the story here related tells how it all came about. The Zobah
campaign (xviii 3 ff.) must have taken place after this episode.
Hadadezer may have attempted to save face by striking eastward,
since his way to the south was blocked, and in so doing encroached
upon territory now under the Israelite king.

The insult administered to David's ambassadors of good will by
the suspicious Hanun drew no immediate reprisal from David. The
Ammonites may have regarded that fact as a sign of weakness on
his part, though according to both Samuel and Chronicles they must
have anticipated trouble eventually for they called upon their Northern neighbors for assistance. All of the Aramaean states, except
Hamath, responded—Aram Naharaim, Maacah, Beth-rehob,
Zobah, and Tob. Tob and Beth-rehob are not specifically mentioned
in Chronicles but are named in II Sam x. On the location of these

Aramaean states see O'Callaghan, *Aram Naharaim,* pp. 124–27. Aram Naharaim appears to be a region rather than a state. All of these states lay to the north and northeast of Israel and, if Damascus is taken into account—it figured in the preceding chapter—formed a solid block of Aramaean allies whose territory stretched from north and east of Lake Huleh through the Antilibanus region into the traditional Aram Naharaim beyond the Euphrates.

The Israelite campaign was a long drawn out affair and several battles took place before they were finally brought into subjection by the forces of David and Joab. After the defeat of the allies, Joab returned to Jerusalem without laying siege to Rabbah. Only after the arrival of Aramaean reinforcements from the far-flung domain of Hadadezer did David himself appear on the scene to deal the coup de grace to the Aramaeans. In the end David was the undisputed master, by treaty or conquest, of an empire that extended from Egypt to the Euphrates and from the Mediterranean to the Arabian desert. Only Ammon remained to be conquered.

There are a few differences in detail between the Chronicler's version and that of II Sam x. For example, he speaks of a thousand talents of silver paid by Hanun to induce the Aramaeans to assist him. Then there are the regular variations in numbers. II Sam x says the allies contributed twenty thousand foot soldiers plus thirteen thousand men; no chariots are mentioned until the results of the battle are given—the men of seven hundred chariots, forty thousand horsemen, and Shophach. The Chronicler's list of Aramaean support includes thirty-two thousand chariots, some horsemen, and the army of the king of Maacah. The victims of the battle were seven thousand charioteers, forty thousand infantrymen, and Shophach.

[Final campaign against Ammon, xx 1–3]: The first three verses of chapter xx are paralleled in II Sam xi 1, xii 26, 30–31. They have to do with the siege and capture of Rabbah, the capital of Ammon, which was the outcome of the insult to the messengers whom David had sent to pay his respects to Hanun upon the death of his father. Joab was the commander, while David remained in Jerusalem. It was during that campaign that the king became involved in the Bathsheba affair which the Chronicler omits because it was so detrimental to David's character and was not relevant to his purpose. The private life of the king has been completely ignored by him because he was concerned only with the official matters which pertained to Israel directly. That he omitted some of the material from his sources may be gathered from the fact that while he has Joab capturing the city he also has a reference to David's returning to Jerusalem after the event. The Samuel source states that Joab raided the land of Ammon and then besieged the capital, even taking "the city of waters" (II Sam xii 27), probably a portion of the city. He advised David to come and direct the final assault against the acropolis so that he might have the honor accruing therefrom. David heeded the advice of his commander and took the crown of the king of Ammon and a large quantity of booty, and put the population into a corvée. One more kingdom was thus added to David's jurisdiction.

[Further conflicts with Philistines, 4–8]: The last verses of the chapter return to the Philistines with whom David had already dealt. How long the threat continued is not stated, but there were doubtless frequent brushes with them during the early part of his reign. Eventually all of their centers were probably subdued. Three episodes are mentioned here. The first refers to war with the Philistines at Gezer, which sounds quite reasonable, despite the fact that II Sam xxi 18 reads Gob (otherwise unknown). While I Kings ix 16 says Pharaoh destroyed Gezer in the reign of Solomon and then presented the ruins to the latter as a marriage dowry, archaeological evidence for such a destruction is not clear. Moreover it assumes that this Canaanite enclave had remained in hostile hands in the Davidic period, which does not seem possible. Cf. query of Noth, *The History of Israel,* p. 214, n. 2. Albright's suggestion still seems the most reasonable, that "Gezer" has been corrupted from "Gerar" in I Kings ix 16; see AASOR 12 (1932), 75, but cf. caveat of Alt, KS, III, p. 412, n. 1. It appears now that the casemate walls are to be attributed to Solomon. Cf. Aharoni, BASOR 154 (April 1959), 35–39; Y. Yadin, IEJ 8 (1958), 80–86. Gezer was probably one of the cities destroyed by Shishak, in the reign of Rehoboam (cf. Albright, BASOR 92 [December 1943], 18).

All three skirmishes with the Philistines center about giants. The whole idea of giants here and in the parallels may be due to traditional belief that Canaan was a land of giants (cf. Gen xv 20). These giants were said to be descendants of Rapha, the eponymous ancestor of the Rephaim. The use of the article with Rapha, "the giants," in vss. 6, 8 points up this fact. According to the Samuel parallel Elhanan slew Goliath, while here he is the slayer of Lahmi, the brother of Goliath. II Sam xxi 19 therefore goes against I Sam xvii where David is said to have killed Goliath during one of Saul's campaigns. The Chronicler thus resolves the problem by crediting Elhanan with dispatching the brother of the giant David had slain. The Samuel text speaks of four descendants of Rapha; our source omits the reference to the number because he lists only three adventures with them. The one involving near tragedy for David was not included here because it undermined the writer's conception of the promise that he and his dynasty were to continue forever.

21. DAVID PUNISHED FOR TAKING THE CENSUS.
JERUSALEM CHOSEN FOR THE TEMPLE
(xxi 1–30, xxii 1)†

XXI 1 Satan rose up against Israel by enticing David to count Israel. 2 So David said to Joab and the princes of the people, "Go, count Israel from Beer-sheba to Dan and bring the result to me so that I may know their number." 3 But Joab replied, "May Yahweh multiply his people to a hundred times what they now are! Do not all of them, my lord, O king, belong to my lord as servants? Why does my lord require this thing? Why should it be the occasion of guilt upon Israel?" 4 However, the king's word prevailed over Joab. So Joab set out, went about through all Israel and then returned to Jerusalem. 5 Joab reported to David the results of the census of the people. All Israel had one million one hundred thousand men capable of drawing the sword; Judah alone had four hundred seventy thousand men capable of drawing the sword. 6 But he did not include Levi and Benjamin because the command of the king was repugnant to Joab. 7 This thing was displeasing in the sight of God, so that he punished Israel. 8 Then David said to God, "I sinned greatly when I did this thing; forgive, now, I pray, the transgression of your servant, for I have acted very foolishly." 9 So Yahweh spoke to Gad, David's seer, as follows: 10 "Go, tell David, thus has Yahweh said: I offer you three [punishments]ᵃ; choose the one which I should impose upon you." 11 When Gad came to David he said to him, "Thus has Yahweh said: choose for yourself 12 whether there shall be threeᵇ years of famine, three months

† I Chron xxi 1–30 ‖ II Sam xxiv 1–25.

ᵃ Hebrew has only the word "three."
ᵇ II Sam xxiv 13 has "seven," but LXX has "three." Samuel adds "in your land."

of flight[c] from the presence of your enemies while their sword overtakes you, or three days of [d]the sword of Yahweh[d], an epidemic in the land, during which time the angel of Yahweh will bring disaster to all the territory of Israel. Determine now what reply I shall give to him who sent me." 13 David said to Gad, "I am in very great anxiety; let me fall into the hands of Yahweh for his mercies are very great, but do not let me fall into the hands of man."[e] 14 So Yahweh let loose a pestilence in Israel during which seventy thousand Israelites succumbed. 15 God also sent the angel to Jerusalem to destroy it but when [he was about] to destroy [it], Yahweh looked upon it and changed his mind about the disaster [which he had threatened]. So he said to the destroying angel, "Enough now; stop." The angel of Yahweh was standing just at the threshing floor of Ornan, the Jebusite. 16 When David lifted up his eyes he saw the angel of Yahweh standing between the earth and the heavens with the drawn sword in his hand stretched out over Jerusalem. Then David and the elders covered themselves with sackcloth and fell down upon their faces. 17 David said to God, "Did I not give the order to count the people? I am the one who sinned and really committed the evil, but these, the flock, what have they done? O Yahweh my God, let your hand be against me and my family but spare your people from the plague." 18 The angel of Yahweh ordered Gad to tell David that David should go up and erect an altar to Yahweh on the threshing floor of Ornan the Jebusite. 19 So David went up in accordance with the word of Gad when he had spoken in the name of Yahweh. 20 Now Ornan had turned and was watching the angel while his four sons hid themselves, for Ornan was threshing wheat 21 when David came to Ornan. When Ornan looked and saw David, he came off the threshing floor and bowed himself down before David until his face touched the ground. 22 David

[c] So with II Sam xxiv 13 and LXX; Hebrew reads "swept away."
[d-d] Omitted in II Sam xxiv 13. Apparently cited in 1QH 6:29. This verse confirms the accuracy of LXX against MT of Samuel.
[e] II Sam xxiv 15, LXX, adds "and David chose the pestilence for himself; and the days of the wheat harvest. . . ." May be misplaced or an explanation of the presence of Ornan at the threshing floor when David arrived.

said to Ornan, "Give me the threshing-floor plot that I may erect an altar to Yahweh upon it. Give it to me at full price, so that the plague may be turned away from the people." 23 Ornan replied to David, "Take it and may my lord, the king, do what seems good in his sight! Behold, I will give the oxen for burnt offerings, the threshing sledges for wood, and the wheat for the meal offering: I will give everything." 24 Then David the king said to Ornan, "No, but I will indeed buy it at full price. I will not offer to Yahweh what belongs to you nor sacrifice a burnt offering that costs me nothing." 25 So David paid Ornan six hundred shekels of gold for the plot. 26 David erected there an altar to Yahweh and offered burnt offerings and peace offerings. He called upon Yahweh who answered him with fire from heaven upon the altar of burnt offering ʲand consumed the burnt offeringʲ. 27 Then Yahweh ordered the angel to put back his sword into its sheath. 28 At that time, when David saw that Yahweh answered him on the threshing floor of Ornan the Jebusite, he offered sacrifice there. 29 The tabernacle which Moses had made in the desert together with the altar of burnt offering were at the high place at Gibeon at that time. 30 But David could not go before it to consult God because he was terrified by the angel's sword.

XXII 1 David said, "This is the house of Yahweh God and this is the altar of burnt offering for Israel."

ʲ–ʲ With LXX; omitted from MT by haplography.

NOTES

xxi 1. *Satan.* Without the article here.

rose up against. For the same construction in Hebrew see Zech iii 1; Ps cix 6; "to stand against," "bring to trial," "tempt," "seek an occasion against." Cf. II Chron xx 23; Dan xi 14 and Vulg. *consurrexit,* "arise," "stand up against."

5. On the interpretation of numbers see COMMENT on Sec. 13. The crucial term is *eleph* (1000). If *eleph* stands for military units we should have the figure of 1100 units for all Israel and 470 for Judah alone. That is about double the number at the time of the amphictyony.

On the basis of 10 men per unit, it would mean a total of roughly 11,000 fighting men—not an impossibly high figure.

12. *overtakes you.* II Sam xxiv 13 reads "while he pursues you."

13. *let me fall.* II Sam "let us fall," etc.

15. *the angel.* Article or suffix (his angel) required by context; cf. vs. 12.

changed . . . threatened]. Literally "was sorry for the evil" (he planned to do).

stop. Literally "let your hand drop."

25. *six hundred shekels of gold.* Something over fifteen pounds. II Sam xxiv 24 "fifty shekels of silver" or 20 ounces.

COMMENT

The purpose of this section is clear, though it must have gone against the writer's grain to relate the story because it failed to jibe with his view of David. Nevertheless one of the central interests of his work was David's concern for the temple for which much war booty had already been set aside. The specific reason for the census is not given. A census for military purposes was authorized by God (Num xxvi). Doubtless it was frowned upon for special reasons, particularly because it was associated with the imposition of military duty on the citizens or estimation of their wealth for purposes of taxation. In this instance it might have been regarded as the basis for the corvée. Census taking could easily be attended by epidemics inadvertently spread by the census takers themselves as they went from town to town. The empirical basis for the story may be the association, vividly remembered, of David's numbering of the people with the outbreak of a severe epidemic which then became the occasion for rituals of confession and penitence designed to alleviate the plague. The plague itself was correctly connected with the census, though the theological inferences are something else again. That Joab and others objected to the census before it was undertaken is not surprising; it was, in all probability, due to a full appreciation of the difficulties involved, especially the recalcitrance of the people which was more pronounced in the country than in the cities. That the prophets should interpret it as divine judgment is to be expected. The sudden abatement of the plague, and the revelation at the time of the preparations for the ritual of confession, then provide the background for the purchase of the future temple site. Despite the obvious legendary accretions and embellishments, the nucleus of the story may be taken as historical.

[The sin of the census, xxi 1–7]: According to the Chronicler it was Satan who motivated the king to undertake the census. He cannot attribute, in his time, the source of evil to God. The idea of the Satan was not new (cf. Job i–ii; Zech iii 1) but his appearance here as an opponent of God is a further development. Elsewhere the Satan is a member of the heavenly court whose business was to accuse the guilty; here he is the instigator, or inciter, to evil and, as the name without the article shows, a personality with a will and purpose of his own (for a discussion of the problem see Rothstein and Hänel, pp. 377–83; A. Lods, "Les origines de la figure de Satan, ses fonctions à la cour céleste," *Mélanges Syriens offerts à Monsieur R. Dussaud,* pp. 649–60; and G. von Rad's article in *Theologisches Wörterbuch zum Neuen Testament,* II, 1935, pp. 71–74). For the writer, the incitement of Satan accounts for the persistence of David despite the violent objection of Joab, though it is to be noted that Satan does not have the power to thwart the purposes of God. The census was taken "from Beer-sheba to Dan," a reversal of the order in II Sam xxiv 2. The fine order of procedure of II Samuel is omitted together with the length of time consumed in the project, because the writer was hurrying on to the main point in his story. The total number of those fit for military service was 1,100,000 of whom 470,000 belonged to Judah. II Sam xxiv 9 has 800,000 for Israel and 500,000 for Judah, a total of 1,300,000, or 200,000 more than the Chronicler records. The difference is due to the fact that Levi and Benjamin were not counted. The basis for the omission of Levi is Num i 49, which forbids a census of Levi. Benjamin was doubtless excluded because the high place of Gibeon was located there (Josh xviii 25 and vs. 28). Cf. Curtis and Madsen, p. 248; Rudolph, p. 145. The difference between those reckoned to Judah in II Samuel and here is because our writer is thinking of the kingdom of Judah, of which 30,000 were apparently attributed to Benjamin (so also Rudolph, p. 144). The Chronicler emphasizes all Israel rather than the two segments of Judah and Israel held together by the crown—a personal rather than organizational union.

[Alternatives of punishment, 8–14]: How David recognized that he had done wrong in taking the census is not disclosed. The Samuel parallel says his conscience troubled or accused him. Both this version and the one in Samuel present the king's confession in full. The prophet Gad offers him three alternative ways to make amends: (a) three years of famine, (b) three months' flight before his enemies, or (c) three days' pestilence. Pressed for an answer, David asked only that he be spared the humiliation of falling into the hands of enemies, literally oppressors, choosing rather to endure the direct stroke of Yahweh because of his great mercy. The choice, otherwise, was equally severe, three days of pestilence being about equivalent to three years of famine, as the number of the unfortunate victims indicates.

[The staying of the pestilence, 15–27]: The pestilence had apparently not yet run its full course since the destroying angel was about to do his work at the capital as he had done throughout the land (II Sam xxiv 15). But Yahweh intervened and stayed the hand of the angel. That was the vision David saw (vs. 16) when he and the elders were on their way to the high place to do penance. The angel appeared suspended in the air over Jerusalem with his sword drawn and was a divine functionary, not a surrogate of Yahweh himself as in earlier stories. The Chronicler has combined two features here: that of destruction (cf. II Kings xix 35) and obstruction (Num xxii 22 ff.) and that of revelation (Num xxii 35). These functions may have been suggested by the angelic figure in the story of Balaam (Num xxii). See Rothstein and Hänel, p. 383. The function of revelation, particularly as it applies to the angelic mediation of the word of Yahweh to Gad (vs. 18), is exactly parallel to that of the angel in Zechariah.

The writer is more pointed in his description of David's confession of guilt than II Sam xxiv 17. David admits that he gave the order for the census and accepts full responsibility. He requests that the people be absolved and the punishment be visited upon him and his house—"spare your people from the plague." The reference to the elders may be a contemporary interpretation of "the servants" who came with the king (II Sam xxiv 20) and points forward to the transaction with Ornan. Cf. transaction of Abraham with Ephron (Gen xxiii 11), and the scene at the city gate at Bethlehem in Ruth iv which involved the transfer of property. II Samuel says nothing of Ornan or his sons seeing the angel. The Chronicler follows protocol by having Ornan bow down before the king, who, contrary to the report of the meeting in II Sam xxiv opens the conversation. It is clear that his model was the Abraham-Ephron deal in Gen xxiii, since the term for the monetary consideration is the same in each case. Ornan offers not only to sell the threshing floor, but also to furnish the offerings necessary for the king's use; even the wheat for a meal offering was involved, in accordance with the regulation of *P* that a meal offering was to be included with every burnt offering (Exod xxix 38 ff.; Num xv 1 ff.). The difference in price (50 shekels of silver for oxen *and* threshing floor in II Samuel; 600 shekels of gold for the threshing floor alone here) may be due to the fact that David could not have paid less for the property of Ornan than Abraham had paid for the cave at Machpelah (400 shekels of silver), because he was regarded as *the* greatest Hebrew of them all. Curtis (Curtis and Madsen, p. 253) suggests that since gold figures so prominently in the temple, the Chronicler characteristically puts the price in terms of gold, with his typical exaggerations (twelve times the amount given in II Samuel). As Rashi speculates, he may have thought of fifty shekels as the contribution for each tribe since the temple was for all Israel. Attention may also be called to the tradition connecting the Mount Moriah of Abraham and the Mount Zion of David, which may be in the background of the writer's mind. According to the lists, David was regarded as a descendant of Abraham through Judah, the son of Jacob. The relationship of Abraham and David, and the apparent or hidden parallels, are probably no accident; they seem to be part of the total scheme of Israelite history, to which the Chronicler attached his own extension.

Thus the first part of the command of Yahweh through the angel to Gad the prophet was carried out. With the help of provisions ready to hand—the oxen, the wood, and the grain—the proper offering was made upon an altar constructed by David on the threshing-floor site. The acceptance of the offering was confirmed by the fire from heaven, a powerful attestation of divine approval (cf. Judg vi 21; I Kings xviii 38; II Chron vii 1). The response of Yahweh indicated the appeasement of his wrath and meant the cessation of the pestilence for Jerusalem. It had already done its work in the rest of the land (II Sam xxiv 25 affirms that the plague was checked in Israel), and hence the offering is interpreted as having efficacy only for staying the plague in the capital.

[How Jerusalem became the cult center for Israel, 28-30, xxii 1]: This is the Chronicler's explanation for the transfer of the cult from Gibeon to Jerusalem. Evidently we are to understand that David and his company were going to Gibeon to consult Yahweh there but were met by the angel of destruction (vs. 30). That experience called for heroic action: the hasty construction of an altar and the offering of a sacrifice thereon. The favorable response of Yahweh to that offering led to the proclamation in xxii 1. The whole episode therefore served to show how Jerusalem was chosen for the temple. For a discussion of the location see Vincent and Steve, *Jerusalem de l'Ancien Testament,* p. 634; Avi-Yonah, *Sepher Yerushalayim,* I, Map 9, opposite p. 160; A. Parrot, *The Temple of Jerusalem,* 1957, opposite p. 19.

22. DAVID'S PREPARATIONS FOR THE TEMPLE. HIS CHARGE TO SOLOMON FOR ITS CONSTRUCTION (xxii 2–19)

XXII 2 Then David ordered all foreigners in the land of Israel to come together and he made them quarrymen to cut out ashlar to build the house of God. 3 David also prepared a large quantity of iron for nails for the doors of the gates and for the clamps, together with a vast quantity of bronze, beyond weighing, 4 and innumerable cedar logs, for the Sidonians and Tyrians brought large quantities of cedar logs to David. 5 For David thought, "My son Solomon is still young and inexperienced and the house to be built for Yahweh must be exceedingly great, the most famous and splendid in all lands; therefore I will make preparations for it." Hence David made such lavish preparations before his death. 6 Then David summoned Solomon his son and commanded him to build the house of Yahweh God of Israel. 7 David said to Solomon, "My son, I was determined to build a house in honor of Yahweh my God, 8 but the word of Yahweh came to me saying, you have spilled much blood and fought great wars; you must not build a house in my honor because you have spilled so much blood in my sight upon the earth. 9 See, a son shall be born to you, he shall be a man of peace and I will give him peace from his enemies on all sides, for Solomon is to be his name and I will bestow prosperity and security upon Israel in his time. 10 He shall build a house in my honor, he shall be my son and I will be his father, and I will establish the throne of his kingdom over Israel forever. 11 Now, my son, may Yahweh be with you that you may be successful in building the house of Yahweh your God, just as he promised concerning you. 12 May Yahweh indeed give you insight and understanding when he gives you charge of Israel that you may observe the law of Yahweh your God. 13 Then you will be suc-

cessful, if you adhere to the statutes and judgments which Yahweh gave to Moses as regulations for Israel; be courageous and
strong; do not be afraid, do not be disheartened! 14 Behold, by
my painful efforts I have provided for the house of God a hundred thousand talents of gold, a million talents of silver, together with bronze and iron beyond calculation, because there
was so much; I have also provided lumber and stones but you
may add to these. 15 In addition you have very many workmen,
quarrymen, masons, carpenters, and all sorts of craftsmen for
every type of work 16 in gold, silver, bronze, and iron. So get
to work and may Yahweh be with you." 17 Then David ordered
all the princes of Israel to assist Solomon his son. 18 "Has not
Yahweh your God been with you and given you peace on all
sides? For he has put all the inhabitants of the land into my
hands and the land is subdued before Yahweh and before his
people. 19 Therefore determine with heart and soul to seek Yahweh your God, rise and build the sanctuary of Yahweh God so
that the ark of the covenant of Yahweh and the holy vessels
of God may be brought into the house built in honor of Yahweh."

NOTES

xxii 2. *and he made them.* Understood.

3. *a large quantity of iron.* After the Philistine conquest iron apparently became plentiful in the land.

7. *in honor.* Literally "to the name."

10. Cf. II Sam vii 13; I Chron xvii 12–13.

in my honor. See NOTE on vs. 7.

11. The blessing of David reminds the reader of I Kings ii 3 and I
Chron xxviii 10.

14. *a hundred thousand talents of gold.* Approximately 3775 tons.

a million talents of silver. Approximately 37,750 tons, or more than
4¼ billion dollars worth.

19. *in honor of.* See NOTE on vs. 7.

COMMENT

There are no parallels to this section elsewhere, except for isolated verses. Either the writer had other sources available or he constructed it on the basis of later traditions which preserved records of what actually took place during the reign of Solomon.

[Preparations for the construction of the temple, xxii 2–5]: These verses reflect a degree of organization and administration hinted at in II Sam xxiv, viii 15–18, xx 24. The census clearly points to the development of a tighter control of affairs in the later years of David's reign, possibly in the wake of unrest in the empire. There were the rebellion of Absalom, the uprising of Sheba, and the Gibeonite affair. Then too there was the persistent desire of David to provide for a temple which required a vast amount of materials and labor. The Chronicler was, on the whole, conservative and therefore modified the extent of the corvée, making it apply only to the foreigners in Israel. The thought of forced labor for Israelites was repugnant to him as is evident from his altering Solomon's decree in I Kings v 13, which established labor battalions out of Israel, to aliens (II Chron ii 17–18, viii 7–10 || I Kings ix 20 ff.). That some sort of corvée, which required census and organization, was levied under David is clear from the fact that there was an official who had charge of it (II Sam xx 24). See I. Mendelsohn, *Slavery in the Ancient Near East,* 1949, pp. 149 f. The forced laborers were set to quarrying ashlar for the walls of the structure. Other materials were also provided in extravagant amounts. As was pointed out above, it was one of David's cherished dreams to bring the cultus to Jerusalem and was, in all probability, present with him from the beginning of his reign. He did not want to repeat the fiasco of Saul, who never paid much attention to the cult. His ever expanding activities, including his wars, made it increasingly apparent that he would have to forgo the actual construction of the temple and content himself with the designation of the site and the gathering of materials. Then too cultic matters could not be hurried; they had to grow. Another reason for the pursuit of his plans, according to the writer, was the immaturity of Solomon. Just how old Solomon was at the time or, indeed, at what age he became king is not known. The Chronicler is hardly interested in age; he is concerned rather with the immensity and complexity of the task committed to Solomon—one which, be it remembered, David himself could not carry out. There may be more than a hint of coregency here since we know from I Kings that Solomon was elevated to the throne before the death of David. How long before is uncertain, but the narrative implies only a short time. It has been suggested that construction of the temple did not begin before the death of David. According to II Chron iii 2 (cf. I Kings iii 1, 7), Solomon opened building operations in the second month of the fourth year of his reign. Therefore, it is argued, there must have been a coregency of about four years. David's determination to have a temple built thus provides a possible motivation for a regency arrangement—to avoid a palace revolution that could jeopardize his plans.

[David's charge to Solomon, 6–16]: The writer's point of view is reflected here. It is obviously his intention to imitate the charge of David to Solomon in I Kings ii 1–9, where, in addition to the counsel concerning Joab, the sons of Barzillai, and Shimei, David exhorts Solomon to be faithful to the law of Moses. That charge is almost incidental here. The chief concern of the Chronicler is the command to build the temple. David goes into the reasons for his own failure to carry through his great ambition—he is a man of war and has spilled much blood (I Kings v 3 says he was too busy fighting his enemies). The chief reason was not his wars as such, but that he was a man of blood, a more or less ritual reason (cf. Goettsberger, p. 163). Underlying the Chronicler's story is a strong psychological revulsion against bloodshed, so that this becomes the compelling reason for the prohibition to build the temple. See also Rudolph, p. 151; he points out the advanced thought expressed here, the significance of which is still not fully appreciated. The wordplay on the name of Solomon in vs. 9 is unmistakable. The Hebrew reads *ky šlmh* ("Solomon") *yhyh šmw w-šlwm* ("peace") *w-šqṭ 'tn 'l-ysr'l bymym* (the underscored words are from the root). The contrast is striking—David a man of war, Solomon a man of peace. Note that concern for the house of God comes before the exhortation to observe the law of Yahweh. This is followed once more by reference to the building supplies on hand—an extraordinarily large number, typical of the Chronicler—and to workmen gathered together for the project.

[Charge to the officials, 17–19]: David's charge to Solomon was a private affair, preceding the public assembly at which he addressed the officials and the people and laid before them his plans for the building of the temple (chs. xxviii, xxix), a ceremonial occasion where the king's will was delivered to Solomon and they were the witnesses. This little pericope is directed to the officials alone; they are exhorted to stand by Solomon as they stood by him, and, in effect, are pledged to that end. King, officials, and people are to work together for the realization of David's heart's desire.

23. PREPARATIONS FOR THE TEMPLE: CLASSIFICATION OF THE LEVITES
(xxiii 1–32)

Classification of the Levites

XXIII 1 When David had become old and full of days, he made Solomon his son king over Israel, 2 and then summoned all the princes of Israel together with the priests and Levites. 3 The Levites of thirty years and over were polled; the number, after they were polled, was thirty-eight thousand men. 4 "Of these," said David, "twenty-four thousand are to direct the administration of the house of Yahweh, six thousand are to be official agents and judges, 5 four thousand are to be gatekeepers, and four thousand are to praise Yahweh with the instruments which I made for praise." 6 David divided them into orders named after the sons of Levi, that is, after Gershon, Kehath, and Merari. 7 Of the Gershunnites were Ladan and Shimei. 8 The sons of Ladan were first Jehiel, then Zetham and Joel, three. 9 The sons of Shimei were Shelomith, Haziel, and Haran, three; these were the chiefs of the family of Ladan. 10 The sons of Shimei were Jahath, Zina, Jeush, and Beriah; these four were the sons of Shimei. 11 Jahath was the first, Zizah the second; because Jeush and Beriah did not have many sons they were reckoned as one family. 12 The sons of Kehath were Amram, Izhar, Hebron, and Uzziel, four. 13 The sons of Amram were Aaron and Moses; Aaron was set apart for him to sanctify[a] the holy of holies, he and his sons forever, to burn incense before Yahweh, to minister to him and to bless in his name forever. 14 Moses, the man of God, and his sons were reckoned with the tribe of Levi. 15 The sons of Moses were Gershom and Eliezer.

[a] Vulg., Syr. "to minister in."

16 Of the sons of Gershom, Shebuel[b] was the first. 17 Of the sons of Eliezer, Rehabiah was the first; Eliezer had no other sons but the sons of Rehabiah were exceedingly numerous. 18 Of the sons of Izhar, Shelomith was the first. 19 The sons of Hebron were first Jerijah, the second Amariah, the third Jahaziel, and the fourth Jekameam. 20 The sons of Uzziel were Micah the first and Isshiah the second. 21 The sons of Merari were Mahli and Mushi, and the sons of Mahli were Eleazar and Kish. 22 Eleazar died without sons but he did have daughters whom their brothers, the sons of Kish, married. 23 The sons of Mushi were Mahli, Eder, and Jeremoth, three. 24 These were the sons of Levi of twenty years and over according to their families and heads of the families, according to their commissions in the list of their several names, who performed[c] the ministry of the house of Yahweh. 25 For David said, "Since Yahweh God of Israel has given rest to his people Israel and has taken up residence in Jerusalem forever, 26 the Levites need no longer carry the tabernacle or any of the objects required for its service—27 (for according to the last words of David that was the list of Levites of twenty years and over) 28 rather their place is beside the sons of Aaron in the service of the house of Yahweh, that is, in the care of the courts and the chambers, the purification of all the holy things, the work for the service of the house of God, 29 the layer bread, the flour for the meal offering, the unleavened wafers, the pan-baked materials, the unmixed materials, and all content and linear measures. 30 Furthermore they are to present themselves every morning to give thanks and praise to Yahweh, also every evening 31 and at the offering of burnt offerings to Yahweh on Sabbaths, new moons, and festivals, appearing regularly before Yahweh in accordance with the numbers required of them. 32 They shall, therefore, have charge of the tent of meeting and of the sanctuary and with the sons of Aaron their brothers of the ministry of the house of Yahweh."

b LXX^AB and xxiv 20 read "Shubael." See NOTE.
c Reading plural for singular with LXX.

NOTES

xxiii 4. *said David*. Insert because of the phrase "I made" in vs. 5.

official agents. For this rendering see Albright, AMJV p. 75, n. 56.

9. Perhaps "Jehiel" instead of "Shimei," with Galling, p. 64, n. 2; cf. also Kittel (see Selected Bibliography, Commentaries). Rehm thinks one of the sons of Ladan. Goettsberger takes "Shelomith . . . Ladan" as an addition belonging to an earlier verse, and "the sons of Shimei" of vs. 10 is then a repetition of 9a. That some such arrangement is called for appears from the notice at the end of vs. 9: "these were the chiefs of Ladan."

16. *Shebuel*. Name occurs on jar-handle stamp from Gibeon, on an eighth-century tomb in Jordan and on an ostracon from Nimrud. Cf. Pritchard, *Hebrew Inscriptions and Stamps from Gibeon*, pp. 3, 11 f.

22. *brothers*. Actually cousins.

25. *has taken up residence*. The verb *škn* is a significant priestly term, to indicate the precise manner of the divine residence. It is connected with *P*'s understanding of the *miškān* and the tabernacling presence of Yahweh with his people. (See F. M. Cross, Jr., "The Priestly Tabernacle," *The Biblical Archaeological Reader*, pp. 224–27.) In view of the flat statement here concerning Yahweh's permanent presence in Jerusalem, the vision of Ezekiel (chs. vii–ix) takes on added significance. This is a different concept from that of Deuteronomy and Jeremiah, neither of whom so closely identify God and name and temple.

27. Probably should follow vs. 24.

28. The work for the service of the house of God had to do with the preparation of the items mentioned, i.e., to see that they met legal requirements. For subordination of Levites to priests see 1QSa, line 23.

29. *the layer bread*. I.e., the presence bread or showbread regularly placed on the table provided for it in the temple.

30. *to give . . . Yahweh*. I.e., to fulfill their obligations as singers.

COMMENT

Preparations for the temple were not complete with arrangements for the material structure alone. While that phase was important, to judge from the space allotted to the building itself, the future nature of the temple service with its personnel was even more crucial. The next four chapters are devoted to the temple service and are to be taken as a unit, though several strata may be reflected in the composition. Most scholars are agreed that these chapters form a unit. Whether they were constructed by the Chronicler himself or are a later insertion is a question difficult to answer. Welch is of the opinion that chapters xxiii–xxvi are so confused that they defy attempts to bring them into any kind of order (*The Work of the Chronicler,* p. 81). We can hardly go further than Burnet who sees some indications that the writer utilized for his composition some traditions which may have been reduced to writing earlier but which, however, bear unmistakable signs of his style of writing (RB 60 [1953], 507). The framework of these chapters follows the order of Ezekiel which may have furnished the compiler's pattern (cf. Cazelles, p. 104, n. e.). But it appears that while he was following ancient practice he was at the same time accommodating himself to the situation current in his time, as will appear from the observations below.

[Introduction, xxiii 1–2]: These verses set the stage for what follows, especially in chapter xxviii. In other words, they introduce the order of service for the nation to be followed by the king and all his administrative officials. As might be expected from the Chronicler, the religious situation receives priority. Note the regular pattern of the writer of citing the functionaries to be dealt with in the reverse order of priority accorded them in what follows. The general terms in which the statement is couched points to the author's purpose of using David's arrangement as the authority for the practices involved.

[Census of the Levites, 3–5]: Provision for the temple services begins with the Levites who were counted in accordance with the precedent given in Numbers (iv 3, 23, 30), that is, from thirty years and up. The total far exceeds that of Num iv 48: 8580. If one again takes the *eleph* (thousand) to mean "unit," there would be a total of thirty-eight units. The complement per unit is not given. Applying the same principle in Numbers, there would be eight units with 580 men. There is an interesting, but probably accidental, correspondence between the administrative officials and the twenty-four courses (ch. xxiv). While the Chronicler's numbers here as elsewhere are exaggerated, there is a reason for it. In his reconstruction of Israel's history, the Davidic period represents a considerably larger population (with correspondingly greater wealth and power) than that of Moses. Of particular interest is the proportion of Levites

assigned to each category, and more especially the small number for
the instruments when earlier so much was made of them (ch. xvi).
If II Chron xxxiv 12 f. is to be credited, the building overseers were
drafted from the Levites, but it is doubtful if any of these categories
refer to building. Cazelles, p. 105, n. b., thinks there is no reference
here to the construction of the temple and that we are to regard
the administration of the house of Yahweh as having to do with
purely musical matters; the twenty-four thousand are then "without
doubt" singers. More likely they refer to temple services, if we are
to judge by the following chapters. The whole direction of this
passage points to the beginnings of the organization of the clergy
which doubtless had its inception in the time of David who was
always tremendously concerned about religious institutions and
orders.

[Organization of the Levites, 6–24]: The organization of Levites
was based on the three traditional families of Levi in the order followed by all the lists (Exod vi 17 f.; Num iii; I Chron vi). In the
list the Gershunnites are represented by Ladan (elsewhere Libni; see
COMMMENT on Sec. 6, vi 1–15; and Möhlenbrink, ZAW 52 [1934],
205 f.) and Shimei. The former has three sons, the latter four. The
second generation of Shimei has four names but they were reckoned
as three families because the latter two sons had but few sons. The
Kehathites are represented by four sons of Kehath but the line of
Aaron was excluded from the Levites at once because of its priestly
functions (vs. 13). On the other hand, Moses is relegated to the
Levites and his line is followed for the descendants of Amram.
Moses' son Gershom had only one son; so also Eliezer whose son
Rehabiah had numerous descendants. Amram's brother Izhar also
had just one son; Hebron had four and Uzziel two. Merari had two
sons. The older, Mahli also had two, though Eleazar had only daughters who married their cousins. The second son of Merari had
three sons. The families serving at the time contemplated in the
document numbered only twenty-two whereas in chapters xxiv, xxv
there were twenty-four courses of priests and musicians. That is
unusual in view of the Chronicler's feeling for the Levites. Perhaps
the whole chapter reflects a fluctuating situation (cf. Rudolph, p.
155) when the Levitical families were depleted; that might be the
reason for vs. 24, which lowers the age limit from thirty to twenty
years (vs. 3 follows the P tradition of Num iii; there is another
tradition in Num viii 24 which sets the lower age at twenty-five).

While the organizational details are doubtless contemporary with the period of the writer, the idea may be correctly attributed to David.

[Duties of the Levites, 25–32]: Verse 27 is out of place since it does not fit the context. It probably is to be placed after vs. 24. With the construction of the temple, the ark would be placed in its permanent abode. Hence there would be no need to carry it about from place to place, nor would it be necessary to move the tabernacle—about which our author speaks, following *P*. In any case more Levites were required to care for the tabernacle than to carry the ark. Consequently the duties of the Levites were altered. According to chapter xv they were assigned cultic responsibilities, particularly those of furnishing music for the services. That was an advancement for them. Here, however, they appear to be downgraded a bit for they are "to stand beside the sons of Aaron," that is, to assist them. Their duties are clearly subordinate to those of the priests. In effect they are made janitors (cf. *P* in Num iii 7 ff., iv 27–33), having charge of preparations for the materials used in the various services, of keeping the house of God clean and in order, and of seeing that the legal requirements are met. The significance of this passage is further stressed in the last verse, that is, that the Levites are in charge of the physical equipment of the sanctuary and with the priests compose the cultic personnel. As such, the situation reflected is that of the period of the writer for which he claims Davidic authority. On the Levitical organization and claims see J. Liver, "Korah, Dathan and Abiram," *Scripta Hierosolymitana,* VIII, 1961, pp. 189–217, especially sec. VII.

24. PREPARATIONS FOR THE TEMPLE: CLASSIFICATION OF THE PRIESTS AND THE OTHER LEVITES
(xxiv 1–31)

Classification of the priests

XXIV 1 The sons of Aaron according to their groups were as follows: the sons of Aaron were Nadab, Abihu, Eleazar, and Ithamar. 2 Nadab and Abihu died before their father and had no sons. Therefore Eleazar and Ithamar filled the office of priest. 3 David, with Zadok of the sons of Eleazar, and Ahimelech of the sons of Ithamar, allocated them to their ministry in accordance with their official classification. 4 Since the sons of Eleazar were found to have more headmen than the sons of Ithamar, they allocated sixteen clan heads to the sons of Eleazar and eight clan heads to the sons of Ithamar. 5 They allocated them by lot, both alike, for there were officials of the cult and officials of God among both the sons of Eleazar and the sons of Ithamar. 6 Shemaiah, the son of Nethanel, the Levitical scribe registered them in the presence of the king, the princes, Zadok the priest, Ahimelech the son of Abiathar, and the heads of the priestly and Levitical families, so that *a*two families*a* were selected for Eleazar for [each] one*b* selected for Ithamar. 7 The first lot came out for Jehoiarib, the second for Jedaiah, 8 the third for Harim, the fourth for Seorim, 9 the fifth for Malchijah, the sixth for Mijamin, 10 the seventh for Hakkoz, the eighth for Abijah, 11 the ninth for Jeshua, the tenth for Shecaniah, 12 the eleventh for Eliashib, the twelfth for Jakim, 13 the thirteenth for Huppah, the fourteenth for Jeshebkab, 14 the fifteenth for Bilgah, the sixteenth for Immer, 15 the seventeenth for Hezir, the eighteenth

a–a Cf. LXX; literally "one family and one." Context demands this translation.
b Reading "one" for first "selected." If this verse represents another tradition the MT may be intended as is, i.e. "Of the family of Eleazar one was selected, and one for [that] of Ithamar."

for Happizzez, 16 the nineteenth for Pethahiah, the twentieth for Jehezkel, 17 the twenty-first for Jachin, the twenty-second for Gamul, 18 the twenty-third for Delaiah, the twenty-fourth for Maaziah. 19 These were their official classifications⁰ for their ministry when they entered the house of Yahweh in accordance with their prescriptions laid down by Aaron their father as Yahweh God of Israel commanded him.

The rest of the Levites

20 Concerning the rest of the Levites. Of the sons of Amram, Shubael; of the sons of Shubael, Jehdeiah. 21 Concerning Rehabiah: of the sons of Rehabiah, Isshiah, the first one. 22 Of the Izharites, Shelomoth; of the sons of Shelomoth, Jahath; 23 Of the sons of Hebron: Jerijah the first, Amariah the second, Jahaziel the third, and Jekameam the fourth. 24 The son of Uzziel was Micah^d; of the sons of Micah, Shamir. 25 The brother of Micah was Isshiah; of the sons of Isshiah, Zechariah. 26 The sons of Merari were Mahli and Mushi; of his sons, Jaaziah his son. 27 The sons of Merari, by his son Jaaziah, were Shoham, Zaccur, and Ibri. 28 Of Mahli there were Eleazar, who had no sons, 29 and Kish; and of the sons of Kish, Jerahmeel. 30 The sons of Mushi were Mahli, Eder, and Jerimoth. These were the Levites according to their families. 31 The family head and his younger brother alike also cast lots before David the king, Zadok, Ahimelech, and the heads of the priestly and Levitical families, just as their brothers, the sons of Aaron [had done].

⁰ Reading plural for singular pointing of MT.
^d LXX^L adds "Mikah the first and Ishshiah the second." Cf. vs. 25. "Sons" may be carried over from the preceding verse.

NOTES

xxiv 5. For a similar rendering see N. Avigad in IEJ 7 (1957), 149. The import of the verse is that both lines of the priesthood—Eleazar and Ithamar—are given equal standing. Num iii 32 makes Eleazar chief of the Levitical overseers in charge of the sanctuary. But Exod xxviii 1 and Lev x 6 do not distinguish between the position of the two lines. The

Chronicler accepts that view so that both could be referred to as "officials of the cult and officials of God." The lot came out with sixteen for Eleazar to eight for Ithamar, because of the numerical preponderance of the former.

10. *Hakkoz.* For a discussion of the Hakkoz family see Avigad, IEJ 7 (1957), 149 f. It persisted into Maccabean times (I Maccabees viii 17).

20. *Shubael.* See NOTE on xxiii 16.

23. *Hebron.* So with xxiii 19.

Jerijah the first. From xxiii 19; it fell out of text here. For another suggestion see Rudolph, *in loco.*

Amariah. Name occurs on jar handles from Gibeon; in Bible only in Chronicles, Ezra, Nehemiah, and Zephaniah.

26. *of his sons.* So, following Rudolph's suggestion.

29. *and Kish.* Cf. xxiii 21.

31. *The family . . . alike.* See NOTE on vs. 5 above.

COMMENT

[The priestly divisions, xxiv 1–19]: The Chronicler's interest in cultic matters may be judged by the fact that he presents no fewer than six lists of priests or priestly families (others are ix 10–12; Neh x 1–8, xi 10–14, xii 1–7, 12–21), besides other references to them. The order of treatment, following Levites, is followed elsewhere in Chronicles (Chron vi, xii, xv, xvi). For the first two verses, the author draws upon the common priestly tradition (cf. Num iii 2–4, xxvi 60–61). Though he recalls the death of Nadab and Abihu before their father, he omits any reference to the cause of their death (he does give the cause of death of Er [ii 3] and Achan-Achar [ii 7]). He was probably concerned only with the reason for just two lines of priestly descent, in contrast with three for the Levites. Assisting David in the appointment of the priestly divisions are Zadok (representing Eleazar) and Ahimelech (representing Ithamar). The relegation of Ahimelech (Abiathar's son) to the line of Ithamar can hardly be historically accurate, if the evidence elsewhere is to be taken seriously. The Chronicler is naturally inclined to the line of Zadok, which was the prevailing one in the days of Solomon and later, as is indicated by his connecting him with Ahitub (vi 8, xviii 16). But according to I Sam xxii 20, Abiathar was a scion (grandson) of the Ahitub line; he was the representative of the Elides who lost their position under Solomon (I Kings ii 27). There was nothing left for our author to do but to follow the position taken earlier, which meant simply to relegate Ahimelech to the family of Ithamar; that of Zadok had pre-empted Eleazar. In any case, serious concern for the genealogical association of the priests with the sons of Aaron probably began in the time of Ezra (cf. Rudolph, *Esra und Nehemia* on Ezra viii 2; Kittel, GVI, III, pp. 401 ff.; Meyer, EJ, pp. 171 f.); Möhlenbrink, ZAW 52 [1934], 206, thinks this list breathes the spirit of historical narrative rather than that of genealogical interest.

The Eleazar line, which had been in favor since the days of Solomon, had twice as many representatives as the Ithamar line which was more or less on the side lines. The matter was resolved, not by demotion, but by the selection of two families of Eleazar for one from that of Ithamar. The registering was done by Shemaiah (otherwise unknown) in the presence of the king, the priests and the chiefs of the priestly and Levitical families. The story reflects, there-fore, the successful outcome of the struggle for proper recognition by the Ithamar family which had apparently been confined to Levitical duties other than those of the priesthood. However the Eleazar family still retained control by virtue of numbers. Why there were twenty-four divisions cannot now be determined; the earlier lists (Neh x, xii) contain only twenty-two.

It must be remembered that these names represent families and not individuals as such (for a sample of the listing of both see Neh xii 12–21). A number of these families continued down into New Testament times. It has been argued that the list comes from Mac-cabean times because Jehoiarib, who has replaced Jedaiah at the head of the list (cf. ix 10), was the family to whom the Maccabees belonged (I Maccabees ii 1, xiv 29). But then there is a tendency in that direction in all the lists except the one noted above (neither, of course, occur in Neh x 1–8). On the other hand the interchange of Jehoiarib for Jedaiah could have been made then and the list could have been much older. The discovery of a fragment of Chroni-cles at Qumran renders a Maccabean date virtually impossible for any part of Chronicles. Such a late date is highly improbable on other grounds, too. Only three of the names of those who returned with Zerubbabel are on the list. They must have been added later in the development of the courses, or they must have died out be-fore the Exile, or the return. It is possible that the list reflects late pre-exilic or exilic times rather than late postexilic practice. The persistence of the priestly families into later post-OT times may be accounted for on the grounds that others returned to Jerusalem at a later date to take up their duties or that the names were revived to conform to older lists. It is possible that the present list was a later addition to the Chronicler's work.

Zechariah was of the family of Abijah (Luke i 5). On a hypogeum in the Kidron Valley was found an inscription. While the inscription itself dates from the first century B.C., the burials had begun two centuries earlier mentioning the sons of Hezir (N. Avigad, *Ancient Monuments in the Kidron Valley* [Jerusalem, 1954], pp. 37–78). That family thus persisted down through the pre-Christian period. Others are mentioned in the Talmud (see Strack and Billerbeck, *Kommentar zum Neuen Testament aus Talmud u. Midrash,* II, 1924, pp. 55–71; E. Schürer, *Geschichte des jüdischen Volkes,* II, 3d ed., 1898, pp. 235–42, 266). Only three of the families of those who returned with Zerubbabel (Ezra ii 36–39 ‖ Neh vii 39–42) are definitely included in this list—Jedaiah, Immer, Harim. Possibly the family of Pashhur is represented by Malchijah (cf. Neh xi 12; I Chron ix 12). Our list represents the end of a period of development and expansion (see Rudolph, pp. 162 f., and Meyer, EJ, pp. 171–72). It is countersigned (vs. 19) by reference to the prescriptions of Aaron; David was responsible only for their arrangement into divisions for service.

[The other Levites, 20–31]: This is a later addition to the list of Levites given in the preceding chapter. It parallels the latter to a large extent but takes it a few steps further in several instances. To the family of Kehath, the line of Shubael (Shebuel) is extended to Jehdeiah, that of Rehabiah to Isshiah, that of Izhar to Jahath. The Hebron line is exactly the same (vs. 23 ‖ xxiii 19), that of Uzziel goes to Shamir, that of Isshiah the second son of Uzziel to Zechariah. The Merari family has the line of Mahli through Kish extended to Jerahmeel, while that of Mushi remains the same (vs. 30a ‖ xxiii 23). A new line is added—that of Jaaziah a third son of Merari; Jaaziah is represented by three sons: Shoham, Zaccur, Ibri. Ten more names are added. Doubtless they reflect the situation at the time of the author. Noteworthy is the absence of the Gershon family; why can only be speculated. Nor can we be certain of the exact time to which the list is to be assigned. The addition of only one name in most instances points to a generation later than the list in chapter xxiii (Benzinger, p. 70, thinks the addition is

Maccabean). But the development of a whole new line in the family
of Merari could mean that a considerably later period is envisioned
since enough time elapsed to allow for its growth and/or the possible
displacement of Mushi. The purpose of this addition may have been
more than simply the changed situation; it may have been due to
the fact that the writer wished to extend the Levitical courses to an
equality with that of the priests and singers, though it is impossible
to get twenty-four courses out of the present text without drastic
juggling and surgery. (Kittel, pp. 86 f., refers to a total of twenty-
four names without Gershon and he believes that points to the purpose of the writer. Josephus [*Antiquities* VII.xiv] also thought there
were twenty-four divisions of Levites.) Yet vs. 31 indicates, by the
use of the same process of selection, that the Levitical families were
of equal importance with the others, that is, the priests and singers.

[Special note on classification of priests]: In Egypt, in the Old
Kingdom period, the priests in the service of the mortuary temples
were distributed into watches (phyles) based on old nautical practices. Temple services were organized in such a manner that each
of the four shifts was responsible for one month's service out of
every four, or a total of three months per year. A staff list of officials
serving in the mortuary temple of Senwosret III (1878–1843 B.C.)
appears in the texts found at Illahun. Nine permanent administrative officials are mentioned together with the rest of the priests who
were divided into four groups (Eg. *sa,* Gr. *phyle,* meaning watch.
Cf. Heb. *mišmārōt* "watches"). Service in a given *sa* was hereditary,
as shown by the family designations extending in some cases through
three or four generations. The practice of service relays was apparently continued down into Ptolemaic times, when it was extended
into five phyles. The three-month-service idea was taken over from
the corvée. See H. Kees, *Das Priestertum im ägyptischen Staat*
(Leiden, 1953), pp. 300–8, and "Die Phylen und ihre Vorsteher
im Dienst der Tempel und Totenstiftungen," *Orientalia* 17 (1948),
71–90, 314–25; and J. Černý, *Ancient Egyptian Religion* (London,
1952), p. 117.

A *mišmarot* manuscript from 4Q at Qumran lists the feasts of the
year with the months in which they occur and the priestly orders
for the Sabbath services. The names of the priestly orders given in
the published fragment in the *Volume du Congrès: Strasbourg,*
1956, p. 25, are Meoziah (Maaziah), Jedaiah, Seorim, Jeshua, and
Joiarib. See further J. T. Milik, *Dix ans de découvertes dans le*

désert de Juda, 1957, pp. 70–74. A fragmentary inscription from Caesarea preserves a numerical sequence of fifteenth, sixteenth, and seventeenth courses (?), which may or may not refer to the priestly orders. *Views of the Biblical World,* IV, 1961, p. 257.

25. PREPARATIONS FOR THE TEMPLE: CLASSIFICATION OF THE MUSICIANS
(xxv 1–31)

The classes of musicians

XXV 1 David and the cult officials selected the sons of Asaph, Heman, and Jeduthun to [lead] the service; they were to prophesy*a* with zithers, with harps, and with cymbals. The list of ministrants and their types of service was as follows: 2 Of the sons of Asaph: Zaccur, Joseph, Nethaniah, and Asarelah; the sons of Asaph were under the direction of Asaph who prophesied under orders of the king. 3 Of Jeduthun there were the sons of Jeduthun: Gedaliah, Zeri, Jeshaiah, Shimei*b*, Hashabiah, and Mattithiah, six, under the direction of their father Jeduthun who prophesied with the zither in connection with the giving of thanks and praise to Yahweh. 4 Of Heman there were the sons of Heman: Bukkiah, Mattaniah, Uzziel, Shebuel, Jerimoth, Hananiah, Hanani, Eliathah, Giddalti Romamti-ezer, Joshbekashah, Mallothi, Hothir, and Mahazioth. 5 All these were the sons of Heman the king's seer, to exalt his horn according to the words of God, for God gave Heman fourteen sons and three daughters. 6 Under the direction of their father, all these were occupied with song to the accompaniment of cymbals, harps, and zithers for the service of the house of God under the orders of the king—Asaph, Jeduthun, and Heman. 7 Together with their brothers trained in the songs of Yahweh, all masters, they numbered two hundred and eighty-eight. 8 They cast lots for relays of service, for the younger as for the older, for the master as for the pupil. 9 The first lot came out for Asaph, for Joseph; the second for Gedaliah, he, his sons, and his brothers, twelve; 10 the third for Zaccur, his sons, and his brothers, twelve;

a So with LXX, Vulg. for MT "prophets."
b Insert with LXX; cf. vs. 17.

11the fourth for Izri, his sons, and his brothers, twelve; 12 the fifth for Nethaniah, his sons, and his brothers, twelve; 13 the sixth for Bukkiah, his sons, and his brothers, twelve; 14 the seventh for Jesarelah, his sons, and his brothers, twelve; 15 the eighth for Jeshaiah, his sons, and his brothers, twelve; 16 the ninth for Mattaniah, his sons, and his brothers, twelve; 17 the tenth for Shimei, his sons, and his brothers, twelve; 18 the eleventh for Azarel, his sons, and his brothers, twelve; 19 the twelfth for Hashabiah, his sons, and his brothers, twelve; 20 the thirteenth for Shubael, his sons, and his brothers, twelve; 21 the fourteenth for Mattithiah, his sons, and his brothers, twelve; 22 the fifteenth for Jeremoth, his sons, and his brothers, twelve; 23 the sixteenth for Hananiah, his sons, and his brothers, twelve; 24 the seventeenth for Joshbekashah, his sons, and his brothers, twelve; 25 the eighteenth for Hanani, his sons, and his brothers, twelve; 26 the nineteenth for Mallothi, his sons, and his brothers, twelve; 27 the twentieth for Eliathah, his sons, and his brothers, twelve; 28 the twenty-first for Hothir, his sons, and his brothers, twelve; 29 the twenty-second for Giddalti, his sons, and his brothers, twelve; 30 the twenty-third for Mahazioth, his sons, and his brothers, twelve; 31 the twenty-fourth for Romamti-ezer, his sons, and his brothers, twelve.

NOTES

xxv 1. *David and the cult officials.* See NOTE on xxiv 5 with reference there; cf. Num viii 25.

3. *Zeri.* To be read "Izri" with vs. 11.

4. *Shebuel.* See NOTE on xxiii 16.

5. *horn.* The horn was the symbol of plenty and strength (I Sam ii 10; Ps cxlviii 14; Lam ii 17).

6. A reflection on vs. 1 or belonging to what follows.

8. *the pupil.* The only occurrence of this term in OT.

9. Probably insert "his sons, and his brothers, twelve" to fill out the total of 288.

18. *Azarel.* So for "Uzziel" in vs. 4; cf. "Uzziah" and "Azariah," variants for same person.

23. *Hananiah.* Name occurs on twenty-one jar handles found at Gibeon (Pritchard, *Hebrew Inscriptions and Stamps from Gibeon*, pp. 8 f., 11). Cf. viii 24; Neh iii 8.

COMMENT

This is an attempt to authenticate the position of the Levitical singers by referring the origin of their position to David. They are meant to be put on an organizational footing just like the priests and Levites. All were regarded as official cult personnel who owed their position to appointment by "David and the cult officials." Special emphasis is placed on Asaph, Heman, and Jeduthun (or Ethan) who were associated with musical guilds. The origin of these guilds goes back to the Canaanites, as is shown by the fact that both Heman and Ethan are referred to as Ezrahites (ii 6; Ps lxxxix, title; see Albright, ARI, p. 210, n. 95). The tradition of David's founding of some kind of musical orders is quite probable because of his interest in music (cf. I Sam xvi 23, xviii 10, xix 9; II Sam i 17 ff., vi 5, 14) and composition of songs. To judge from cultic practices reflected in the Psalms and elsewhere, music was closely associated with worship; that it was highly developed by the eighth century is shown by the fact that Sennacherib accepted male and female singers as tribute from Hezekiah.

Certain types of prophecy too were linked to the cult (see Mowinckel, *Psalmenstudien*, III, 1923; A. R. Johnson, *The Cultic Prophet in Ancient Israel*, 1944; A. C. Welch, *Prophet and Priest in Old Israel*, 1936, especially Ch. IV). The references to cult prophecy in vss. 1–5 follow an old pattern. The cult prophets who met Saul after his first interview with Samuel (I Sam x 5–13) were coming down from the high place (cf. also I Sam xix 18–24). A good illustration of how cult prophecy operated is found in II Chron xx where Jahaziel prophesied in answer to Jehoshaphat's prayer; and Jahaziel was a Levite. There is some evidence that Levites took the place of cult prophets, as may be seen in the parallel passages of II Kings xxiii 2 and II Chron xxxiv 30. In any case, at the time of the compiler of their list, cult prophecy must have been well established and claimed for its authority the appointment of classes of musicians in the service by none other than David. That they were regarded as Levites is certain from II Chron v 12, xxix 12 ff. Asaph and Jeduthun are mentioned with the Levites in Neh xi 17 f.; neither Heman nor Ethan are named in Ezra-Nehemiah. The latter is assigned to Gershom in I Chron vi 42 and another

Ethan to Merari in vi 44, xv 17, 19. The order in vs. 1 is the one generally followed in Chronicles (II Chron v 12, xxix 12 ff., xxxv 15), but Asaph is frequently named first where he is mentioned with one or both of his brothers (but "Heman, Kalkol, and Darda" in I Kings iv 31 ‖ I Chron ii 6; and Heman is first in xv 19; xvi 41, 42). Here even the first lot comes out for him. It has been observed that at the time of writing Asaph no longer played the leading role (Rudolph, p. 168), mainly on the basis of the number of families attributed to him. Asaph was represented by four families, Jeduthun by six, and Heman by fourteen. Two Psalm titles (xxxix, lxii) contain the name of Jeduthun, twelve that of Asaph (l, lxxiii–lxxxiii), one that of Heman (lxxxviii), and one that of Ethan. That proves nothing as to their origin; it simply indicates the persistence of a tradition indicative of the tenacity of the names in cultic affairs. At least five of these Psalms (l, lxxv, lxxvi, lxxxi, lxxxii) contain prophetic elements. Cf. Gunkel and Begrich, *Einleitung in die Psalmen*, pp. 329–81. On the other hand, the reference to prophesying may signify prophetic (poetic) inspiration (cf. Mowinckel, *Psalmenstudien*, III, p. 26). Only the family of Asaph occurs among the returnees from Babylon (Ezra ii 41 ‖ Neh vii 44; Ezra iii 10); in Neh xi 17 f. the families of Asaph and Jeduthun are mentioned. I Esdras i 15, v 27, 59 speaks only of Asaph, though that may be due to the sources but Josephus says the Levites and the sons of Asaph sang hymns at the laying of the foundations of the temple (*Antiquities* XI.iv). Certainly one would expect references to Heman in the later literature if he became the most important of the Levitical musicians. The emphasis upon Heman here may be due to the fact that he is said to have been the king's seer, for the seers are very prominent in Chronicles. Or it may be because of the desire to fill the number of twenty-four divisions of musicians which was done by making names out of a psalm thus obscured. There have been many attempts to interpret 4b as a psalm. They go as far back as H. Ewald (1870); E. Kautzsch (ZAW 6 [1886], 260) thought at least a part of the complex of names was poetic. P. Haupt devoted an article—"Die Psalmverse I Chr. 25:4," (ZAW 34 [1914], 142–45)—to it. H. Torczyner also treated it in JBL 68 (1949), 247–49, with a number of modifications. For other suggestions and variations on the theme see the commentaries. As it now stands, with only slight change in vocalization and word division, it can be rendered as follows:

Be gracious to me, Yahweh, be gracious to me;
My God art thou;
I have magnified, and I will exalt [my] helper;
Sitting [in] adversity I said,
Clear signs give plentifully.

It may be that we have here incipits of hymns sung by the Levitical singers. The existence of hymn catalogues has now been demonstrated in abundance. Cf. H. Gressmann, AOB, pp. 326 ff.; S. N. Kramer, BASOR 88 (December 1942), 10–19; W. F. Albright, HUCA 23, Pt. I (1950–51), 1–39. On line 1 of the preceding translation, cf. Pss li 3, lvi 2, lvii 2 (all introductory passages); on line 2, cf. Ps lxiii 2; on line 3, cf. Pss xxxiv 4, cxv 9–11. For the last two lines there is no satisfactory parallel.

Whatever may have been the original status of 4b, it is quite clear that the compiler interpreted the nine Hebrew words as names, as shown by his list below. If they were a psalm fragment or incipits originally, he interpreted them, intentionally or unintentionally, as names to fill out the number of sons necessary to Heman to fill out the complement of twenty-four names essential for the number of divisions of singers to correspond with those of the priests. In the conduct of the temple services the singers were nearly as important as the priests, though their importance apparently receded afterward since Josephus and later writers make no mention of them. Inasmuch as the choice by lot is completely artificial, the whole scheme may be no more than a pious hope. If so, it is an excellent illustration of the writer's magnification of temple personnel whose origins are traced back to David.

26. PREPARATIONS FOR THE TEMPLE: CLASSIFICATION OF THE GATEKEEPERS AND TREASURY OFFICIALS
(xxvi 1–28)†

XXVI 1 For the divisions of the gatekeepers, of the Korahites there was Meshelemiah the son of Kore, of the sons of Asaph.*a* 2 The sons of Meshelemiah were Zechariah his firstborn son, Jediael the second, Zebadiah the third, Jathniel the fourth, 3 Elam the fifth, Jehohanan the sixth, and Eliehoenai the seventh. 4 The sons of Obed-edom were Shemaiah his firstborn son, Jehozabad the second, Joah the third, Sachar the fourth, Nethanel the fifth, 5 Ammiel the sixth, Issachar the seventh, and Peullethai the eighth—for God had blessed him. 6 Shemaiah his son also fathered sons who exercised leadership in their family because they were men of outstanding quality. 7 The sons of Shemaiah were Othni, Rephael, Obed, and Elzabad whose brothers Elihu and Semachiah*b* were outstanding men. 8 All these were sons of Obed-edom who with their sons and brothers were men of standing and qualified for service; altogether Obed-edom had sixty-two [sons and brothers]. 9 Meshelemiah had eighteen outstanding sons and brothers. 10 The sons of Hosah, of the sons of Merari, were Shimri the head, who was not the first-born son though his father made him head, 11 Hilkiah the second, Tebaliah the third, and Zechariah the fourth; Hosah had thirteen sons and brothers in all. 12 These divisions of the gatekeepers, allocated according to their head

† I Chron xxvi 1–28: cf. I Chron ix 17–27, xvi 37–43, Ezra ii 42, Neh vii 45, xi 19.

a LXXᴮ has "Abia-Saphar." The Hebrew consonants would be *'bysp*, which could be vocalized as "Abiasaph" or "Ebiasaph." MT has "Ebiasaph" in ix 19. "Ebiasaph" may be right since it is difficult to believe that Meshelemiah belonged to the family of celebrated temple musicians.
b Also found in Weidner texts and Lachish ostraca.

men, had obligations, just like their brothers, to minister in the house of Yahweh. 13 They cast lots for each gate in the same way whether their family was small or great. 14 The lot for the east [gate] fell to Shelemiah; and when they cast lots for⁰ Zechariah his son, a clever counselor, his lot came out for the north [gate]; 15 that for Obed-edom for the south [gate] and that for his sons for the storehouses; 16 and that for Hosah for the west [gate], with the Shallecheth᙭ Gate on the upper road. The corresponding guards were as follows: 17 for the east gate six per day᙭, for the north gate four per day, for the south gate four per day, for the storehouses ᶠtwo eachᶠ, 18 for the Parbar at the west gate four for the road and two for Parbar. 19 These were the divisions of the gatekeepers of the sons of Korah and the sons of Merari.

Other Levitical officials

20 The Levites, ᵍtheir brothers,ᵍ who had charge of the treasures of God's house and of the treasures of consecrated gifts, were 21 the sons of Ladan belonging to the Gershunnites—of Ladan were the heads of the families of Ladan the Gershunnite —that is, the Jehielites. 22 The sons of the Jehielites, Zetham and Joel his brother, had charge of the treasures of the house of Yahweh. 23 Over [the assignments pertaining to] the Amramites, the Izharites, the Hebronites, and the Uzzielites was 24 Shebuelʰ, the son of Gershom, the son of Moses, who was chief overseer of the treasures; 25 and his brothers [of the line of] Eliezer were Rehabiah his son, Jeshaiah his son, Joram his

⁰ So with LXX, Vulg.
ᵈ Known only from this passage. LXXᴮ reads ". . . to Iossa to the west, with the gate of the [priest's] chamber of the upper road"; Vulg. reads "near the gate that leads to the road of ascent." The Vrs. thus read liškāh or liškat ("room") for "Shallecheth." They may be correct; the MT can be explained as a metathesis. Cf. LXX of I Chron ix 26, xxiii 28, xxviii 12; II Chron xxxi 11; I Esdras ix 1. See also Vincent and Steve, Jerusalem de l'Ancien Testament, p. 607; J. Simons, Jerusalem in the Old Testament, 1952, p. 426.
ᵉ With LXX; MT has "Levites"; a scribal error.
ᶠ⁻ᶠ So for MT "two, two." There were apparently two storehouses (cf. Neh xii 25).
ᵍ⁻ᵍ So with LXX for Heb. Ahaiah.
ʰ xxiii 16 has "Shubael"; so also LXXᴬ and Vulg.

son, Zichri his son, and Shelomoth his son. 26 That Shelomoth and his brothers had charge of the consecrated treasures which David the king, the family heads, the captains of the thousands and the hundreds, and the commanders of the army had dedicated. 27 They had dedicated the booty acquired in war to the service of the house of God. 28 Also everything that Samuel the seer, Saul the son of Kish, Abner the son of Ner, and Joab the son of Zeruiah had dedicated—in fact everything that had been dedicated—was in charge of Shelomoth and his brothers.

NOTES

xxvi 8. *sixty-two*. See xvi 38, which has "sixty-eight" for Obed-edom.

14, 15. *[gate]*. Added for clarification of context.

16. *and*. Omitting "Shuppim" as dittography of preceding word.

18. *Parbar*. Term occurs in a Lydian inscription from Sardis, with the same meaning as here (E. Littmann, *Sardis*, VI, Pt. I, 1916, and *Kleinasiatische Forschungen*, I, 1930, pp. 18 ff.). J. M. Allegro thinks item 31 of the Copper Scroll confirms the meaning attributed to it— open pavilion, summer house, treasury (*The Treasure of the Copper Scroll*, 1960, p. 117). Here it probably refers to a place of some kind.

21. Verse is corrupt and difficult.

25, 28. *Shelomoth*. So for "Shelomith," as in xxiii 9, 18, xxiv 22, xxvi 26.

COMMENT

Like the preceding sections, this one deals with cultic officials of a more or less peripheral nature. That they were looked upon as important is shown by the fact that they were classified as Levites. Yet they were regarded as of a somewhat lower order, as may be seen from the position they occupy in the general scheme of temple ministrants (for arrangements for service in the Qumran community, see "Additions to Manual of Discipline," in D. Barthelemy and J. T. Milik, *Qumran Cave I*, 1955, pp. 108–18). This chapter also belongs to a later stratum of this section of the Bible because the gatekeepers apparently did not have Levitical status in Ezra ii 42, 70, vii 24, x 24; Neh x 28, xi 19. The normal order of treatment is here followed, that is, the gatekeepers coming after the musicians (for the reverse see xxiii 3–5; Neh vii 73, x 28, 39).

[The gatekeepers, xxvi 1–19]: Chronicles has three lists of gate-keepers (ix 17 ff., xvi 37 ff., and here) of which this is the most extensive. I Chron xvi 37 ff. mentions only two—Obed-edom and Hosah. That in ix 17 ff. has four families—Shallum, Akkub, Talmon, and Ahiman; Shallum is succeeded by his son Zechariah and their lineage is traced back to Korah. The total number of persons is given as 212. Ezra ii 42 (|| Neh vii 45) lists six families—Shallum, Ater, Talmon, Akkub, Hatita, Shobai—with a total of 138 (139) persons. Neh xi 19 gives only Akkub and Talmon with 172 persons; xii 25 has three—Meshullam, Talmon, and Akkub. According to Ezra x 24, Shallum and Telem (Talmon) had married foreign wives. Look-ing at the lists as a whole, those in Ezra and Nehemiah and I Chron ix 17 ff., with slight expansions are fairly similar, though it would appear that the latter is later because it connects the gatekeeper families with the Levites. Our list seems to be a combination of ix 17 ff. and xvi 37 ff., with additions bringing it up to the date of the compiler. An interesting feature is the progress of the family of Obed-edom which was apparently unsuccessful in attaining higher aspirations (cf. Rudolph, p. 174). While the Meshelemiah family numbered only eighteen and the family of Hosah thirteen, Obed-edom had sixty-two. This fact may have been the reason for his position—"for God had blessed him" (vs. 5b). A curious feature here is the noticeable decline in the number of gatekeeper families —ninety-three.

The allotments came out in such a way that two gates fell to the family of Shelemiah and one each for Obed-edom and Hosah. Perhaps some justification was required for the double assignment of Shelemiah which was done by pointing out that Zechariah was "a clever counselor." The importance of their function is indicated by the notice that they had duties to perform in the administration of the house of Yahweh "just like their brothers." The whole procedure also indicates that the writer was thinking of an existent temple complex which in his time would have been the second one. It has been pointed out that there was no south gate in the period of the Solomonic temple because the palace adjoined it on that side, which obviated the need for a guard there. The references to a south gate in Ezekiel (xl 24, 28) is part of a vision of things to come, though it probably cannot be ruled out altogether. If there was a south gate in the period of the first temple, Rothstein and Hänel, pp. 468, 472, may be right in regarding Obed-edom's assignment thereto as due to his close relationship with David. The guard detail for gates, storehouses, and Parbar is given in vss. 17–18. Because of its importance, six guards are assigned to the east gate; to each of the others, four. Thus the family of Shelemiah was responsible for ten guards, Obed-edom for eight, and Hosah for six, a total of twenty-four for each day.

[Other Levitical officials, 20–28]: One group (20–28) was charged with the care of the temple treasury, which had custody of two types of possessions. One had to do with "the treasures of God's house," that is, the offerings and the implements of worship (cf. ix 28–29, xxiii 28–29). The other consisted of "the treasures of consecrated gifts" which is explained by vss. 27 f. The first office was committed to the Gershunnites, the second to the Amramites. The reference to the contributions of Samuel, Saul, Abner, and Joab certainly does not sound like the Chronicler, who had nothing good to say about Saul. On the other hand, it may actually carry further one of his fundamental conceptions which is expressed in the constantly recurring phrase "all Israel," or "all the congregation of Israel." If that is really the case, this addition serves to strengthen that principle by emphasizing the combined contributions of seers, kings, and generals toward the central religious institution of the nation.

27. DAVID'S CIVIL AND MILITARY ARRANGEMENTS
(xxvi 29–32, xxvii 1–34)

XXVI 29 Of the Izharites, Chenaniah and his sons were designated to perform outside duties for Israel as official agents and
judges. 30 Of the Hebronites, Hashabiah and his brothers, seventeen hundred outstanding men, were in charge of the administration of Israel in the territory west of the Jordan pertaining
to all the affairs of Yahweh and the service of the king. 31 Of
Jerijah, the head of the Hebronites—there were sought and
found among the Hebronites, according to their lineage and
families, men of outstanding quality at Jazer in Gilead in the
fortieth year of David's reign—32 and his brothers there were
twenty-seven hundred outstanding men, heads of families,
whom David the king placed in charge of the Reubenites, the
Gadites, and the half-tribe of Manassites in matters pertaining
to God and the king.
XXVII 1 This is the roster of the sons of Israel by family
heads, captains of the thousands and the hundreds together with
their official agents who served the king in every matter pertaining to the divisions on duty in monthly relays throughout all
the months of the year; each division consisted of twenty-four
thousand men. 2 Jashobeam the son of Zabdiel was in charge of
the first division assigned for the first month: his division had
twenty-four thousand men. 3 He belonged to the family of Perez
and was the chief of all the army captains for the first month;
4 Dodai the Ahohite was in charge of a division for the second
month;[a] his division had twenty-four thousand men. 5 Benaiah,
the son of Jehoiada the chief priest, was the captain of the third
army for the third month; his division had twenty-four thousand

---

[a] Hebrew adds "and his division and Mikloth the leader." LXX[B] omits the
addition.

men. 6 That Benaiah was a mighty man among the thirty and over the thirty; his division was in charge of Ammizabad his son. 7 Asahel the brother of Joab, and Zebadiah his son after him, was fourth for the fourth month; his division had twenty-four thousand men. 8 Captain Shamhuth the Izrahite was the fifth for the fifth month; his division had twenty-four thousand men. 9 Ira, the son of Ikkesh the Tekoite, was sixth for the sixth month; his division had twenty-four thousand men. 10 Helez the Pelonite, one of the Ephraimites, was seventh for the seventh month; his division had twenty-four thousand men. 11 Sibbecai the Hushathite, of the Zerahites, was eighth for the eighth month; his division had twenty-four thousand men. 12 Abiezer the Anathothite, of the Benjaminites, was ninth for the ninth month; his division had twenty-four thousand men. 13 Maharai the Netophathite, of the Zerahites, was tenth for the tenth month; his division had twenty-four thousand men. 14 Benaiah the Pirathonite, of the Ephraimites, was eleventh for the eleventh month; his division had twenty-four thousand men. 15 Heldai the Netophathite, of Othniel, was the twelfth for the twelfth month; his division had twenty-four thousand men. 16 In charge of the tribes of Israel were chief Eliezer, the son of Zichri, for the Reubenites; Shephatiah the son of Maacah for the Simeonites; 17 Hashabiah the son of Kemuel for the Levites; Zadok for Aaron; 18 Elihu, one of the brothers of David, for Judah; Omri the son of Michael for Issachar, 19 Ishmaiah the son of Obadiah for Zebulun; Jerimoth the son of Azriel for Naphtali; 20 Hoshea the son of Azaziah for the Ephraimites; Joel the son of Pedaiah for the half-tribe of Manasseh; 21 Iddo the son of Zechariah for the Gilead half of Manasseh; Jaasiel the son of Abner for Benjamin; 22 and Azarel the son of Jeroham for Dan. These were the captains of the tribes of Israel. 23 But David did not count those twenty years old or under because Yahweh had promised to make Israel as numerous as the stars of the heavens. 24 Joab the son of Zeruiah had begun to count them but never finished; in as much as wrath came upon Israel because of it, the number was not recorded in the book*b* of the chronicles of

b So with LXX for Heb. "number," "list," "record."

King David. 25 Azmaveth the son of Adiel was in charge of the supplies of the king; Jehonathan the son of Uzziah was in charge of the supplies in the country, in the cities, in the villages, and in the fortresses. 26 Ezri the son of Chelub was in charge of the farmers who tilled the soil. 27 Shimei the Ramathite was in charge of vineyards and Zabdi the Shiphmite was in charge of products of the vineyards stored in the wine cellars. 28 Baal-hanan the Gaderite was in charge of the olive and sycamore trees in the Shephelah and Joash had charge of the oil supplies. 29 Shitrai the Sharonite was in charge of the cattle grazing on the plains of Sharon and Shaphat the son of Adlai was in charge of the cattle in the valleys. 30 Obil the Ishmaelite was in charge of the camels and Jehdeiah the Meronothite was in charge of the she-asses. 31 Jaziz the Hagrite was in charge of the flocks. All these were overseers of the property belonging to King David. 32 Jehonathan, David's uncle, who was a counselor, a wise man, and a scribe, and Jehiel the son of Hachmoni took care of the king's sons. 33 Ahithophel was the king's counselor and Hushai the Archite the friend of the king—34 Ahithophel was succeeded by Jehoiada the son of Benaiah—and Abiathar. Joab was the commander of the king's army.

NOTES

xxvi 29. *official agents.* See NOTE on xxiii 4.

31. *the fortieth year.* This is an interesting reference to the length of his reign because it tends to confirm it and points to its correctness, since nothing is served by such a reference.

32. *in matters . . . king.* I.e., over sacred and royal business. The Levitical cities were administrative and fiscal centers. See COMMENT on Sec. 6, 54–81.

xxvii 1. *official agents.* See NOTE on xxiii 4.

monthly relays. Literally ". . . which came and went month by month."

2. *Jashobeam.* xi 11 makes Jashobeam chief of the three.

8. *the Izrahite.* Cf. vs. 11 "Zerahite."

21. *the Gilead half of Manasseh.* Literally "for half-Manasseh in Gilead."

24. *wrath.* I.e., the divine wrath or displeasure (cf. Num i 53).

25. *Azmaveth.* On name see AASOR 4 (1924), 157.

the supplies of the king. Those in Jerusalem, as shown by the second half of the verse.

27. *in charge of vineyards.* May be pointed to read "keepers of the vineyards," parallel with farmers in vs. 26.

wine cellars. On meaning of the term "wine cellars," see M. Dahood, *Biblica* 40 (1959), 164. For the wine cellars at Gibeon, see J. B. Pritchard, BA 23 (1960), 28.

28. *the Shephelah.* I.e., the low hill country to the southwest of Jerusalem.

34. *Abiathar.* This must be the priest Abiathar who was among the original coterie of David (I Sam xxii 20).

COMMENT

It is obvious that this section has nothing to do with the preparations for the construction of the temple, with which xxiii–xxvi 28 are concerned. The source for the section may be a compilation of Davidic accounts referred to in vs. 24 and which contained both historical and fictional material.

[The Izharites and Hebronites, xxvi 29–32]: They were placed in charge of secular affairs. The former were designated to perform "outside obligations," which probably means duties coming under royal jurisdiction and so were outside the strictly priestly and Levitical functions connected with the cultus. According to II Chron xix 4–11, in the time of Jehoshaphat, priests and Levites were appointed to judicial posts. Josephus (*Antiquities* IV.viii.14) speaks of two Levites being appointed as assistants for each judge and since he refers this order to Moses the practice must have been old at the time. While the tradition ascribed to David here is obviously anachronistic, Albright (AMJV, p. 77, n. 59) thinks it reflects an accurate view of a significant function of the Levites in the later monarchy. The Hebronites were assigned administrative duties, for the king and the cult, in connection with the Transjordan tribes. Just what the functional relationship between the "official agents and judges" and the administrators of the tribes on the other side of the Jordan was is not clear. It has been argued that the whole practice of priestly Levitical administration reflects the Maccabean period when the priests were in control. It is more likely that it is somehow connected with Neh xi 16, though the outside duty there may refer

specifically to Levitical functions outside the cult proper. More than
that cannot be said but it surely antedates the Maccabean period.
It must be remembered that the sacred and secular sometimes in-
termingled indistinguishably. Moreover, there must be a vast mixture in Chronicles (as attested in this chapter) of materials of every
conceivable date from the time of David down to postexilic times.

[A list of divisional commanders of the monthly relays, xxvii
1–15]: The list corresponds closely to that of David's mighty men
(xi 11–47 ‖ II Sam xxiii 8–39). Here, however, they are commanders of divisions whose duty it was to serve the king in monthly
relays. That fact makes it clear that the writer did not copy it from
chapter xi but was dependent on a parallel list. Jashobeam stands
first in all three lists. According to xi 12 Eleazar is named as one of
the three; here it is his father, Dodai. Benaiah is no longer in
command of his division but his son Ammizabad is; so also in the
division of Asahel, who was followed by his son Zebadiah. There is
far more identification of family relationships here than in the earlier
chapter. The number twelve and its multiples are persistent throughout the Chronicler's work. In view of the twelve tribes and the
twelve months of court service, the rest fits in quite well. The number
twenty-four for the various groups of priests and temple servants
suggests relays of two weeks each. The whole plan appears to have
an empirical basis. Perhaps David had already divided Judah into
twelve administrative districts; then Solomon finished the organizational structure by extending it to Israel. That would provide a basis
for the twenty-four number system. The other orders then followed
the same pattern, if not immediately, then later. Again on the basis
of the *eleph* ("thousand") meaning unit, there is a total of 288
units. How many persons there were per unit is not known. Whatever the origin of the list, it indicates organization to a more than
ordinary extent. E. Junge sees a reflection here of the reorganization
of the army under Josiah (*Der Wiederaufbau des Heerwesens des
Reiches Juda unter Josia,* 1937, pp. 64 ff.) which was stationed at
fortified centers throughout the land. Here, however, there is no
reference to fortified places and the divisions appear to have been
for service at Jerusalem. David probably had no more than strategic
fortifications and was certainly without the elaborate divisional system with its monthly relays. Rothstein and Hänel, p. 495, think the
system of numbers follows the analogy of the singers but that it
may possibly have been due in part to the monthly details for the

provisioning of Solomon's court (I Kings iv 7 ff.). In any event as it now stands, it credits David with auspicious plans for the administration of the kingdom and while he was hardly responsible for the elaborate details and the numbers connected with the divisions, there may be truth in the over-all idea of organization, especially as it concerned the standing army. The troubles that beset the last years of David's reign doubtless caused him to reflect on the condition of his kingdom, which was not enviable. It is quite possible that the census was taken in preparation for the carrying out of just such organizational plans as are hinted at here.

[The tribal chiefs, 16–22]: The tribal chiefs listed belong to the Davidic period, according to the writer. Perhaps the only actual reflection of that period is the reference to the tribal system which obtained in that period. Many of the names are found only in the work of the Chronicler, though that does not automatically make them late. The twelve-tribe system is retained (cf. Num i) but the order is not the same, nor are the tribal arrangements within the twelve-unit system. The tribe of Levi is retained with special mention of Zadok as an Aaronite. Asher and Gad are omitted and to compensate for their omission Manasseh is divided into the districts in Cisjordan and Transjordan. The fact that Zadok is classified as an Aaronite points to the lateness of the list as it stands, since he was not so regarded until the time of Ezra. The nucleus of the list may be quite old, however, to judge from the inclusion of Reuben, Simeon, and Elihu, a brother of David. Or it could be a fabrication, which seems most unlikely. Perhaps Levi was retained because of the Chronicler's strong feeling for the Levites, though this chapter was a later addition to his work by one somewhat imbued with his spirit. The priestly line is naturally stressed too, but it appears subsidiary to Levi.

[The incompleted census, 23–24]: The sections above list the monthly relays of the army and the heads of the tribes. This little notice describes why there are no census figures for the nation as a whole. Two reasons are given for this deficiency, apart from the observation that those under twenty were not counted. Both reasons are religious in character; the one affirms that it was because of David's trust in the promise of Yahweh (Gen xv 5), the other that Joab never finished the census because the divine wrath fell upon the nation and hence the results of that part of it which was completed were not recorded in the official annals of the king. This

does not coincide with earlier reports. Chapter xxi 5 does record the
results of Joab's census, exclusive of Levi and Benjamin (xxi 6)
and the official record of II Sam xxiv 9 also contains figures pur-
porting to give the total number of persons for Israel and Judah.
See the commentaries on xxi 1–7. It is an attempt to smooth
out a bit the contradiction between chapter xxi and the next passage
and may be a later addition. In any case, not counting persons
under twenty years means that at least an attempt was made at a
census but even an attempt to do so would hardly harmonize
with the declaration of David's faith in the promises of God (cf.
Num i 3 for similar age limit); twenty years was the age limit for
full participation in the Qumran community (1QSa, col. i, line 10).
That age must have been the time for ordinary persons to enter upon
full responsibilities in civic life.

[Administrators of crown property, 25–31]: There is no indication of taxation in the time of David. His expenditures were met by
income from the crown property which began to accumulate in his
outlaw days and was largely the fruit of conquest. While the loose
spoils of war were dedicated to Yahweh, some of the land and
other property, such as cattle, camels, etc., were retained for the
use of the court. Storehouses for spoils of war were set up both at
Jerusalem and in the provinces. Azmaveth was the keeper of the
royal supplies in Jerusalem and Jehonathan had charge of those
in the provinces. But the management of the crown property was
very important, too—the farmers, the vineyards with the processing
and storing of wine, the olive and sycamore groves, the cattle
ranches, and the camels and she-asses. The far-reaching domain of
the king is striking—but much produce was required to support the
personnel and multitudinous activities of the court (cf. De Vaux,
Les Institutions de l'Ancien Testament, I, pp. 190 ff.). There can
hardly be doubt as to the antiquity of the list. The names are old,
the conditions reflected are not those prevalent in the age of Solomon or later. On the management of crown property, see M. Noth,
"Das Krongut der israelitischen Könige und seine Verwaltung,"
ZDPV 50 (1927), especially pp. 217, 230–40.

[Personal counselors, 32–34]: Along with public counselors and
administrative officials (cf. xviii 14–17 || II Sam viii 15–18, xx 23–
26), David had private advisers. Jehonathan, David's uncle, is
mentioned only here in the Bible. He and Jehiel (only here) were
in charge of the sons of the king, that is, over their upbringing,

education, etc. From earlier sources we learn of the position of Ahithophel (II Sam xv 12) and his subsequent defection (II Sam xvi 15–xvii 23). His counsel to Absalom was defeated by that of Hushai, another trusted friend of the king. On the Egyptian title of "friend of the king," "well-beloved friend of the king" and "near-est friend of the king" see A. Erman, *Life in Ancient Egypt* (Eng. tr. by H. M. Tirard), 1894, p. 72. Rudolph points out that the meaning changed under Solomon (I Kings iv 5) from honorific to official. It probably carries with it the function of adviser to the king. See now H. Donner, "Der Freund des Königs," ZAW 73 (1961), 269–75, and A. H. Gardiner, *Ancient Egyptian Onomastica*, I, 1947, p. 20,* No. 74.

After his suicide, Ahithophel was succeeded by Jehoiada the son of Benaiah known only from this passage. This may point to the date of the source—late in the reign of David. Abiathar is certainly the long-time associate of David (I Sam xxii 20 ff.). He is not referred to as priest, which is due to the Chronicler's view that the legitimate priesthood of the cult is assured only through the line of Zadok, Abiathar's rival.

28. DAVID'S FINAL INSTRUCTIONS AND CONTRIBUTIONS FOR THE TEMPLE. CONTRIBUTIONS OF OTHERS
(xxviii 1–21, xxix 1–9)

XXVIII 1 David summoned all the officials of Israel to Jerusalem—the tribal chiefs, the divisional chiefs in the royal service, the captains of the thousands and the hundreds, and the overseers of all the property and cattle belonging to the king and his sons—including the court officials, the mighty men, and every man of standing. 2 Then David the king rose to his feet and said, "Listen to me, my brothers and my people. I desired to build a permanent abode*a* for the ark of the covenant of Yahweh and for the footstool of our God. But when I prepared to build it, 3 God said to me, 'You must not build a house for my name because you are a man of wars and have shed blood.' 4 Thus Yahweh God of Israel chose me out of all my family to be king over Israel forever; having selected Judah as leader and my family of the house of Judah, it pleased him to make me king over all Israel in preference to all the [other] sons of my father. 5 From all my sons—for Yahweh gave me many sons— he selected Solomon my son to occupy the throne of Yahweh's rule over Israel. 6 He further said to me, 'Solomon your son shall build my house and my courts, for I have chosen him to be my son and I will be his father. 7 I will maintain his kingdom forever if he executes vigorously my commandments and my judgments as he does now.' 8 Now in the sight of all Israel, the congregation of Yahweh, and in the hearing of our God, [I charge you] to observe and adhere closely to all the commandments of Yahweh your God in order that you may retain possession of the good land and bequeath it to your sons after

---

a Heb. "house of rest"; in contrast to the movable quarters, tent, in which it was located until now (cf. Ps cxxxii 8, 14).

you forever. 9 And you, Solomon my son, recognize the God of
your father*b* and serve him with a whole heart and ready mind—
for Yahweh looks into all hearts and perceives every purpose of
their*c* thoughts. If you seek him he will disclose himself to you
but if you forsake him he will reject you forever. 10 Behold now,
Yahweh has chosen you to build a house for the sanctuary;
work resolutely." 11 Then David handed over to Solomon his
son the plan for the portico, the *d*plan for the temple*d*, its storehouses, its upper chambers, its inner rooms, and the propitia-
tory; 12 along with the plan for everything that came to his
mind through the spirit [of God] for the courts of the house
of Yahweh and for all the surrounding rooms, for the storehouses of the house of God and the storehouses of the consecrated gifts; 13 for the divisions of the priests and Levites, for
all the ministerial service required for the house of Yahweh,
for all the cult objects of the house of Yahweh; 14 for the gold
by weight for all the gold cult objects used for each service,
*e*for the silver*e* by weight for all the silver cult objects used
for each service; 15 for the gold by weight for the golden lampstands and each of its lamps and *e*for the silver*e* by weight
for the silver lampstands and its lights in accordance with the
use of each light; 16 for the gold by weight for the tables for the
layer bread for each table as well as silver for the silver tables;
17 for the pure gold for the forks, the bowls and the jars, for
the gold by weight for each of the golden basins and for the
silver by weight for each of the silver basins; 18 and for the refined gold by weight for the incense altar; also for the gold for
the model of the chariot of cherubs that with outstretched
wings cover the ark of the covenant of Yahweh. 19 All this is in
the document conveying the order of Yahweh *f*by which*f* he
revealed the works of the pattern. 20 David then said to Solomon
his son, "Be courageous and resolute in your work; do not be

b LXX "fathers."
c Adding suffix for clarity; word omitted by LXX*AB*.
d–d So with Vulg., Syr., and adding *tabnīt* ("plan"), required by the sign of the
accusative. Heb. ". . . the plan for the portico and its houses."
e–e Omitted by haplography.
f–f Reading third person suffix for first person. MT has "upon" or "concerning"
me.

afraid or disheartened, for Yahweh God, my God, is with you; he will neither forsake you nor abandon you until all the work for the administration of the house of Yahweh is finished. 21 And there are the divisions of the priests and the Levites for every type of service for the house of God and you have at your disposal men of every skill for all the work, together with the officials and all the people as you may require."

Contributions for the temple construction

XXIX 1 David the king said to the whole congregation, "Solomon my son, whom alone God had chosen, is still young and immature and the work is colossal, for the temple is not for man but for Yahweh God. 2 With all the resources at my command, I have provided for the house of my God gold for what is to be made of gold, silver for what is to be made of silver, bronze for what is to be made with bronze, iron for what is to be made of iron, lumber for what is to be made of wood, in addition to a large quantity of carnelian *with fillings*, *blocks of hard mortar with mosaic pebbles*, all kinds of precious stones, and alabaster. 3 Moreover, because of my deep interest in the house of my God I gave my personal possessions of gold and silver for the house of my God—over and above all that I provided for the sanctuary—4 to the amount of three thousand talents of gold, of the gold from Ophir, and seven thousand talents of refined silver to overlay 'the walls of the houses', 5 the gold is for the objects of gold and the silver for the objects of silver and for all the artistic work. Who, then, is ready to consecrate himself to Yahweh today?" 6 Then the chiefs of the families, the chiefs of the tribes of Israel, the captains of the thousands and the hundreds, and the officers in the service of the king volunteered 7 to give five thousand talents and ten thousand darics of gold, ten thousand talents of silver, eighteen thousand talents of bronze and one hundred thousand talents of iron. 8 Whoever possessed pre-

g–g Uncertain. RSV "for setting." LXX "of filling." Vulg. "quasi."
h–h LXX "very costly stones." Vulg. *stibinos*. Heb. "finely crushed or pulverized stones." See NOTE.
i–i Apparently the inside of the rooms of the temple. LXX "of the house," which would refer to the sanctuary proper.

cious stones presented them to the treasury of the house of Yahweh in the custody of Jehiel the Gershunnite. 9 Then the people rejoiced because of their voluntary gifts, for they had presented their freewill offerings with a whole heart. David the king also rejoiced very greatly.

NOTES

xxviii 2. *footstool.* Cf. Ps cxxxii 7; Isa lxvi 1; Lam ii 1. For the footstool of a king's throne see ANEP, Figs. 460, 463 and R. D. Barnett, *Assyrian Palace Reliefs*, n. d., Fig. 47.

11. *storehouses.* Word occurs only here in the Bible; Persian loan word meaning supply room or treasury.

12. *the spirit [of God].* Cf. L. Köhler, *Old Testament Theology*, 1957, pp. 111–19, especially p. 115d. The usual rendering—everything that came into his mind—is not adequate here since the term for spirit (*rūᵃḥ*) is not used of man but always of God by the Chronicler. Cf. Rudolph, p. 186; Cazelles, p. 122, n. f.

17. *for the gold . . . for the silver.* Insert to harmonize with preceding verse.

19. *the document.* Apparently more than verbal instruction from David to Solomon was involved. The term used here points to a written document, possibly even a model of some kind. As vs. 11 indicates, this was the thing David handed to Solomon. See Bewer, FAB, pp. 75 f.

xxix 2. *blocks . . . pebbles.* The translation is only approximate. Mosaics were laid in cement or mortar which was made of powdered gypsum or limestone mixed with resin.

4. Something above 113 tons of gold and over 214 tons of silver.

Ophir. On location, see Albright, ARI, p. 133; Montgomery, *Arabia and the Bible*, pp. 38 f. The words *zhb 'pr* "gold of Ophir" appears on an ostracon found at Tell Qasile which dates from the end of the Israelite period (cf. BA 14 (1951), 49).

7. Five thousand talents of gold was 188-plus tons; 10,000 darics of gold, 185-plus pounds. The daric was a Persian coin well known to the author of Chronicles. It was first issued by Darius I and weighed 130 grains. There was no coined money in the time of David. This passage and Ezra-Nehemiah are the first in the Bible to mention coined money (cf. A. G. Barrois, IB, I, 1952, p. 157; G. E. Wright, *Biblical Archaeology*, 1957, p. 203). Ten thousand talents of silver was about 377.5 tons; 18,000 talents of bronze about 679.5 tons; and 100,000 talents of iron about 3775 tons.

COMMENT

This section (xxviii 1–xxix 9) joins directly with xxiii 2a and continues the story of what transpired when David assembled the political and military leaders to witness the transfer of the kingdom to his son Solomon. The author does not draw upon the Kings parallel dealing with the accession of Solomon because of his idealistic conception of David and his kingdom. He passed over the experiences in David's life that militated against his view—the Bathsheba incident, the rebellion of Absalom, family troubles. To follow in the footsteps of his father, Solomon's accession could not be marred by the distasteful Adonijah affair. From the Chronicler's point of view the divine plan was clear and unequivocal. So he draws upon other sources which he expands into an elaborate story requisite for his conception of the Davidic kingdom in extenso.

[Address to the people and to Solomon, xxviii 1–10]: For the Chronicler the chief concern in the transition of the kingdom from David to Solomon was religious. It is, therefore, a bit strange that the priest and Levites are not specifically included in the formal summons for this important occasion; that they were present is clear from other references (xxix 21). Perhaps the preceding chapters had something to do with the omission or part of their purpose may have been to make up for it. Since the main purpose of the Chronicler centers about the religious institutions of Israel, it is likely that the officials of Israel are cited in order to accentuate their role in the construction and maintenance of the temple. Cf. I. Kings ii 2–4 where Solomon is charged to obey the law of Moses to assure that his throne remain secure. The Chronicler may have interpreted that injunction in a broader and narrower sense—in the broader sense, it was inclusive of the officialdom of the nation, in the narrower sense, to follow the law of Moses meant support for the religious institutions (cf. vss. 7, 8). Since the strictly religious officials were already committed to building and caring for the temple, it was necessary only to demand the support of the political leaders. The address of the king is based on earlier sources which the writer elaborated extensively. On his desire to build a house for Yahweh, see II Sam vii 2–3 ‖ I Chron xvii 1–2. The reason David was not permitted to build the temple was because he was a man of war, with blood on his hands (cf. xxii 8)—a fact completely ignored in chapter xvii. The artful way in which the facts of the succession are portrayed illustrate the method and ability of the author. God chose David but behind that choice lies the selection of Judah and within Judah the family of Jesse. As Judah had been chosen from the twelve sons of Israel, the family of Jesse (Perez) from the five families of Judah (cf. ii 4b, iv 1; Ruth iv 18–22), and David in preference to all the other sons of Jesse (I Sam xvi), so Solomon was selected from the many sons of David to occupy the throne and perpetuate the dynasty. From the vantage point of the writer, such a succession of events were acts of God, not just circumstances of history. But the Davidic line could not survive without the relationship to God maintained in the time of David. Note the father-child emphasis (vs. 6); two elements were strongly operative here—the conception of the king as son of God and the ethical principles of the prophets. The whole address converges upon Solomon, who is exhorted to hold fast to the commandments of Yahweh that the land may remain in Israel's possession forever and that the succession may be secure. But all that had but one aim for the Chronicler, that is, for the purpose of building the sanctuary, the abode of Yahweh, symbolical of his presence in the land among his people.

[The presentation of the plans for the temple to Solomon, 11–19]: As pointed out in the NOTE on vs. 19, the transmission of the plan for the temple was not simply an oral communication; apparently underlying this narrative is a written record or plan (vs. 19) which was part of the official records of the temple (see Maisler, IEJ 2 [1952], 86 f.). Nevertheless all that was involved is credited to the divinely inspired mind of David. Perhaps the plan for the tabernacle devised by Bezalel and his helpers (Exod xxxi 1–11, xxxv 30–35) was in the mind of the writer. The fact that he went beyond the conceptions of the Deuteronomist, who attributes everything to Solomon so far as planning and execution of the project were concerned (I Kings v, vi), points to a later view represented in the priestly writings and particularly in Ezekiel (chs. xl ff.). As such the plan envisaged by the writer includes everything connected with the sacred structure—the portico, the main structure with the storehouses, the various chambers, the adytum, as well as the courts around it. But that is not all; the details for the cult objects are set down meticulously, even to the amount of gold and silver for each. It has been suggested that vss. 14–18 were an addition. In the Kings story the vessels were of gold or bronze; silver is not mentioned. Here gold and silver are mentioned in such a way as to make it appear as if there were two sets of vessels. There was only one table for the layer bread in the old temple; here the plural is used, doubtless under the influence of II Chron iv 8 which speaks of ten tables made for the temple. All of this superlative plan emphasizes the Chronicler's deep concern for the temple and places David in the same position with reference to it as that which Moses occupied with reference to the tabernacle. The chariot of cherubs brings to mind the famous throne-chariot of Ezekiel (chs. i, x, xliii 3–4).

[David's final charge to Solomon, 20–21]: This is David's third exhortation to Solomon (cf. xxii 11 ff., xxviii 9–10); the author thereby means to impress upon the new king and the people the seriousness of the undertaking to build the temple as well as the dominant interest in the project sustained by David. He utilizes the language of the Deuteronomist attributed to Moses (Deut xxxi 6, 8; Josh i 5) to inspire Solomon to courage and determination in the sure faith that Yahweh will not forsake him. In carrying out the work, he will have the assistance of the priests and Levites and in addition men of skill, officials, and others required for the task. One eye of the king was on Solomon but the other certainly upon those directed to assist him so as to inspire their loyalty and devotion to him in the execution of the enterprise with which he was charged.

[Material contributions of David, the officials, and others, xxix 1–9]: Though David reminds the assembly of Solomon's lack of experience in political affairs, his chief interest (vs. 3) centers about the house of Yahweh. The Chronicler here combines his own views with those of David (known from other sources and noted earlier). The dominant concern for both was the temple for the construction of which David had devoted all his resources. He calls attention to the resources of his kingdom from which he provided all sorts of materials—gold, silver, bronze, iron, wood, and precious stones. So great was his desire to achieve his goal that he dedicated his personal possessions to that end (the $s^e gull\bar{a}h$ was the private possession of the king. Cf. M. Greenberg, JAOS 71 [1951], 172–74). The quantity was enormous, perhaps purposely stated in such extravagant terms because this was to be the most magnificent building in the kingdom. Again both gold and silver figure in the catalogue of gifts. Such a vast array of contributions on the part of the king stimulated the officials to offer their gifts, whose total was about a

third greater than the king's. In addition precious stones were offered
freely. The accumulated offerings of the kingdom, David, the officials and the people were turned over to Jehiel (cf. xxiii 8). The
freely offered contributions of king and people brought great joy to
all.

29. DAVID'S PRAYER OF THANKSGIVING. SOLOMON BECOMES KING
(xxix 10–25)

XXIX 10 Thus David blessed Yahweh in the sight of the whole congregation. David said, "Blessed be you, O Yahweh God of Israel our father, for ever and ever. 11 Yours, O Yahweh, is the greatness, the power, the glory, the pre-eminence, and the majesty, yes everything in heaven and on earth; yours is the kingdom and you have exalted yourself as head over all. 12 Riches and wealth come from you; you rule over all; in your hand are power and might; and you are able to magnify and strengthen everyone. 13 Now, our God, we give thanks to you and praise your majestic name. 14 For who am I and who are my people, that we should be able to volunteer like this; rather everything comes from you and we have given you [only] what has come from your hand. 15 We are but strangers in your sight and sojourners as were all our fathers; our days on the earth are like a shadow and without security. 16 O Yahweh, our God, all this wealth which we have provided to build a house for you for your holy name has come from your hand because all of it belongs to you. 17 Because I know, my God, that you examine the mind and desire uprightness, I have freely given all these things in the integrity of my purpose and now I have joyfully watched your people, who are present here, contribute willingly to you. 18 O Yahweh God of Abraham, Isaac, and Israel our fathers, preserve the desire for such dispositions forever in the heart of your people and direct their heart toward yourself. 19 And give to Solomon my son an undivided heart that he may keep your commandments, your stipulations, and your statutes, carry them all out, and construct the temple for which I have provided." 20 David said to the whole congregation, "Bless Yahweh your

God." Then the whole congregation blessed Yahweh God of their fathers, bowed down and did homage to Yahweh and to the king.

The accession of Solomon

21 The next day they slaughtered sacrifices and offered burnt offerings to Yahweh for all Israel—a thousand bulls, a thousand rams, a thousand sheep in addition to their libations and sacrifices in abundance—22 and they ate and drank before Yahweh that day with great joy. Then they made Solomon the son of David king *a second time* and anointed him for Yahweh as leader and Zadok as priest. 23 Solomon occupied the throne of Yahweh as king in place of David his father and he was successful; all Israel obeyed him, 24 and all the chiefs, the leading citizens, as well as all the sons of King David submitted themselves to King Solomon. 25 Yahweh highly exalted Solomon in the sight of all Israel and bestowed upon him such royal dignity as no king *over Israel* before him possessed.

a–a Omitted by LXX^B. Probably stands here because of xxiii 1.
b–b Omitted by LXX^AB, perhaps correctly, as there were only two kings over Israel before Solomon. Cf. II Chron i 12.

NOTES

xxix 10. *Israel.* I.e., Jacob. The Chronicler regularly refers to Jacob as Israel.

15. *our days . . . a shadow.* An inscription from the tomb of Neferhotep reads in part:

As for the duration of what is done on earth,
It is a kind of dream.

security. On the meaning of *miqweh* as abode see G. R. Driver, JTS, N.S. 3 (1952), 310; on the meaning given here cf. P. A. H. de Boer, OTS 10 (1954), 239 f.

22. *as leader. Nāgīd.* This is a special term for leader, and appears to be the official title of the earliest kings, still distinguishing them from the kings of the surrounding countries. It seems to be connected with anointing, and is used of anointed leaders like the priest. It appears also to be a favored word with the Chronicler in whose writings it occurs twenty-two times (used only forty-four times in OT, eleven in the work of the Deuteronomist).

COMMENT

[David's prayer of thanksgiving, xxix 10–20]: The presentation
of such a wealth of gifts called forth David's praise and thanksgiving
to Yahweh who was the bestower of it all in the first place. Verses
10 and 18 recall the blessings Yahweh had given to the patriarchs
who counted their possessions as gifts from God and whenever they
surveyed them gave credit to him for his goodness and grace. Thus
Jacob refers to the generosity and protection of God (Gen xxx 43,
xxxi 7, xxxiii 11), and the attitude of Abraham and Isaac parallels
that of Jacob (Gen xiii 2, xxiv 1, xxvi 12–14). The praise thus
showered upon Yahweh was not an empty gesture, because what
David said about his beneficence was demonstrated before the eyes
of all at that very moment. They could not have responded as they
did without the material goods that came from God's hand. Hence
God was really providing the requisites for his own house. Yet he
did not do it directly, but rather through the willingness of his people. God, who knows what is in the heart of man, is aware of the
spontaneity of the offerings of king and people and David prays
that the desire for such disposition may remain with the people of
Israel forever. He implores Yahweh to keep Solomon true and
loyal to the ideals with which he had been charged, that is, to remain faithful to the commandments of Yahweh and especially to
carry out the plans for the building of the temple. Then he calls
upon the congregation to bless Yahweh for what he has done. The
congregation responded with alacrity, blessed Yahweh, and did
homage to both Yahweh and the king.

On the Chronicler's prayers, see O. Plöger, "Reden und Gebete
im deuteronomistischen und chronistischen Geschichtswerk," in
Festschrift für Günther Dehn (Neukirchen, 1957), pp. 35–49.

[Solomon's accession to the throne, 21–25]: While one not know-
ing about the events related in I Kings i, ii would hardly suspect any
opposition to the elevation of Solomon to the throne of David, they
are obviously in the background of the writer's mind. His observation about the magnitude of the celebration attendant upon the
anointing of Solomon may have been influenced by the story of
Adonijah's abortive venture (cf. I Kings i 9, 19, 25). There was
tremendous rejoicing by the Solomon partisans after his anointing

(I Kings i 40, 45a) but no great sacrificial ceremonies are mentioned in connection with it, as in the anointment of Adonijah. The officiation at the anointing ceremony of Zadok necessitated his elevation to the high priesthood and may be a reflection of I Kings i 39, ii 35. I Kings (i 46, ii 12) twice refers to Solomon's enthronement; in the second passage it is stated that he was very firmly established. Here the statement in vs. 23 that "he was successful; all Israel obeyed him" apparently grows out of the writer's knowledge of the circumstances surrounding the succession to the throne. Particularly striking is the clause, "all Israel obeyed him." Equally noteworthy is vs. 24 which affirms that not only did the chiefs and mighty men submit to his authority, but that "all the sons of King David" did likewise. Perhaps the closest contact with the Kings story is the assertion that Yahweh bestowed upon Solomon such royal dignity as no king over Israel before him enjoyed (cf. I Kings i 37b, 47, iii 12). There is certainly nothing unhistorical or visionary in the story. It is a unit and sets forth the pertinent facts as they relate to the accession of Solomon whose chief responsibility was the maintenance of the Davidic line and the construction of the temple. Just because certain events in the career of individuals are not mentioned specifically by the Chronicler does not mean they were unknown to him or piously glossed over. They were a matter of record and everybody knew about them. He has chronicled the history of the kingdom from a religious point of view and follows a straight line rather than detours that would detract from his objective. His is a positive approach and hence he omits the aberrations that might raise doubts in the minds of his hearers (readers).

30. SUMMARY OF DAVID'S REIGN
(xxix 26–30)†

XXIX 26 David the son of Jesse was king over all Israel. 27 He was king over Israel for a period of forty years; he was king at Hebron seven years and he was king in Jerusalem thirty-three years. 28 He died in good old age, full of days, wealth, and honor and Solomon his son became king in his place. 29 The history of David the king from beginning to end is written down in the records of Samuel the seer, in the records of Nathan the prophet, and in the records of Gad the seer; 30 in addition, there is the record of all the affairs of his kingdom, of his mighty deeds and of the times through which he, Israel, and all the kings of the lands passed.

† I Chron xxix 26–30 ‖ I Kings ii 10=12.

NOTES

xxix 30. *all the kings.* Literally "royalty," as Phoen. *mmlkt.*

COMMENT

This is a summary of the barest facts about David and his kingdom, similar to those standing at the conclusion of the reign of each of the kings with whom the work of the Chronicler deals. Once more he notes that David had been king over *all Israel.* He does not even speak of the fact that his reign at Hebron embraced only Judah (cf. I Kings ii 11); he simply says he reigned over Israel for seven years from Hebron and for thirty-three years from Jerusalem. Verse 28 points out that he attained everything that an Israelite king could wish—truly a sign that Yahweh was with him and had blessed

him. Whether the sources utilized for his account of David were only
those recorded in Samuel and I Kings (so most commentators) or
whether they were actual archives cannot be determined with
absolute certainty. The "kings of the lands" probably refers to the
states whose crowns he wore and the kings with whom he came
in contact in the course of his long reign—Philistia, Moab, the
Aramaean states, Edom, Ammon, and Tyre.

INDEX OF PLACE AND PERSONAL NAMES

NOTES

1. The transcriptional spelling is generally that appearing in the first reference. Important variations are, however, noted where they do occur.

2. This index lists place and personal names, though it is recognized that it is often difficult, perhaps impossible, in some cases to make the distinction. The twelve tribes of Israel are designated by their personal names.

3. The general practice has been followed in transcriptions—

'=*aleph*	s=*samek*
'=*ayin*	ṣ=*tsade*
ḥ=*heth*	ś=*sin*
h=*he*	š=*shin*
ṭ=*teth*	y=*yod*
t=*taw*	

No attempt has been made to distinguish between consonants with or without *dagesh*.

PLACE NAMES

Abdon (*'bdwn*) I Chron vi 74.
Adullam (*'dlm*) I Chron xi 15; II Chron xi 7; Neh xi 30.
Aijah (*'yh*) I Chron vii 28; Neh xi 31.
Aijalon (*'ylwn*) I Chron vi 69, viii 13; II Chron xi 10, xxviii 18.
Ain (*'yn*) I Chron iv 32.
Alemeth (*'lmt*) I Chron vi 60.
Anathoth (*'ntwt*) I Chron vi 60; Ezra ii 23; Neh vii 27, xi 32.

Anem (*'nm*)   I Chron vi 73.
Aner (*'nr*)   I Chron vi 70.
Aroer (*'r'r*)   I Chron v 8.
Ashan (*'šn*)   I Chron iv 32, vi 59.
Ashtaroth (*'štrwt*)   I Chron vi 71.
Assyria (*'šwr*)   I Chron v 6,26(*bis*); II Chron xxviii 16,20,21,
   xxx 6, xxxii 1,4,7,10,21,22, xxxiii 11; Ezra vi 22; Neh ix 32.
Avith (*'wyt* [Q(ere)])   I Chron i 46.

Baalath (*b'lt*)   I Chron iv 33, xiii 6; II Chron viii 6.
Baal-hermon (*b'l-ḥrmwn*)   I Chron v 23.
Baal-meon (*b'l-m'wn*)   I Chron v 8.
Baal-perazim (*b'l-prṣym*)   I Chron xiv 11(*bis*).
Baka-bushes (*hbk'ym*)   I Chron xiv 14,15.
Bashan (*bšn*)   I Chron v 11,12,16,23, vi 62,71; Neh ix 22.
Beer-sheba (*b'r-šb'*)   I Chron iv 28, xxi 2; II Chron xix 4, xxiv 1,
   xxx 5; Neh xi 27,30.
Beth-ashbea (*byt-'šb'*)   I Chron iv 21.
Beth-biri (*byt-br'y*)   I Chron iv 31.
Bethel (*byt-'l*)   I Chron vii 28; II Chron xiii 19; Ezra ii 28; Neh vii
   32, xi 31.
Beth-horon (*byt-ḥwrwn*)   I Chron vi 68, vii 24; II Chron viii 5,
   xxv 13.
Bethlehem (*byt lḥm*)   I Chron iv 22, xi 16,17,18,26; II Chron
   xi 6; Ezra ii 21; Neh vii 26.
Beth-marcaboth (*byt mrkbwt*)   I Chron iv 31.
Beth-shean (*byt š'n*)   I Chron vii 29.
Beth-shemesh (*byt šmš*)   I Chron vi 59; II Chron xxv 21,23, xxviii
   18.
Bethuel (*btw'l*)   I Chron iv 30.
Bezer (*bṣr*)   I Chron vi 78.
Bileam (*bl'm*)   I Chron vi 70.
Bilhah (*blhh*)   I Chron iv 29.
Bozrah (*bṣrh*)   I Chron i 44.

Carmel (*krml*)   I Chron iii 1.
Cozeba (*kzb'*)   I Chron iv 22.
Cun (*kwn*)   I Chron xviii 8.

Daberath (*dbrt*) I Chron vi 72.

Damascus (*drmśq*) I Chron xviii 5,6; II Chron xvi 2, xxiv 23, xxviii 5,23.

Debir (*dbyr*) I Chron vi 58.

Dinhabah (*dnhbh*) I Chron i 43.

Dor (*dwr*) I Chron vii 29.

Edom (*'dwm*) I Chron i 43,51,54, xviii 11,12,13(*bis*); II Chron viii 17, xx 2 (MT *rm*), xxi 8, xxv 19,20.

Egypt (*mṣrym*) I Chron xiii 5, xvii 21; II Chron i 17, v 10, vi 5, vii 8,22, ix 26,28, x 2(*bis*), xii 2,9, xx 10, xxvi 8, xxxv 20, xxxvi 3,4(*bis*); Neh ix 9,17 (with Greek), 18.

Eshtemoa (*'štm'*) I Chron vi 57.

Etam (*'yṭm*) I Chron iv 32; II Chron xi 6.

Euphrates (*prt*) I Chron v 9, xviii 3; II Chron xxxv 20.

Ezem (*'ṣm*) I Chron iv 29.

Gaash (*g'š*) I Chron xi 32.

Galilee (*glyl*) I Chron vi 76.

Gath (*gt*) I Chron vii 21, viii 13, xviii 1, xx 6,8; II Chron xi 8, xxvi 6.

Gath-rimmon (*gt rmwn*) I Chron vi 69.

Geba (*gb'*) I Chron vi 60, viii 6; II Chron xvi 6; Ezra ii 26; Neh vii 30, xi 31, xii 29.

Gederah (*gdrh*) I Chron iv 23.

Gedor (*gdwr; gdr*) I Chron iv 39, xii 8.

Geshur (*gšwr*) I Chron iii 2.

Gezer (*gzr*) I Chron vi 67, vii 28, xiv 16, xx 4.

Gibeah (*gb'h*) I Chron xi 31; II Chron xiii 2.

Gibeon (*gb'wn*) I Chron viii 29, ix 35, xiv 16, xvi 39, xxi 29; II Chron i 3,13; Neh iii 7, vii 25.

Gilead (*gl'd*) I Chron ii 22, v 9,10,16, vi 80, xxvi 31, xxvii 21.

Golan (*gwln*) I Chron vi 71.

Gozan (*gwzn*) I Chron v 26.

Habor (*ḥbwr*) I Chron v 26.

Halah (*ḥlḥ*) I Chron v 26.

Hamath (*ḥmt*) I Chron xiii 5, xviii 3,9; II Chron vii 8, viii 4.

Hammon (*ḥmwn*) I Chron vi 76.

Hara (*hr'*) I Chron v 26.

Hazar-shual (*ḥṣr šw'l*) I Chron iv 28; Neh xi 27.

Hazar-susim (*ḥṣr swsym*) I Chron iv 31.

Hebron (*ḥbrwn*) I Chron iii 1,4, vi 55,57, xi 1,3(*bis*), xii 24, 39, xxix 27; II Chron xi 10.

Heshbon (*ḥšbwn*) I Chron vi 81; Neh ix 22.

Hilen (*ḥlyn*) I Chron vi 58.

Hormah (*ḥrmh*) I Chron iv 30.

Hukok (*ḥwqq*) I Chron vi 75.

Jabesh (*ybyš*) I Chron x 12(*bis*).

Jabesh-gilead (*ybyš gl'd*) I Chron x 11.

Jabez (*y'bṣ*) I Chron ii 55.

Jahzah (*yhṣh*) I Chron vi 78.

Jattir (*ytr*) I Chron xi 57.

Jazer (*y'zyr*) I Chron vi 81, xxvi 31.

Jebus (*ybws*) I Chron xi 4,5.

Jericho (*yrḥw*) I Chron vi 78, xix 5; II Chron xxviii 15; Ezra ii 34; Neh iii 2, vii 36.

Jerusalem (*yrwšlm*) I Chron iii 4,5, vi 10,15,32, viii 28,32, ix 3, 34,38, xi 4, xiv 3,4, xv 3, xviii 7, xix 15, xx 1,3, xxi 4,15,16, xxiii 25, xxviii 1, xxix 27; II Chron i 4,13,14,15, ii 6,15, iii 1, v 2, vi 6, viii 6, ix 1,25,27,30, x 18, xi 1,5,14,16, xii 2,3,4,5,7, 8,13(*bis*), xiv 14, xv 10, xvii 13, xix 1,4,8(*bis*), xx 5,15,17, 18,20,27(*bis*), 28,31, xxi 5,11,13,20, xxii 1,2, xxiii 2, xxiv 1,6, 9,18,23, xxv 1(*bis*), 23(*bis*), 27, xxvi 3(*bis*), 9,15, xxvii 1,8, xxviii 10,24,27, xxix 1,8, xxx 1,2,5,11,13,14,21,26(*bis*), xxxi 4, xxxii 2,9(*bis*), 10,12,18,19,22,23,25,26,33, xxxiii 1,4,7,9,13,15, xxxiv 1,3,5,6,9,22,29,30,32(*bis*), xxxv 1,18,24(*bis*), xxxvi 1,2, 3,4,5,9,10,11,14,19,23; Ezra i 2,3(*bis*), 4,5,7,11, ii 1,68,70, iii 1,8(*bis*), iv 6,7,8,12,20,23,24, v 1,2,14,15,16,17, vi 3,5(*bis*), 9,12,18, vii 7,8,9,13,14,15,16,17,19,27, viii 29,30,31,32, ix 9, x 7(*bis*), 9; Neh i 2,3, ii 11,12,13,17(*bis*), 20, iii 8,9,12, iv 1,2, 16, vi 7, vii 2,3(*bis*), 6, viii 15, xi 1(*bis*), 2,3,4,6,22, xii 27 (*bis*), 28,29,43, xiii 7,15,16,19,20.

Jezreel (*yzr'l*) I Chron iii 1; II Chron xxii 6(*bis*).

Jokmeam (*yqm'm*) I Chron vi 68.

Jordan (*yrdn*) I Chron vi 78, xii 16,38, xix 17, xxvi 30; II Chron iv 17.

Kabzeel (*qbṣ'l*) I Chron xi 22.
Kedemoth (*qdmwt*) I Chron vi 79.
Kedesh (*qdš*) I Chron vi 72,76.
Kiriathaim (*qrytym*) I Chron vi 76.
Kiriath-jearim (*qryt y'rym*) I Chron xiii 5,6; II Chron i 4; Neh
  vii 29.

Libnah (*lbnh*) I Chron vi 57; II Chron xxi 10.
Lod (*ld*) I Chron viii 12; Ezra ii 33; Neh vii 37, xi 35.

Maacah (*m'kh*) I Chron xix 6,7.
Mahanaim (*mḥnym*) I Chron vi 80.
Manahath (*mnḥt*) I Chron viii 6.
Mashal (*mšl*) I Chron vi 74.
Masrekah (*mśrqh*) I Chron i 47.
Medeba (*mydb'*) I Chron xix 7.
Megiddo (*mgdw*) I Chron vii 29; II Chron xxxv 22.
Menuhoth (*mnḥwt*) I Chron ii 52.
Mephaath (*myp't*) I Chron vi 79.
Midian (*mdyn*) I Chron i 46.
Millo (*mlw'*) I Chron xi 8; II Chron xxxii 5.
Moab (*mw'b*) I Chron i 46, viii 8, xviii 2,11.
Moladah (*mwldh*) I Chron iv 28; Neh xi 26.
Mt. Ephraim (*hr' prym*) I Chron vi 67; II Chron xiii 4, xv 8, xix 4.
Mt. Gilboa (*hr glb'*) I Chron x 1,8.
Mt. Hermon (*hr ḥrmwn*) I Chron v 23.
Mt. Seir (*hr š'yr*) I Chron iv 42; II Chron xx 10,22,23.

Naaran (*n'rn*) I Chron vii 28.
Naharaim (*nhrym*) I Chron xix 6.
Nebo (*nbw*) I Chron v 8.
Netaim (*nṭ'ym*) I Chron iv 23.

Ono (*'wnw*) I Chron viii 12; Ezra ii 33; Neh vi 2, vii 37, xi 35.
Ophir (*'wpyr*) I Chron xxix 4; II Chron viii 18, ix 10.

Pai (*p'y*) I Chron i 50.
Parbar (*prbr*) I Chron xxvi 18(*bis*).
Pas-dammim (*ps dmym*) I Chron xi 13.
Perez-uzza (*prṣ 'z'*) I Chron xiii 11.

Rabbah (*rbh*) I Chron xx 1(*bis*).
Ramoth (*r'mwt*) I Chron vi 73,80.
Rehob (*rḥb*) I Chron vi 75.
Rehoboth (*rḥbwt*) I Chron i 48.
Rephaim (*rp'ym*) I Chron xi 15, xiv 9.
Rimmon (*rmwn*) I Chron iv 32.
Rimmono (*rmwnw*) I Chron vi 77.

Salecah (*slkh*) I Chron v 11.
Senir (*śnyr*) I Chron v 23.
Shaaraim (*š'rym*) I Chron iv 31.
Shallecheth Gate (*š'r šlkt*) I Chron xxvi 16.
Sharon (*šrwn*) I Chron v 16, xxvii 29.
Shechem (*škm*) I Chron vi 67, vii 28; II Chron x 1(*bis*).
Shephelah (*šplh*) I Chron xxvii 28; II Chron i 15, ix 27, xxvi 10,
    xxviii 18.

Taanach (*t'nk*) I Chron vii 29.
Tabor (*tbwr*) I Chron vi 77.
Teman (*tymn*) I Chron i 45.
Tibhath (*tbḥt*) I Chron xviii 8.
Tochen (*tkn*) I Chron iv 32.
Tolad (*twld*) I Chron iv 29.
Transjordan (*'br yrdn*) I Chron vi 78.
Tyre (*ṣr*) I Chron xiv 1; II Chron ii 10.

Uzzen-sheerah (*'zn š'rh*) I Chron vii 24.

Valley of Salt (*gy' hmlḥ*) I Chron xviii 12; II Chron xxv 11.

Ziklag (*ṣyqlg*) I Chron iv 30, xii 1,21; Neh xi 28.
Zion (*ṣywn*) I Chron xi 5; II Chron v 2.
Zobah (*ṣwbh*) I Chron xviii 3,5,9, xix 6.

PERSONAL AND OTHER NAMES

Aaron (*'hrn*) I Chron vi 3(*bis*), 49,50,54,57, xii 28, xv 4, xxiii
    13(*bis*), 28,32, xxiv 1(*bis*), 19,31, xxvii 17; II Chron xiii 9,10,
    xxix 21, xxxi 19, xxxv 14(*bis*); Ezra vii 5; Neh x 29, xii 47.

Abdi (*'bdy*)   I Chron vi 44; II Chron xxix 12; Ezra x 26.
Abdiel (*'bdy'l*)   I Chron v 15.
Abdon (*'bdwn*)   I Chron viii 23,30, ix 36; II Chron xxxiv 20.
Abiathar (*'bytr*)   I Chron xv 11, xviii 16, xxiv 6, xxvii 34.
Abida (*'byd'*)   I Chron i 33.
Abiel (*'by'l*)   I Chron xi 32.
Abiezer (*'by'zr*)   I Chron vii 18, xi 28, xxvii 12.
Abigail (*'bygyl*)   I Chron ii 16,17, iii 1.
Abihail (*'byhyl*)   I Chron ii 29, v 14; II Chron xi 18.
Abihu (*'byhw'*)   I Chron vi 3, xxiv 1,2.
Abihud (*'byhwd*)   I Chron viii 3.
Abijah (*'byh*)   I Chron iii 10, vi 28, vii 8, xxiv 10; II Chron xi
    20,22, xii 16, xiii 1,2,3,4,15,17,19,21,22,23; Neh x 8, xii 4,17.
Abimael (*'bym'l*)   I Chron i 22.
Abimelech (*'bymlk*)   I Chron xviii 16.
Abinadab (*'byndb*)   I Chron ii 13, viii 33, ix 39, x 2, xiii 7.
Abishai (*'bšy*)   I Chron ii 16, xi 20, xviii 12, xix 11,15.
Abishua (*'byšw'*)   I Chron vi 4,5,50, viii 4; Ezra vii 5.
Abishur (*'byšwr*)   I Chron ii 28,29.
Abital (*'byṭl*)   I Chron iii 3.
Abitub (*'byṭwb*)   I Chron viii 11.
Abner (*'bnr*)   I Chron xxvi 29, xxvii 21.
Abraham (*'brhm*)   I Chron i 27,28,32,34, xvi 16, xxix 18; II
    Chron xx 7, xxx 6; Neh ix 7.
Abram (*'brm*)   I Chron i 27; Neh ix 7.
Absalom (*'bšlwm*)   I Chron iii 2; II Chron xi 20,21.
Achar (*'kr*)   I Chron ii 7.
Achbor (*'kbwr*)   I Chron i 49.
Achsah (*'ksh*)   I Chron ii 49.
Adaiah (*'dyh*)   I Chron vi 41, viii 21, ix 12; II Chron xxiii 1;
    Ezra x 29,39; Neh xi 5,12.
Adam (*'dm*)   I Chron i 1.
Adbeel (*'db'l*)   I Chron i 29.
Addar (*'dr*)   I Chron viii 3.
Adiel (*'dy'l*)   I Chron iv 36, ix 12, xxvii 25.
Adina (*'dyn'*)   I Chron xi 42.
Adlai (*'dly*)   I Chron xxvii 29.
Adnah (*'dnh*)   I Chron xii 21.
Adonijah (*'dnyh*)   I Chron iii 2; II Chron xvii 8; Neh x 17.
Aharah (*'ḥrḥ*)   I Chron viii 1.

Aharhel (*'ḥrḥl*)   I Chron iv 8.

Ahashtarite (*'ḥštry*)   I Chron iv 6.

Ahaz (*'ḥz*)   I Chron iii 13, viii 35,36, ix 42; II Chron xxvii 9,
xxviii 1,16,19,21,22,24,27, xxix 19.

Ahaziah (*'ḥzyhw*)   I Chron ii 11; II Chron xx 35,37, xxi 1(*bis*),
2,6,7,8(*bis*), 9(*bis*), 10,11(*bis*), xxv 23 (with Greek; MT
yhw'ḥz).

Ahban (*'ḥbn*)   I Chron ii 29.

Aher (*'ḥr*)   I Chron vii 12.

Ahi (*'ḥy*)   I Chron v 15.

Ahiam (*'ḥy'm*)   I Chron xi 35.

Ahian (*'ḥyn*)   I Chron vii 19.

Ahiezer (*'ḥy'zr*)   I Chron xii 3.

Ahihud (*'ḥyhd*)   I Chron viii 7.

Ahijah (*'ḥyh*)   I Chron ii 25, viii 7, xi 36; II Chron ix 29, x 15;
Neh x 27.

Ahilud (*'ḥylwd*)   I Chron xviii 15.

Ahimaaz (*'ḥym'z*)   I Chron vi 8,9,53.

Ahiman (*'ḥymn*)   I Chron ix 17.

Ahimelech (*'ḥymlk*)   I Chron xxiv 3,6,31.

Ahimoth (*ḥymwt*)   I Chron vi 25.

Ahinoam (*'ḥyn'm*)   I Chron iii 1.

Ahio (*'ḥyw*)   I Chron viii 31, ix 37, xiii 7.

Ahishahar (*'ḥyšḥr*)   I Chron vii 10.

Ahithophel (*'ḥytpl*)   I Chron xxvii 33,34.

Ahitub (*'ḥyṭwb*)   I Chron vi 7,8,11,12,52, ix 11, xviii 16; Ezra
vii 2; Neh xi 11.

Ahlai (*'ḥly*)   I Chron ii 31, xi 41.

Ahoah (*'ḥwḥ*)   I Chron viii 4.

Ahohite (*'ḥwḥy*)   I Chron xi 12,29, xxvii 4.

Ahumai (*'ḥwmy*)   I Chron iv 2.

Ahuzzam (*'ḥzm*)   I Chron iv 6.

Aiah (*'yh*)   I Chron i 40.

Akkub (*'qwb*)   I Chron iii 24, ix 17; Ezra ii 42,45; Neh vii 45,
viii 7, xi 19, xii 25.

Alemeth (*'lmt*)   I Chron vii 8, viii 36, ix 42.

Aliah (*'lyh*)   I Chron i 51.

Alian (*'lyn*)   I Chron i 40.

Allon (*'lwn*)   I Chron iv 37.

Almodad (*'lmwdd*)   I Chron i 20.

Amal (*'ml*) I Chron vii 35.

Amalek (*'mlq*) I Chron i 36, iv 43, xviii 11.

Amariah (*'mryh*) I Chron vi 7(*bis*), 11(*bis*), 52, xxiii 19, xxiv 23; II Chron xix 11, xxxi 15; Ezra vii 3, x 42; Neh x 4, xii 2,13.

Amasa (*'mš'*) I Chron ii 17(*bis*); II Chron xxviii 12.

Amasai (*'mśy*) I Chron vi 25,35, xii 19, xv 24; II Chron xxix 12.

Amaziah (*'mṣyhw*) I Chron iii 12, iv 34, vi 45; II Chron xxiv 27, xxv 1,5,9,10,11,13,14,15,17,18,20,21,23,25,26,27, xxvi 1,4.

Ammiel (*'my'l*) I Chron iii 5, xxvi 5.

Ammihud (*'myhwd*) I Chron vii 26, ix 4.

Amminadab (*'myndb*) I Chron ii 10(*bis*), vi 22, xv 10,11.

Ammizabad (*'myzbd*) I Chron xxvii 6.

Ammon (*'mwn*) I Chron xviii 11, xix 2,3,6(*bis*), 7,9,11,15,19, xx 1,3; II Chron xx 1,10,22,23, xxvii 5(*tris*).

Ammonite (*'mwny*) I Chron xi 39; II Chron xii 13 (fem.), xxiv 26 (fem.); Ezra ix 1; Neh ii 10,19, iv 1, xiii 1,23 (fem.).

Amnon (*'mnn*) I Chron iii 1, iv 20.

Amon (*'mwn*) I Chron iii 14; II Chron xviii 25, xxxiii 20,21,22, 23,25; Neh vii 59.

Amorite (*'mry*) I Chron i 14; II Chron viii 7; Ezra ix 1; Neh ix 8.

Amram (*'mrm*) I Chron vi 2,3,18, xxiii 12,13, xxiv 20, **xxvi** 23 (Amramites); Ezra x 34.

Amzi (*'mṣy*) I Chron vi 46; Neh xi 12.

Anah (*'nh*) I Chron i 38,40,41.

Anamim (*'nmym*) I Chron i 11.

Anani (*'nny*) I Chron iii 24.

Anathoth (*'ntwt*) I Chron vii 8; Neh x 20.

Anathothite (*'ntwty*) I Chron xi 28, xii 3, xxvii 12.

Aniam (*'ny'm*) I Chron vii 19.

Anthothijah (*'nttyh*) I Chron viii 24.

Anub (*'nwb*) I Chron iv 8.

Appaim (*'pym*) I Chron ii 30,31.

Arad (*'rd*) I Chron viii 15.

Arah (*'rḥ*) I Chron vii 39; Ezra ii 5; Neh vi 18, vii 10.

Aram (*'rm*) I Chron i 17, ii 23, vii 34.

Aramaean (*'rmyh, 'rm*) I Chron vii 14, xviii 5,6(*bis*), xix 6,10, 12,14,15,16(*bis*), 17,18(*bis*), 19; II Chron xxii 5 (as in II Kings viii 28), xxiv 23,24.

Aran (*'rn*) I Chron i 42.

Arbathite (*'rbty*) I Chron xi 32.

Archite (*'rky*)   I Chron xxvii 33.

Ardon (*'rdwn*)   I Chron ii 18.

Arkite (*'rqy*)   I Chron i 15, xxvii 33.

Arnan (*'rnn*)   I Chron iii 21.

Aroerite (*'r'ry*)   I Chron xi 44.

Arpachshad (*'rpkšd*)   I Chron i 17,18,24.

Arvadite (*'rwdy*)   I Chron i 16.

Asa (*'s'*)   I Chron iii 10, ix 16; II Chron xiii 23, xiv 1,7,9,10,11, 12, xv 2(*bis*), 8,10,16,(*bis*), 17,19, xvi 1(*bis*), 2,4,6,7,10,11, 12,13, xvii 2, xx 32, xxi 12.

Asahel (*'šh'l*)   I Chron ii 16, xi 26, xxvii 7; II Chron xvii 8, xxxi 13; Ezra x 15.

Asaiah (*'šyh*)   I Chron iv 36, vi 30, ix 5, xv 6,11; II Chron xxxiv 20.

Asaph (*'sp*)   I Chron vi 39(*bis*), ix 15, xv 17,19, xvi 5(*bis*), 7,37, xxv 1,2(*tris*), 6,9, xxvi 1; II Chron v 12, xx 14, xxix 13, 30, xxxv 15(*bis*); Ezra ii 41, iii 10; Neh ii 8, vii 44, xi 17,22, xii 35,46.

Asarelah (*'šr'lh*)   I Chron xxv 2.

Asharel (*'šr'l*)   I Chron iv 16.

Ashbel (*'šbl*)   I Chron viii 1.

Asher (*'šr*)   I Chron ii 2, vi 62,74, vii 30,40, xii 37; II Chron xxx 11.

Ashhur (*'šḥwr*)   I Chron ii 24, iv 5.

Ashkenaz (*'šknz*)   I Chron i 6.

Ashterathite (*'štrty*)   I Chron xi 44.

Ashvath (*'šwt*)   I Chron vii 33.

Asiel (*'šy'l*)   I Chron iv 35.

Asriel (*'šry'l*)   I Chron vii 14.

Asshur (*'šwr*)   I Chron i 17.

Assir (*'syr*)   I Chron vi 22,23,37.

Atarah (*'ṭrh*)   I Chron ii 26.

Athaliah (*'tlyh*)   I Chron viii 26; II Chron xxii 2,10,11,12, xxiii 12,13,21, xxiv 7; Ezra viii 7.

Atroth-beth-joab (*'ṭrwt-byt-yw'b*)   I Chron ii 54.

Attai (*'ty*)   I Chron ii 35,36, xii 12; II Chron xi 20.

Azarel (*'zr'l*)   I Chron xii 7, xxv 18, xxvii 22; Ezra x 41; Neh xi 13, xii 36.

Azariah (*'zryh*)   I Chron ii 8,38,39, iii 12, vi 9(*bis*), 10,11,13,14, 36, ix 11; II Chron xv 1, xxi 2(*bis*), xxiii 1(*bis*), xxvi 17,20;

xxviii 12, xxix 12(*bis*), xxxi 10,13; Ezra vii 1,3; Neh iii 23,24, vii 7, viii 7, x 3, xii 33.

Azaz (*'zz*) I Chron v 8.

Azaziah (*'zzyhw*) I Chron xv 21, xxvii 20; II Chron xxxi 13.

Azel (*'ṣl*) I Chron viii 37,38(*bis*), ix 43,44(*bis*).

Aziel (*'zy'l*) I Chron xv 20.

Azmaveth (*'zmwt*) I Chron viii 36, ix 42, xi 33, xii 3, xxvii 25.

Azriel (*'zry'l*) I Chron v 24, xxvii 19.

Azrikam (*'zryqm*) I Chron iii 23, viii 38, ix 14,44; II Chron xxviii 7; Neh xi 15.

Azubah (*'zwbh*) I Chron ii 18,19; II Chron xx 31.

Baal (*b'l*) I Chron v 5, viii 30, ix 36; II Chron xvii 3, xxiii 17 (*bis*), xxiv 7, xxviii 2, xxxiii 3.

Baal-hanan (*b'l-ḥnn*) I Chron i 49,50, xxvii 28.

Baanah (*b'nh*) I Chron xi 30; Ezra ii 2; Neh vii 7, x 28.

Baara (*b'r*) I Chron viii 8.

Baaseiah (*b'śyh*) I Chron vi 40.

Baharumite (*bḥrwmy*) I Chron xi 33.

Bakbakkar (*bqbqr*) I Chron ix 15.

Bani (*bny*) I Chron vi 46, ix 4; Ezra ii 10, viii 10 (with Greek), x 29,34; Neh iii 17, viii 7, ix 4(*bis*), 5, x 14,15, xi 22.

Bariah (*bryḥ*) I Chron iii 22.

Bathshua (*bt-šw'*) I Chron ii 3, iii 5.

Bealiah (*b'lyh*) I Chron xii 6.

Becher (*bkr*) I Chron vii 6,8.

Bedad (*bdd*) I Chron i 46.

Bedan (*bdn*) I Chron vii 17.

Beeliada (*b'lyd'*) I Chron xiv 7.

Beera (*b'r*) I Chron vii 37.

Beerah (*b'rh*) I Chron v 6.

Bela (*bl'*) I Chron i 43,44, v 8, vii 6,7, viii 1,3.

Benaiah (*bnyhw*) I Chron iv 36, xi 22,24,31, xv 18,20,24, xvi 5,6, xviii 17, xxvii 5,6,14,34; II Chron xx 14, xxxi 13; Ezra x 25,30,35,43.

Ben-hanan (*bn-ḥnn*) I Chron iv 20.

Benjamin (*bnymn*) I Chron ii 2, vi 60,65, vii 6,10, viii 1,40, ix 3,7, xi 31, xii 2,17,30, xxi 6, xxviii 21; II Chron xi 1,3,10,12,23, xiv 7, xv 2,8,9, xvii 17, xxv 5, xxxi 1, xxxiv 9,32; Ezra i 5, iv 1, x 9,32; Neh iii 23, xi 4,7,31,36, xii 34.

Benjaminite (*bnymyny*)   I Chron xxvii 12.

Ben-zoheth (*bn-zwḥt*)   I Chron iv 20.

Beor (*b'wr*)   I Chron i 43.

Beracah (*brkh*)   I Chron xii 3.

Beraiah (*br'yh*)   I Chron viii 21.

Berechiah (*brkyh*)   I Chron iii 20, vi 39, ix 16, xv 17,23; II Chron
   xxviii 12; Neh iii 4,30, vi 18.

Bered (*brd*)   I Chron vii 20.

Beri (*bry*)   I Chron vii 36.

Beriah (*bry'h, br'h*)   I Chron vii 23,30,31, viii 13,16, xxiii 10,11.

Berothite (*brty*)   I Chron xi 39.

Beth-gader (*byt-gdr*)   I Chron ii 51.

Bethlehem (*byt-lḥm*)   I Chron ii 51,54, iv 4.

Beth-rapha (*byt-rp'*)   I Chron iv 12.

Beth-rechab (*byt-rkb*)   I Chron ii 55.

Beth-zur (*byt-ṣwr*)   I Chron ii 45.

Bezalel (*bṣl'l*)   I Chron ii 20; II Chron i 5; Ezra x 30.

Bezer (*bṣr*)   I Chron vii 37.

Bilgah (*blgh*)   I Chron xxiv 14; Neh xii 5,18.

Bilhah (*blhh*)   I Chron vii 13.

Bilhan (*blhn*)   I Chron i 42, vii 10(*bis*).

Bimhal (*bmhl*)   I Chron vii 33.

Binea (*bn ''*)   I Chron viii 37, ix 43.

Birzvaith (*brzwt,* [Kethib])   I Chron vii 31.

Bithiah (*btyh*)   I Chron iv 8.

Boaz (*b'z*)   I Chron ii 11,12; II Chron iii 17.

Bocheru (*bkrw*)   I Chron viii 38; ix 44.

Bukki (*bqy*)   I Chron vi 5(*bis*), 51; Ezra vii 4.

Bukkiah (*bqyhw*)   I Chron xxv 4,13.

Bunah (*bwnh*)   I Chron ii 25.

Buz (*bwz*)   I Chron v 14.

Caleb (*klb*)   I Chron ii 18,19,24,42,46,48,49,50, iv 15, vi 56.

Calcol (*klkl*)   I Chron ii 6.

Canaan (*kn'n*)   I Chron i 8,13, xvi 18.

Canaanitess (*kn'nyt*)   I Chron ii 3.

Caphtorim (*kptrym*)   I Chron i 12.

Carmelite (*krmly*)   I Chron xi 37.

Carmi (*krmy*)   I Chron ii 7, iv 1, v 3.

Casluhim (*kslḥym*)   I Chron i 12.

Chelub (*klwb*) I Chron iv 11, xxvii 26.

Chelubi (*klwby*) I Chron ii 9.

Chenaanah (*kn'nh*) I Chron vii 10; II Chron xviii 10,23.

Chenaniah (*knnyhw*) I Chron xv 22,27, xxvi 29.

Cheran (*krn*) I Chron i 41.

Cherethite (*krty*) I Chron xviii 17.

Chidon (*kydn*) I Chron xiii 9.

Cush (*kwš*) I Chron i 8,9,10.

Dagon (*dgwn*) I Chron x 10.

Dan (*dn*) I Chron ii 2, xxi 2, xxvii 22; II Chron ii 13, xvi 4, xxx 5.

Daniel (*dny'l*) I Chron iii 1; Ezra viii 2; Neh x 7.

Danites (*dny*) I Chron xii 36.

Dara (*dr'*) I Chron ii 6.

David (*dwyd*) I Chron ii 15, iii 1,9, iv 31, vi 31, vii 2, ix 22, x 14, xi 1,3(*bis*), 4,5(*tris*), 6,7(*bis*), 9,10,11,13,15,16,17,18(*bis*), 25, xii 1,9,17,18,19(*bis*), 20,22,23,24,32,34,39(*tris*), 40, xiii 1,2,5,6, 8,11,12,13(*bis*), xiv 1,2,3,8(*tris*), 10,11(*bis*), 12,14,16,17, xv 1, 2,3,4,11,16,25,27(*bis*), 29(*bis*), xvi 2,7,43, xvii 1(*bis*), 2,4,7,15, 16,18,24, xviii 1,2,4(*bis*), 5,6(*tris*), 7,8,9,10,11,13(*bis*), 14,17, xix 2(*tris*), 3,4,5,6,8,17(*bis*), 18,19, xx 1,2(*bis*), 3,7,8, xxi 1,2, 5,8,9,10,11,13,16(*bis*), 17,18(*bis*), 19,21(*tris*), 22,23,24,25,26, 28,30, xxii 1,2,3,4,5(*bis*), 6,7,17, xxiii 1,4,6,25,27, xxiv 3,31, xxv 1, xxvi 26,31,32, xxvii 18,23,24,31,32, xxviii 1,2,11,20, xxix 1,9,10(*bis*), 20,22,23,24,26,29; II Chron i 1,4,8,9, ii 2,6,11,13, 16, iii 1(*bis*), v 1,2, vi 4,6,7,8,10,16,17,42, vii 6(*bis*), 10,17,18, viii 11(*bis*), 14(*bis*), ix 31, x 16(*bis*), 19, xi 17,18, xii 16, xiii 5, 6,8,23, xvi 14, xxi 1,7(*bis*), 12,20, xxiii 3,9,18, xxiv 16,25, xxvii 9, xxviii 1, xxix 2,25,26,27,30, xxx 26, xxxii 5,30,33, xxxiii 7,14, xxxiv 2,3, xxxv 3,15; Ezra iii 10, viii 2,20; Neh iii 15,16, xii 24, 36,37(*bis*), 45,46.

Dedan (*ddn*) I Chron i 9,32.

Delaiah (*dlyh*) I Chron iii 24, xxiv 18; Ezra ii 60; Neh vi 10, vii 62.

Diklah (*dqlh*) I Chron i 21.

Diphath (*dypt*) I Chron i 6.

Dishan (*dyšn*) I Chron i 38.

Dishon (*dyšwn*) I Chron i 38,41(*bis*), 42.

Dodai (*dwdy*) I Chron xxvii 4.

Dodo (*dwdw*)   I Chron xi 12,26.
Dumah (*dwmh*)   I Chron i 30.

Ebal (*'ybl*)   I Chron i 22,40.
Eber (*'br*)   I Chron i 18,19,25, v 13, viii 12,22; Neh xii 20.
Ebiasaph (*'bysp*)   I Chron vi 23,37, ix 19.
Eder (*'dr*)   I Chron viii 15, xxiii 23, xxiv 30.
Eglah (*'glh*)   I Chron iii 3.
Egyptian (*mṣry*)   I Chron ii 34, xi 23(*tris*); Ezra ix 1.
Ehud (*'hwd*)   I Chron vii 10.
Ehud (*ḥwd*)   I Chron viii 6.
Eker (*'qr*)   I Chron ii 27.
Elah (*'lh*)   I Chron i 52, iv 15(*bis*), ix 8.
Elam (*'ylm*)   I Chron i 17, viii 24, xxvi 3; Ezra ii 7,31, vii 7, x 2
    [Q(ere)], 26; Neh vii 12,34, x 15, xii 42.
Eldaah (*'ld'h*)   I Chron i 33.
Elead (*'l'd*)   I Chron vii 21.
Eleadah (*'l'dh*)   I Chron vii 20.
Eleasah (*'l'śh*)   I Chron ii 39,40, viii 37, ix 43; Ezra x 22.
Eleazar (*'l'zr*)   I Chron vi 3,4,50, ix 20, xi 12, xxiii 21,22, xxiv
    1,2,3,4(*bis*), 5,6,28; Ezra vii 5, viii 33, x 25; Neh xii 42.
Elhanan (*'lḥnn*)   I Chron xi 26, xx 5.
Eliab (*'ly'b*)   I Chron ii 13, vi 27, xii 10, xv 18,20, xvi 5; II
    Chron xi 18.
Eliada (*'lyd'*)   I Chron iii 8; II Chron xvii 17.
Eliahba (*'lyḥb'*)   I Chron xi 33.
Eliashib (*'lyšyb*)   I Chron iii 24, xxiv 12; Ezra x 6,24,27,36; Neh
    iii 1,20,21(*bis*), xii 10(*bis*), 22,23, xiii 4,7,28.
Eliathah (*'ly'th*)   I Chron xxv 4,27.
Eliel (*'ly'l*)   I Chron v 24, vi 34, viii 20,22, xi 46,47, xii 12, xv 9,
    11; II Chron xxxi 13.
Eliehoenai (*'lyhw'yny*)   I Chron xxvi 3; Ezra viii 4.
Elienai (*'ly'ny*)   I Chron viii 20.
Eliezer (*'ly'zr*)   I Chron vii 8, xv 24, xxiii 15,17(*bis*), xxvi 25,
    xxvii 16; II Chron xx 37; Ezra viii 16, x 18,23,31.
Elihu (*'lyhw', 'lyhw*)   I Chron xii 21, xxvi 7, xxvii 18.
Elijah (*'lyh*)   I Chron viii 27.
Elioenai (*'lyw'yny, 'lyw'ny*)   I Chron iii 23,24, iv 36, vii 8; Ezra x
    22,27; Neh xii 41.
Eliphal (*'lypl*)   I Chron xi 35.

Eliphaz (*'lypz*)   I Chron i 35,36.

Eliphelehu (*'lyplhw*)   I Chron xv 18,21.

Eliphelet (*'lyplṭ*)   I Chron iii 6,8, viii 39, xiv 7; Ezra viii 13.

Elishah (*'lyšh*)   I Chron i 7.

Elishama (*'lyšm'*)   I Chron ii 41, iii 6,8, vii 26, xiv 7; II Chron xvii 8.

Elishua (*'lšw'*)   I Chron xiv 5.

Elizaphan (*'lyṣpn*)   I Chron xv 8; II Chron xxix 13.

Elkanah (*'lqnh*)   I Chron vi 23,25,26,27,34,35,36, ix 16, xii 7, xv 23; II Chron xxviii 7.

Elnaam (*'ln'm*)   I Chron xi 46.

Elpaal (*'lp'l*)   I Chron viii 11,12,18.

Elpelet (*'lplṭ*)   I Chron xiv 5.

Eluzai (*'l'wzy*)   I Chron xii 6.

Elzabad (*'lzbd*)   I Chron xii 13, xxvi 7.

Enoch (*ḥnwk*)   I Chron i 3,33, v 3.

Enosh (*'nwš*)   I Chron i 1.

Ephah (*'yph*)   I Chron i 33, ii 46,47.

Epher (*'pr*)   I Chron i 33, iv 17, v 24.

Ephlal (*'pll*)   I Chron ii 37(*bis*).

Ephraim (*'prym*)   I Chron vi 66, vii 20,22, ix 3, xii 31, xxvii 10, 14,20; II Chron xv 9, xvii 2, xxv 7,10,23, xxviii 7,12, xxx 1,10, 18, xxxi 1, xxxiv 6,9.

Ephrath (*'prt*)   I Chron ii 19.

Ephrathah (*'prth*)   I Chron ii 24,50, iv 4.

Er (*'r*)   I Chron ii 3(*bis*), iv 21.

Era (*'r'*)   I Chron vii 38.

Esau (*'św*)   I Chron i 34,35.

Eshbaal (*'šb'l*)   I Chron viii 33, ix 39.

Eshban (*'šbn*)   I Chron i 41.

Eshek (*'šq*)   I Chron viii 39.

Eshtaolite (*'št'ly*)   I Chron ii 53.

Eshtemoa (*'štm'*)   I Chron iv 17,19.

Eshton (*'štwn*)   I Chron iv 11,12.

Etam (*'yṭm*)   I Chron iv 3.

Ethan (*'ytn*)   I Chron ii 6,8, vi 42,44, xv 17,19.

Ethnan (*'tnn*)   I Chron iv 7.

Ethni (*'tny*)   I Chron vi 41.

Ezbai (*'zby*)   I Chron xi 37.

Ezbon (*'ṣbwn*)   I Chron vii 7.

Ezer (*'ṣr*) I Chron i 38,42.
Ezer (*'zr*) I Chron iv 4, vii 21, xii 10; Neh iii 19, xii 42.
Ezrah (*'zrh*) I Chron iv 17.
Ezri (*'zry*) I Chron xxvii 26.

Gad (*gd, gdy*) I Chron ii 2, v 11,18,26, vi 63, 80, xii 15, xxi 9,
    11,13,18,19, xxix 29; II Chron xxix 25.
Gaderite (*gdry*) I Chron xxvii 28.
Gadite (*gdy*) I Chron xii 9,38, xxvi 32.
Galal (*gll*) I Chron ix 15,16; Neh xi 17.
Gamul (*gmwl*) I Chron xxiv 17.
Gareb (*grb*) I Chron xi 40.
Garmite (*grmy*) I Chron iv 19.
Gatam (*g'tm*) I Chron i 36.
Gazez (*gzz*) I Chron ii 46(*bis*).
Gedaliah (*gdlyhw*) I Chron xxv 3,9; Ezra x 18.
Gederathite (*gdrty*) I Chron xii 5.
Gedor (*gdr, gdwr*) I Chron iv 4,18, viii 31, ix 37.
Ge-harashim (*gy' ḥršym*) I Chron iv 14.
Gera (*gr'*) I Chron viii 3,5,7.
Gershom (*gršm, gršwm*) I Chron vi 16,17,20,43,62,71, xv 7,
    xxiii 15,16, xxvi 24; Ezra viii 2.
Gershon (*gršwn*) I Chron vi 1, xxiii 6.
Gershunnite (*gršny*) I Chron xxiii 7, xxvi 21(*bis*), xxix 8; II
    Chron xxix 12.
Geshan (*gyšn*) I Chron ii 47.
Geshur (*gšwr*) I Chron ii 23.
Gether (*gtr*) I Chron i 17.
Gibea (*gb''*) I Chron ii 49.
Gibeathite (*gb'thy*) I Chron xii 3.
Gibeon (*gb'wn*) I Chron viii 29, ix 35.
Gibeonite (*gb'wny*) I Chron xii 4; Neh iii 7.
Giddalti (*gdlty*) I Chron xxv 4,29.
Gilead (*gl'd*) I Chron ii 21,23, v 14, vii 14,17.
Girgashite (*grgšy*) I Chron i 14; Neh ix 8.
Gittite (*gty*) I Chron xiii 13, xx 5.
Gizonite (*gzwny*) I Chron xi 34.
Gog (*gwg*) I Chron v 4.
Goliath (*glyt*) I Chron xx 5.

Gomer (*gmr*) I Chron i 5,6.
Guni (*gwny*) I Chron v 15, vii 13.

Hachmoni (*ḥkmwny*) I Chron xi 11, xxvii 32.
Hadad (*ḥdd*) I Chron i 30,46,47,50,51.
Hadadezer (*ḥddʿzr*) I Chron xviii 3,5,7,9,10(*bis*), xix 16,19.
Hadoram (*hdwrm*) I Chron i 21, xviii 10; II Chron x 18.
Haggiah (*ḥgyh*) I Chron vi 30.
Haggith (*ḥgyt*) I Chron iii 2.
Hagri (*hgry*) I Chron xi 38.
Hagrites (*hgrʾym, hgry*) I Chron v 10,19,20, xxvii 31.
Hakkoz (*hqwz*) I Chron xxiv 10; Ezra ii 61; Neh iii 4,21, vii 63.
Ham (*ḥm*) I Chron i 4,8, iv 40.
Hamathite (*ḥmty*) I Chron i 16.
Hammath (*ḥmt*) I Chron ii 55.
Hammolecheth (*hmlkt*) I Chron vii 18.
Hammuel (*ḥmwʾl*) I Chron iv 26.
Hamran (*ḥmrn*) I Chron i 41.
Hamul (*ḥmwl*) I Chron ii 5.
Hanan (*ḥnn*) I Chron viii 23,38, ix 44, xi 43; Ezra ii 46; Neh vii 49, viii 7, x 11,23,27, xiii 13.
Hanani (*ḥnny*) I Chron xxv 4,25; II Chron xvi 7, xix 2, xx 34; Ezra x 20; Neh i 2, xii 36.
Hananiah (*ḥnnyh*) I Chron iii 19,21, viii 24, xxv 4,23; II Chron xxvi 11; Ezra x 28; Neh iii 8,30, x 24, xii 12,41.
Hanniel (*ḥnyʾl*) I Chron vii 39.
Hanun (*ḥnwn*) I Chron xix 2(*bis*), 3,4,6; Neh iii 13,30.
Happizzez (*hpṣṣ*) I Chron xxiv 15.
Haran (*ḥrn*) I Chron ii 46(*bis*).
Haran (*hrn*) I Chron xxiii 9.
Hararite (*hrry*) I Chron xi 34,35.
Hareph (*ḥrp*) I Chron ii 51, iv 3.
Harim (*ḥrm*) I Chron xxiv 8; Ezra ii 32,39, x 21,31; Neh iii 11, vii 35,42, x 6,28, xii 15.
Harnepher (*ḥrnpr*) I Chron vii 36.
Haroeh (*hrʾh*) I Chron ii 52.
Harorite (*hrwry*) I Chron xi 27.
Harum (*hrwm*) I Chron iv 8.
Haruphite (*hrwpy,* [Q(ere)]) I Chron xii 6.
Hasadiah (*ḥsdyh*) I Chron iii 20.

218   INDEX OF

Hashabiah (*ḥšbyh*)   I Chron vi 45, ix 14, xxv 3,19, xxvi 30, xxvii
    17; II Chron xxxv 9; Ezra viii 19,24; Neh iii 17, x 12, xi 15,22,
    xii 21,24.
Hashem (*ḥšm*)   I Chron xi 34.
Hashshub (*ḥšwb*)   I Chron ix 14; Neh iii 11,23, x 24, xi 15.
Hashubah (*ḥšwbh*)   I Chron iii 20.
Hassenuah (*hsn'h, hsnw'h*)   I Chron ix 7; Neh xi 9.
Hatath (*ḥtt*)   I Chron iv 13.
Hattush (*ḥṭwš*)   I Chron iii 22; Ezra viii 2; Neh iii 10, x 5, xii 2.
Havilah (*ḥwylh*)   I Chron i 9,23.
Hazarmaveth (*ḥṣrmwt*)   I Chron i 20.
Haziel (*ḥzy'l*)   I Chron xxiii 9.
Hazzelelponi (*ḥṣllpwny*)   I Chron iv 3.
Hazzobebah (*hṣbbh*)   I Chron iv 8.
Heber (*ḥbr*)   I Chron iv 18, vii 31,32, viii 17.
Hebron (*ḥbrwn*)   I Chron ii 42,43, vi 2,18, xv 9, xxiii 12,19, xxiv
    23.
Hebronite (*ḥbrwny*)   I Chron xxvi 23,30,31(*bis*).
Helah (*ḥl'h*)   I Chron iv 5,7.
Heldai (*ḥldy*)   I Chron xxvii 15.
Heled (*ḥld*)   I Chron xi 30.
Helem (*hlm*)   I Chron vii 35.
Helez (*ḥlṣ*)   I Chron ii 39(*bis*), xi 27, xxvii 10.
Heman (*hymn*)   I Chron ii 6, vi 33, xv 17,19, xvi 41,42, xxv 1,
    4(*bis*), 5(*bis*), 6; II Chron v 12, xxix 14, xxxv 15.
Hepher (*ḥpr*)   I Chron iv 6, xi 36.
Heresh (*ḥrš*)   I Chron ix 15.
Heth (*ḥt*)   I Chron ix 15.
Hezekiah (*ḥzqyhw*)   I Chron iii 13, iv 41; II Chron xxviii 12,
    17, xxix 1,18,20,27,30,31,36, xxx 1,18,20,22,24, xxxi 2,8,9,11,
    13,20, xxxii 2,8,9,11,12,15,16,17,20,22,23,24,25,26(*bis*), 27,30
    (*bis*), 32,33, xxxiii 3; Ezra ii 16; Neh vii 21, x 18.
Hezir (*ḥzyr*)   I Chron xxiv 15; Neh x 21.
Hezro (*ḥṣrw*)   I Chron xi 37.
Hezron (*ḥṣrwn*)   I Chron ii 5,9,18,21,24(*bis*), 25, iv 1, v 3.
Hilkiah (*ḥlqyh*)   I Chron vi 13(*bis*), 45, ix 11, xxvi 11; II Chron
    xxiv 9,14,15(*bis*), 18,20,22, xxxv 8; Ezra vii 1; Neh viii 4, xi
    11, xii 7,21.
Hiram (*ḥyrm*)   I Chron xiv 1; II Chron iv 11, ix 10.

Hittite (*ḥty*) I Chron xi 41; II Chron i 17, viii 7; Ezra ix 1; Neh ix 8.

Hivites (*ḥwy*) I Chron i 15; II Chron viii 7.

Hizki (*ḥzqy*) I Chron viii 17.

Hizkiah (*ḥzqyh*) I Chron iii 23.

Hod (*hwd*) I Chron vii 37.

Hodaivah, Hodaviah (*hdywhw, hwdwyh*) I Chron iii 24, v 24, ix 7; Ezra ii 40.

Hodesh (*ḥdš*) I Chron viii 9.

Hodiah (*hwdyh*) I Chron iv 19; Neh viii 7, ix 5, x 11,14,19.

Homam (*hwmm*) I Chron i 39.

Hori (*ḥry*) I Chron i 39.

Hosah (*ḥsh*) I Chron xvi 38, xxvi 10,11,16.

Hoshama (*hwšmʿ*) I Chron iii 18.

Hoshea (*hwšʿ*) I Chron xxvii 20; Neh x 24.

Hotham (*ḥwtm*) I Chron vii 32, xi 44.

Hothir (*hwtyr*) I Chron xxv 4,28.

Hul (*ḥwl*) I Chron i 17.

Huppah (*ḥph*) I Chron xxiv 13.

Huppim (*ḥpm*) I Chron vii 12,15.

Hur (*ḥwr*) I Chron ii 19,20,50, iv 1,4; II Chron i 5; Neh iii 9.

Hurai (*ḥry*) I Chron xi 32.

Huram (*ḥwrm*) I Chron viii 5; II Chron ii 2,10,11, iv 11(*bis*), viii 2,18.

Huri (*ḥwry*) I Chron v 14.

Hushah (*ḥwšh*) I Chron iv 4.

Hushai (*ḥwšy*) I Chron xxvii 33.

Husham (*ḥwšm*) I Chron i 45,46.

Hushathite (*ḥšty*) I Chron xi 29, xx 4, xxvii 11.

Hushim (*ḥšm, ḥšym*) I Chron vii 12, viii 8,11.

Ibhar (*ybḥr*) I Chron iii 6, xiv 5.

Ibneiah (*ybnyh*) I Chron ix 8.

Ibnijah (*ybnyh*) I Chron ix 8.

Ibri (*ʿbry*) I Chron xxiv 27.

Ibsam (*ybśm*) I Chron vii 2.

Idbash (*ydbš*) I Chron iv 3.

Iddo (*ydw, yʿdy, ʿdw, ʿdwʾ, ʾdw*) I Chron vi 21, xxvii 21; II Chron ix 29, xii 15, xiii 22; Ezra v 1, vi 14, viii 17(*bis*); Neh xii 4,16.

Igal (*ygʾl*) I Chron iii 22.

(*bis*), 17,21,24,25,27,29,32,33, vii 3,6,8,10,18, viii 2,7,8,9,11, ix
8,30, x 1,3,16(*tris*), 17,18,19, xi 3,13,16(*bis*), xii 1,6,13, xiii
4,5(*bis*), 12,15,16,17,18, xv 3,4,9,13,17, xvi 1,3,7,11, xvii 1,4,
xviii 3,4,5,7,8,9,16,17,19,25,28,29(*bis*), 30,31,32,33,34, xix 8,
xx 7,10,19,29,34,35, xxi 2,4,6,13(*bis*), xxii 5, xxiii 2, xxiv 5,6,
9,16, xxv 6,7(*bis*), 9,17,18,21,22,23,25,26, xxvii 7, xxviii 2,3,5,
8,13,19,23,26,27, xxix 7,10,24(*bis*), 27, xxx 1(*bis*), 5(*bis*), 6
(*tris*), 21,25(*bis*), 26, xxxi 1(*bis*), 5,6,8, xxxii 17,32, xxxiii 2,7,
8,9,16,18(*bis*), xxxiv 7,9,21,23,26,33(*bis*), xxxv 3(*tris*), 4,17,
18(*bis*), 25,27, xxxvi 8,13; Ezra i 3, ii 2,59,70, iii 1,2,10,11, iv
1,3(*bis*), v 1,11, vi 14,16,17(*bis*), 21(*bis*), 22, vii 6,7,11,13,
15,28, viii 18,25,29,35(*bis*), ix 1,4,15, x 1,2,5,10,25; Neh i 6
(*bis*), ii 10, vii 7,61,72(*bis*), viii 1,14,17, ix 1,2, x 40, xi 3,20,
xii 47, xiii 2,3,18,26(*bis*).

Issachar (*yśśkr*)   I Chron ii 1, vi 62,72, vii 1,5, xii 33,41, xxvi 5,
xxvii 18; II Chron xxx 18.

Isshiah (*yšyh*)   I Chron vii 3, xii 7, xxiii 20, xxiv 21,25(*bis*);
Ezra x 31.

Ithai (*'yty*)   I Chron xi 31.

Ithamar (*'ytmr*)   I Chron vi 3, xxiv 1,2,3,4(*bis*), 5,6; Ezra viii 2.

Ithmah (*ytmh*)   I Chron xi 46.

Ithran (*ytrn*)   I Chron i 41, vii 37.

Ithream (*ytr'm*)   I Chron iii 3.

Ithrite (*ytry*)   I Chron ii 53, xi 40(*bis*).

Izhar (*yṣhr*)   I Chron vi 2,18,38, xxiii 12,18, xxiv 22.

Izharite (*yṣhry*)   I Chron xxvi 23,29.

Izliah (*yzly'h*)   I Chron viii 18.

Izrahiah (*yzrḥyh*)   I Chron vii 3(*bis*).

Izrahite (*yzrḥ*)   I Chron xxvii 8.

Izri (*yṣry*)   I Chron xxv 11.

Jaakan (*y'qn*)   I Chron i 42.

Jaakob (*y'qb*)   see Jacob.

Jaakobah (*y'qbh*)   I Chron iv 36.

Jaareshiah (*y'ršyh*)   I Chron viii 27.

Jaasiel (*y'śy'l*)   I Chron xi 47, xxvii 21.

Jaaziah (*y'zyhw*)   I Chron xxiv 26,27.

Jaaziel (*y'zy'l*)   I Chron xv 18.

Jabez (*y'bṣ*)   I Chron iv 9(*bis*), 10.

Jacan (*y'kn*)   I Chron v 13.

Jediael (*ydy''l*)   I Chron vii 6,10,11, xi 45, xii 21, xxvi 2.

Jedithun (*ydytwn*)   I Chron xvi 38.

Jeduthun (*ydwtwn*)   I Chron ix 16, xvi 41,42(*bis*), xxv 1,3(*tris*), 6; II Chron v 12, xxix 14, xxxv 15; Neh ix 17 (Kethib, *ydytwn*).

Jehallelel (*yhll'l*)   I Chron iv 16; II Chron xxix 12.

Jehdeiah (*yhdyhw*)   I Chron xxiv 20, xxvii 30.

Jehezkel (*yhzq'l*)   I Chron xxiv 16.

Jehiah (*yhyh*)   I Chron xv 24.

Jehiel (*yhy'l*)   I Chron xv 18,20, xvi 5, xxiii 8, xxvi 21,22 (*yhy'ly*), xxvii 32, xxix 8; II Chron xxi 2, xxix 14 (Kethib, *yhw'l*), xxxi 13, xxv 8; Ezra viii 9, x 2,21,26.

Jehizkiah (*yhzqyhw*)   II Chron xxviii 12. See Hezekiah.

Jehoaddah (*yhw'dh*)   I Chron viii 36(*bis*).

Jehohanan (*yhwhnn*)   I Chron xxvi 3; II Chron xvii 15, xxiii 1, xxviii 12; Ezra x 6,28; Neh vi 18, xii 13,18,42.

Jehoiada (*yhwyd'*)   I Chron xi 22,24, xii 28, xviii 17, xxvii 5, 34; II Chron xxii 11, xxiii 1,8(*bis*), 9,11,14,16,18, xxiv 2,3,6, 12,14(*bis*), 15,17,20,22,25.

Jehoiakim (*yhwyqym*)   I Chron iii 15,16; II Chron xxxvi 4,5,8.

Jehoiarib (*yhwyryb*)   I Chron ix 10, xxiv 7.

Jehonathan (*yhwntn*)   I Chron viii 33,34, ix 39,40, xx 7, xxvii 25,32; II Chron xvii 8.

Jehoshaphat (*yhwšpṭ*)   I Chron iii 10, xviii 15; II Chron xvii 1,3, 5,10,11,12, xviii 1,3,4,6,7(*bis*), 9,17,28,29,31(*bis*), xix 1,2,4, 8, xx 1,2,3,5,15,18,20,25,27,30,31,34,35,37, xxi 1,2(*bis*), 12, xxii 9.

Jehozabad (*yhwzbd*)   I Chron xxvi 4; II Chron xvii 18, xxiv 26.

Jehozadak (*yhwṣdq*)   I Chron vi 14,15.

Jehu (*yhw'*)   I Chron ii 38(*bis*), iv 35, xii 3; II Chron xix 2, xx 34, xxii 7,8,9, xxv 17.

Jehubbah (*yhbh*)   I Chron vii 34.

Jeiel (*y'y'l, y'w'l*)   I Chron v 7, viii 29, ix 35, xi 44, xv 18,21, xvi 5(*bis*); II Chron xx 14, xxvi 11, xxxv 9; Ezra viii 13, x 43.

Jekameam (*yqm'm*)   I Chron xxiii 19, xxiv 23.

Jekamiah (*yqmyh*)   I Chron ii 41(*bis*), iii 18.

Jekuthiel (*yqwty'l*)   I Chron iv 18.

Jephunneh (*ypnh*)   I Chron iv 15, vi 56, vii 38.

Jerah (*yrh*)   I Chron i 20.

Jerahmeel (*yrhm'l*)   I Chron ii 9,25,26,27,33,42, xxiv 29.

Jered (*yrd*)   I Chron iv 18.

Jeremiah (*yrmyh*) I Chron v 24, xii 5,11,14; II Chron xxxv 25, xxxvi 12,21,22; Ezra i 1; Neh x 3, xii 1,12,34.

Jeremoth (*yrmwt*) I Chron vii 8, viii 14, xxiii 23, xxv 22; Ezra x 26.

Jeribai (*yryby*) I Chron xi 46.

Jeriel (*yry'l*) I Chron vii 2.

Jerijah (*yryhw*) I Chron xxiii 19, xxiv 23, xxvi 31.

Jerimoth (*yrymwt*) I Chron vii 7, xii 6, xxiv 30, xxv 4, xxvii 19; II Chron xi 18, xxxi 13.

Jerioth (*yry'wt*) I Chron ii 18.

Jeroboam (*yrb'm*) I Chron v 17; II Chron ix 29, x 2,3,12,15, xi 4,14, xii 15, xiii 1,2,3,4,6,8,13,15,20.

Jeroham (*yrḥm*) I Chron vi 27,34, viii 27, ix 8,12, xii 8, xxvii 22; II Chron xxiii 1; Neh xi 12.

Jeshaiah (*yš'yh*) I Chron iii 21, xxv 3,15, xxvi 25; Ezra viii 7,19; Neh xi 7.

Jesharelah (*yśr'lh*) I Chron xxv 14.

Jeshebeab (*yšb'b*) I Chron xxiv 13.

Jesher (*yšr*) I Chron ii 18.

Jeshishai (*yšyšy*) I Chron v 14.

Jeshohaiah (*yšwḥyh*) I Chron iv 36.

Jeshua (*yšw'*) I Chron xxiv 11; II Chron xxxi 15; Ezra ii 2,6, 36,40, iii 2,8,9, iv 3, v 2, viii 33, x 18; Neh iii 19, vii 7,11,39, 43, viii 7,17, ix 4,5, x 10, xii 1,7,8,10,24,26.

Jesimiel (*yśym'l*) I Chron iv 36.

Jesse (*yšy, 'yšy*) I Chron ii 12,13, x 14, xii 19, xxix 26; II Chron x 16, xi 18.

Jether (*ytr*) I Chron ii 17,32(*bis*), iv 17, vii 38.

Jetheth (*ytt*) I Chron i 51.

Jetur (*ytwr*) I Chron i 31, v 19.

Jeuel (*y'w'l*) I Chron ix 6; II Chron xxix 13 ([Q(ere)], *y'y'l*).

Jeush (*y'ws*) I Chron i 35, vii 10 (Kethib, *y'yš*), viii 39, xxiii 10, 11; II Chron xi 19.

Jeuz (*y'wṣ*) I Chron viii 10.

Jezer (*yṣr*) I Chron vii 13.

Jeziel (*yzy'l;* Kethib, *yzw'l*) I Chron xii 3.

Jezreel (*yzr''l*) I Chron iv 3.

Joab (*yw'b*) I Chron ii 16, iv 14, xi 6,8,20,26,39, xviii 15, xix 8,10,14,15, xx 1(*bis*), xxi 2,3,4(*bis*), 5,6, xxvi 28, xxvii 7,24,34; Ezra ii 6, viii 9; Neh vii 11.

Joah (*yw'ḥ*) I Chron vi 21, xxvi 4; II Chron xxix 12(*bis*), xxxiv 8.

Joash (*yw'š, yw'š*) I Chron iii 11, iv 22, vii 8, xii 3, xxvii 28; II Chron xviii 25, xxii 11, xxiv 1,2,4,22,24, xxv 17,18,20,21,23 (*bis*), 25(*bis*).

Jobab (*ywbb*) I Chron i 23,44,45, viii 9,18.

Joel (*yw'l*) I Chron iv 35, v 4,8,12, vi 28,33,36, vii 3, xi 38, xv 7,11,17, xxiii 8, xxvi 22, xxvii 20; II Chron xxix 12; Ezra x 43; Neh xi 9.

Joelah (*yw''lh*) I Chron xii 8.

Joezer (*yw'zr*) I Chron xii 7.

Joha (*ywḥ'*) I Chron viii 16, xi 45.

Johanan (*ywḥnn*) I Chron iii 15,24, vi 9,10, xii 5,13; Ezra viii 12; Neh xii 22,23.

Jokim (*ywqym*) I Chron iv 22.

Jokshan (*yqšn*) I Chron i 32(*bis*).

Joktan (*yqṭn*) I Chron i 19,20,23.

Jonathan (*ywntn*) I Chron ii 32, 33, x 2, xi 34; Ezra viii 6, x 15; Neh xii 11(*bis*), 14, xii 35.

Jorai (*ywry*) I Chron v 13.

Joram (*ywrm*) I Chron iii 11, xxvi 25; II Chron xxii 5,7.

Jorkeam (*yrq'm*) I Chron ii 44.

Joseph (*ywsp*) I Chron ii 2, v 1,2, vii 29, xxv 2,9; Ezra x 42; Neh xii 14.

Joshah (*ywšh*) I Chron iv 34.

Joshaphat (*ywšpṭ*) I Chron xi 43, xv 24.

Joshaviah (*ywšwyh*) I Chron xi 46.

Joshbekashah (*yšbqšh*) I Chron xxv 4,24.

Joshibiah (*ywšbyh*) I Chron iv 35.

Joshua (*yhwš'*) I Chron vii 27.

Josiah (*y'šyhw*) I Chron iii 14,15; II Chron xxxiii 25, xxxiv 1, 33, xxxv 1,7,16,18,19,20(*bis*), 22,23,24,25(*bis*), xxxvi 1.

Jotham (*ywtm*) I Chron ii 47, iii 12, v 17; II Chron xxvi 21,23, xxvii 1,6,7,9.

Jozabad (*ywzbd*) I Chron xii 5,21(*bis*); II Chron xxxi 13, xxxv 9; Ezra viii 33, x 22,23; Neh viii 7, xi 16.

Judah (*yhwdh*) I Chron ii 1,3(*bis*), 10, iv 1,21,27,41, v 2,17, vi 15,55,65, ix 1,3,4, xii 17,25, xiii 6, xxi 5, xxvii 18, xxviii 4 (*bis*); II Chron ii 6, ix 11, x 17, xi 1,3(*bis*), 5,10,12,14,17,23, xii 4,5,12, xiii 1,13,14,15(*tris*), 16,18, xiv 3,4,5,6,7,11, xv 2,8, 9,15, xvi 1(*bis*), 6,7,11, xvii 2(*bis*), 5,6,7,9(*bis*), 10,12,13,14,

19, xviii 3,9,28, xix 1,5,11, xx 3,4(*bis*), 5,13,15,17,18,20,22,24, 27,31,35, xxi 3(*bis*), 8,10,11(*bis*), 12,13,17, xxii 1,6,8,10, xxiii 2(*bis*), 8, xxiv 5,6,9,17,18,23, xxv 5(*bis*), 10,12,13,17,18,19,21 (*bis*), 22,23,25,26,28, xxvi 1,2, xxvii 4,7, xxviii 6,9,10,17,18,19 (*bis*), 25,26, xxix 8,21, xxx 1,6,12,24,25(*bis*), xxxi 1(*bis*), 6(*bis*), 20, xxxii 1,8,9,12,23,25,32,33, xxxiii 9,14,16, xxxiv 3,5,9,11,21, 24,26,29,30, xxxv 18,21,24,27, xxxvi 4,8,10,14,23; Ezra i 2,3,5,8, ii 1(*bis*), iii 9, iv 1,4,6, v 1,8, vii 14, ix 9, x 7,9,23; Neh ii 5,7, iv 4,10, v 14, vi 7,17,18, vii 6, xi 3,4(*bis*), 9,20,24,25,36, xii 8,31,32,34,36,44, xiii 12,15,16,24.

Jushab-hesed (*ywšb-ḥsd*) I Chron iii 20.

Kedar (*qdr*) I Chron i 29.

Kedemah (*qdmh*) I Chron i 31.

Kehath (*qht*) I Chron vi 1,2,16,18,22,38,61,66,70, xv 5, xxiii 6, 12.

Kehathite (*qhty*) I Chron vi 33,54, ix 32; II Chron xx 19, xxix 12, xxxiv 12.

Keilah (*q'ylh*) I Chron iv 19.

Kemuel (*qmw'l*) I Chron xxvii 17.

Kenan (*qynn*) I Chron i 2.

Kenath (*qnt*) I Chron ii 33.

Kenaz (*qnz*) I Chron i 36,53, iv 13,15.

Kenites (*qynym*) I Chron ii 55.

Keturah (*qṭwrh*) I Chron i 32,33.

Kirjath-jearim (*qryt-y'rym*) I Chron ii 50,52,53.

Kish (*qyš*) I Chron viii 30,33(*bis*), ix 36,39(*bis*), xii 1, xxiii 21, 22, xxiv 29(*bis*), xxvi 28; II Chron xxix 12.

Kishi (*qyšy*) I Chron vi 44.

Kittim (*ktym*) I Chron i 7.

Korah (*qrḥ, qrḥy*) I Chron i 35, ii 43, vi 22,37, ix 19, xxvi 19.

Korahites (*qrḥym*) I Chron ix 19,31, xii 7, xxvi 1; II Chron xx 19.

Kore (*qwr'*) I Chron ix 19, xxvi 1; II Chron xxxi 14.

Koz (*qwṣ*) I Chron iv 8.

Kushaiah (*qwšyhw*) I Chron xv 17.

Laadah (*l'dh*) I Chron iv 21.

Ladan (*l'dn*) I Chron vii 26, xxiii 7,8,9, xxvi 21(*tris*).

Lahad (*lhd*) I Chron iv 2.

Lahmi (*lḥmy*) I Chron xx 5.

Lamech (*lmk*) I Chron i 3.

Lecah (*lkh*) I Chron iv 21.

Lehabim (*lhbym*) I Chron i 11.

Levi (*lwy*) I Chron ii 1, vi 1,16,38,43,47, ix 18, xxi 6, xxiii 6, 14,24; Ezra viii 18.

Levite(s) (*lwy, lwym*) I Chron vi 19,48,64, ix 2,14,26,31,33,34, xii 27, xiii 2, xv 2,4,11,12,14,15,16,17,22,26,27, xvi 4, xxiii 2,3, 26,27, xxiv 6(*bis*), 20,30,31, xxvi 20, xxvii 17, xxviii 13,21; II Chron v 4,5,12, vii 6, viii 14,15, xi 13,14, xiii 9,10, xvii 8 (*bis*), xix 8, xx 14,19, xxiii 2,4,6,7,8,18, xxiv 5(*bis*), 6,11, xxix 4,5,12,16,25,26,30,34(*bis*), xxx 15,16,17,21,22,25,27, xxxi 2 (*bis*), 4,8,12,14,17,19, xxxiv 9,12(*bis*), 13,30, xxxv 3,5,8,9(*bis*), 10,11,14,15,18; Ezra i 5,40, ii 70, iii 8(*bis*), 9,10,12, vi 16,18,20, vii 7,13,24, viii 15,20,29,30,33, ix 1, x 5,15,23; Neh iii 17, vii 1,43,72, viii 7,9,11,13, ix 4,5, x 1,10,29,35,38(*bis*), 39(*bis*), 40, xi 3,15,16,18,20,22,36, xii 1,8,22,23,24,27,28,30,44(*bis*), 47 (*bis*), xiii 5,10(*bis*), 13,22,29,30.

Libni (*lbny*) I Chron vi 17,20,29.

Likhi (*lqḥy*) I Chron vii 19.

Lotan (*lwṭn*) I Chron i 38,39(*bis*).

Lud (*lwd*) I Chron i 17.

Ludim (*lwdyym*) I Chron i 11.

Maacah (*m'kh*) I Chron ii 48, iii 2, vii 15,16, viii 29, ix 35, xi 43, xxvii 16; II Chron xi 20,21,22, xv 16.

Maacathite (*m'kty*) I Chron iv 19.

Maasai (*m'śy*) I Chron ix 12.

Maaseiah (*m'śyhw*) I Chron xv 18,20; II Chron xxiii 1, xxvi 11, xxviii 7, xxxiv 8; Ezra x 18,21,22,30; Neh iii 23, viii 4,7, x 26, xi 5,7, xii 41,42.

Maaz (*m'ṣ*) I Chron ii 27.

Maaziah (*m'zyhw*) I Chron xxiv 18; Neh x 9.

Machbannai (*mkbny*) I Chron xii 14.

Machbenah (*mkbnh*) I Chron ii 49.

Machir (*mkyr*) I Chron ii 21,23, vii 14,15,16,17.

Madai (*mdy*) I Chron i 5.

Madmannah (*mdmnh*) I Chron ii 49.

Magdiel (*mgdy'l*) I Chron i 54.

Magog (*mgwg*) I Chron i 5.

Mahalalel (*mhll'l*) I Chron i 2; Neh xi 4.

Maharai (*mhry*) I Chron xi 30, xxvii 13.

Mahath (*mḥt*) I Chron vi 35; II Chron xxix 12, xxxi 13.

Mahavites (*mḥwym*) I Chron xi 46.

Mahazioth (*mḥzy'wt*) I Chron xxv 4,30.

Mahlah (*mḥlh*) I Chron vii 18.

Mahli (*mḥly*) I Chron vi 19,29,47, xxiii 21(*bis*), 23, xxiv 26,28, 30; Ezra viii 18.

Malcham (*mlkm*) I Chron viii 9.

Malchiel (*mlky'l*) I Chron vii 31.

Malchijah (*mlkyh*) I Chron vi 40, ix 12, xxiv 9; Ezra x 25(*bis*), 31; Neh iii 11,14,31, viii 4, x 4, xi 12, xii 42.

Malchiram (*mlkyrm*) I Chron iii 18.

Malchishua (*mlky-šw'*) I Chron viii 33, ix 39, x 2.

Mallothi (*mlwty*) I Chron xxv 4,26.

Malluch (*mlwk*) I Chron vi 44; Ezra x 29,32; Neh x 5,28, xii 2, 14 (Kethib, *mlwky*).

Manahath (*mnḥt*) I Chron i 40.

Manahathite (*mnḥty*) I Chron ii 54.

Manasseh (*mnšh, mnšy*) I Chron ii 13, v 18,26, vi 61,62,70,71, vii 14,17,29, ix 3, xii 20,21(*bis*), 32,38, xxxi 32, xxvii 20,21; II Chron xv 9, xxx 1,10,11,18, xxxi 1, xxxii 33, xxxiii 1,9,10, 11, 13,14,18,20,22(*bis*), 23, xxxiv 6,9; Ezra x 30,33.

Maon (*m'wn*) I Chron ii 45(*bis*).

Mareshah (*mršh*) I Chron ii 42, iv 21.

Massa (*mś'*) I Chron i 30.

Matred (*mṭrd*) I Chron i 50.

Mattaniah (*mtnyh*) I Chron ix 15, xxv 4,16; II Chron xx 14, xxix 13; Ezra x 26,27,30,37; Neh xi 17,22, xii 8,25,35, xiii 13.

Mattithiah (*mttyh*) I Chron ix 31, xv 18,21, xvi 5, xxv 3,21; Ezra x 43; Neh viii 4.

Mecherathite (*mkrty*) I Chron xi 36.

Medan (*mdn*) I Chron i 32.

Mehetabel (*mḥyṭb'l*) I Chron i 50; Neh vi 10.

Mehir (*mḥyr*) I Chron iv 11.

Melech (*mlk*) I Chron viii 35, ix 41.

Meonothai (*m'wnty*) I Chron iv 13,14.

Meraioth (*mrywt*) I Chron vi 6,7,52, ix 11; Ezra vii 3; Neh xi 11, xii 15.

Merari (*mrry*) I Chron vi 1,16,19,29,44,47,63,77, ix 14, xv 6, 17, xxiii 6,21, xxiv 26,27, xxvi 10,19; II Chron xxix 12, xxxiv 12; Ezra viii 19.

Mered (*mrd*) I Chron iv 17,18.

Meribbaal (*mryb-b'l*) I Chron viii 34(*bis*), ix 40(*bis*).

Meronothite (*mrnty*) I Chron xxvii 30; Neh iii 7.

Mesha (*myš', myš'*) I Chron ii 42, viii 9.

Meshech (*mšk*) I Chron i 5,17.

Meshelemiah (*mšlmyh*) I Chron ix 21, xxvi 1,2,9.

Meshillemith (*mšlmyt*) I Chron ix 12.

Meshobab (*mšwbb*) I Chron iv 34.

Meshullam (*mšlm*) I Chron iii 19, v 13, viii 17, ix 7,8,11,12; II Chron xxxiv 12; Ezra viii 16, x 15,29; Neh iii 4,6,30, vi 18, viii 4, x 8,21, xi 7,11, xii 13,16,25,33.

Methuselah (*mtwšlḥ*) I Chron i 3.

Mezahab (*my-zhb*) I Chron i 50.

Mezobaite (*mṣbyh*) I Chron xi 47.

Mibhar (*mbḥr*) I Chron xi 38.

Mibsam (*mbśm*) I Chron i 29, iv 25.

Mibzar (*mbṣr*) I Chron i 53.

Midian (*mdyn*) I Chron i 32,33.

Mijamin (*mymn*) I Chron xxiv 9; Ezra x 25; Neh x 8, xii 5.

Mica (*myk'*) I Chron ix 15; Neh x 12, xi 22.

Micah (*mykh*) I Chron v 5, viii 34,35, ix 40,41, xxiii 20, xxiv 24(*bis*), 25; II Chron xviii 14, xxxiv 20; Neh xi 17.

Micaiah (*mykyh, mykhw*) II Chron xiii 2, xvii 7, xviii 7,8,12,13, 23,24,25,27; Neh xii 35,41.

Michael (*myk'l*) I Chron v 13,14, vi 40, vii 3, viii 16, xii 21, xxvii 18; II Chron xxi 2; Ezra viii 8.

Michal (*mykl*) I Chron xv 29.

Michri (*mkry*) I Chron ix 8.

Mikloth (*mqlwt*) I Chron viii 31,32, ix 37,38.

Mikneiah (*mqnyhw*) I Chron xv 18,21.

Miriam (*mrym*) I Chron iv 17, vi 3.

Mirmah (*mrmh*) I Chron viii 10.

Misham (*mš'm*) I Chron viii 12.

Mishma (*mšm'*) I Chron i 30, iv 25,26.

Mishmannah (*mšmnh*) I Chron xii 11.

Mishraite (*mšr'y*) I Chron ii 53.

Mithnite (*mtny*) I Chron xi 43.

Mizraim (*mṣrym*) I Chron i 8,11.

Mizzah (*mzh*) I Chron i 37.

Moab—Moabite (*mw'b, mw'by*) I Chron iv 22, xi 22,46, xviii 2; II Chron xx 1,10,22,23, xxiv 26; Ezra ix 1; Neh xiii 1,23.

Molid (*mwlyd*) I Chron ii 29.

Moses (*mšh*) I Chron vi 3,49, xv 15, xxi 29, xxii 13, xxiii 13, 14,15, xxvi 24; II Chron i 3, v 10, viii 13, xxiii 18, xxiv 6,9, xxv 4, xxx 16, xxxiii 8, xxxiv 14, xxxv 6,12; Ezra iii 2, vi 18, vii 6; Neh i 7,8, viii 1,14, ix 14, x 30, xiii 1.

Moza (*mwṣ'*) I Chron ii 46, viii 36,37, ix 42,43.

Mushi (*mšy, mwšy*) I Chron vi 19,47, xxiii 21,23, xxiv 26,30.

Naam (*n'm*) I Chron iv 15.

Naaman (*n'mn*) I Chron viii 4,7.

Naarah (*n'rh*) I Chron iv 5,6(*bis*).

Naarai (*n'ry*) I Chron xi 37.

Nadab (*ndb*) I Chron ii 28,30, vi 3, viii 30, ix 36, xxiv 1,2.

Naham (*nḥm*) I Chron iv 19.

Naharai (*nḥry*) I Chron xi 39.

Nahash (*nḥš*) I Chron xix 1,2.

Nahath (*nḥt*) I Chron i 37, vi 26; II Chron xxxi 13.

Nahor (*nḥwr*) I Chron i 26.

Nahshon (*nḥšwn*) I Chron ii 10,11.

Naphish (*npyš*) I Chron i 31, v 19.

Naphtali (*nptly*) I Chron ii 2, vi 62,76, vii 13, xii 35,41, xxvii 19; II Chron xvi 4, xxxiv 6.

Naphtuhim (*npthym*) I Chron i 11.

Nathan (*ntn*) I Chron ii 36(*bis*), iii 5, xi 38, xiv 4, xvii 1,2,3,15, xxix 29; II Chron ix 29, xxix 25; Ezra viii 16, x 39.

Neariah (*n'ryh*) I Chron iii 22,23, iv 42.

Nebaioth (*nbywt*) I Chron i 29.

Nebuchadnezzar (*nbkdn'ṣr, nbwkdn'ṣr*) I Chron vi 15; II Chron xxxvi 6,7,10,13; Ezra i 7, ii 1, v 12,14; vi 5; Neh vii 6.

Nedabiah (*ndbyh*) I Chron iii 18.

Nemuel (*nmw'l*) I Chron iv 24.

Nepheg (*npg*) I Chron iii 7, xiv 6.

Ner (*nr*) I Chron viii 33, ix 36,39, xxvi 28.

Nethaniah (*ntnyh*) I Chron xxv 2,12; II Chron xvii 8.

Nethanel (*ntn'l*) I Chron ii 14, xv 24, xxiv 6, xxvi 4; II Chron xvii 7, xxxv 9; Ezra x 22; Neh xii 21,36.

Netophathite (*nṭwpty*) I Chron ii 54, ix 16, xi 30(*bis*), xxvii 13,15; Neh xii 28.
Nimrod (*nmrwd*) I Chron i 10.
Noah (*nḥ*) I Chron i 4.
Nodab (*nwdb*) I Chron v 19.
Nogah (*ngh*) I Chron iii 7, xiv 6.
Nohah (*nwḥh*) I Chron viii 2.
Non (*nwn*) I Chron vii 27; Neh viii 17.

Obadiah (*'bdyh*) I Chron iii 21, vii 3, viii 38, ix 16,44, xii 10, xxvii 19; II Chron xvii 7, xxxiv 12; Ezra viii 9; Neh x 6, xii 25.
Obed (*'wbd*) I Chron ii 12(*bis*), 37,38, xi 47, xxvi 7; II Chron xxiii 1.
Obed-edom (*'bd-'dm*) I Chron xiii 13,14(*bis*), xv 18,21,24,25, xvi 5,38(*bis*), xxvi 4,8(*bis*), 15; II Chron xxv 24.
Obil (*'wbyl*) I Chron xxvii 30.
Ohel (*'hl*) I Chron iii 20.
Oholibamah (*'hlybmh*) I Chron i 52.
Omar (*'wmr*) I Chron i 36.
Omri (*'mry*) I Chron vii 8, ix 4, xxvii 18; II Chron xxii 2.
Onam (*'wnm*) I Chron i 40, ii 26,28.
Onan (*'wnn*) I Chron ii 3.
Ophir (*'pyr*) I Chron i 23.
Ophrah (*'prh*) I Chron iv 14.
Oren (*'rn*) I Chron ii 25.
Ornan (*'rnn*) I Chron xxi 15,18,20(*bis*), 21(*bis*), 22,23,24,25, 28; II Chron iii 1.
Othni (*'tny*) I Chron xxvi 7.
Othniel (*'tny'l*) I Chron iv 13(*bis*), xxvii 15.
Ozem (*'ṣm*) I Chron ii 15,25.

Pallu (*plw'*) I Chron v 3.
Pasach (*psk*) I Chron vii 33.
Paseah (*psḥ*) I Chron iv 12; Ezra ii 49; Neh iii 6, vii 51.
Pashhur (*pšḥwr*) I Chron ix 12; Ezra ii 38, x 22; Neh vii 41, x 4, xi 12.
Pathrusim (*ptrsym*) I Chron i 12.
Pedaiah (*pdyh*) I Chron iii 18,19, xxvii 20; Neh iii 25, viii 4, xi 7, xiii 13.

Rehoboam (*rḥb'm*) I Chron iii 10; II Chron ix 31, x 1,3,6,12, 13,17,18(*bis*), xi 1(*bis*), 3,5,17,18,21,22, xii 1,2,5,10,13(*bis*), 15(*bis*), 16, xiii 7(*bis*).

Rekem (*rqm*) I Chron ii 43,44, vii 16.

Rephah (*rph*) I Chron vii 25.

Rephael (*rp'l*) I Chron xxvi 7.

Rephaiah (*rpyh*) I Chron iii 21, iv 42, vii 2, ix 43; Neh iii 9.

Resheaph (*ršp*) I Chron vii 25.

Reu (*r'w*) I Chron i 25.

Reuben (*r'wbn*) I Chron ii 1, v 1,3,18, vi 63,78.

Reubenite (*r'wbny*) I Chron v 6,26, xi 42(*bis*), xii 38, xxvi 32, xxvii 16.

Reuel (*r'w'l*) I Chron i 35,37, ix 8.

Ribai (*ryby*) I Chron xi 31.

Rinnah (*rnh*) I Chron iv 20.

Rizia (*rṣy'*) I Chron vii 39.

Rodanim (*rwdnym*) I Chron i 7.

Rohgah (*rwhgh*) I Chron vii 34.

Romamti-ezer (*rmmty-'zr*) I Chron xxv 4,31.

Sabta (*sbt'*) I Chron i 9.

Sabteca (*sbtk'*) I Chron i 9.

Sachar (*śkr*) I Chron xi 35, xxvi 4.

Sachiah (*śkyh*) I Chron viii 10.

Sallu (*slw', slw*) I Chron ix 7; Neh xi 7, xii 7.

Salma (*šlm'*) I Chron ii 11(*bis*), 51,54.

Samlah (*śmlh*) I Chron i 47,48.

Samuel (*šmw'l*) I Chron vi 28,33, vii 2, ix 22, xi 3, xxvi 28, xxix 29; II Chron xxxv 18.

Saraph (*śrp*) I Chron iv 22.

Satan (*śṭn*) I Chron xxi 1.

Saul (*š'wl*) I Chron i 48,49, iv 24, v 10, vi 24, viii 33(*bis*), ix 39 (*bis*), x 2(*bis*), 3,4(*bis*), 5,6,7,11,12,13, xi 2, xii 1,2,20(*bis*), 24,30(*bis*), xiii 3, xv 29, xxvi 28.

Seba (*sb'*) I Chron i 9.

Segub (*śgwb*) I Chron ii 21,22.

Seir (*ś'yr*) I Chron i 38; II Chron xxv 11,14.

Seled (*sld*) I Chron ii 30(*bis*).

Semachiah (*smkyhw*) I Chron xxvi 7.

Seorim (*ś'rym*) I Chron xxiv 8.

Serah (*śrḥ*) I Chron vii 30.

Seraiah (*śryh*) I Chron iv 13,14,35, vi 14(*bis*); Ezra ii 2, vii 1; Neh x 3, xi 11, xii 1,12.

Serug (*śrwg*) I Chron i 26.

Seth (*št*) I Chron i 1.

Shaalbonite (*š'lbny*) I Chron xi 33.

Shaaph (*š'p*) I Chron ii 47,49.

Shageh (*šgh*) I Chron xi 34.

Shaharaim (*šḥrym*) I Chron viii 8.

Shallum (*šlwm*) I Chron ii 40,41, iii 15, iv 25, vi 12,13, vii 13, ix 17(*bis*), 19,31; II Chron xxviii 12, xxxiv 22; Ezra ii 42, vii 2, x 24,42; Neh iii 12, vii 45.

Shama (*šm'*) I Chron xi 44.

Shamhuth (*šmhwt*) I Chron xxvii 8.

Shamir (*šmwr* [Kethib], *šmyr* [Q(ere)]) I Chron xxiv 24.

Shamma (*šm'*) I Chron vii 37.

Shammah (*šmh*) I Chron i 37.

Shammai (*šmy*) I Chron ii 28(*bis*), 32,44,45, iv 17.

Shammoth (*šmwt*) I Chron xi 27.

Shammua (*šmw'*) I Chron xiv 4; Neh xi 17, xii 18.

Shamsherai (*šmšry*) I Chron viii 26.

Shapham (*špm*) I Chron v 12.

Shaphat (*špṭ*) I Chron iii 22, v 12, xxvii 29.

Sharonite (*šrwny*) I Chron xxvii 29.

Shashak (*ššq*) I Chron viii 14,25.

Shavsha (*šwš'*) I Chron xviii 16.

Shealtiel (*š'lty'l*) I Chron iii 17; Ezra iii 2,8, v 2; Neh xii 1.

Sheariah (*š'ryh*) I Chron viii 38, ix 44.

Sheba (*šb', šb'*) I Chron i 9,22,32, v 13.

Shebaniah (*šbnyhw*) I Chron xv 24; Neh iv 4,5, x 5,11,13, xii 14.

Sheber (*šbr*) I Chron ii 48.

Shebuel (*šbw'l*) I Chron xxiii 16, xxv 4, xxvi 24.

Shecaniah (*šknyh*) I Chron iii 21,22, xxiv 11; II Chron xxxi 15; Ezra viii 3,5, x 2; Neh vi 18, xii 3.

Shechem (*škm*) I Chron vii 19.

Sheerah (*š'rh*) I Chron vii 24.

Shehariah (*šḥryh*) I Chron viii 26.

Shelah (*šlḥ, šlh*) I Chron i 18(*bis*), 24, ii 3, iv 21.

Shelemiah (*šlmyhw*) I Chron xxvi 14; Ezra x 39,41; Neh iii 30, xiii 13.

Sheleph (*šlp*) I Chron i 20.

Shelesh (*šlš*) I Chron vii 35.

Shelomith (*šlmyt*) I Chron iii 19, xxiii 9 [Q(ere), Kethïb, *šlmwt*], 18; II Chron xi 20; Ezra viii 10.

Shelomoth (*šlmwt*) I Chron xxiv 22(*bis*), xxvi 25 [Kethib, Q(ere), *šlmyt*], 26,28.

Shem (*šm*) I Chron i 4,17,24.

Shema (*šm'*) I Chron ii 43,44, v 8, viii 13; Neh viii 4.

Shemaah (*šm'h*) I Chron xii 3 (Kethib, *hsm'h*).

Shemaiah (*šm'yh*) I Chron iii 22(*bis*), iv 37, v 4, ix 14,16, xv 8,11, xxiv 6, xxvi 4,6,7; II Chron xi 2, xii 5,7,15, xvii 8, xxix 14, xxxi 15, xxxv 9; Ezra viii 13,16, x 21,31; Neh iii 29, vi 10, x 9, xi 15, xii 6,18,34,35,36,42.

Shemariah (*šmryhw*) I Chron xii 6; II Chron xi 19; Ezra x 32, 41.

Shemed (*šmd*) I Chron viii 12.

Shemer (*šmr*) I Chron vi 46, vii 34.

Shemida (*šmyd'*) I Chron vii 19.

Shemiramoth (*šmyrmwt*) I Chron xv 18,20.

Shenazzar (*šn'ṣr*) I Chron iii 18.

Shephatiah (*šptyh*) I Chron iii 3, ix 8, xii 6, xxvii 16; II Chron xxi 2; Ezra ii 4,57, viii 8; Neh vii 9,59, xi 4.

Shephi (*špy*) I Chron i 40.

Shephuphan (*špwpn*) I Chron viii 5.

Sheresh (*šrš*) I Chron vii 16.

Sheshan (*ššn*) I Chron ii 31(*bis*), 34(*bis*), 35.

Sheva (*šw'*) I Chron ii 49.

Shilonite (*šylwny*) I Chron ix 5; II Chron ix 29, x 15; Neh xi 5.

Shilshah (*šlšh*) I Chron vii 37.

Shimea (*šm''*) I Chron ii 13, iii 5, vi 30,39, xx 7.

Shimeah (*šm'h*) I Chron viii 32.

Shimeam (*šm'm*) I Chron ix 38.

Shimeathites (*šm'tym*) I Chron ii 55.

Shimei (*šm'y*) I Chron iii 19, iv 26,27, v 4, vi 17,29,42, viii 21, xxiii 7,9,10(*bis*), xxv 3,17, xxvii 27; II Chron xxix 14, xxxi 12, 13; Ezra x 23,33,38.

Shimon (*šymwn*) I Chron iv 20.

Shimrath (*šmrt*) I Chron viii 21.

Shimri (*šmry*) I Chron iv 37, xi 45, xxvi 10; II Chron xxix 13.

Shimron (*šmrwn*) I Chron vii 1.

Shiphi (*šp'y*) I Chron iv 37.

Shiphmite (*špmy*) I Chron xxvii 27.

Shitrai (*šṭry*) I Chron xxvii 29.

Shiza (*šyz'*) I Chron xi 42.

Shobab (*šwbb*) I Chron ii 18, iii 5, xiv 4.

Shobal (*šwbl*) I Chron i 38,40, ii 50,52, iv 1,2.

Shoham (*šhm*) I Chron xxiv 27.

Shomer (*šwmr*) I Chron vii 32.

Shophach (*šwpk*) I Chron xix 16,18.

Shua (*šw''*) I Chron vii 32.

Shuah (*šwḥ*) I Chron i 32.

Shual (*šw'l*) I Chron vii 36.

Shubael (*šwb'l*) I Chron xxiv 20(*bis*), xxv 20.

Shuhah (*šwḥh*) I Chron iv 11.

Shumathite (*šmty*) I Chron ii 53.

Shuppim (*špm, špym*) I Chron vii 12,15.

Shuthelah (*šwtlḥ*) I Chron vii 20,21.

Sibbecai (*sbky*) I Chron xi 29, xx 4, xxvii 11.

Sidon (*ṣydwn*) I Chron i 13.

Sidonians (*ṣydnym*) I Chron xxii 4; Ezra iii 7.

Simeon (*šm'wn*) I Chron ii 1, iv 24,42, vi 65, xii 26, xxvii 16;
    II Chron xv 9.

Sinite (*syny*) I Chron i 15.

Sippai (*spy*) I Chron xx 4.

Sismai (*ssmy*) I Chron ii 40(*bis*).

Soco (*śwkw*) I Chron iv 18.

Solomon (*šlmh*) I Chron iii 5,10, vi 10,32, xiv 4, xviii 8, xxii 5,
    6,7,9,17, xxiii 1, xxviii 5,6,9,11,20, xxix 1,19,22,23,24,25,28;
    II Chron i 1,2,3,5,6,7,8,11,13,14,16,18, ii 1,2,10,16, iii 1,3, iv
    11,16,18,19, v 1(*bis*), 2,6, vi 1,13, vii 1,5,7(*bis*), 8,10,11(*bis*),
    12, viii 1,3,6,8,9,10,11,12,16,17,18(*bis*), ix 1(*tris*), 2(*bis*), 3,9,
    10,12,13,14,15,20(*bis*), 22,23,25,28,29,30,31, x 2, xi 3,17(*bis*),
    xii 9, xiii 6,7, xxx 26, xxxiii 7, xxxv 3,4; Ezra ii 55,58; Neh vii
    57,60, xi 3, xii 45, xiii 26.

Sopherim (*sprym*) I Chron ii 55.

Suah (*swḥ*) I Chron vii 36.

Sucathites (*śwktym*) I Chron ii 55.

Tahan (*thn*) I Chron vii 25.
Tahath (*tht*) I Chron vi 24,37, vii 20(*bis*).
Tahrea (*thr'*) I Chron ix 41.
Talmai (*tlmy*) I Chron iii 2.
Talmon (*tlmn, tlmwn*) I Chron ix 17; Ezra ii 42; Neh vii 45, xi 19, xii 25.
Tamar (*tmr*) I Chron ii 4, iii 9.
Tappuah (*tph*) I Chron ii 43.
Tarea (*t'r'*) I Chron viii 35.
Tarshish (*tršyšh, tršyš*) I Chron i 7, vii 10.
Tebaliah (*tblyhw*) I Chron xxvi 11.
Tehinnah (*thnh*) I Chron iv 12.
Tekoa (*tqw'*) I Chron ii 24, iv 5.
Tekoite (*tqw'y*) I Chron xi 28, xxvii 9; Neh iii 5,27.
Telah (*tlh*) I Chron vii 25.
Tema (*tym'*) I Chron i 30.
Teman (*tymn*) I Chron i 36,53.
Temeni (*tymny*) I Chron iv 6.
Terah (*trh*) I Chron i 26.
Tilgath-pilneser (*tlgt-pln'sr; tlgt-plnsr*) I Chron v 6,26; II Chron xxviii 20.
Tilon (Kethib, *twlwn;* Q[ere], *tylon*) I Chron iv 20.
Timma (*tmn'*) I Chron i 36,39,51.
Tiras (*tyrs*) I Chron i 5.
Tirathites (*tr'tym*) I Chron ii 55.
Tirhanah (*trhnh*) I Chron ii 48.
Tiria (*tyry'*) I Chron iv 16.
Tizite (*tysy*) I Chron xi 45.
Toah (*twh*) I Chron vi 34.
Togarmah (*twgrmh*) I Chron i 6.
Tola (*twl'*) I Chron vii 1,2(*bis*).
Tou (*t'w*) I Chron xviii 9,10.
Tubal (*tbl*) I Chron i 5.
Tyrian (*sry*) I Chron xxii 4; II Chron ii 13; Ezra iii 7; Neh xiii 16.

Ulam (*'wlm*) I Chron vii 16,17, viii 39,40.
Ulla (*'l*) I Chron vii 39.
Unni (*'ny, 'nw*) I Chron xv 18,20; Neh xii 9 [Q(ere)].
Ur (*'wr*) I Chron xi 35.

Uri (*'wry*) I Chron ii 20(*bis*); II Chron i 5; Ezra x 24.
Uriah (*'wryh*) I Chron xi 41; Ezra viii 33; Neh iii 4,21, viii 4.
Uriel (*'wry'l*) I Chron vi 24, xv 5,11; II Chron xiii 2.
Uthai (*'wty*) I Chron ix 4; Ezra viii 14.
Uz (*'wṣ*) I Chron i 17,42.
Uzal (*'wzl*) I Chron i 21.
Uzza (*'z'*) I Chron viii 7, xiii 7,9,10,11; Ezra ii 49; Neh vii 51.
Uzzah (*'zh*) I Chron vi 29.
Uzzi (*'zy*) I Chron vi 5,6,51, vii 2,3,7, ix 8; Ezra vii 4; Neh xi 22, xii 19,42.
Uzzia (*'zy'*) I Chron xi 44.
Uzziah (*'zyh*) I Chron vi 24, xxvii 25; II Chron xxvi 1,3,8,9,11, 14,18(*bis*), 19,21,22,23, xxvii 2; Ezra x 21; Neh xi 4.
Uzziel (*'zy'l*) I Chron iv 42, vi 2,18, vii 7, xv 10; xxiii 12,20, xxiv 24, xxv 4, xxvi 23; II Chron xxix 14; Neh iii 8.

Zaavan (*z'wn*) I Chron i 42.
Zabad (*zbd*) I Chron ii 36,37, vii 21, xi 41; II Chron xxiv 26; Ezra x 27,33,43.
Zabdi (*zbdy*) I Chron viii 19, xxvii 27; Neh xi 17.
Zabdiel (*zbdy'l*) I Chron xxvii 2; Neh xi 14.
Zaccur (*zkwr*) I Chron iv 26, xxiv 27, xxv 2,10; Neh iii 2, x 13, xii 35, xiii 13.
Zadok (*ṣdwq*) I Chron vi 8(*bis*), 12(*bis*), 53, ix 11, xii 29, xv 11, xvi 39, xviii 16, xxiv 3,6,31, xxvii 17, xxix 22; II Chron xxvii 1, xxxi 10; Ezra vii 2; Neh iii 4,29, x 22, xi 11, xiii 13.
Zanoah (*znwḥ*) I Chron iv 18.
Zaza (*zz'*) I Chron ii 33.
Zebadiah (*zbdyh*) I Chron viii 15,17, xii 8, xxvi 2, xxvii 7; II Chron xvii 8, xix 11; Ezra viii 8, xx 20.
Zebulun (*zblwn*) I Chron ii 1, vi 63,77, xii 34,41, xxvii 19; II Chron xxx 10,11,18.
Zechariah (*zkryhw*) I Chron v 7, ix 21,37, xv 18,20,24, xvi 5, xxiv 25, xxvi 2,11,14, xxvii 21; II Chron xvii 7, xx 14, xxi 2, xxiv 20, xxvi 5, xxix 1,13, xxxii 12, xxxv 8; Ezra v 1, vi 14, viii 3,11,16, x 26; Neh viii 4, xi 4,5,12, xii 16,35,41.
Zecher (*zkr*) I Chron viii 31.
Zedekiah (*ṣdqyhw*) I Chron iii 15,16; II Chron xviii 10,23, xxxvi 10,11; Neh x 2.
Zelek (*ṣlq*) I Chron xi 39.

Zelophehad (*ṣlphd*) I Chron vii 15(*bis*).

Zemarite (*ṣmry*) I Chron i 16.

Zemirah (*zmyrh*) I Chron vii 8.

Zephaniah (*ṣpnyh*) I Chron vi 36.

Zephi (*ṣpy*) I Chron i 36.

Zerah (*zrḥ*) I Chron i 37,44, ii 4,6, iv 24, vi 21,41, ix 6; II Chron xiv 8; Neh xi 24.

Zerahiah (*zrḥyh*) I Chron vi 6(*bis*), 51; Ezra vii 4, viii 4.

Zerahite (*zrḥy*) I Chron xxvii 11,13.

Zereth (*ṣrt*) I Chron iv 7.

Zeri (*ṣry*) I Chron xxv 3.

Zerubbabel (*zrbbl*) I Chron iii 19(*bis*); Ezra ii 2, iii 2,8, iv 2,3, v 2; Neh vii 7, xii 1,47.

Zeruiah (*ṣrwyh*) I Chron ii 16(*bis*), xi 6,39, xviii 12,15, xxvi 28, xxvii 24.

Zetham (*ztm*) I Chron xxiii 8, xxvi 22.

Zethan (*zytn*) I Chron vii 10.

Zia (*zyʿ*) I Chron v 13.

Zibeon (*ṣbʿwn*) I Chron i 38,40.

Zibia (*ṣbyʾ*) I Chron viii 9.

Zichri (*zkry*) I Chron viii 19,23,27, ix 15, xxvi 25, xxvii 16; II Chron xvii 16, xxiii 1, xxviii 7; Neh xi 9, xii 17.

Zillethai (*ṣlty*) I Chron viii 20, xii 21.

Zimmah (*zmh*) I Chron vi 20,42; II Chron xxix 12.

Zimran (*zmrn*) I Chron i 32.

Zimri (*zmry*) I Chron ii 6, viii 36(*bis*), ix 42(*bis*).

Zina (*zynʾ*) I Chron xxiii 10.

Ziph (*zyp*) I Chron ii 42, iv 16.

Ziphah (*zyph*) I Chron iv 16.

Ziza (*zyzʾ*) I Chron iv 37; II Chron xi 20.

Zizah (*zyzh*) I Chron xxiii 11.

Zohar (Q[ere] for Kethib, *yṣhr*) I Chron iv 7.

Zoheth (*zwḥt*) I Chron iv 20.

Zophah (*ṣwph*) I Chron vii 35,36.

Zophai (*ṣwpy*) I Chron vi 26.

Zorathite (*ṣrʿty*) I Chron ii 53, iv 2.

Zorite (*ṣrʿy*) I Chron ii 54.

Zuph (Q[ere] for Kethib, *ṣyp*) I Chron vi 35.

Zur (*ṣwr*) I Chron viii 30, ix 36.

KEY TO THE TEXT